THIRD EDITION

JavaScript Cookbook

Adam D. Scott, Matthew MacDonald,
and Shelley Powers

Beijing · Boston · Farnham · Sebastopol · Tokyo

JavaScript Cookbook, Third Edition

by Adam D. Scott, Matthew MacDonald, and Shelley Powers

Published by O'Reilly Media, Inc., 1005 Gravenstein Highway North, Sebastopol, CA 95472.

O'Reilly books may be purchased for educational, business, or sales promotional use. Online editions are also available for most titles (*http://oreilly.com*). For more information, contact our corporate/institutional sales department: 800-998-9938 or *corporate@oreilly.com*.

Acquisitions Editor: Jennifer Pollock	**Indexer:** Potomac Indexing, LLC
Development Editor: Angela Rufino	**Interior Designer:** David Futato
Production Editor: Katherine Tozer	**Cover Designer:** Karen Montgomery
Copyeditor: Sonia Saruba	**Illustrator:** Kate Dullea
Proofreader: James Fraleigh	

July 2021:   Third Edition

Revision History for the Third Edition
2021-07-16:   First Release

See *http://oreilly.com/catalog/errata.csp?isbn=9781492055754* for release details.

978-1-492-05575-4

[LSI]

Table of Contents

Preface. xi

Part I.   The JavaScript Language

1. Setting Up a Development Environment. 1
    1.1 Choosing a Code Editor   2
    1.2 Using the Developer Console in Your Browser   4
    1.3 Running Blocks of Code in the Developer Console   7
    1.4 Using Strict Mode to Catch Common Mistakes   9
    1.5 Filling in HTML Boilerplate with Emmet Shortcuts   11
    1.6 Installing the npm Package Manager (with Node.js)   13
    1.7 Downloading a Package with npm   16
    1.8 Updating a Package with npm   20
    1.9 Setting Up a Local Test Server   21
    1.10 Enforcing Code Standards with a Linter   24
    1.11 Styling Code Consistently with a Formatter   28
    1.12 Experimenting in a JavaScript Playground   31

2. Strings and Regular Expressions. 35
    2.1 Checking for an Existing, Nonempty String   35
    2.2 Converting a Numeric Value to a Formatted String   38
    2.3 Inserting Special Characters   40
    2.4 Inserting Emojis   42
    2.5 Using Template Literals for Clearer String Concatenation   43
    2.6 Performing a Case-Insensitive String Comparison   45
    2.7 Checking If a String Contains a Specific Substring   46
    2.8 Replacing All Occurrences of a String   47

2.9 Replacing HTML Tags with Named Entities   48
2.10 Using a Regular Expression to Replace Patterns in a String   49
2.11 Extracting a List from a String   52
2.12 Finding All Instances of a Pattern   54
2.13 Removing Whitespace from the Beginning and End of a String   57
2.14 Converting the First Letter of a String to Uppercase   58
2.15 Validating an Email Address   59

3. Numbers. 61
3.1 Generating Random Numbers   61
3.2 Generating Cryptographically Secure Random Numbers   63
3.3 Rounding to a Specific Decimal Place   65
3.4 Preserving Accuracy in Decimal Values   66
3.5 Converting a String to a Number   68
3.6 Converting a Decimal to a Hexadecimal Value   70
3.7 Converting Between Degrees and Radians   71
3.8 Calculating the Length of a Circular Arc   71
3.9 Manipulating Very Large Numbers with BigInt   72

4. Dates. 75
4.1 Getting the Current Date and Time   75
4.2 Converting a String to a Date   77
4.3 Adding Days to a Date   79
4.4 Comparing Dates and Testing Dates for Equality   80
4.5 Calculating the Time Elapsed Between Two Dates   82
4.6 Formatting a Date Value as a String   84

5. Arrays. 87
5.1 Checking If an Object Is an Array   88
5.2 Iterating Over All the Elements in an Array   88
5.3 Checking If Two Arrays Are Equal   90
5.4 Breaking Down an Array into Separate Variables   93
5.5 Passing an Array to a Function That Expects a List of Values   94
5.6 Cloning an Array   95
5.7 Merging Two Arrays   97
5.8 Copying a Portion of an Array by Position   98
5.9 Extracting Array Items That Meet Specific Criteria   100
5.10 Emptying an Array   101
5.11 Removing Duplicate Values   102
5.12 Flattening a Two-Dimensional Array   103
5.13 Searching Through an Array for Exact Matches   104
5.14 Searching Through an Array for Items That Meet Specific Criteria 105

5.15 Removing or Replacing Array Elements   107
5.16 Sorting an Array of Objects by a Property Value   108
5.17 Transforming Every Element of an Array   109
5.18 Combining an Array's Values in a Single Calculation   110
5.19 Validating Array Contents   112
5.20 Creating a Collection of Nonduplicated Values   113
5.21 Creating a Key-Indexed Collection of Items   114

6. Functions. 117
6.1 Passing a Function as an Argument to Another Function   117
6.2 Using Arrow Functions   121
6.3 Providing a Default Parameter Value   124
6.4 Creating a Function That Accepts Unlimited Arguments   125
6.5 Using Named Function Parameters   126
6.6 Creating a Function That Stores its State with a Closure   129
6.7 Creating a Generator Function That Yields Multiple Values   131
6.8 Reducing Redundancy by Using Partial Application   135
6.9 Fixing this with Function Binding   138
6.10 Implementing a Recursive Algorithm   141

7. Objects. 145
7.1 Checking if an Object Is a Certain Type   145
7.2 Using an Object Literal to Bundle Data   147
7.3 Checking If an Object Has a Property   150
7.4 Iterating Over All the Properties of an Object   152
7.5 Testing for an Empty Object   154
7.6 Merging the Properties of Two Objects   155
7.7 Customizing the Way a Property Is Defined   156
7.8 Preventing Any Changes to an Object   159
7.9 Intercepting and Changing Actions on an Object with a Proxy   161
7.10 Cloning an Object   164
7.11 Making a Deep Copy of an Object   166
7.12 Creating Absolutely Unique Object Property Keys   168
7.13 Creating Enums with Symbol   170

8. Classes. 173
8.1 Creating a Reusable Class   173
8.2 Adding Properties to a Class   177
8.3 Giving a Class a Better String Representation   182
8.4 Using the Constructor Pattern to Make a Custom Class   183
8.5 Supporting Method Chaining in Your Class   186
8.6 Adding Static Methods to a Class   188

8.7 Using a Static Method to Create Objects   190
8.8 Inheriting Functionality from Another Class   192
8.9 Organizing Your JavaScript Classes with Modules   197

9. **Asynchronous Programming.** **201**
9.1 Updating the Page During a Loop   202
9.2 Using a Function That Returns a Promise   204
9.3 Promisifying an Asynchronous Function That Uses a Callback   208
9.4 Executing Multiple Promises Concurrently   211
9.5 Waiting for a Promise to Finish with Await and Async   214
9.6 Creating an Asynchronous Generator Function   218
9.7 Using a Web Worker to Perform a Background Task   220
9.8 Adding Progress Support to a Web Worker   224

10. **Errors and Testing.** **227**
10.1 Catching and Neutralizing an Error   227
10.2 Catching Different Types of Errors   230
10.3 Catching Asynchronous Errors   232
10.4 Detecting Unhandled Errors   233
10.5 Throwing a Standard Error   237
10.6 Throwing a Custom Error   239
10.7 Writing Unit Tests for Your Code   241
10.8 Tracking Test Code Coverage   247

Part II.   JavaScript in the Browser

11. **Browser Tools.** **253**
11.1 Debugging JavaScript   253
11.2 Analyzing Runtime Performance   255
11.3 Identifying Unused JavaScript   257
11.4 Using Lighthouse to Measure Best Practices   259

12. **Working with HTML.** **263**
12.1 Accessing a Given Element and Finding Its Parent and Child Elements   263
12.2 Traversing the Results from querySelectorAll() with forEach()   266
12.3 Adding Click Functionality to an Element   267
12.4 Finding All Elements That Share an Attribute   269
12.5 Accessing All Elements of a Specific Type   269
12.6 Discovering Child Elements Using the Selectors API   272
12.7 Changing an Element's Class Value   273
12.8 Setting an Element's Style Attribute   274

12.9 Adding Text to a New Paragraph   276
12.10 Inserting a New Element in a Specific DOM Location   278
12.11 Checking If a Checkbox Is Checked   279
12.12 Adding Up Values in an HTML Table   280
12.13 Deleting Rows from an HTML Table   283
12.14 Hiding Page Sections   285
12.15 Creating Hover-Based Pop-Up Info Windows   287
12.16 Validating Form Data   289
12.17 Highlighting Form Errors and Accessibility   292
12.18 Creating an Accessible Automatically Updated Region   298

13. Fetching Remote Data.   301
13.1 Requesting Remote Data with Fetch   301
13.2 Using XMLHttpRequest   305
13.3 Submitting a Form   306
13.4 Populating a Selection List from the Server   310
13.5 Parsing Returned JSON   314
13.6 Fetching and Parsing XML   316
13.7 Sending Binary Data and Loading into an Image   318
13.8 Sharing HTTP Cookies Across Domains   319
13.9 Using Websockets to Establish a Two-Way Communication Between
     Client and Server   320
13.10 Long Polling a Remote Data Source   322

14. Data Persistence.   325
14.1 Persisting Information with Cookies   325
14.2 Using sessionStorage for Client-Side Storage   328
14.3 Creating a localStorage Client-Side Data Storage Item   334
14.4 Persisting Larger Chunks of Data on the Client Using IndexedDB 338
14.5 Simplifying IndexedDB with a Library   341

15. Working with Media.   345
15.1 Adding JavaScript to SVG   345
15.2 Accessing SVG from a Web Page Script   348
15.3 Creating an SVG Bar Chart with D3   350
15.4 Integrating SVG and the Canvas Element in HTML   354
15.5 Running a Routine When an Audio File Begins Playing   356
15.6 Controlling Video from JavaScript with the video Element   357

16. Writing Web Applications.   361
16.1 Bundling JavaScript   361
16.2 JavaScript and the Mobile Web   363

16.3 Writing a Progressive Web Application   366
16.4 Testing and Profiling a Progressive Web Application   373
16.5 Getting the Value of the Current URL   377
16.6 Redirecting a URL   379
16.7 Copying Text to a User's Clipboard   380
16.8 Enabling a Mobile-Like Notification in the Desktop Browser   382
16.9 Loading a File Locally in the Browser   385
16.10 Extending the Possible with Web Components   388
16.11 Choosing a Front-End Framework   391

Part III.   Node.js

17. Node Basics.   397
17.1 Managing Node Versions with Node Version Manager   397
17.2 Responding to a Simple Browser Request   400
17.3 Interactively Trying Out Node Code Snippets with REPL   402
17.4 Reading and Writing File Data   405
17.5 Getting Input from the Terminal   410
17.6 Getting the Path to the Current Script   412
17.7 Working with Node Timers and Understanding the Node Event Loop   413

18. Node Modules.   419
18.1 Searching for a Specific Node Module via npm   420
18.2 Converting Your Library into a Node Module   421
18.3 Taking Your Code Across Module Environments   422
18.4 Creating an Installable Node Module   425
18.5 Writing Multiplatform Libraries   431
18.6 Unit Testing Your Modules   435

19. Managing Node.   439
19.1 Using Environment Variables   439
19.2 Managing Callback Hell   441
19.3 Accessing Command-Line Functionality Within a Node Application   444
19.4 Passing Command-Line Arguments   447
19.5 Creating a Command-Line Utility with Help from Commander   448
19.6 Keeping a Node Instance Up and Running   451
19.7 Monitoring Application Changes and Restarting During Local
     Development   452
19.8 Scheduling Repeat Tasks   454
19.9 Testing the Performance and Capability of Your WebSockets Application 455

20. **Remote Data.** **457**
    20.1 Fetching Remote Data   457
    20.2 Screen Scraping   459
    20.3 Accessing JSON-Formatted Data via a RESTful API   461

21. **Building Web Applications with Express.** **465**
    21.1 Using Express to Respond to Requests   465
    21.2 Using the Express-Generator   469
    21.3 Routing   474
    21.4 Working with OAuth   476
    21.5 OAuth 2 User Authentication with Passport.js   486
    21.6 Serving Up Formatted Data   491
    21.7 Building a RESTful API   492
    21.8 Building a GraphQL API   496

Index. **501**

Preface

As I sat down to work on the latest edition of *JavaScript Cookbook*, I considered the "cookbook" metaphor carefully. What makes a great food cookbook? Browsing the cookbooks on a shelf in my dining room, I noted that my favorites not only have delicious recipes, but they are also full of opinionated hard-earned advice. A cookbook rarely seeks to teach you *every* recipe for beef bourguignon; rather it teaches you the technique and recipe that the author has found works best for them, typically with a bit of advice thrown in for good measure. It's with this concept in mind that we put together this collection of JavaScript recipes. The advice in this book comes from three seasoned pros, but it is ultimately the culmination of *our* unique experiences. Any other group of developers would have likely produced a similar, but different book.

JavaScript has developed into an amazing and powerful multipurpose programming language. With this collection in hand you will be able to solve all sorts of problems that you encounter and may even begin to develop recipes of your own.

Book Audience

To encompass the many subjects and topics reflective of JavaScript in use today, we had to start with one premise: this is not a book for someone brand new to programming. There are so many good books and tutorials for those looking to learn to program with JavaScript that we felt comfortable targeting the *practicing developer*, someone looking to solve specific problems and challenges with JavaScript.

If you've been playing around with JavaScript for several months, maybe tried your hand with a little Node or web development, you should be comfortable with the book material. Additionally, if you're a developer who primarily works in another programming language, but find yourself needing to use JavaScript from time to time, this should be a helpful guide. Finally, if you're a working JavaScript developer who sometimes gets stuck on some of the idiosyncrasies of the language, this should act as a useful resource.

Book Organization

There are two types of readers of this book. The first is someone who reads it cover to cover, picking up tidbits of applicable knowledge along the way. The second is someone who dips their toes in as needed, seeking out the solution to a specific challenge or category of problem that they face. We attempted to organize the book in such a way that it would be useful to both types of readers, organizing it into three sections:

- Part I, *The JavaScript Language*, covers recipes for JavaScript as a programming language.
- Part II, *JavaScript in the Browser*, covers JavaScript in its natural habitat: the browser.
- Part III, *Node.js*, looks at JavaScript specifically through the lens of Node.js.

Each chapter of the book is broken down into several individual "recipes." A recipe is composed of several parts:

Problem
    This defines a common development scenario where JavaScript may be used.

Solution
    A solution to the problem, with a code sample and minimal description.

Discussion
    An in-depth discussion of the code sample and techniques.

Additionally, a recipe may contain recommendations for further reading in a "See Also" section, or additional techniques in an "Extra" section.

Conventions Used in This Book

The following typographical conventions are used in this book:

Italic
    Indicates new terms, URLs, email addresses, filenames, and file extensions.

Bold
    Indicates UI items such as menu items and buttons to be selected or clicked.

`Constant width`
    Indicates computer code in a broad sense, including commands, arrays, elements, statements, options, switches, variables, attributes, keys, functions, types, classes, namespaces, methods, modules, properties, parameters, values, objects, events, event handlers, XML tags, HTML tags, macros, the contents of files, and the output from commands.

Constant width bold

> Shows commands or other text that should be typed literally by the user.

Constant width italic

> hows text that should be replaced with user-supplied values or by values determined by context.

 This element signifies a general note.

 This element signifies a tip or suggestion.

 This element indicates a warning or caution.

Websites and pages are mentioned in this book to help you locate online information that might be useful. Normally both the address (URL) and the name (or title, or appropriate heading) of a page are mentioned. Some addresses are relatively complicated. You may locate such pages more easily using your favorite search engine to search for a page by its name. This may also help if the page cannot be found by its address; the URL may have changed, but the name may still work.

Using Code Examples

Supplemental material (code examples, exercises, etc.) is available for download at *https://github.com/javascripteverywhere/cookbook*.

This book is here to help you get your job done. In general, if example code is offered with this book, you may use it in your programs and documentation. You do not need to contact us for permission unless you're reproducing a significant portion of the code. For example, writing a program that uses several chunks of code from this book does not require permission. Selling or distributing examples from O'Reilly books does require permission. Answering a question by citing this book and quoting example code does not require permission. Incorporating a significant amount of example code from this book into your product's documentation does require permission.

We appreciate, but do not require, attribution. An attribution usually includes the title, author, publisher, and ISBN. For example: *JavaScript Cookbook*, Third Edition, by Adam D. Scott, Matthew MacDonald, and Shelley Powers. Copyright 2021 Adam D. Scott and Matthew MacDonald, 978-1-492-05575-4.

If you feel your use of code examples falls outside fair use or the permission given here, feel free to contact us at *permissions@oreilly.com*.

O'Reilly Online Learning

 For more than 40 years, *O'Reilly Media* has provided technology and business training, knowledge, and insight to help companies succeed.

Our unique network of experts and innovators share their knowledge and expertise through books, articles, and our online learning platform. O'Reilly's online learning platform gives you on-demand access to live training courses, in-depth learning paths, interactive coding environments, and a vast collection of text and video from O'Reilly and 200+ other publishers. For more information, visit *http://oreilly.com*.

How to Contact Us

Please address comments and questions concerning this book to the publisher:

O'Reilly Media, Inc.
1005 Gravenstein Highway North
Sebastopol, CA 95472
800-998-9938 (in the United States or Canada)
707-829-0515 (international or local)
707-829-0104 (fax)

We have a web page for this book, where we list errata, examples, and any additional information. You can access this page at *https://oreil.ly/js-cookbook-3e*.

Email *bookquestions@oreilly.com* to comment or ask technical questions about this book.

For news and information about our books and courses, visit *http://oreilly.com*.

Find us on Facebook: *http://facebook.com/oreilly*

Follow us on Twitter: *http://twitter.com/oreillymedia*

Watch us on YouTube: *http://www.youtube.com/oreillymedia*

Acknowledgments

This is the third edition of the *JavaScript Cookbook*. The first two editions were written by Shelley Powers. This edition was written and updated by Adam Scott and Matthew MacDonald. Adam and Matthew would like to thank their editors, Angela Rufino and Jennifer Pollock, who shepherded the project through all its growing pains; and their top-shelf tech reviewers, Sarah Wachs, Schalk Neethling, and Elisabeth Robson, who offered many sharp insights and helpful suggestions. Adam would also like to thank John Paxton for his support and conversation during the early drafts of this edition.

Shelley thanks her editors, Simon St. Laurent and Brian McDonald, and her tech reviewers, Dr. Axel Rauschmayer and Semmy Purewal.

Collectively we all thank the O'Reilly production staff for their ongoing help and support.

## PART I

The JavaScript Language

## CHAPTER 1

Setting Up a Development Environment

You may have heard it said that the "tools make the developer." While that's something of an exaggeration, no one wants to be left in front of a wall of JavaScript code without their favorite tools to edit, analyze, and debug it.

When you're setting up your own development environment, the first tool you'll consider is a code editor. Even the most basic editor adds essentials like autocompletion and syntax highlighting—two simple features that prevent piles of potential mistakes. Modern code editors add many more features, such as integration with a source control service like GitHub, line-by-line debugging, and smart refactoring. Sometimes these features will snap into your editor with a plug-in. Sometimes you'll run them from the terminal or as part of a build process. But no matter how you use your tools, assembling the right combination to suit your coding style, development environment, and project types is part of the fun. It's like a home improvement pro collecting tools, or an aspiring chef investing in just the right cooking gear.

Tool choices aren't static. As a developer, your preferences may shift. You'll grow your kit as you evolve and as new tools prove themselves useful. This chapter explores the minimum toolset that every JavaScript developer should consider before they tackle a project. But there's plenty of room to choose between different, broadly equivalent options. And, as many a wise person has remarked, there's no accounting for taste!

 In this chapter, we're putting on our advocacy hat. You'll see some of our favorite tools, and references to other, equally good options. But we don't attempt to cover *every* tool, just some excellent default choices you can start with.

1.1 Choosing a Code Editor

Problem

You want to write code in an editor that understands JavaScript syntax.

Solution

If you're in a hurry, you won't go wrong with our favorite choice, Visual Studio Code (often shortened to just *VS Code*). You can download this free, open source editor for Windows, Macintosh, or Linux.

If you have time to research, there are a number of other editors you might consider. The list in Table 1-1 is far from complete, but shows some of the most consistently popular editors.

Table 1-1. Desktop code editors

Editor	Supported platforms	Open source	Cost	Notes
Visual Studio Code (*https://code.visual studio.com*)	Windows, Macintosh, Linux	Yes	Free	A great choice for any language, and our first choice for JavaScript development
Atom (*https://atom.io*)	Windows, Macintosh, Linux	Yes	Free	Most of the chapters in this book were written using Atom with plug-ins for AsciiDoc support
WebStorm (*https://jetbrains.com/webstorm*)	Windows, Macintosh, Linux	No	Free for open source developers and educational users, otherwise roughly $60 per year for an individual	A heavier-weight environment that's closer to a traditional IDE than a code editor
Sublime Text (*https://sublime text.com*)	Windows, Macintosh, Linux	No	A one-time payment of $80 for an individual, although there is no license enforcement or time limit	A popular editor with a reputation for fast performance with massive text files
Brackets (*http://brackets.io*)	Windows, Macintosh	Yes	Free	An Adobe-sponsored project that's focused on web development

No matter what code editor you choose, you'll follow a similar process to start a new project. Begin by creating a new folder for your project (like *test-site*). Then, in your code editor, look for a command like **File > Open Folder**, and choose the project folder you created. Most code editors will immediately show the contents of the project folder in a handy list or tree panel, so you can quickly jump between files.

Having a project folder also gives you a place to put the packages you use (Recipe 1.7) and store application-specific configuration files and linting rules (Recipe 1.10). And

---

if your editor has a built-in terminal ("Extra: Using a Terminal and Shell" on page 14), it always starts in the current project folder.

Discussion

Recommending a best editor is a little like *me* choosing *your* dessert. Personal taste is definitely a factor, and there are at least a dozen reasonable choices. Most of the suggestions listed in Table 1-1 tick off all the important boxes, meaning they're:

- Cross-platform, so it doesn't matter what operating system you're using.
- Plug-in-based, so you can snap in whatever features you need. Many of the tools mentioned in this book (like the Prettier code formatter described in Recipe 1.10) have plug-ins that integrate with different editors.
- Multilanguage, allowing you to go beyond HTML, CSS, and JavaScript to write code in other programming languages (with the right plug-in).
- Community-driven, which gives you confidence that they'll be maintained and improved long into the future.
- Free, or available for a modest cost.

Our top choice, VS Code, is a Microsoft-built code editor with native JavaScript support. In fact, the editor itself is *written* in JavaScript, and hosted in Electron. (More precisely, it's written in TypeScript, a stricter superset of JavaScript that's transpiled into JavaScript before it's distributed or executed.)

In many ways, VS Code is the younger, trendier sibling to Microsoft's sprawling Visual Studio IDE, which is also available in a free Community edition, and also supports JavaScript coding. But VS Code strikes a better balance for developers that aren't already working with the Microsoft .NET stack. That's because it starts out lightweight, but is endlessly customizable through its library with thousands of community plug-ins (*https://oreil.ly/RvMZ9*). In Stack Overflow's developer survey, VS Code regularly ranks as the most popular code editor across as languages.

See Also

For an introduction to VS Code's basic features and overall organization, there's an excellent set of introductory videos (*https://oreil.ly/iiRhA*). In this chapter, you'll also learn how to use Emmet shortcuts in VS Code (Recipe 1.5), and how to add the ESLint (Recipe 1.10) and Prettier (Recipe 1.11) plug-ins.

1.2 Using the Developer Console in Your Browser

Problem

You want to see the errors that occur in your web page and the messages you write to the console.

Solution

Use the developer console in your browser. Table 1-2 shows how to load the developer tools in every modern desktop browser.

Table 1-2. Shortcut key to load the developer console

Browser	Operating system	Shortcut
Chrome	Windows or Linux	F12 or Ctrl+Shift+J
Chrome	Macintosh	Cmd-Option-J
Edge	Windows or Linux	F12 or Ctrl+Shift+J
Firefox	Windows or Linux	F12 or Ctrl+Shift+J
Firefox	Macintosh	Cmd-Shift-J
Safari[a]	Macintosh	Cmd-Option-C
Opera	Windows	Ctrl+Shift+J
Opera	Macintosh	Cmd-Option-J

[a] Before you can use the developer console in Safari, you must enable it. To do so, choose **Safari Menu > Preferences** from the menu, click the **Advanced** tab, and check **Show Develop menu in the menu bar**.

The developer tools are usually presented as a tabbed group of panes at the right or bottom of the web browser window. The Console panel is the one that shows the messages you output with `console.log()` and any unhandled errors.

Here's the full code for a page that writes to the console and then fails with an error:

```
<!DOCTYPE html>
<html lang="en">
  <head>
    <meta charset="UTF-8" />
    <meta name="viewport" content="width=device-width, initial-scale=1.0" />
    <meta http-equiv="X-UA-Compatible" content="ie=edge" />
    <title>Log and Error Test</title>
  </head>
  <body>
    <h1>Log and Error Test</h1>

<script>
  console.log('This appears in the developer console');
</script>
```

```
<script>
  // This will cause an error that appears in the console
  const myNumber =
</script>
  </body>
</html>
```

Figure 1-1 shows the output in the developer console. The logged message appears first, followed by the error (a `SyntaxError` for "Unexpected end of input"). Errors are displayed in red lettering, and Chrome helpfully adds links next to each message, so you can quickly view the source code that caused the message. Lines in your web pages and script files are numbered automatically. In this example, that makes it easy to distinguish between the source of the message (line 13) and the source of the error (the closing `</script>` tag on line 19).

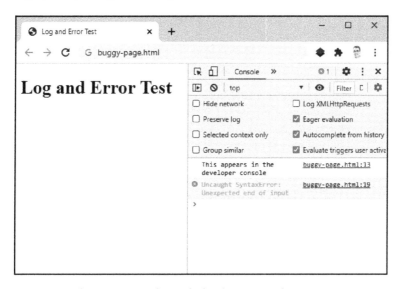

Figure 1-1. Viewing the output in Chrome's developer console

Discussion

We use `console.log()` throughout this book, often to write quick testing messages. However, there are other `console` methods you can use. Table 1-3 lists some of the most useful.

Table 1-3. Console methods

Method	Description
console.warn(object)	Similar to console.log(), but outputs text with a yellow background.
console.error(object)	Similar to console.log(), but outputs text with a red background. It's typically used to log error objects.
console.assert(expression, object)	If the expression is false, the message is written to the console along with a stack trace.
console.trace()	Displays a stack trace.
console.count(label)	Displays the number of times you've called this method with this label.
console.dir(object)	Displays all the properties of an object in an expandable, tree-like list.
console.group()	Starts a new group with the title you supply. The following console messages are indented underneath this heading, so they appear to be part of one logically related section. You use console.group End() to end the group.
console.time(label)	Starts a timer with a label you use to identify it.
console.timeEnd(label)	Stops the timer associated with the label and displays the elapsed time.

The consoles in modern browsers sometimes use *lazy evaluation* with objects and arrays. This issue may appear if you output an object with console.log(), then change it, and then output the same object a second time. If you do this from the script code in a web page, you'll often find that both calls to console.log() emit the same changed object, even though the first call preceded the actual change!

To avoid this quirk, you can explicitly convert your object to a string before you log it. This trick works because the console doesn't use lazy evaluation with strings. This technique isn't always convenient (for example, it doesn't help if you want to log a complete array that contains objects), but it does let you work around most cases.

Of course, the console is only one panel (or tab) in the developer tools. Look around, and you'll find quite a bit of useful functionality packed into the other panels. The exact arrangement and naming depends on your browser, but here are some highlights in Chrome:

Elements

Use this panel to view the HTML markup for specific parts of your page, and inspect the CSS rules that apply to individual elements. You can even *change* markup and styles (temporarily) to quickly test potential edits.

Sources
> Use this panel to browse all the files the current page is using, including Java-Script libraries, images, and style sheets.

Network
> Use the panel tab to watch the size and download time of your page and its resources, and to view the asynchronous messages being sent over the wire (for example, as part of a `fetch` request).

Performance
> Use this panel to start tracking the time your code takes to execute (see Recipe 11.2).

Application
> Use this panel to review all the data the current site is storing with cookies, in local storage or with the IndexedDB API.

You can play around with most of these panels to get an idea about how they work, or you can review Google's documentation (*https://oreil.ly/cZ6AP*).

See Also

Recipe 1.3 explains how to run ad hoc bits of code in the developer console.

1.3 Running Blocks of Code in the Developer Console

Problem

You want to try out a snippet of code without opening an editor and creating HTML and JavaScript files.

Solution

Use the developer console in your browser. First, open the developer tools (as explained in Recipe 1.2). Make sure the Console panel is selected. Then, paste or type your JavaScript.

Press Enter to run your code immediately. If you need to type multiple lines of code, press Shift+Enter at the end of each line to insert a soft return. Only press Enter when you're finished and you want to run your full block of code.

Often, you'll want to modify the same piece of code and rerun it. In all modern browsers, the developer console has a history feature that makes this easy. To use it, press the up arrow key to show the previously executed code block. If you want to see the code you ran before *that*, press the up arrow multiple times.

Figure 1-2 shows an example with a code block that didn't run successfully the first time because of a syntax error. The code was then called up in the history, edited, and executed, with the output (15) appearing underneath.

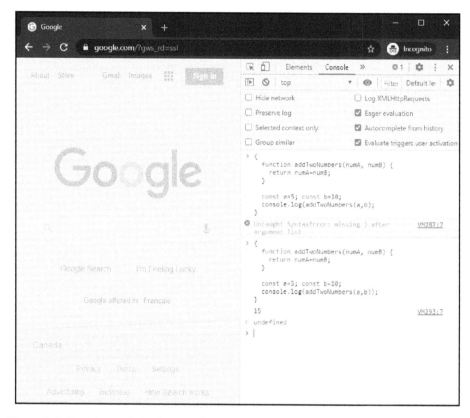

Figure 1-2. Running code in the console

The history feature only works if you *don't* start typing in any new code. If the console command line isn't empty, the up arrow key will just move through the current code block rather than stepping back through the history.

Discussion

In the developer console, you can enter JavaScript code exactly as you would in a script block. In other words, you can add functions and call them, or define a class and then instantiate it. You can also access the document object, interact with HTML elements in the current page, show alerts, and write to the console. (The messages will appear directly below.)

There's one potential stumbling block when using the console for longer code examples. You may run into a naming clash, because JavaScript won't allow you to define the same variables or function names in the same scope more than once. For example, consider a simple block of code like this:

```
const testValue = 40+12;
console.log(testValue);
```

This works fine if you run it once. But if you call it back up in the history to make a modification (by pressing the up arrow), and you try to run it again, you'll get an error informing you that `testValue` is already declared. You could rename your variable, but if you're trying to perfect a snippet of code with multiple values and functions, this renaming gets awkward fast. Alternatively, you could execute the command `location.reload()` to refresh the page, but that can be slow for complex pages, and you might lose some page state you're trying to keep.

Fortunately, there's a simpler solution. Simply enclose your entire block of code in an extra set of braces to create a new naming scope. You can then safely run the code multiple times, because each time a new context is created (and then discarded).

```
{
  const testValue = 40+12;
  console.log(testValue);
}
```

See Also

Recipe 11.1 explores the art of debugging in the developer console. Recipe 11.2 shows how to use the developer console for performance analysis.

1.4 Using Strict Mode to Catch Common Mistakes

Problem

You want to disallow potentially risky features, like automatic variable creation and some statements that fail silently.

Solution

Add the `use strict` directive at the top of your JavaScript code file, like this:

```
'use strict';
```

Alternatively, consider writing your JavaScript in a *module*, which is always loaded in strict mode (Recipe 8.9).

Discussion

JavaScript has a (somewhat deserved) reputation for tolerating sloppy code practices. The problem is that languages that ignore minor rule breaking put developers at a disadvantage. After all, you can't fix a problem that you never notice.

The following example demonstrates an example of JavaScript gone bad. Can you find the mistake?

```
// This function adds a list of consecutive numbers
function addRange(start, end) {
  let sum = 0;
  for (let i = start; i < end+1; i++) {
    sum += i;
  }
  return sum;
}

// Add numbers from 10 to 15
let startNumber = 10;
let endNumber = 15;
console.log(addRange(startNumber,endNumber));    // Displays 75

// Now add numbers from 1 to 5
startnumber = 1;
endNumber = 5;
console.log(addRange(startNumber,endNumber));    // Displays 0, but we expect 15
```

Although the code runs without an error, the results aren't what we expect. The problem occurs in this line:

```
startnumber = 1;
```

The issue here is that JavaScript creates variables whenever you assign a value, even if you don't explicitly define the variable. So if you assign to startnumber when you really want startNumber, JavaScript quietly creates a new startnumber variable. The end result is that the value you intended to assign to startNumber vanishes into another variable, never to be seen or used again.

To catch this problem, add the strict mode directive to the top of the file, before the function code:

```
'use strict';
```

Now a ReferenceError occurs when JavaScript reaches the startnumber assignment. This interrupts your code, ending the script. However, the error appears in red lettering in the developer console, explaining the problem and the line number where it happened. Now, a fix is trivially easy.

Strict mode catches a number of small but pernicious errors. Some examples include:

- Assignments to undeclared variables
- Duplicate parameter names (like `function(a, b, a)`) or object literal property names (as in `{a: 5, a: 0}`)
- Attempts to assign values to special keywords like `Infinity` or `undefined`
- Attempts to set read-only properties (Recipe 7.7) or change frozen objects (Recipe 7.8)

Many of these actions would fail without strict mode. However, they would fail *silently*, potentially leading to a maddening situation where your code doesn't work the way you expect it to, and you have no idea why.

 You may be able to configure your editor to insert the `use strict` directive to every new code file. For example, Visual Studio Code has at least three small extensions (*https://oreil.ly/ye0o7*) that offer to perform this task.

Strict mode catches a relatively small set of errors. Most developers also use a linting tool (Recipe 1.10) to catch a much broader range of bugs and potentially risky actions. In fact, developers rely on linters to such an extent that they sometimes don't bother to apply strict mode at all. However, it's always recommended to have strict mode as a basic level of protection against shooting yourself in the foot.

See Also

For the full details on what strict mode won't accept, see the strict mode documentation (*https://oreil.ly/Z7QhF*). To see how to use modules, which always execute in strict mode, see Recipe 8.9.

1.5 Filling in HTML Boilerplate with Emmet Shortcuts

Problem

You want to add a common chunk of HTML boilerplate without painstakingly typing each start and end tag.

Solution

Emmet is an editor feature that automatically changes predefined text abbreviations into standard blocks of HTML. Some code editors, like Visual Studio and WebStorm, support Emmet natively. Other editors, like Atom and Sublime Text, require the use of an editor plug-in. You can usually find the right plug-in by searching the plug-in library for "Emmet," but if you're in doubt, there's a master list of Emmet-supporting plug-ins (*https://emmet.io/download*).

To use Emmet, create a new file and save it with a *.html* or *.htm* extension, so your code editor recognizes it as an HTML document. Then, type one of Emmet's abbreviations, followed by the Tab key. (In some editors, you might use a different shortcut, like Enter or Ctrl+E, but the Tab key is most common.) Your text will be automatically expanded into the corresponding block of markup.

For example, the Emmet abbreviation `input:time` expands into this markup:

```
<input type="time" name="" id="" />
```

Figure 1-3 shows how VS Code recognizes an Emmet abbreviation as you type it. VS Code provides autocomplete support for Emmet, so you can see possible choices, and it adds the note "Emmet Abbreviation" to the autocomplete menu to signal that you aren't writing HTML, but an Emmet shortcut that will be *translated* into HTML.

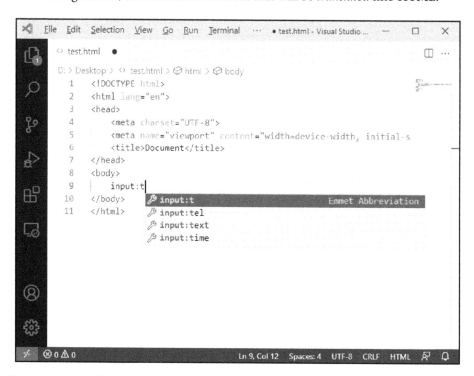

Figure 1-3. Using Emmet in VS Code

Discussion

Emmet provides a straightforward syntax, but it's surprisingly flexible. You can write more complicated expressions that create nested combinations of elements, set attributes, and incorporate sequential numbers into names. For example, to create a bulleted list with five items, you use the abbreviation ul>li*5, which adds the following block of markup:

```
<ul>
    <li></li>
    <li></li>
    <li></li>
    <li></li>
    <li></li>
</ul>
```

Or, you can create the starting skeleton for an HTML5 web page (the modern standard) with the shortcut html:5.

```
<!DOCTYPE html>
<html lang="en">
<head>
    <meta charset="UTF-8" />
    <meta name="viewport" content="width=device-width, initial-scale=1.0">
    <title>Document</title>
</head>
<body>

</body>
</html>
```

All of these features are described in the Emmet documentation (*https:// docs.emmet.io*). If you're in a hurry, start with the patterns in the useful cheatsheet.

1.6 Installing the npm Package Manager (with Node.js)

Problem

You want to install npm, so you can easily download JavaScript libraries from the npm registry and add them to web projects.

Solution

The Node Package Manager (npm) hosts the largest (and currently most popular) software registry in the world. The easiest way to get software from the npm registry is using npm, which is bundled with Node.js. To install Node, download an installer for your operating system (Windows, MacOS, or Linux) from the Node website (*https://nodejs.org*).

Once you finish installing Node, you can test that it's available using the command line. Open a terminal window and type the command node -v. To check if npm is installed, type npm -v. You'll see the version number of both packages:

```
$ node -v
v14.15.4
$ npm -v
6.14.10
```

Discussion

npm is included with Node.js, a JavaScript runtime environment and web server. You might use Node to run a server-side JavaScript framework like Express, or to build a JavaScript desktop application with Electron. But even if you don't plan to use Node, you'll almost certainly still install it just to get access to the npm package manager.

The Node Package Manager is a tool that can download packages from the npm registry, a free catalog that tracks tens of thousands of JavaScript libraries. In fact, you'll be hard-pressed to find a computer that's used for JavaScript development that *doesn't* have an installation of Node and npm.

The work of a package manager goes beyond simply downloading useful libraries. The package manager also has the responsibility of tracking what libraries your project is using (called *dependencies*), downloading the packages *they* depend on (sometimes called subdependencies), storing versioning information, and distinguishing between test and production builds. Thanks to npm, you can take a completed application to another computer and install all the dependencies it needs with a single command, as explained in Recipe 1.7.

Although npm is currently the most popular package manager for JavaScript, it's not the only one you might encounter. Yarn (*https://yarnpkg.com*) is favored by some developers who find it offers faster package installation. Pnpm (*https://pnpm.io*) is another option that aims to be command-line compatible with npm, while requiring less diskspace and offering better installation performance.

See Also

To install a package with npm, see Recipe 1.7.

If you're using Node for development (not just npm), you should consider installing it with nvm, the Node version manager. That way you can easily switch between different Node versions and quickly update your installation when new releases are available (which is often). For more information, see Recipe 17.1. And if you need help to get started running code in the Node environment, Chapter 17 has many more examples.

Extra: Using a Terminal and Shell

To run Node or npm, you use the *terminal*. Technically, a terminal is a text-based interface that communicates with a *shell* to execute commands. Many different terminal programs exist, along with many different shells. The terminal and shell program that you use depends on your operating system (and your personal preference, because there are plenty of third-party alternatives).

Here are some of the most common terminal and shell combinations you'll encounter:

- On a Macintosh computer, go to **Applications**, open the **Utilities** folder, and choose **Terminal**. This launches the default terminal program, which uses bash as its shell.

- On a Linux computer, the terminal program depends on the distro. There's often a shortcut named Terminal, and it almost always uses the bash shell.

- On Windows, you can launch PowerShell from the Start menu. Technically, PowerShell is the shell and it's wrapped in a terminal process called conhost. Microsoft is developing a modern conhost replacement called Windows Terminal, which early adopters can install from the Windows Store (or download from GitHub (*https://github.com/microsoft/terminal*)). Microsoft also includes the bash shell as part of its Windows Subsystem for Linux (*https://oreil.ly/N7EWS*), although that's a relatively recent addition to the operating system.

- Code editors sometimes include their own terminals. For example, if you open the terminal window in VS Code (use the Ctrl + ` shortcut [that's a backtick, not a single quote] or choose **View > Terminal** from the menu) you get VS Code's integrated terminal window. By default, it communicates with PowerShell on Windows and bash on other systems, although you can configure its settings.

When we direct you to use a terminal command, you can use the terminal window in your code editor, the terminal program that's specific to your computer, or one of the many third-party terminal and shell applications. They all get the same environment variables (which means they have access to Node and npm once they're installed), and they all have the ability to run programs in the current path. You can also use your terminal for the usual filesystem maintenance tasks, like creating folders and files.

In this book, when we show the commands you should type in a terminal (as in Recipe 1.6), we preceded them with the $ character. This is the traditional prompt for bash. However, different shells have different conventions. If you're using PowerShell you'll see a folder name followed by the > character instead (as in C:\Projects \Sites\WebTest>). Either way, the commands you use to run utilities (like npm) don't change.

1.7 Downloading a Package with npm

Problem

You want to install a specific software package from the npm registry.

Solution

First, you must have npm on your computer (see Recipe 1.6 for instructions). Assuming you do, open a terminal window ("Extra: Using a Terminal and Shell" on page 14), and go to the project directory for your website.

Next, you should create a *package.json* file, if your application doesn't already have one. You don't actually need this file to install packages, but it does become important for some other tasks (like restoring your packages to another development computer). The easiest way to create a *package.json* file is with npm's `init` command:

```
$ npm init -y
```

The `-y` parameter (for *yes*) means that npm will simply choose default values rather than prompt you for specific information about your application. If you don't include the `-y` parameter, you'll be asked a variety of questions about your application (its package name, description, version, license, and so on). However, you don't need to fill in any of these details at first (or at all), so it's perfectly acceptable to press Enter to leave each field blank and create the basic *package.json* boilerplate. For more information about the descriptive information inside *package.json*, see "Extra: Understanding package.json" on page 18.

Once you've initialized your application, you're ready to install a package. You must know the exact name of the package you want to install. By convention, npm names are made up of dash-separated lowercase words, like `fs-extra` or `react-dom`. To install your package of choice, run the `npm install` command with the package name. For example, here's how you would install the popular Lodash library:

```
$ npm install lodash
```

npm adds the packages you install to the *package.json* file. It also records more detailed versioning information about each package in a file named *package-lock.json*.

When you install a package, npm downloads its files and places them in a folder named *node_modules*. For example, if you install Lodash in a project folder named *test-site*, the Lodash script files will be placed in the folder *test-site/node_modules/lodash*.

You can remove a package by name using `npm uninstall`:

```
$ npm uninstall lodash
```

Discussion

The genius of npm (or any package manager) becomes apparent when you have a typical web project with half a dozen or more packages, each of which depends on additional packages. Because all these dependencies are tracked in the *package-lock.json* file, it's easy to figure out what a web application needs. You can see a full report by executing this command from your project folder:

```
$ npm list
```

It's also easy to re-download these packages on a new computer. For example, if you copy your website to another computer with the *package.json* and *package-lock.json* files, but without the *node_modules* folder, you can install all the dependent packages like this:

```
$ npm install
```

So far, you've seen how to install packages *locally* (as part of the current web application). npm also allows packages to be installed *globally* (in a system-specific folder, so the same version is available to all the web applications on your computer). For most software packages, local installation is best. It gives you the flexibility to control the exact version of a package that you use, and it lets you use different versions of the same package with different applications, so you never break compatibility. (This potential problem becomes magnified when one package depends on the specific version of *another* package.) However, global installation is useful for certain types of packages, particularly development tools that have command-line utilities. Some examples of packages that are sometimes installed globally include `create-react-app` (used to create a new React project), `http-server` (used to run a test web server), `typescript` (used to compile TypeScript code into JavaScript), and `jest` (used to run automated tests on your code).

To see all the global npm packages installed on your computer, run this command:

```
`npm list -g --depth 0`
```

Here, the `--depth` parameter makes sure that you only see the top layer of global packages, not the other packages that these global packages use. npm has additional features that we won't cover here, including the ability to:

- Designate some dependencies as *developer dependencies*, meaning they're required for development but not deployment (like a unit testing tool). You'll see this technique in Recipes 1.9 and 1.10.

- Audit your dependencies by searching the npm registry for reports of known vulnerabilities, which it may be able to fix by installing new versions (*https://oreil.ly/XJkEM*).

- Run command-line tasks through a bundled utility called npx. You can even launch tasks automatically by adding them to *package.json*, like prepping your site for production deployment or starting a web server during development testing. You'll see this technique with the test server in Recipe 1.9.

npm isn't the only package manager that JavaScript developers use. Yarn is a similar package manager that was initially developed by Facebook. It has a performance edge in some scenarios, due to the way that it downloads packages in parallel and uses caching. Historically, it's also enforced stricter security checks. There's no reason *not* to use Yarn, but npm remains significantly more popular in the JavaScript community.

To learn everything there is to know about npm, you can spend some quality time with the npm developer docs (*https://docs.npmjs.com*). You can also take a peek at Yarn (*https://yarnpkg.com*).

Extra: Understanding package.json

The *package.json* file is an application configuration file that was introduced with Node, but is now used for a variety of purposes. It stores descriptive information about your project, its creator, and its license, which becomes important if you ever decide to publish your project as a package on npm (a topic covered in Recipe 18.2). The *package.json* file also tracks your dependencies (the packages your application uses) and can store extra configuration steps for debugging and deployment.

It's a good practice to begin by creating a *package.json* file whenever you start a new project. You can create the file by hand, or using the npm init -y command, which is what we use in the examples in this chapter. Your newly generated file will look something like this (assuming your project folder is named *test_site*):

```
{
  "name": "test_site",
  "version": "1.0.0",
  "description": "",
  "main": "index.js",
  "scripts": {
    "test": "echo \"Error: no test specified\" && exit 1"
  },
  "keywords": [],
  "author": "",
  "license": "ISC"
}
```

As you may notice, the *package.json* file uses the JSON (JavaScript Object Notation) format. It holds a comma-separated list of property settings, all wrapped inside {} braces. You can edit *package.json* in your code editor at any time.

When you install a package with npm, that dependency is recorded in *package.json* using a property named dependencies. For example, if you install Lodash, the *package.json* file will look like this:

```
{
  "name": "test_site",
  "version": "1.0.0",
  "description": "",
  "main": "index.js",
  "scripts": {
    "test": "echo \"Error: no test specified\" && exit 1"
  },
  "keywords": [],
  "author": "",
  "license": "ISC",
  "dependencies": {
    "lodash": "^4.17.20"
  }
}
```

Don't confuse *package.json* with *package-lock.json*. The *package.json* file stores basic project settings and lists all the packages you use. The *package-lock.json* file specifies the exact version and checksum of every package you use (and the version and checksum of each package *those* packages use). For example, here's the automatically created *package-lock.json* file after you install Lodash:

```
{
  "name": "test-site",
  "version": "1.0.0",
  "lockfileVersion": 1,
  "requires": true,
  "dependencies": {
    "lodash": {
      "version": "4.17.20",
      "resolved": "https://registry.npmjs.org/lodash/-/lodash-4.17.20.tgz",
      "integrity": "sha512-PlhdFcillOINfeV7Ni6oF1TAEayyZBoZ8bcshTHqOYJYlrqzRK5h
agpagky5o4HfCzzd1TRkXPMFq6cKk9rGmA=="
    }
  }
}
```

In other words, *package-lock.json* "locks" your packages to a specific version. This is useful if you're deploying your project to another computer, and you want to install exactly the same versions of every package that you used during development.

There are two common reasons you might edit your application's *package.json* file. First, you might want to add more descriptive details for completeness before you share the project with anyone else. You'll definitely want to make sure this information is correct if you're planning to share your package in the npm registry (Recipe 18.2). Second, you might decide to configure command-line tasks for debugging, like starting a test server (Recipe 1.9). For a complete, property-by-property description of what you can put in *package.json*, refer to the npm documentation (*https://oreil.ly/n9PkO*).

1.8 Updating a Package with npm

Problem

You want to update an npm package to a newer version.

Solution

For minor updates, use `npm update`. You can name the specific package you want to update, or ask npm to check for new versions of *every* package your site uses, and update them all in one fell swoop:

```
$ npm update
```

npm will examine the *package.json* file and update every dependency and subdependency. It will also download any missing packages. Finally, it will update the *package-lock.json* file to match the new versions.

Discussion

It's a good practice to regularly update the packages you use. However, not all updates can happen automatically. npm updates follow the rules of *semver* (semantic versioning). npm will install updates that have greater patch numbers (for example, updating `2.1.2` to `2.1.3`) or minor version numbers (`2.1.2` to `2.2.0`), but it won't upgrade a dependency if the new release changes the major version number (`2.1.2` to `3.0.0`). This behavior guards against breaking changes when you update or deploy your application.

You can review what updates are available for all of your dependencies using the `npm outdated` command:

```
$ npm outdated
```

This produces output like this:

```
Package                 Current   Wanted   Latest   Location
-------                 -------   ------   ------   --------
eslint                   7.18.0   7.25.0   7.25.0   my-site
eslint-plugin-promise     4.2.1    4.3.1    5.1.0   my-site
lodash                  4.17.20  4.17.21  4.17.21   npm-test
```

The `Wanted` column shows available updates that will be installed the next time you run `npm update`. The `Latest` column shows the most recent version of the package. In the example above, both `lodash` and `eslint` can be updated to the latest package version. But the `eslint-plugin-promise` package will only be updated to version 4.3.1. The latest version, 5.1.0, changes the major version number, which means that according to the rules of semver it can't be applied automatically.

 This is a slight simplification, because npm gives you the ability to specify versioning policies more specifically in the *package.json* file. But in practice, this is the way that almost all npm updates will work. For more information about npm versioning, see the npm documentation (*https://oreil.ly/NX8js*).

If you want to update a dependency to use a new major version, you need to do it deliberately. Options include editing the *package.json* file by hand (slightly painful) or using a tool that can do it for you, like `npm-check-updates` (*https://oreil.ly/0JcMt*). The `npm-check-updates` tool allows you to review your dependencies, see what updates are available, and choose to update the *package.json* file to allow a new major version update. Once you've done that, call `npm update` to download the new version.

1.9 Setting Up a Local Test Server

Problem

You want to test your web pages during development, without local security restrictions, and without deploying them to a live web server.

Solution

Install a local test server on your computer. The test server will handle requests and send web pages to your browser, just like a real web server. The only difference is that the test server won't accept remote connections from other computers.

There are many choices for a test server (see the Discussion section). However, two simple, reliable choices are the `http-server` and `lite-server` packages that you can install through npm. We use `lite-server` here, because it adds a live update feature that automatically refreshes the page in the browser when you save changed code in your editor.

Before you install `lite-server`, it helps to have a sample web page to request. If you haven't already done so, make a project folder and configure it with the `npm init -y` command (Recipe 1.7). Then, add a file named *index.html* with a basic content. If you're in a hurry, here's a minimal but valid HTML document you can use to test where your code is running:

```
<!DOCTYPE html>
<html lang="en">
```

```
  <head>
    <meta charset="utf-8">
    <title>Test Page</title>
  </head>
  <body>
    <p>This is the index page</p>
    <script>
if (window.location.protocol === 'file:') {
  console.log('Running as local file!');
}
else if (window.location.host.startsWith('localhost')) {
  console.log('Running on a local server');
}
else {
  console.log('Running on a remote web server');
}
    </script>
  </body>
</html>
```

Now you're ready to make this document accessible to your browser through a test server.

To install `lite-server`, use npm with the `--save-dev` option. That way it's marked as a *developer dependency* that won't be deployed in a production build.

```
npm install lite-server --save-dev
```

Now you can run `lite-server` directly from a terminal window using npm's package runner, npx:

```
npx lite-server
```

This launches `lite-server`, opens a new browser tab, and requests *http://localhost: 3000* (where 3000 is whatever port `lite-server` acquires dynamically). The `lite-server` attempts to return *index.html*, or just displays "Cannot GET /" if you don't have a file with that name. If you used the sample page from this section, you'll see the "This is the index page" message on the page and "Running on a local server" in the developer console. If you don't have an *index.html* page in your test site, you can load up a different page by editing the URL in the address bar (for example, *http://localhost:3000/someOtherPage.html*).

Now try making some changes. The `lite-server` instance watches your project folder. Whenever you change a file, it automatically forces the browser to refresh the page. In the terminal, you'll see a "Reloading Browsers" message whenever this happens.

To end the server, press Ctrl+C at the terminal (Command-C on a Macintosh) and answer Y. Or, close the terminal window (or use the Kill Terminal trashcan icon in VS Code).

Behind the scenes, `lite-server` uses a popular browser automation tool called BrowserSync (*https://oreil.ly/tAwyk*) to implement its live reloading. The only requirement is that your web page must have a `<body>` section. (Create a super-simple test page without that detail, and you won't see the automatic refreshing behavior.)

Discussion

You can save a web page on your local computer, open it in a web browser, and run its code. However, web browsers greatly restrict pages that are opened from the local filesystem. Entire features are unavailable and will fail quietly (like web workers, ES modules, and certain Canvas operations). To avoid hitting these security barriers or—even worse—being confused at why code isn't working the way you expect, it's always better to run your web pages from a test web server.

While testing, it's common to use a development server. There are many options, and your decision will depend somewhat on the other server-side technologies that you plan to use. For example, if you want to run PHP code in your web pages, you'll need a web server that supports it. If you plan to build part of the backend of your application using JavaScript or a JavaScript-powered server-side framework like Express, you'll need to use Node.js. But if you're running web pages with traditional client-side JavaScript, a simple server that sends static files is enough, like `http-server` or `lite-server`. There are many more and code editors often have their own plug-in-based test server. For example, if you're using Visual Studio Code you can search the extension library for the popular Live Server plug-in (*https://oreil.ly/NIrRK*).

In the Solution section, you saw how to run `lite-server` with `npx`. However, a more convenient setup is to make a *development run task* that automatically starts the server. You can do that by editing the *package.json* file and adding the following instruction to the `scripts` section:

```
{
...
  "scripts": {
    "dev": "lite-server"
  }
}
```

The `scripts` section holds executable tasks that you want to run regularly. These might include verifying your code with a linter, checking it into source control, packaging your files for deployment, or running a unit test. You can add as many scripts as you need—for example, it's common to use one task to run your application, another to test it with an automated testing tool (Recipe 10.7), another to prepare it for distribution, and so on. In this example, the script is named `dev`, which is a convention that identifies a task you plan to use while developing your application.

Once you've defined a script in *package.json*, you can run it with the `npm run` command at the terminal:

```
npm run dev
```

This launches `lite-server` with `npx`.

Some code editors have additional support for this configuration detail. For example, if you open the *package.json* file in VS Code you'll see that a "Debug" link is added just above the `dev` setting. Click this link and VS Code opens a new terminal and launches `lite-server` automatically.

See Also

To learn more about using Node as a test server, see the recipes in Chapter 17. For more information about running tasks with npm, you can read this good overview (*https://oreil.ly/nq31H*).

1.10 Enforcing Code Standards with a Linter

Problem

You want to standardize your JavaScript code, follow best practices, and avoid common pitfalls that can lead to bugs.

Solution

Check your code with a *linter*, which warns you when you deviate from the rules you've chosen to follow. The most popular JavaScript linter is ESLint.

To use ESLint, you first need npm (see Recipe 1.6). Open a terminal window in your project folder. If you haven't already created the *package.json* file, get npm to create it now:

```
$ npm init -y
```

Next, install the `eslint` package using the `--save-dev` option, because you want ESLint to be a *developer dependency* that's installed on developer computers, but not deployed to a production server:

```
$ npm install eslint --save-dev
```

If you don't already have an ESLint configuration file, you need to create one now. Use npx to run the ESLint setup:

```
$ npx eslint --init
```

ESLint will ask you a series of questions to assess the type of rules it should enforce. Often, it presents a small menu of choices, and you must use the arrow keys to pick the option you want.

The first question is "How would you like to use ESLint?" Here you have three options, arranged from least strict to most strict:

Check syntax only
> Uses ESLint to catch errors. It's not any stricter than the error-highlighting feature in most code editors.

Check syntax and find problems
> Enforces ESLint's recommended practices (*https://eslint.org/docs/rules*) (the ones marked with a checkmark). This is an excellent starting point, and you can override individual rules to your preference later on.

Check syntax, find problems, and enforce code style
> Is a good choice if you want to use a specific JavaScript style guide, like Airbnb (*https://github.com/airbnb/javascript*), to enforce a broader set of style conventions. If you choose this option, you'll be asked to pick the style guide later in the process.

Next, you'll be asked a series of technical questions: are you using modules, the React or Vue framework, or the TypeScript language? Choose JavaScript modules to get support for the ES6 modules standard described in Recipe 8.9, and choose No for other questions unless you're using the technology in question.

Next, you'll be asked "Where does your code run?" Choose Browser for a traditional website with client-side JavaScript code (the usual), or Node if you're building a server-side application that runs in the Node.js server.

If you've chosen to use a style guide, JavaScript will now prompt you to pick one from a small list of choices. It then installs these rules automatically using one or more separate packages, provided you allow it.

Finally, ESLint asks "What format do you want your config file to be in?" All the format choices work equally well. We prefer to use JSON for symmetry with the *package.json* file, in which case ESList stores its configuration in a file named *.eslintrc.json*. If you use a JavaScript configuration file, the extension is *.js*, and if you choose a YAML configuration file, the extension is *.yaml*.

Here's what you'll see in the *.eslintrc.json* file if you've asked ESLint to "check syntax and find problems" without the addition of a separate style guide:

```
{
  "env": {
      "browser": true,
      "es2021": true
```

```
    },
    "extends": "eslint:recommended",
    "parserOptions": {
      "ecmaVersion": 12,
      "sourceType": "module"
    },
    "rules": {
  }
}
```

Now you can ESLint to check your files in the terminal:

```
npx eslint my-script.js
```

But a far more practical option is to use a plug-in that integrates ESLint with your code editor. All the code editors introduced in Recipe 1.1 support ESLint, and you can browse the full list of ESLint-supporting plug-ins (*https://oreil.ly/isQMA*).

To add ESLint to your code editor, go to its plug-in library. For example, in Visual Studio Code you begin by clicking **Extensions** in the left panel, and then searching the library for "eslint," then clicking **Install**. Once you've installed ESLint, you will need to officially allow it through the plug-in's settings page (or by clicking the light-bulb icon that appears when you open a code file in the editor, and then choosing **Allow**). You may also need to install ESLint globally across your entire computer so the plug-in can find it:

```
$ npm install -g eslint
```

Once ESLint is enabled, you'll see the squiggly underlines that denote ESLint errors and warnings. Figure 1-4 shows an example where ESLint detects a `case` in a `switch` statement that falls through to the next `case`, which isn't allowed in ESLint's standard settings. The "eslint" label in the pop-up identifies that this message is from the ESLint plug-in, not VS Code's standard error checking.

> If ESLint isn't catching the issues that you expect it to catch, it could be due to *another* error in your file, possibly even one in a different section of code. Try resolving any outstanding issues, and then recheck your file.

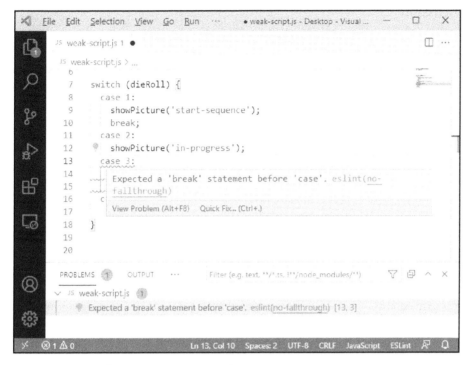

Figure 1-4. ESLint flags an error in VS Code

Click **Quick Fix** (or the lightbulb icon in the margin) to learn more about the problem or attempt a fix (if possible). You can also disable checking for this issue in the current line or file, in which case your override is recorded in a special comment. For example, this disables the rule against declaring variables that you don't use:

```
/* eslint-disable no-unused-vars */
```

If you must override ESLint with comments, it's probably best to be as targeted and judicious as possible. Instead of disabling checking for an entire file, override it for a single, specific line, like this:

```
// eslint-disable-next-line no-unused-vars
let futureUseVariable;
```

or this (replacing `eslint-disable-next-line` with `eslint-disable-line`):

```
let futureUseVariable;  // eslint-disable-line no-unused-vars
```

If you want to resume checking for the issue, just remove the comment.

Discussion

JavaScript is a permissive language that gives developers a great deal of flexibility. Sometimes this flexibility can lead to problems. For example, it can hide errors or cause ambiguity that makes the code harder to understand. A linter works to prevent these problems by enforcing a range of standards, even if they don't correspond to outright errors. It flags potential issues in the making, and suspicious practices that don't trigger your code editor's error checker but may eventually come back to haunt you.

ESLint is an *opinionated* linter, which means it flags issues that you may not consider problems, like variables you declare but don't use, parameter values you change in a function, empty conditional blocks, and regular expressions that include literal spaces (to name just a few). If you want to allow some of these, you have the power to override any of these settings in the ESLint configuration file (or on a file-by-file or line-by-line basis with a comment). But usually you'll just decide to change your ways to get along, knowing that ESLint's choices will eventually avoid a future headache.

ESLint also has the ability to correct certain types of errors automatically, and enforce style conventions (like tabs versus spaces, single quotes versus double quotes, brace and indent styles, and so on). Using the ESLint plug-in for an editor like VS Code, you can configure it to perform these corrections automatically when you save your file. Or, you can use ESLint to flag potential problems only, and use a formatter (Recipe 1.11) to enforce code style conventions.

If you work in a team, you may simply receive a preordained ESLint configuration file to use. If not, you need to decide which set of ESLint defaults to follow. You can lean more about ESLint recommended set (*https://eslint.org/docs/rules*) (used in this recipe), which provides examples of nonconforming code for every issue the ESLint can check. If you want to use a more thorough JavaScript style guide, we recommend the popular Airbnb JavaScript Style Guide (*https://github.com/airbnb/javascript*), which can be installed automatically with `eslint -init`.

1.11 Styling Code Consistently with a Formatter

Problem

You want to format your JavaScript consistently to improve readability and reduce ambiguity.

Solution

Use the Prettier code formatter to automatically format your code according to the rules you've established. Prettier enforces consistency on style details like indentation, use of single and double quotes, spacing inside brackets, spacing for function parameter lists, and the wrapping of long code lines. But unlike a linter (Recipe 1.10), Prettier doesn't flag these issues for you to fix them. Instead, it applies its formatting automatically every time you save your JavaScript code, HTML markup, or CSS style rules.

Although Prettier exists as a package you can install with npm and use at the command line, it's much more useful to use a plug-in for your code editor. All the code editors introduced in Recipe 1.1 have a Prettier plug-in. Most of them are listed at the Prettier website (*https://oreil.ly/weRb5*).

To add Prettier to your code editor, go to its plug-in library. For example, in Visual Studio Code you click **Extensions** in the left panel, search the library for "prettier," and then click **Install**.

Once you've installed Prettier, you'll be able to use it when you're editing a code file. Right-click next to your code in the editor and choose **Format Document**. You can configure the plug-in settings to change a small set of options (like the maximum allowed width before code lines are split, and whether you prefer spaces to tabs).

 In VS Code, you can also configure Prettier to run automatically every time you save a file. To activate this behavior, choose **File > Preferences > Settings**, go to the **Text Editor > Formatting** section, and choose **Format On Save**.

Discussion

Although many code editors have their own automatic formatting features, a code formatter goes beyond these. For example, the Prettier formatter strips away any custom formatting. It parses all the code and reformats it according to the conventions you've set, with almost no consideration to how it was originally written. (Blank lines and object literals are the only two exceptions.) This approach guarantees that the same code is always presented in the same way, and that code from different developers is completely consistent. And like a linter, the rules for a code formatter are defined in a configuration file, which means you can easily distribute them to different members of a team, even if they're using different code editors.

The Prettier formatter takes particular care with line breaks. By default, the maximum line length is set to 80, but Prettier will allows some lines to stretch a bit longer if it avoids a confusing line break. And if a line break is required, Prettier does it intelligently. For example, it would prefer to fit a function call into one line:

```
myFunction(argA(), argB(), argC());
```

But if that isn't practical, it doesn't just wrap the code however it fits. It chooses the most pleasing arrangement it understands:

```
myFunction(
  reallyLongArg(),
  omgSoManyParameters(),
  IShouldRefactorThis(),
  isThereSeriouslyAnotherOne()
);
```

Of course, no matter how intelligent a formatter like Prettier is, you may prefer your own idiosyncratic code arrangements. It's sometimes said that "Nobody loves what Prettier does to their syntax. Everyone loves what Prettier does to their coworkers' syntax." In other words, the value of an aggressive, opinionated formatter like Prettier is the way it unifies different developers, cleans up legacy code, and irons out bizarre habits. And if you decide to use Prettier, you'll have the unchecked freedom to write your code without thinking about spacing, line breaks, or presentation. In the end, your code will still be converted to the same canonical form.

 If you're not entirely certain that you want to use a code formatter, or you're not sure how to configure its settings, spend some time in the Prettier playground (*https://oreil.ly/TKam1*) to explore how it works.

A linter like ESLint and a formatter like Prettier have some overlap. However, their goals are different and their use is complementary. If you're using both ESLint and Prettier, you should keep the ESLint rules that catch suspicious coding practices, but disable the ones that enforce formatting conventions about indents, quotes, and spacing. Fortunately, this is easy to do by adding an extra ESLint configuration rule that turns off potential settings that could conflict with Prettier. And the easiest way to do that is by adding the `eslint-config-prettier` package to your project:

```
$ npm install --save-dev eslint-config-prettier
```

Lastly, you need to add `prettier` to the `extends` section in your *.eslintrc.json* file. The `extends` section will hold a list wrapped in square brackets, and `prettier` should be at the very end. Here's an example:

```
{
  "env": {
      "browser": true,
      "es2021": true
  },
  "extends": ["eslint:recommended", "prettier"],
  "parserOptions": {
    "ecmaVersion": 12,
    "sourceType": "module"
  },
  "rules": {
  }
}
```

To review the most recent installation instructions, check out the documentation for the `eslint-config-prettier` package (*https://oreil.ly/AgxiF*).

1.12 Experimenting in a JavaScript Playground

Problem

You want to quickly test or share a code idea without building a project and spinning up your desktop code editor.

Solution

Use a JavaScript *playground*, which is a website where you can edit and run JavaScript code. There are well over a dozen JavaScript playgrounds, but Table 1-4 lists five of the most popular.

Table 1-4. JavaScript playgrounds

Website	Notes
JSFiddle (*https://jsfiddle.net*)	Arguably the first JavaScript playground, JSFiddle is still at the forefront with features for simulating asynchronous calls and GitHub integration.
JS Bin (*https://jsbin.com*)	A classic playground with a simple tab-based interface that lets you pop different sections (JavaScript, HTML, CSS) into view one at a time. The code for JS Bin is also available as an open source project.
CodePen (*https://codepen.io*)	One of the more attractively designed playgrounds, with an emphasis on the social (popular examples are promoted in the CodePen community). Its polished interface is particularly suitable for novice users.
CodeSandbox (*http://codesandbox.io*)	One of the newer playgrounds, it uses an IDE-like layout that feels a lot like a web-hosted version of Visual Studio Code.
Glitch (*https://glitch.com*)	Another IDE-in-a-browser, Glitch is notable for its VS Code plug-in, which lets you switch between editing in a browser playground or using your desktop editor on the same project.

All these JavaScript playgrounds are powerful, practical choices. They all work similarly, although they can look strikingly different. For example, compare the dense developer cockpit of JSFiddle (Figure 1-5) to the more spaced-out editor in CodePen (Figure 1-6).

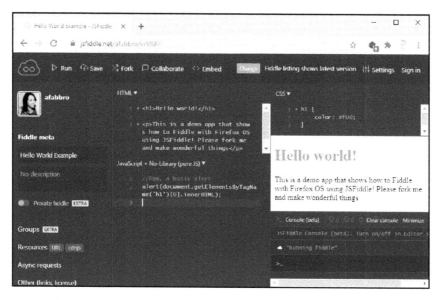

Figure 1-5. The JavaScript playground JSFiddle

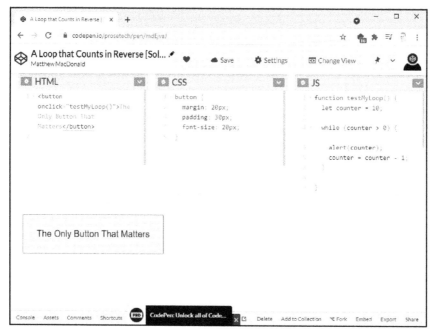

Figure 1-6. A simple example in CodePen

Here's how you use a JavaScript playground. When you visit the site, you can start coding immediately at a blank page. Even though your JavaScript, HTML, and CSS are presented separately, you don't need to explicitly add a `<script>` element to connect your JavaScript or a `<link>` element for your style sheet. These details are already filled into the markup of your page or, more commonly, are an implicit part of boilerplate that's hidden behind the scenes.

All JavaScript playgrounds let you see the page you're working on beside your code window. In some (like CodePen), the preview is refreshed automatically as you make changes. In others (like JSFiddle), you need to explicitly click a Play or Run button to reload your page. If you write messages with `console.log()`, some JavaScript playgrounds send that directly to the browser console (like CodePen), while others can also show it in a dedicated panel that's visible on the page (like JSFiddle).

When you're finished you can save your work, at which point you receive a newly generated, shareable link. However, it's a better idea to sign up for an account first, so you're able to return to the JavaScript playground, find all the examples you've created, and edit them. (If you save an example anonymously, you can't edit it, although you can use it as a starting point to build another example.) All the playgrounds listed in Table 1-4 let you create an account and save your work for free.

 The exact terminology for the kind of example you create in a JavaScript playground varies based on the site. It might be called a fiddle, a pen, a snippet, or something else.

Discussion

JavaScript playgrounds are a useful idea that's been picked up by more than a dozen websites. Almost all of them share some important characteristics:

- They're free to use. However, many have a subscription option for premium features, like being able to save your work and keep it private.

- You can save your work indefinitely. This is particularly handy if you want to share a quick mock-up or collaborate on a new experiment with others.

- They support a wide range of popular JavaScript libraries and frameworks. For example, you can quickly add Lodash, React, or jQuery to your example, just by picking it from a list.

- You can edit HTML, JavaScript, and CSS all in one window. Depending on the playground, it may be divided into panels that are all visible at once (like JSFiddle) or tabs that you switch between (like JS Bin). Or, it may be customizable (like CodePen).

- They provide some level of autocompletion, error checking, and syntax high-lighting (colorizing different code ingredients), although it's not as complete as what you'll get in a desktop code editor.

- They provide a preview of your page so you can jump easily between coding and testing.

JavaScript playgrounds also have limits. For example, you may not be able to host other resources like images, interact with backend services like databases, or use asynchronous requests with `fetch`.

JavaScript playgrounds should also be distinguished from full cloud-based programming environments. For example, you can use VS Code online in a completely hosted environment called GitHub Codespaces (*https://oreil.ly/Vo95d*), or AWS Cloud9 from Amazon (*https://oreil.ly/tvTZq*), or Google Cloud (*https://oreil.ly/fqWuW*). None of these products are free, but all are appealing if you want to set up a specific development environment that you can use in your browser, on different devices, and with no setup or performance concerns.

## CHAPTER 2

Strings and Regular Expressions

Here's a trivia question for your next JavaScript party: how many data types are there in the world's most popular language?

The answer is *eight*, but they might not be what you expect. JavaScript's eight data types are:

- `Number`
- `String`
- `Boolean`
- `BigInt` (for very large integers)
- `Symbol` (for unique identifiers)
- `Object` (the root of every other JavaScript type)
- `undefined` (a variable that hasn't been assigned a value)
- `null` (a missing object)

The recipes in this book feature all of these ingredients. In this chapter, you'll turn your focus to the text-manipulating power of strings.

2.1 Checking for an Existing, Nonempty String

Problem

You want to verify that a variable is defined, is a string, and is not empty before you use it.

Solution

Before you start working with a string, you often need to validate that it's safe to use. When you do, there are different questions you might ask.

If you want to make sure that your variable is a string (not just a variable that can be *converted* to a string), you use this test:

```
if (typeof unknownVariable === 'string') {
  // unknownVariable is a string
}
```

If you want to check that you have a nonempty string (not the zero-length string ''), you can tighten your verification like this:

```
if (typeof unknownVariable === 'string' && unknownVariable.length > 0) {
  // This is a genuine string with characters or whitespace in it
}
```

Optionally, you may want to reject strings that are made up of whitespace only, in which case you can use the `String.trim()` method:

```
if (typeof unknownVariable === 'string' && unknownVariable.trim().length > 0) {
  // This is a genuine string that is not empty or all whitespace
}
```

The order of your conditions is important. JavaScript uses *short-circuit evaluation.* That means it will only evaluate the second condition (the length check) if the first condition (the type check) succeeds. This is important because the length check will fail if `unknownVariable` is a different type of variable, like a number.

```
// This test is only safe if we already know unknownVariable is a string
if (unknownVariable.length > 0)
```

There's a potential gap when using the `typeof` operator. It's possible to circumvent the string test by using a `String` object instead of a string literal:

```
const unknownVariable = new String('test');
```

Now the `typeof` operator will return *object* instead of *string*, because the string primitive is wrapped in a `String` object.

In modern JavaScript, creating a `String` object instance is discouraged for reasons like this. You're better off removing this practice from any code you encounter than coding around it. However, if you need to accommodate possible `String` objects, you can use a more complex test like this:

```
if (typeof unknownVariable === 'string' ||
    String.prototype.isPrototypeOf(unknownVariable)) {
  // It's a string primitive or a string wrapped in an object.
}
```

This code checks that one of two conditions are met: either you have a string primitive or an object that has the same prototype as `String`.[1]

Discussion

The type-checking test in this recipe uses the `typeof` operator. It returns the type name of the variable as a lowercase string. The possible values are:

- `undefined`
- `boolean`
- `number`
- `bigint`
- `string`
- `symbol`
- `function`
- `object`

These values match the list at the beginning of this chapter, but with two small differences. First, there's no *null*, because null values return the string *object* instead. (This is considered a bug by many, but it's kept for historical reasons.) Second, there's an added *function* data type, even though a function is technically a special case of object.

Occasionally, you'll see the following old-fashioned string-validation technique. It doesn't require a variable to actually *be* a string. It simply verifies that your value can be treated as a string, and that it isn't the empty string.

```
if (unknownVariable) {
  /* We get here as long as:
     unknownVariable has been declared
     unknownVariable is not null
     unknownVariable is not the empty string ''
  */
}
```

This works because `null` values, `undefined` values, and empty strings (`''`) are all *falsy* in JavaScript. If you evaluate any of them in a conditional expression, they are treated as false.

---

1 In JavaScript, a *prototype* is a template for a specific type of object. In a more traditional object-oriented language, we would say that objects with the same prototype are instances of the same class. Chapter 8 has many recipes that explore prototypes in JavaScript.

This approach has a potential blindspot with the number 0, which always evaluates to `false`, skipping the `if` block. To be safe, it's better to explicitly convert your numeric variables to strings, as described in Recipe 2.2.

2.2 Converting a Numeric Value to a Formatted String

Problem

You want to create a string representation of a number.

Solution

JavaScript is a loosely typed language, and it will automatically convert any value to a string when it needs to—for example, if you compare a number to a string or join a number to a string with the + operator. In fact, one of the easiest tricks that JavaScript developers use to convert numbers to strings is to simply concatenate an empty string on the beginning or end of the value:

```
const someNumber = 42;
const someString = someNumber + '';
```

However, modern practice favors *explicit* variable conversions. Every JavaScript object has a built-in `toString()` method, including the `Number` object. You can call it like this:

```
const someNumber = 42;
const someString = someNumber.toString();
```

Often, you need to customize the string representation of your number. For example, you might want a fixed number of decimal places (like 30.00 instead of 30). This might also involve rounding (for example, from 30.009 to 30.01).

JavaScript has three utility methods built into the number data type that can help you. All of them create string representations of a number:

`Number.toFixed()`
> Lets you specify the number of digits to keep after the decimal point.

`Number.toExponential()`
> Uses scientific notation, and lets you specify the number of digits to show after the decimal point.

`Number.toPrecision()`
> Lets you specify the number of significant digits to keep, without considering how large or small your number is.

If you aren't familiar with *significant digits*, it's a scientific concept used to make sure calculations keep an appropriate degree of precision. It also helps to make sure a measurement is not represented in a way that implies more precision than it actually has. (For example, your average weight may be 162.5 pounds, but it's probably not meaningful to say it's 162.503018 pounds, nor is it helpful to round it to 200 pounds.) Wikipedia explains the concept in detail (*https://oreil.ly/vrrPr*).

Here's an example that demonstrates all three string conversion methods:

```
const someNumber = 1242.0055;

// Ask for exactly 2 decimal points. Numbers will be rounded if necessary.
const fixedString = someNumber.toFixed(2);
// fixedString = '1242.01'

// Ask for 5 significant digits. Scientific notation is used if necessary.
const precisionString = someNumber.toPrecision(5);
// precisionString = '1242.0'

// Ask for scientific notation with 2 decimal plates.
const scientificString = someNumber.toExponential(2);
// scientificString = '1.24e+3'
```

If you want to apply formatting like commas, a currency symbol, or some other locale-specific details, you need the help of the `Intl.NumberFormat` object. Once you create an instance and configure it appropriately, you can use the `Intl.NumberFormat` to perform your number-to-string conversion.

For example, to format a number as a US currency string, you use code like this:

```
const formatter =
  new Intl.NumberFormat('en-US', { style: 'currency', currency: 'USD' });

const someNumber = 1242.0005;
const moneyString = formatter.format(someNumber);
// moneyString = '$1,242.00'
```

Discussion

A *locale* represents a specific geographic or cultural region. Locale identifiers combine a language code and a region string. The locale *en-US* represents the English language in the United States of America. The local *en_CA* is English in Canada, *fr-CA* is French in Canada, *ja-JP* is Japanese in Japan, and so on.

Depending on your locale, there are some standard number formatting rules that apply. For example, numbers in English language regions often use commas to separate thousands (as in *1,200.00*), while commas in French language regions often use commas instead of a decimal point (as in *1 200,00*). If you create a `Intl.NumberFor` `mat` object without any constructor arguments, you get the locale settings of the current computer:

```
const formatter = new Intl.NumberFormat();
```

You can also create an `Intl.NumberFormat` object for a specific locale, with no extra options:

```
const formatter = new Intl.NumberFormat('en-US');
```

In the *en-US* region, this object will add comma separators, but it won't apply a fixed number of decimal points or add a currency symbol.

The `Intl.NumberFormat` object supports a number of options. You can change the way negative numbers are displayed, set minimum and maximum numbers of digits, show percentages, and choose different numbering systems in some languages. You can find comprehensive information in the Mozilla Developer Network reference (*https://oreil.ly/JEF4Q*).

You may see an older version of this technique that uses the `Number.toLocale` `String()` method. Here's an example:

```
const someNumber = 1242.0005;
const moneyString = someNumber.toLocaleString(
  'en-US', { style: 'currency', currency: 'USD' });
```

This approach is perfectly valid, although if you plan to format a long series of numbers, creating and reusing a single `Intl.NumberFormat` object will perform better.

See Also

If you need formatting support that's more extensive than what `Intl.NumberFormat` provides, you can use a third-party library like Numeral.js (*https://github.com/adamw draper/Numeral-js*).

2.3 Inserting Special Characters

Problem

You want to insert a special character, such as a line break, into a string.

Solution

The simplest approach with many special characters is simple: just paste the character you want into your editor. For example, if you need a copyright symbol (©), first find the character in a desktop utility like charmap (on a Windows computer) or just search for "copyright symbol" in Google. Select the symbol, copy it, and then paste it into your code.

If you want to use a character that wouldn't normally be allowed in your code (according to the syntax rules of JavaScript), you need to use one of its *escape sequences*—special character code combinations that aren't interpreted literally.

For example, if you're using apostrophes to delimit your strings, you can't put an apostrophe character directly *in* your string. Instead, you need to use the \' escape sequence, like this:

```
const favoriteMovie = 'My favorite movie is \'The Seventh Seal\'.';
```

Now `favoriteMovie` holds the text *My favorite movie is 'The Seventh Seal'*.

Discussion

The escape sequences in JavaScript all begin with the *backslash character* (\). This character signals that what follows is a sequence of characters that needs special handling. Table 2-1 lists the other escape sequences that JavaScript recognizes.

Table 2-1. Escape sequences

Sequence	Character
\'	Single quote
\"	Double quote
\\	Backslash
\n	Newline
\t	Horizontal tab
\b	Nondestructive backspace*
\f	Form feed*
\r	Carriage return[a]
\ddd	Octal sequence (3 digits: *ddd*)
\xdd	Hexadecimal sequence (2 digits: *dd*)
\udddd	Unicode sequence (4 hex digits: *dddd*)

[a] Some escape sequences (like the ones used for backspaces and form feeds) are holdovers from the original ASCII character standard and C language. Unless you're dealing with a legacy scenario (like sending input to a terminal), these escape sequences aren't likely to be useful in JavaScript.

The last three escape sequences in Table 2-1 are patterns that require you to supply a numeric value. For example, if you don't want to use the copy-and-paste trick to add a copyright symbol, you can insert it by using the \u escape sequence and the copyright symbol's Unicode value:

```
const copyrightNotice = 'This page \u00A9 Shelley Powers.';
```

Now the `copyrightNotice` string is set to *This page © Shelley Powers.*

See Also

For information about inserting even more specialized characters in your strings, see Recipe 2.4. For an alternate approach to dealing with line breaks without using \n, see Recipe 2.5.

2.4 Inserting Emojis

Problem

You want to insert an extended Unicode character that has a 4-byte encoding, like an emoji or certain types of accented non-English letters.

Solution

If you simply want to create a string with an emoji, the copy-and-paste trick from Recipe 2.3 usually works. In a modern code editor, you can write code like this:

```
const hamburger = '🍔';
const hamburgerStory = 'I like hamburgers' + hamburger;
```

Your code font doesn't even need to support emojis, because your code editor will fall back on the emoji support provided by your operating system. (Of course, issues can still occur. For example, you might see a square "missing character" icon on an older system where the emoji isn't available.)

Another option is to use the Unicode value for the emoji. The problem is that you can't use a standard \u escape sequence to get an emoji, because every emoji is stored as a 4-byte value. (By comparison, the Unicode characters that map to the keys of your keyboard are usually encoded as 2-byte values.)

The solution is to use the `String.fromCodePoint()` method:

```
const hamburgerStory = 'I like hamburgers' + String.fromCodePoint(0x1F354);
```

The hamburger emoji has the hexadecimal code U+1F354. To use it with `fromCodePoint()`, replace the prefix *U+* with *0x*.

Once you've created an emoji-enhanced string, you can write it to the developer console or show it in a web page, just as you would with an ordinary string composed of ordinary characters.

Discussion

As of 2020, there are just over three thousand emojis in the world. You can see them, with their corresponding hexadecimal values at the Full Emoji List (*https://oreil.ly/IIguA*). Just because an emoji exists doesn't mean it will be supported on the devices where you plan to use it, so test for compliance early.

If you need to do string processing with strings that may include emojis, other issues can crawl out of the woodwork. For example, what do you expect this code will find?

```
const hamburger = '🍔';
const hamburgerLength = hamburger.length;
```

Even though the `hamburger` string is just one character, to your code the length appears to be 2 because the hamburger emoji takes twice as many bytes in memory. This is an unpleasant *leaky abstraction* (*https://oreil.ly/nlmvi*) and a limitation of JavaScript's support for Unicode.

There are workarounds that people have invented to deal with emoji issues, like incorrect lengths and problems iterating over characters or slicing strings. But making a home brew solution is risky, because there are often strange edge cases. Instead, consider a JavaScript library with emoji support like Grapheme Splitter (*https://github.com/orling/grapheme-splitter*) if you need to manipulate emoji-enriched text.

2.5 Using Template Literals for Clearer String Concatenation

Problem

You want a simpler, clearer way to write long string concatenation operations.

Solution

A common task in programming is to combine bits of static text with variables to create a single, longer string. The traditional way to assemble this kind of string is with the concatentation operator +, as shown here:

```
const employeeDetail = 'Our team includes ' + firstName + ' ' + lastName +
  ' who works on the ' + team + " team. They/'ve been a team member since "
  + hireDate + '!';
```

It's not awful, but it can get awkward, particularly as the fixed bits of text get longer. It's also surprisingly easy to forget to add spaces around the variables.

A different approach is to use *template literals*, a type of string literal that allows embedded expressions. To create a template literal, just replace your standard string delimiters (apostrophes or double quotes) with the backtick (`) character:

```
const greeting = `Hello world from a template literal!`;
```

Now you can insert your variables directly into your template literal. All you need to do is wrap each variable in curly braces, preceded by a dollar sign, like ${firstName}. This is called an *expression*.

The advantage of the template literal approach becomes clearer when you look at a full example:

```
employeeDetail = `Our team includes ${firstName} ${lastName} who works on the
${team} team. They've been a team member since ${hireDate}!`;
```

It's even clearer when you use a modern code editor that colorizes the curly brace expressions, making the variables stand out from the literal text.

Template literals also preserve line breaks. In the examples shown here, you can't see this effect, because we've wrapped the code to fit the page. But if you deliberately hit Enter to put hard line breaks in your template literal, those breaks will be preserved in the string, exactly as if you'd used the \n newline escape sequence (see Recipe 2.3).

 Many JavaScript styte guides, including Airbnb (*https://github.com/ airbnb/javascript*), have rules that discourage string concatenation and favor template literals. You can use a linter like ESLint (Recipe 1.10) to enforce this practice in your code.

Discussion

When you use expressions in a template literal, you aren't limited to inserting variables as they are. In fact, you can use any code expression that JavaScript can evaluate. For example, consider this code:

```
const calculation = `The sum of 5 + 3 is ${5+3}`;
```

Here, JavaScript executes the addition in the expression {5+3}, gets the result, and creates the string *The sum of 5 + 3 is 8.*

If you want to do something more complex, like format strings or manipulate objects, you can use an expression that calls a function. For example, if you've created a get DaysSince() function for calculating the difference between dates (see Recipe 4.5), you can use it in a template literal like this:

```
function getDaysSince(date) {
  const today = new Date();
  const oneDay = 24 * 60 * 60 * 1000; // hours*minutes*seconds*milliseconds
  return Math.round(Math.abs((today - date) / oneDay));
```

```
    }

    employeeDetail = `Our team includes ${firstName} ${lastName}. They've been a
    team member since ${hireDate}! That's ${getDaysSince(hireDate)} days.`;
```

The only limit is practical—in other words don't make your expressions so complex that the resulting template literal is more difficult to read than code that uses the traditional string-concatenation approach.

Currently, JavaScript has no built-in way to format numbers, dates, and currency values inside template literal expressions. Plenty of people have speculated that future versions of JavaScript will add this capability. There's even a JavaScript library that uses an awkward extensibility feature called *tagged templates* (*https://github.com/ skolmer/es2015-i18n-tag*) to wedge it in.

2.6 Performing a Case-Insensitive String Comparison

Problem

You want to see if two strings match, while treating uppercase and lowercase letters as the same.

Solution

The off-the-cuff approach is to use the `String.toLowerCase()` method on both strings, and compare the result, like this:

```
    const a = "hello";
    const b = "HELLO";

    if (a.toLowerCase() === b.toLowerCase()) {
      // We end up here, because the lowercase versions of both strings match
    }
```

This approach is fairly reliable, but it can suffer from edge cases with different languages, accents, and special characters. (For example, check out the potential problems (*https://oreil.ly/CiALB*) with Turkish.)

An alternate, bulletproof approach is to use the `String.localeCompare()` method with `sensitivity` set to *accent*, as shown here:

```
    const a = "hello";
    const b = "HELLO";

    if (a.localeCompare(b, undefined, { sensitivity: 'accent' }) === 0) {
      // We end up here, because the case-insensitive strings match.
    }
```

Discussion

If `localeCompare()` deems that two strings match, it returns 0. Otherwise it returns a positive or negative integer indicating whether the compared string falls before or after the referenced string in the sort order. (Because we're using `localeCompare()` to test for equality, the sort order isn't important, and you can ignore it.)

The second parameter of `localeCompare()` holds a string that specifies the locale (as explained in Recipe 2.2). If you pass `undefined`, then `localeCompare()` uses the locale of the current computer, which is almost always what you want.

To perform a case-insensitive comparison, you need to set the `sensitivity` property. There are two values that can work. If you set `sensitivity` to *accent*, characters that have different accents (like *a* and *á*) are treated as unequal. But if you set `sensitiv ity` to *base*, you'll get a more permissive case-insensitive comparison that treats all accented letters as matches.

2.7 Checking If a String Contains a Specific Substring

Problem

You want to check if one string contains another substring.

Solution

If you simply need a yes-or-no test, you can use the `String.includes()` method:

```
const searchString = 'infinitely';
const fullText = 'I know not where I was born, save that the castle was' +
  ' infinitely old and infinitely horrible.';

if (fullText.includes(searchString)) {
  // The search string was found
}
```

Optionally, you can tell the `includes()` method where to start its search by character position. For example, pass in the value 5 and the search skips to the sixth character in the string, and continues to the end:

```
const searchString = 'infinitely';
const fullText = 'I know not where I was born, save that the castle was' +
  ' infinitely old and infinitely horrible.';

if (fullText.includes(searchString, 70)) {
  // Still true, because the search skips the first 'infinitely' and
  // hits the second one.
}
```

Discussion

The search that `includes()` performs is case-sensitive. If you want a case-insensitive search, you can call `toLowerCase()` on both strings first:

```
const searchString = 'INFINITELY';
const fullText = 'I know not where I was born, save that the castle was' +
  ' infinitely old and infinitely horrible.';

if (fullText.toLowerCase().includes(searchString.toLowerCase())) {
  // The search string was found
}
```

The `includes()` method doesn't provide any information about where a match occurs. If you want this information, consider using the `String.indexOf()` method instead, which is described in Recipe 2.11.

2.8 Replacing All Occurrences of a String

Problem

You want to find all occurrences of a specific substring in a string, and replace them with something else.

Solution

You can use the `String.replaceAll()` method to make the change in one step. All you need is a substring to search for and another string to swap in its place:

```
const storyText = 'I know not where I was born, save that the castle was' +
  ' infinitely old and infinitely horrible.';

const changedStory = storyText.replaceAll('infinitely', 'somewhat');

console.log(changedStory);
```

If you run this code, you'll see the altered string "I know not where I was born, save that the castle was somewhat old and somewhat horrible." appear in the developer console.

Discussion

The `replaceAll()` method has the ability to use a regular expression for searching instead of an ordinary string. You can see how this works in Recipe 2.10.

See Also

Consult Recipes 2.11 and 2.12 to see how you can find matches in a string and examine each one, instead of just replacing them outright.

2.9 Replacing HTML Tags with Named Entities

Problem

You want to insert markup into a web page, and escape the markup (so the browser *displays* the angle brackets rather than interpreting them as HTML tags). This could be because you want to show some example HTML markup, for example, in a tutorial article. Or it may be because you need to safely sanitize outside data, like text submitted by a user or pulled out of a database.

Solution

Use the `String.replaceAll()` method to convert angle brackets (< >) into the named HTML entities < and >. You'll need to perform two steps, one for each substitution:

```
const originalPieceOfHtml = '<p>This is a <span>paragraph</span></p>';

// Get a new string with no < characters
let safePieceOfHtml = originalPieceOfHtml.replaceAll('<', '&lt;');

// Get a new string with no > characters
safePieceOfHtml = safePieceOfHtml.replaceAll('>', '&gt;');

// Show it in the page
document.getElementById('placeholder').innerHtml = safePieceOfHtml;
```

If you examine the string now, you'll find it holds the text "<p>This is a paragraph</p>", which will appear as you expect (with angle brackets shown) in the web page.

You can perform both string substitutions in one step, as long as you can keep the code readable:

```
const safePieceOfHtml =
  originalPieceOfHtml.replaceAll('<', '&lt;').replaceAll('>', '&gt;');
```

The first `replaceAll()` returns a new string, and the code calls `replaceAll()` on that second string to get a *third* string in this case. This technique of calling a method on a value that's returned from a method is called *method chaining*.

Discussion

HTML escaping is critically important if you're inserting raw text into a web page. If you don't perform this step, you've left open a gaping security hole. In fact, you should make sure all text content is escaped before you show it in a web page, even if you think that text doesn't contain any HTML entities (for example, even if it's just set as a literal in your code). There's no telling when someone might change the code and substitute a text value from somewhere else.

That said, doing HTML escaping on your own usually isn't the best approach. You need to do it if you are deliberately creating a string that mingles your HTML tags with outside content. But ideally you'll put text in your web page using an element's `textContent` property instead of its `innerHTML` property. When you use `textContent`, the browser escapes the content automatically, which means you don't need to use `String.replaceAll()`.

See Also

See Chapter 12 for more information about using the HTML DOM to insert text content into a web page.

2.10 Using a Regular Expression to Replace Patterns in a String

Problem

You want to search a string for a pattern, rather than an exact sequence of characters. You then want to create a new string, with the pattern replaced.

Solution

You can use the `String.replace()` or `String.replaceAll()` methods, both of which support regular expressions.

A *regular expression* is a sequence of characters that defines a text pattern. Regular expressions are a standard that's implemented in JavaScript and many other programming languages. Table 2-2 gives a brief introduction to regular expression syntax.

For example, consider the regular expression pattern *t\w{2}e*. This translates into *look for any sequence of characters beginning with t, ending with e, and containing two other alphanumeric characters*. The solution matches *time*, but also matches *tame*.

Here's the code that uses this regular expression:

```
const originalString = 'Now is the time, this is the tame';
const regex = /t\w{2}e/g;
const newString = originalString.replaceAll(regex, 'place');

// newString = 'Now is the place, this is the place'
```

Notice that the regular expression isn't written a string. Instead, it's a literal that begins and ends with a slash (/). JavaScript recognizes this syntax and creates a RegEx object that uses your expression.

The g at the end of the regular expression is an additional detail called the *global flag*. It indicates that you are searching the whole string for matches. If you don't include the g flag, you'll receive an error when you call replaceAll(). However, you can use a regular expression without the global flag when you use the replace() method to change just one occurrence of a pattern.

Discussion

If you'd rather create a regular expression without using the / delimiter, there's another option. Instead of writing a regular expression literal, you can explicitly create a RegEx object, like this:

```
const regex = new RegExp('t\\w{2}e', 'g');
const newString = originalString.replaceAll(regex, 'place');
```

When you use this approach, you don't include the surrounding slashes around the regular expression, but you do need to escape any backslashes in the pattern (by replacing / with //). In addition, the global flag becomes a second argument to the RegExp constructor, instead of being added to the end of the regular expression.

You might find that escaping backslashes is awkward or confusing in long, complicated regular expressions. If so, you can get around the escaping requirement with a template literal (introduced in Recipe 2.5). The trick is to combine your template literal with the String.raw() method. Remember to use backticks (`) around the expression string instead of apostrophes or quotes:

```
// Although String.raw is a method, it has no parentheses after it,
// and it uses the specialized backtick syntax shown here.
const regex = new RegExp(String.raw`t\w{2}e`, 'g');
```

Extra: Regular Expressions

Regular expressions are made up of regular characters that are used alone or in combination with special characters. For instance, the following is a regular expression for a pattern that matches against a string that contains the word *technology* and the word *book*, in that order, and separated by one or more whitespace characters:

```
const regex = /technology\s+book/;
```

The backslash character (\) serves two purposes: either it's used with a regular character, to designate that it's a special character, or it's used with a special character, such as the plus sign (+), to designate that the character should be treated literally. In this case, the backslash is used with *s*, which transforms the letter *s* to a special character designating a whitespace character (space, tab, line feed, or form feed). The +\s+ special character is followed by the plus sign, \s, which is a signal to match the preceding character (in this example, a whitespace character) one or more times. This regular expression would work with the following:

```
technology book
```

It would also work with the following:

```
technology      book
```

It would not work with the following, because there is no whitespace between the words:

```
technologybook
```

It doesn't matter how much whitespace is between *technology* and *book*, because of the use of \s+. However, using the plus sign does require at least one whitespace character.

Table 2-2 shows the most commonly used special characters in JavaScript applications.

Table 2-2. Regular expression special characters

Character	Matches	Example
^	Matches beginning of input	/^This/ matches *This is…*
$	Matches end of input	/end$/ matches *This is the end*
*	Matches zero or more times	/se*/ matches *seeee* as well as *se*
?	Matches zero or one time	/ap?/ matches *apple* and *and*
+	Matches one or more times	/ap+/ matches *apple* but not *and*
{n}	Matches exactly *n* times	/ap{2}/ matches *apple* but not *apie*
\{n,\}	Matches *n* or more times	/ap{2,}/ matches all p's in *apple* and *appple* but not *apie*
\{n,m\}	Matches at least *n*, at most *m* times	/ap{2,4}/ matches four p's in *appppple*
.	Any character except newline	/a.e/ matches *ape* and *axe*
[...]	Any character within brackets	/a[px]e/ matches *ape* and *axe* but not *ale*
[^...]	Any character but those within brackets	/a[^px]/ matches *ale* but not *axe* or *ape*
\b	Matches on word boundary	/\bno/ matches the first *no* in *nono*
\B	Matches on nonword boundary	/\Bno/ matches the second *no* in *nono*

Character	Matches	Example
\d	Digits from 0 to 9	/\d{3}/ matches *123* in *Now in 123*
\D	Any nondigit character	/\D{2,4}/ matches *Now '* in *'Now in 123;*
\w	Matches word character (letters, digits, underscores)	/\w/ matches *j* in *javascript*
\W	Matches any nonword character (not letters, digits, or underscores)	\/W/ matches *%* in *100%*
\n	Matches a line feed	
\s	A single whitespace character	
\S	A single character that is not whitespace	
\t	A tab	
(x)	Capturing parentheses	Remembers the matched characters

Regular expressions are powerful but can be tricky. They're only covered lightly in this book. If you want more in-depth coverage of regular expressions, you can read the excellent *Regular Expressions Cookbook* by Jan Goyvaerts and Steven Levithan (O'Reilly), or consult an online reference (*https://github.com/ziishaned/learn-regex*).

2.11 Extracting a List from a String

Problem

You have a string with several sentences, one of which includes a list of items. The list begins with a colon (:), ends with a period (.), and separates each item with a comma (,). You want to extract just the list.

Before:

```
This is a list of items: cherries, limes, oranges, apples.
```

After:

```
['cherries','limes','oranges','apples']
```

Solution

The solution requires two actions: extract the string containing the list of items, and then convert this string into a list.

Use the `String.indexOf()` method twice—first to locate the colon, and again to find the first period following the colon:

```
const sentence = 'This is one sentence. This is a sentence with a list of items:' +
  'cherries, oranges, apples, bananas. That was the list of items.';
```

```
const start = sentence.indexOf(':');
const end = sentence.indexOf('.', start + 1);
```

Using these two locations and the `String.slice()` method, you can extract the string you want:

```
const list = sentence.slice(start + 1, end);
// list = 'cherries, oranges, apples, bananas'
```

You could write a loop that uses the `indexOf()` method to look for commas, and the `slice()` method to split the `list` string into smaller pieces, one for each item. But there's an easier approach. You can break the string into an array using the `String.split()` method:

```
let fruits = list.split(',');
// now fruits has these elements: ['cherries', ' oranges', ' apples', ' bananas']
```

When you call `split()`, you must choose a delimiter. It could be a space, a comma, a series of dashes, or something else. The delimiter is used to carve up the string into smaller pieces, and it won't appear in the results.

Discussion

The result of splitting the extracted string is an array of list items. However, the items may come with artifacts (in this case, an extra leading space in all but the first string). Fortunately, it's easy to clean them up.

One obvious approach is to iterate over the array of strings and manually trim each one, using the technique described in Recipe 2.13. This works, but there's an easier approach.

The trick is to use the `Array.map()`, which runs a piece of code you supply on each element in the array. You need just a single line of code to call the `trim()` method:

```
fruits = fruits.map(s => s.trim());
// now fruits has these elements: ['cherries', 'oranges', 'apples', 'bananas']
```

If you aren't familiar with the arrow syntax used to supply the trimming function in this example, you can read a more detailed explanation of this technique in Recipe 6.2.

See Also

Another way to find matches in a string is to use regular expressions. For example, depending on the way your list is structured, you might be able to use a regular expression that grabs words that fall in between commas. Regular expressions are introduced in Recipe 2.10, and using regular expressions to perform a search is covered in Recipe 2.12.

2.12 Finding All Instances of a Pattern

Problem

You want to find all instances of a pattern within a string and iterate over them.

Solution

Use a regular expression with the `String.matchAll()` method. The `matchAll()` method returns an iterator that lets you loop over all the matches.

The next example uses a regular expression to find any word that begins with *t* and ends with *e*, with any number of characters in between. It uses the template literal syntax from Recipe 2.5 to build a new string with results:

```
const searchString = 'Now is the time and this is the time and that is the time';
const regex = /t\w*e/g;

const matches = searchString.matchAll(regex);
for (const match of matches) {
  console.log(`at ${match.index} we found ${match[0]}`);
}
```

Here are the results from this code:

```
at 7 we found the
at 11 we found time
at 28 we found the
at 32 we found time
at 49 we found the
at 53 we found time
```

Discussion

When you search with `matchAll()`, each match is an object. As you iterate over your matches, you can examine the matched text (`match[0]`), and the index where the match was found (`match.index`).

Here's something that looks a little peculiar in the current example. Even though you're looking at one result at a time, you use `match[0]` to get the first item from an array. This array exists because a regular expression can *capture* multiple portions of a match using parentheses. You can then reference these captured sections later. For example, imagine you write a regular expression that matches a row of information about a person. With capturing, you can easily grab separate pieces of information from each match, like that person's name and birth date. When you use this technique with `matchAll()`, the matched substrings are provided as `match[1]`, `match[2]`, and so on.

And if you don't want to iterate over the results right away, you can dump everything into an array using the spread operator:

```
const searchString = 'Now is the time and this is the time and that is the time';
const regex = /t\w*e/g;

// Put the 6 match objects into an array
const matches = [...searchString.matchAll(regex)];
```

Now you can use `foreach` to loop through your `matches` array at another time. But remember, `matches` isn't just an array of matching text. It's an array of match *objects*. As you saw in the original example, each match object has a position (`match.index`) and an array with one or more matched groups of text (starting with `match[0]`).

Extra: Highlighting Matches

Let's take a look at a more detailed example that shows how you might find and highlight text matches on a web page. Figure 2-1 shows the application in action on William Wordsworth's poem, "The Kitten and the Falling Leaves."

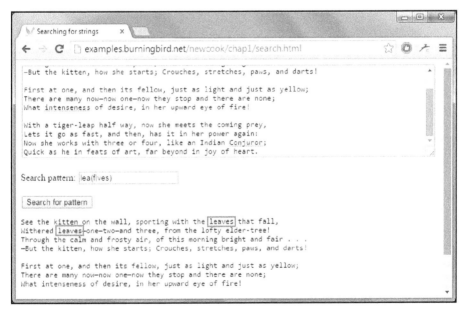

Figure 2-1. Application finding and highlighting all matched strings

This page has a `textarea` and an input text box for entering both a search string and a regular expression. The pattern is used to create a `RegExp` object, which is then applied against the text in the `textarea` using `matchAll()`, just as in the previous (much shorter) example.

As the code examines the matches, it creates a string, consisting of both the unmatched text and the matched text. The matched text is surrounded by a `<span>` element, with a CSS class used to highlight the text. The resulting string is then inserted into the page, using the `innerHTML` property of a `<div>` element (see Example 2-1).

Example 2-1. Highlight all matches in a text string

```
<!DOCTYPE html>
<html lang="en">
  <head>
    <meta charset="UTF-8" />
    <meta name="viewport" content="width=device-width, initial-scale=1.0" />
    <meta http-equiv="X-UA-Compatible" content="ie=edge" />
    <title>Finding All Instances of a Pattern</title>

    <style>
      .found {
        background-color: #ff0;
      }
      body {
        margin: 15px;
      }
      textarea {
        width: 100%;
        height: 350px;
      }
    </style>
  </head>
  <body>
    <h1>Finding All Instances of a Pattern</h1>

    <form id="textsearch">
      <textarea id="incoming">
      </textarea>
      <p>
        Search pattern: <input id="pattern" type="text">
      </p>
    </form>
    <button id="searchSubmit">Search for pattern</button>
    <div id="searchResult"></div>

    <script>
    document.getElementById("searchSubmit").onclick = function() {
        // Get the pattern
        const pattern = document.getElementById('pattern').value;
        const regex = new RegExp(pattern, 'g');

        // Get the text to search
        const searchText = document.getElementById('incoming').value;
```

```
        let highlightedResult = "<pre>";
        let startPosition = 0;
        let endPosition = 0;

        // Find each match, and build the result
        const matches = searchText.matchAll(regex);
        for (const match of matches) {
            endPosition = match.index;

            // Get all of the string up to the match, and concatenate
            highlightedResult += searchText.slice(startPosition, endPosition);

            // Add matched text, using a CSS class for formatting
            highlightedResult += "<span class='found'>" + match[0] + "</span>";
            startPosition = endPosition + match[0].length;
        }

        // Finish off the result string
        highlightedResult += searchText.slice(startPosition);
        highlightedResult += "</pre>";

        // Show the highlighted text in the page
        document.getElementById("searchResult").innerHTML = highlightedResult;
    }
    </script>
  </body>
</html>
```

In Figure 2-1 this page performs a search with this regular expression:

```
lea(f|ves)
```

The bar (|) is a conditional test, and will match a word based on the value on either side of the bar. So *leaf* matches, as well as *leaves*, but not *leap*.

2.13 Removing Whitespace from the Beginning and End of a String

Problem

You want to trim extra spaces that pad the beginning or end of a string.

Solution

Use the `String.trim()` method. It removes all whitespace from both ends of a string, including spaces, tabs, no-break spaces, and line terminator characters.

```
const paddedString = '     The road is long, with many a winding turn.   ';
const trimmedString = paddedString.trim();
```

```
// trimmedString = 'The road is long, with many a winding turn.'
```

Discussion

The `trim()` method is straightforward, but not customizable. If you have even slightly more complex string alteration requirements, you'll need to use a regular expression.

One common problem that thwarts the `trim()` method is removing excess whitespace *inside* a string. The `replaceAll()` method can accomplish this task with relative ease using a regular expression with the `\s` character to match whitespace:

```
const paddedString = 'The road is long,    with many a    winding turn.';
const trimmedString = paddedString.replaceAll(/\s\s+/g, ' ');

// trimmedString = 'The road is long, with many a winding turn.'
```

Of course, unwanted artifacts are possible even after processing bad data with extra spaces. For example, if there are multiple spaces where you don't want *any* space ('is long ,   with') you'll still be left with a single space after you run the replacement ('is long , with'). The only way to deal with issues like these is to manually step through each match, as demonstrated in Recipe 2.12.

See Also

Regular expression syntax is described in Recipe 2.10.

2.14 Converting the First Letter of a String to Uppercase

Problem

You want to make the first letter of a string an uppercase letter, without changing the rest of the string.

Solution

Split off the first letter and capitalize it with `String.toUpper()`. Join the uppercase letter to the remainder of the string, which you can get with `String.slice()`:

```
const original = 'if you cut an orange, there is a risk it will orbisculate.';
const fixed = original[0].toUpperCase() + original.slice(1);

// fixed = 'If you cut an orange, there is a risk it will orbisculate.';
```

Discussion

To get a single character from a string, you can use the string's indexer, as in `original[0]`. This gets the character in position 0 (which is the first character).

```
const firstLetter = original[0];
```

Alternatively, you can use the `String.charAt()` method, which works in exactly the same way.

To get a fragment of a string, you use the `slice()` method. When calling `slice()`, you must always specify the index where you want to start your string extraction. For example, `text.slice(5)` starts at index position 5, continues to the end of the string, and copies that section of the text into a new string.

If you don't want `slice()` to continue to the end of the string, you can supply an optional second parameter with the index where the string copying should stop:

```
// Get a string from index position 5 to 10.
const substring = original.slice(5, 10);
```

The example in this recipe changed a single letter to uppercase. If you want to change an entire sentence to use initial capitals (called *title case*), it's a more complex problem. You might decide to split the string into separate words, trim each word, and then join the results, using a variation of the technique from Recipe 2.11.

See Also

You can use `slice()` in conjunction with `indexOf()` to find the location of specific bits of text that you want to extract. For an example, see Recipe 2.11.

2.15 Validating an Email Address

Problem

You want to catch and reject common errors in email addresses.

Solution

Regular expressions are useful for more than searching. You can also use them to validate strings by testing if a string matches a given pattern. In JavaScript, you test if a string matches a regular expression using the `RegEx.test()` method.

```
const emailValid = "abeLincoln@gmail.com";
const emailInvalid = "abeLincoln@gmail .com";
const regex = /\S+@\S+\.\S+/;

if (regex.test(emailValid)) {
```

```
    // This code is executed, because the email passes.
  }
  if (regex.test(emailInvalid)) {
    // This code is not executed, because the email fails.
  }
```

Discussion

Programmers use many different regular expressions to validate email addresses. The best ones capture obvious mistakes and spurious values, but don't get too complex. Overly strict regular expressions have, from time to time, inadvertently disallowed valid mail addresses. And even if an email address checks out with the most stringent test possible, there's no way to know if it's truly *correct* (at least not without sending an email message and requesting a confirmation).

The regular expression in this recipe requires that an email has a sequence of at least one nonwhitespace character, followed by the @ character, followed by one or more nonwhitespace characters, followed by a period (.), followed again by one or more nonwhitespace characters. It catches obviously invalid emails like *tomkhangmail.com* or *tomkhan@gmail*.

Often, you won't write a regular expression for validation yourself. Instead, you'll use a prewritten expression that matches your data. For a massive collection of regular expression resources, visit the Awesome Regex page (*https://github.com/aloisdg/awesome-regex*).

See Also

Regular expression syntax is described in Recipe 2.10.

## CHAPTER 3

Numbers

There are few ingredients more essential to everyday programming than numbers. Many modern languages have a set of different numeric data types to use in different scenarios, like integers, decimals, floating point values, and so on. But when it comes to numbers, JavaScript reveals its rushed, slightly improvised creation as a loosely-typed scripting language.

Until recently, JavaScript had just a single do-everything numeric data type called Num ber. Today, it has two: the standard Number you use almost all of the time, and the very specialized BigInt that you only consider when you need to deal with huge whole numbers. You'll use both in this chapter, along with the utility methods of the Math object.

3.1 Generating Random Numbers

Problem

You want to generate a random whole number that falls in a set range (for example, from 1 to 6).

Solution

You can use the Math.random() method to generate a floating-point value between 0 and 1. Usually, you'll scale this fractional value and round it, so you end up with an integer in a specific range. Assuming your range spans from some minimum number min to a maximum number max, here's the statement you need:

```
randomNumber = Math.floor(Math.random() * (max - min + 1) ) + min;
```

For example, if you want to pick a random number between 1 and 6, the code becomes:

```
const randomNumber = Math.floor(Math.random()*6) + 1;
```

Now possible values of randomNumber are 1, 2, 3, 4, 5, or 6.

Discussion

The Math object is stocked full of static utility methods you can call at any time. This recipe uses Math.random() to get a random fractional number, and Math.floor() to truncate the decimal portion, leaving you with an integer.

To understand how this works, let's consider a sample run-through. First, Math.random() picks a value between 0 and 1, like *0.374324823*:

```
const randomNumber = Math.floor(0.374324823*6) + 1;
```

That number is multiplied by the number of values in your range (in this example, 6), becoming *2.245948938*:

```
const randomNumber = Math.floor(2.245948938) + 1;
```

Then the Math.floor() function truncates this to just *2*:

```
const randomNumber = 2 + 1;
```

Finally, the starting number of the range is added, giving the final result of *3*. Repeat this calculation and you'll get a different number, but it will always be an integer from the range we've set of 1 to 6.

See Also

The Math.floor() method is only one way to round numbers. See Recipe 3.3 for more.

It's important to understand that numbers generated by Math.random() are *pseudorandom*, which means they can be guessed or reverse engineered. They are not random enough for cryptography, lotteries, or complex modelling. For more about the difference, see Recipe 3.2. And if you need a way to generate a repeatable sequence of pseudorandom numbers, refer to "Extra: Building a Repeatable Pseudorandom Number Generator" on page 133.

3.2 Generating Cryptographically Secure Random Numbers

Problem

You want to create a random number that can't be easily reverse engineered (guessed).

Solution

Use the `window.crypto` property to get an instance of the `Crypto` object. Use the `Crypto.getRandomValues()` method to generate random values that have more *entropy* than those produced by `Math.random()`. (In other words, they are much less likely to be repeated or predicted—see the Discussion section for full details.)

The `Crypto.getRandomValues()` method works differently from `Math.random()`. Rather than giving you a floating-point number between 0 and 1, `getRandomValues()` fills an array with random integers. You can choose whether these integers are 8-bit, 16-bit, or 32-bit, and whether they are signed or unsigned. (A signed data type can be negative or positive, whereas an unsigned number is only positive.)

There is an accepted workaround to convert the output of `getRandomValues()` to a fractional value between 0 and 1. The trick is to divide the random value by the maximum possible number that data type can contain:

```
const randomBuffer = new Uint32Array(1);
window.crypto.getRandomValues(randomBuffer);
const randomFraction = randomBuffer[0] / (0xffffffff + 1);
```

You can now work with `randomFraction` in the same way that you work with the number returned from `Math.random()`. For example, you can convert it to a random integer in a specific range, as explained in Recipe 3.1:

```
// Use the random fraction to make a random integer from 1-6
const randomNumber = Math.floor(randomFraction*6) + 1;
console.log(randomNumber);
```

If you're running your code in the Node.js runtime environment, you won't have access to a `window` object. However, you can get access to a very similar implementation of the Web Crypto API using this code:

```
const crypto = require('crypto').webcrypto;
```

Discussion

There's a lot to unpack in this example. First, even if you don't dig deeper into *how* this code works, you need to be aware of a few important details about the implementation of `Crypto.getRandomValues()`:

- Technically, `Crypto` creates pseudorandom numbers that are generated by a mathematical formula, like those provided by `Math.random()`. The difference is that these numbers are considered *cryptographically strong*, because the random number generator is seeded with a truly random value. The benefit of this tradeoff is that `getRandomValues()` has similar performance to `Math.random()`. (It's fast.)

- There's no way to know how the `Crypto` object is seeded, because that's up to the implementation (for web page code, that means the browser manufacturer), which in turn relies on functionality in the operating system. Usually, the seed is created using a combination of recently recorded details about keyboard timings, mouse movements, and hardware readings.

- No matter how good your random numbers are, if your JavaScript code is running in a browser, it's exposed to a great number of attacks. After all, there's nothing to stop a malicious party from seeing your code and creating an altered copy that bypasses all random number generation. If your code is running on a server, the situation is different.

Now let's look closer at how `getRandomValues()` works. Before you call `getRandomValues()`, you must create a *typed array*, which is an array-like object that can only hold values of a specific data type. (We say *array-like* because it behaves like an array, but it isn't an instance of the official `Array` type.) JavaScript provides several strongly typed array objects you can use: like `Uint32Array` (for an array of unsigned 32-bit integers), `Uint16Array`, `Uint8Array`, and the signed counterparts `Int32Array`, `Int16Array`, and `Int8Array`. You create this array to be as big as you want, and `getRandomValues()` will fill the whole buffer.

In this recipe, we make room for just one value in the `Uint32Array`:

```
const randomBuffer = new Uint32Array(1);
window.crypto.getRandomValues(randomBuffer);
```

The final step is to divide this random value by the maximum possible unsigned 32-bit integer, which is 4,294,967,295. This number is cleaner in its hexadecimal representation, 0xffffffff:

```
const randomFraction = randomBuffer[0] / (0xffffffff + 1);
```

As this code shows, you also need to add 1 to the maximum value. That's because the random value could theoretically land exactly on the maximum integer value. If it did, the randomFraction would become 1, which differs from Math.random() and most other random number generators. (And a tiny unexpected variation from the norm is something that can lead to a incorrect assumption, and then a bug further down the road.)

3.3 Rounding to a Specific Decimal Place

Problem

You want to round a number to a certain precision (for example, 124.793 to 124.80 or 120).

Solution

You can use the Math.round() method to round a number to the nearest whole number:

```
const fractionalNumber = 19.48938;
const roundedNumber = Math.round(fractionalNumber);

// Now roundedNumber is 19
```

Oddly enough, the round() method doesn't take an argument that lets you specify a number of decimal places to keep. If you want a different degree of precision, it's up to you to multiply your number by the appropriate power of 10, round it, and then divide it by the same power of 10 after rounding. Here's the general formula for this operation:

```
const numberToRound = fractionalNumber * (10**numberOfDecimalPlaces);
let roundedNumber = Math.round(numberToRound);
roundedNumber = roundedNumber / (10**numberOfDecimalPlaces);
```

For example, if you want to round to two decimal places, the code becomes this:

```
const fractionalNumber = 19.48938;
const numberToRound = fractionalNumber * (10**2);
let roundedNumber = Math.round(numberToRound);
roundedNumber = roundedNumber / (10**2);

// Now roundedNumber is 19.49
```

If you want to round *left* of decimal place (for example, to the nearest tens, hundreds, and so on), just use a negative number for numberOfDecimalPlaces. For example, –1 rounds to the nearest 10, –2 rounds to the nearest 100, and so on.

Discussion

The `Math` object has several static methods for turning fractional values into integers. The `floor()` method removes all decimal digits, rounding a number down to the nearest whole number. The `ceil()` method does the reverse, and always rounds a fractional number up to the next whole number. The `round()` method rounds to the closest whole number.

There are two important points you need to know about how `round()` works:

- An exact value of 0.5 is always rounded up, even though it is equally distant from both the next lower and next higher integer. In finance and science, different rounding techniques are often used to remove this bias (such as rounding some 0.5 values up and others down). But if you want that behavior in JavaScript, you need to implement it yourself or use a third-party library.

- When rounding negative numbers, JavaScript rounds –0.5 up *toward zero*. That means that –4.5 is rounded to –4, which is different than the rounding implementation in many other programming languages.

See Also

Rounding numbers is one way to get a numeric value closer to an appropriate display format. If you're using rounding to prepare a number to show to a user, you may also be interested in the `Number` formatting methods described in Recipe 2.2.

3.4 Preserving Accuracy in Decimal Values

Problem

All numbers in JavaScript are floating point values, which suffer minute rounding errors with certain operations. In some applications (for example, when dealing with amounts of money), these errors may not be acceptable.

Solution

Floating point rounding errors are a well-understood phenomenon that exists in almost every programming language. To see it in JavaScript, run the following code:

```
const sum = 0.1 + 0.2;
console.log(sum);      // displays 0.30000000000000004
```

You can't avoid the rounding error, but you can minimize it. If you're working with a currency type that has two decimal places of precision (like dollars), consider multiplying all values by 100 to avoid dealing with decimals. Instead of writing code like this:

```
const currentBalance = 5382.23;
const transactionAmount = 14.02;

const updatedBalance = currentBalance - transactionAmount;

// Now updatedBalance = 5368.209999999999
```

Use currency variables like this:

```
const currentBalanceInCents = 538223;
const transactionAmountInCents = 1402;

const updatedBalanceInCents = currentBalanceInCents - transactionAmountInCents;

// Now updatedBalanceInCents = 536821
```

This solves the problem for operations that work out to exact whole numbers, like adding and subtracting numbers of cents. But what happens when you need to calculate tax or interest? In these situations you'll end up with fractional values no matter what, and you need to do what businesses and banks do—round your values immediately after your transaction:

```
const costInCents = 4899;

// Calculate 11% tax, and round the result to the nearest cent
const costWithTax = Math.round(costInCents*1.11);
```

Discussion

The floating point rounding issue stems from the fact that some decimal values can't be stored in binary representation without rounding. The same problem occurs with decimal numbering systems (for example, try to write the result of 1/3). The difference with floating point numbers is that the effect is *counterintuitive*. We don't expect to have trouble adding 0.1 and 0.2, because in decimal notation both fractions can be represented exactly.

Although other programming languages experience the same phenomenon, many of them include an alternate data type for decimal or currency values. JavaScript does not. However, there is a proposal for a new Decimal type (*https://github.com/tc39/proposal-decimal*), which could be incorporated into a future version of the JavaScript language.

See Also

If you perform a lot of financial calculations, you can simplify your life by using a third-party library like *bignumber.js* (*https://github.com/MikeMcl/bignumber.js*), which provides a customized numeric data type that works a lot like the ordinary Number, but preserves exact precision for a fixed number of decimal places.

3.5 Converting a String to a Number

Problem

You want to parse a number in a string and convert it to the number data type.

Solution

It's always safe to convert a number into a string, because that operation can't fail. The reverse task—converting a string into a number, so you can use it in calculations—is a more delicate affair.

The canonical approach is to use the Number() function:

```
const stringData = '42';
const numberData = Number(stringData);
```

The Number() function won't accept formatting like currency symbols and comma separators. It *will* allow extra spaces at the beginning and end of the string. The Num ber() function also converts empty strings or strings with only whitespace to the number 0. This might be a reasonable default (for example, if you're retrieving user input from a text box), but it's not always appropriate. To avoid this case, consider testing for a whitespace-only string before you call Number():

```
if (stringData.trim() === '') {
  // This is an all-whitespace or empty string
}
```

If a conversion fails, the Number() function assigns the value NaN (for *not a number*) to your variable. You can test for this failure by calling the Number.isNaN() method immediately after you use Number():

```
const numberData = Number(stringData);

if (Number.isNaN(numberData)) {
  // It's safe to process this data as a number
}
```

The isFinite() method is almost the same as isNaN(), except it avoids strange edge cases, like 1/0, which returns a value of infinity. If you use the isNaN() method on infinity, it somewhat dubiously returns false.

An alternate approach is to use the parseFloat() method. It's a slightly looser conversion that tolerates text after the number. However, parseFloat() is stricter with blank strings, which it refuses.

```
console.log(Number('42'));                // 42
console.log(parseFloat('42'));            // 42

console.log(Number('12 goats'));          // NaN
console.log(parseFloat('12 goats'));      // 12

console.log(Number('goats 12'));          // NaN
console.log(parseFloat('goats 12'));      // NaN

console.log(Number('2001/01/01'));        // NaN
console.log(parseFloat('2001/01/01'));    // 2001

console.log(Number(' '));                 // 0
console.log(parseFloat(' '));             // NaN
```

Discussion

Developers use some conversion tricks that are functionally equivalent to the Number() function, like multiplying a string by 1 (numberInString*1) or using the unary operator (+numberInString). But using Number() or parseFloat() is preferred for clarity.

If you have a formatted number (like *2,300*), you need to do more work to convert it. The Number() method will return NaN, and parseFloat() will stop at the comma and treat it as 2. Unfortunately, although JavaScript has an Intl.NumberFormat object that can *create* formatted strings from numbers (see Recipe 2.2), it doesn't provide parsing functionality for the reverse operation.

You can use regular expressions to take care of tasks like removing commas from a string (see Recipe 2.8). But a home brew solution can be risky, because some locales use commas to separate thousands, while others use them to separate decimals. In situations like these, a well-used, well-tested JavaScript library like Numeral (*http:// numeraljs.com*) is a better choice.

3.6 Converting a Decimal to a Hexadecimal Value

Problem

You have a decimal value, and need to find its hexadecimal equivalent.

Solution

Use the `Number.toString()` method, with an argument that specifies the base you are converting *to*:

```
const num = 255;

// displays ff, which is hexadecimal equivalent for 255
console.log(num.toString(16));
```

Discussion

By default, numbers in JavaScript are base 10, or decimal. However, they can also be converted to a different *radix*, including hexadecimal (16) and octal (8). Hexadecimal numbers begin with 0x (a zero followed by lowercase x). Octal numbers used to begin with just a zero (0), but now should begin with a zero and then a Latin letter *O* (upper or lowercase):

```
const octalNumber = 0o255;  // equivalent to 173 decimal
const hexaNumber = 0xad;    // equivalent to 173 decimal
```

A decimal number can be converted to another radix, in a range from 2 to 36:

```
const decNum = 55;
const octNum = decNum.toString(8);   // value of 67 octal
const hexNum = decNum.toString(16);  // value of 37 hexadecimal
const binNum = decNum.toString(2);   // value of 110111 binary
```

To complete the octal and hexadecimal presentation, you'll need to concatenate the 0o to the octal, and the 0x to the hexadecimal value. But remember, once you've converted your number into a string, don't expect to use it in any sort of numeric calculation, no matter how it's formatted.

Although decimals can be converted to any base number (between a range of 2 to 36), only the octal, hexadecimal, and decimal numbers can be manipulated directly as numbers.

3.7 Converting Between Degrees and Radians

Problem

You have an angle in degrees. To use the value in the `Math` object's trigonometric functions, you need to convert the degrees to radians.

Solution

To convert degrees to radians, multiply the degree value by (`Math.PI/180`):

```
const radians = degrees * (Math.PI / 180);
```

So if you have a 90 degree angle, the calculation becomes:

```
const radians = 90 * (Math.PI / 180);
console.log(radians);    // 1.5707963267948966
```

To convert radians to degrees, multiply the radians value by (`180/Math.PI`):

```
const degrees = radians * (180 / Math.PI);
```

Discussion

All the trigonometric methods of the `Math` object (`sin()`, `cos()`, `tan()`, `asin()`, `acos()`, `atan()`, and `atan2()`) take values in radians, and return radians as a result. Yet it's not unusual for people to provide values in degrees rather than radians, as degrees are the more familiar unit of measure.

3.8 Calculating the Length of a Circular Arc

Problem

Given the radius of a circle, and the angle of an arc in degrees, find the length of the arc.

Solution

Use `Math.PI` to convert degrees to radians, and use the result in a formula to find the length of the arc:

```
// angle of arc is 120 degrees, radius of circle is 2
const radians = degrees * (Math.PI / 180);
const arclength = radians * radius; // value is 4.18879020478...
```

Discussion

The length of a circular arc is found by multiplying the circle's radius times the angle of the arc, in radians.

If the angle is given in degrees, you'll need to convert the degree to radians first, before multiplying the angle by the radius. This calculation is frequently used when drawing shapes in SVG, as covered in Chapter 15.

3.9 Manipulating Very Large Numbers with BigInt

Problem

You need to work with very large integers (above 2^{53}), without losing precision.

Solution

Use the `BigInt` data type, which can hold integers of any size, limited only by system memory (or the `BigInt` implementation of the JavaScript engine you're using).

You can create a `BigInt` in two ways. You use the `BigInt()` function, like this:

```
// Create a BigInt and set it to 10
const bigInteger = BigInt(10);
```

Or you can add the letter *n* to the end of a number:

```
const bigInteger = 10n;
```

This example shows the difference between an ordinary `Number` and the `BigInt` for very large values:

```
// Ordinarily, large integers suffer from imprecision
const maxInt = Number.MAX_SAFE_INTEGER // Probably about 9007199254740991
console.log(maxInt + 1);  // 9007199254740992 (reasonable)
console.log(maxInt + 2);  // 9007199254740992 (not a typo, this seems wrong)
console.log(maxInt + 3);  // 9007199254740994 (sure)
console.log(maxInt + 4);  // 9007199254740996 (wait, what now?)

// BigInts behave more reliably
const bigInt = BigInt(maxInt);
console.log(bigInt + 1n);  // 9007199254740992 (as before)
console.log(bigInt + 2n);  // 9007199254740993 (this is better)
console.log(bigInt + 3n);  // 9007199254740994 (still good)
console.log(bigInt + 4n);  // 9007199254740995 (excellent!)
```

When you log a `BigInt` to the developer console, it appears with an *n* appended to its value (as in *9007199254740992n*). This convention makes it easy to recognize `BigInt` values. But if you just want the numeric value of your `BigInt`, you simply need to convert it to text first, with `BigInt.toString()`.

Discussion

JavaScript's native `Number` type conforms to the IEEE-754 specification for 64-bit, double-precision floating-point numbers. The standard has acceptable, known limitations and inaccuracies. One practical limitation is that integers cannot be accurately represented past 2^{53}. Beyond this point, inaccuracies in representation which had previously been confined to the right of the decimal place (see Recipe 3.4) jump over to the left of the decimal place. Put another way, as the JavaScript engine counts higher, the chance for inaccuracy grows. Once we are past 2^{53}, the inaccuracy is larger than 1 and shows up in calculations with integral numbers, not just decimal values.

JavaScript has a partial solution to this problem with the `BigInt` type, introduced as part of the ECMAScript 2020 specification. A `BigInt` is an arbitrarily sized integer that allows you to represent exceedingly large numbers. Practically speaking, there is no upper limit to the bit width of a `BigInt`.

Almost all of the operators you are used to using with regular numbers can be used on a `BigInt`, including addition (+), subtraction (-), multiplication (*), division (/), and exponentiation (**). However, `BigInt` is an integer and does not store fractional values. When you perform a division operation, `BigInt` quietly discards the decimal portion:

```
const result = 10n / 6n;    // result is 1.
```

`BigInts` and `Numbers` are not interchangeable nor are they interoperable. But they can be converted to one another using the `Number()` and `BigInt()` functions:

```
let bigInteger = 10n;
let integer = Number(bigInteger);   // Number is 10

integer = 20;
bigInteger = BigInt(integer);        // bigInteger is 20n
```

You need to perform a conversion if you want to use a `BigInt` with a method that expects a `Number`, like the methods of the `Math` object. Similarly, you need to perform a conversion if you want to use a `Number` in a calculation with another `BigInt`.

If you attempt to convert a `Number` that holds a fractional value into a `BigInt`, you'll receive a `RangeError`. You can avoid this possibility by rounding first:

```
const decimal = 10.8;
const bigInteger = BigInt(Math.round(decimal));    // bigInteger is 11n
```

Remember to keep operations consistent with the type. Sometimes what seems like a simple operation can fail because you accidentally combine a `BigInt` with an ordinary number:

```
let x = 10n;
x = x * 2;     // throws a TypeError because x is a BigInt and 2 is a Number
x += 1;        // also throws a TypeError

x = x * 2n;    // x is now 20n, as expected
x += 1n;       // x is 21
```

You can compare a `BigInt` value against a `Number` value using the standard comparison operators (`<`, `>`, `<=`, `>=`). If you want to test if a `BigInt` and a number are equal, use the loose equality operators (`==` and `!=`). Strict equality (`===`) will always return `false`, because `BigInt` and `Number` are different data types. Or, better yet, explicitly convert your `Number` to a `BigInt` and then compare it with `===`.

One last thing to consider with `BigInt`: it is not (at publishing time) serializable to JSON. Attempts to call `JSON.stringify()` on a `BigInt` yield a syntax error. You have several options to consider as a solution. You could monkey-patch your `BigInt` implementation with an appropriate `toJSON()` method:

```
BigInt.prototype.toJSON = function() { return this.toString() }
```

You could also use a library like granola (*https://github.com/kanongil/granola*), which provides JSON-compatiable stringifiers for a number of values, including `BigInt`.

CHAPTER 4

Dates

JavaScript has surprisingly capable date features, which are wrapped in the somewhat old-fashioned `Date` object. As you'll see, the `Date` object has quirks and hidden traps —like the way it counts months starting at 0 and parses year information differently depending on the locale settings of the current computer. But once you learn to navigate these stumbling blocks, you'll be able to accomplish a number of common, useful operations, like counting the days between two dates, formatting dates for display, and timing events.

4.1 Getting the Current Date and Time

Problem

You need to get the current date or time.

Solution

JavaScript includes a `Date` object that provides good support for manipulating date information (and more modest support for performing date calculations). When you create a new `Date` object, it is automatically populated with the current day and time, down to the nearest millisecond:

```
const today = new Date();
```

Now it's simply a matter of extracting the information you want from your `Date` object. The `Date` object has a long list of methods that can help you in this task. Table 4-1 lists the most important methods. Notice that the counting used by different methods isn't always consistent. Months and weekdays are numbered starting at 0, while days are numbered starting at 1.

Table 4-1. Date methods for getting pieces of date information

Method	Gets	Possible values
getFullYear()	The year	A four-digit number like 2021
getMonth()	The month number	0 to 11, where 0 represents January
getDate()	The day of the month	1 to 31
getDay()	The day of the week	0 to 6, where 0 represents Sunday
getHours()	The hour of the day	0 to 23
getMinutes()	The minute	0 to 59
getSeconds()	The seconds	0 to 59
getMilliseconds()	The milliseconds (one thousandth seconds)	0 to 999

Here's an example that displays some basic information about the current date:

```
const today = new Date();

console.log(today.getFullYear());  // example: 2021
console.log(today.getMonth());     // example: 02 (March)
console.log(today.getDay());       // example: 01 (Monday)

// Do a little extra string processing to make sure minutes are padded with
// a leading 0 if needed to make a two-digit value (like '05' in the time 4:05)
const hours = today.getHours();
const minutes = today.getMinutes().toString().padStart(2, '0');
console.log('Time ' + hours + ':' + minutes);   // example: 15:32
```

 The Date methods listed in Table 4-1 exist in two versions. The versions shown in the table use the local time settings. The second set of methods adds the prefix *UTC* (as in getUTCMonth() and getUTCSeconds()). They use *Coordinated Universal Time*, the global time standard. If you need to compare dates from different time zones (or ones that have different conventions for following *daylight saving time*), you must use the UTC methods. Internally, the Date object always uses UTC.

Discussion

The Date() object has several constructors. The empty constructor creates a Date object for the current date and time, as you've just seen. But you can also create a Date object for a different date by specifying the year, month, and day, like this:

```
// February 10, 2021:
const anotherDay = new Date(2021, 1, 10);
```

Once again, be wary of the inconsistent counting (months start at 0, while days start at 1). That means the `anotherDay` variable above represents February 10, *not* January 10.

Optionally, you can tack on up to four more parameters to the `Date` constructor for hours, minutes, seconds, and milliseconds:

```
// February 1, 2021, at 9:30 AM:
const anotherDay = new Date(2021, 1, 1, 9, 30);
```

As you'll see in this chapter, JavaScript's built-in `Date` object has some well-known limitations and a few quirks. If you need to perform extensive date operations in your code, such as calculating date ranges, parsing different types of date strings, or shifting dates between time zones, the best practice is to use a tested third-party date library, such as *day.js* (*https://github.com/iamkun/dayjs*) or *date-fns* (*https://date-fns.org*).

See Also

Once you have a date, you may want to use it in date calculations, as explained in Recipe 4.4. You may also be interested in turning a date into a formatted string (Recipe 4.6), or a date-containing string into a proper `Date` object (Recipe 4.2).

4.2 Converting a String to a Date

Problem

You have date information in a string, but you want to convert it to a `Date` object so you can manipulate it in your code or perform date calculations.

Solution

If you're fortunate, you'll have your date string in the ISO 8601 standard timestamp format (like "2021-12-17T03:24:00Z"), which you can pass directly to the `Date` constructor:

```
const eventDate = new Date('2021-12-17T03:24:00Z');
```

The *T* in this string separates the the date from the time, and the *Z* at the end of the string indicates it's a universal time using the UTC time zone, which is the best way to ensure consistency on different computers.

There are other formats that the `Date` constructor (and the `Date.parse()` method) may recognize. However, they are now strongly discouraged, because their implementations are not consistent across different browsers. They may appear to work in a test example, but they run into trouble when different browsers apply different locale-specific settings, like daylight saving time.

If your date isn't in the ISO 8601 format, you'll need to take a manual approach. Extract the different date components from your string, then use those with the `Date` constructor. You can make good use of `String` methods like `split()`, `slice()`, and `indexOf()`, which are explored in more detail in the recipes in Chapter 2.

For example, if you have a date string in the format *mm/dd/yyyy*, you can use code like this:

```
const stringDate = '12/30/2021';

// Split on the slashes
const dateArray = stringDate.split('/');

// Find the individual date ingredients
const year = dateArray[2];
const month = dateArray[0];
const day = dateArray[1];

// Apply the correction for 0-based month numbering
const eventDate = new Date(year, month-1, day);
```

Discussion

The `Date` object constructor doesn't perform much validation. Check your input before you create a `Date` object, because the `Date` object may accept values that you would not. For example, it will allow day numbers to roll over (in other words, if you set 40 as your day number, JavaScript will just move your date into the next month). The `Date` constructor will also accept strings that may be parsed inconsistently on different computers.

If you attempt to create a `Date` object with a nonnumeric string, you'll receive an "Invalid Date" object. You can test for this condition using `isNaN()`:

```
const badDate = '12 bananas';

const convertedDate = new Date(badDate);

if (Number.isNaN(convertedDate)) {
  // We end up here, because the date object was not created successfully
} else {
  // For a valid Data instance, we end up here
}
```

This technique works because `Date` objects are actually *numbers* behind the scenes, a fact explored in Recipe 4.4.

See Also

Recipe 4.6 explains the reverse operation—taking a `Date` object and converting it to a string.

4.3 Adding Days to a Date

Problem

You want to find a date that's a specific number of days before or after another date.

Solution

Find the current day number with `Date.getDate()`, then change it with `Date.set Date()`. The `Date` object is smart enough to roll over to the next month or year as needed.

```
const today = new Date();
const currentDay = today.getDate();

// Where will be three weeks in the future?
today.setDate(currentDay + 21);
console.log(`Three weeks from today is ${today}`);
```

Discussion

The `setDate()` method isn't limited to positive integers. You can use a negative number to shift a date backward. You may want to use the other *setXxx()* methods to modify a date, like `setMonths()` to move it forward or backward one month at a time, `setHours()` to move it by hours, and so on. All these methods roll over just like `setDate()`, so adding 48 hours will move a date exactly two days forward.

The `Date` object is *mutable*, which makes its behavior look distinctly old-fashioned. In more modern JavaScript libraries, you would expect a method like `setDate()` to return a new `Date` object. But what it actually does is change the *current* `Date` object. This happens even if you declare a date with `const`. (The `const` prevents you from setting your variable to point to a different `Date` object, but it doesn't stop you from altering the currently referenced `Date` object.) To safely avoid potential problems, you can clone your date before operating on it. Just use `Date.getTime()` to get the underlying millisecond count that represents your date and use it to create a new object:

```
const originalDate = new Date();

// Clone the date
const futureDate = new Date(originalDate.getTime());

// Change the cloned date
```

```
futureDate.setDate(originalDate.getDate()+21);
console.log(`Three weeks from ${originalDate} is ${futureDate}`);
```

See Also

Recipe 4.5 shows how to calculate the time period between two dates.

4.4 Comparing Dates and Testing Dates for Equality

Problem

You need to see if two `Date` objects represent the same calendar date, or determine if one date is before another.

Solution

You can compare `Date` objects just like you compare numbers, with the < and > operators:

```
const oldDay = new Date(1999, 10, 20);
const newerDay = new Date(2021, 1, 1);

if (newerDay > oldDay) {
  // This is true, because newerDay falls after oldDay.
}
```

Internally, dates are stored as numbers. When you use the < or > operator, they are automatically converted to numbers and compared. When you run this code, you are comparing the millisecond value for `oldDay` (943,074,000,000) to the millisecond value for `newerDay` (1,612,155,600,000).

The equality operator (=) works differently. It tests the object reference, not the object *content*. (In other words, two `Date` objects are equal only if you are comparing two variables that point to the same instance.)

If you want to test if two `Date` objects represent the same moment in time, you need to convert them to numbers yourself. The clearest way to do this is by calling `Date.getTime()`, which returns the millisecond number for a date:

```
const date1 = new Date(2021, 1, 1);
const date2 = new Date(2021, 1, 1);

// This is false, because they are different objects
console.log(date1 === date2);

// This is true, because they have the same date
console.log(date1.getTime() === date2.getTime());
```

Despite its name, `getTime()` does not return *just* the time. It returns the millisecond number that is an exact representation of that Date object's date *and* time.

Discussion

Internally, a Date object is just an integer. Specifically, it's the number of milliseconds that have elapsed since January 1, 1970. The millisecond number can be negative or positive, which means that the Date object can represent dates from the distant past (roughly 271,821 BCE) to the distant future (year 275,760 CE). You can get the millisecond number by calling `Date.getTime()`.

Two Date objects are only the same if they match exactly, down to the millisecond. Two Date objects that represent the same date but have a different time component won't match. This can be a problem, because you may not realize that your Date object contains time information. This is a common issue when creating a Date object for the current day (Recipe 4.1).

To avoid this issue, you can remove the time information using `Date.setHours()`. Despite its name, the `setHours()` method accepts up to four parameters, allowing you to set the hour, minute, second, and millisecond. To create a date-only Date object, set all these components to 0:

```
const today = new Date();

// Create another copy of the current date
// The day hasn't changed, but the time may have already ticked on
// to the next millisecond
const todayDifferent = new Date();

// This could be true or false, depending on timing factors beyond your control
console.log(today.getTime() === todayDifferent.getTime());

// Remove all the time information
todayDifferent.setHours(0,0,0,0);
today.setHours(0,0,0,0);

// This is always true, because the time has been removed from both instances
console.log(today.getTime() === todayDifferent.getTime());
```

See Also

For more math with dates, see Recipes 4.5 and 4.3.

4.5 Calculating the Time Elapsed Between Two Dates

Problem

You need to calculate how many days, hours, or minutes separate two dates.

Solution

Because dates are numbers (in milliseconds, see Recipe 4.4), calculations with them are relatively straightforward. If you subtract one date from another, you get the number of milliseconds in between:

```
const oldDate = new Date(2021, 1, 1);
const newerDate = new Date(2021, 10, 1);

const differenceInMilliseconds = newerDate - oldDate;
```

Unless you're timing short operations for performance testing, the number of milliseconds isn't a particularly useful unit. It's up to you to divide this number to convert it into a more meaningful number of minutes, hours, or days:

```
const millisecondsPerDay = 1000*60*60*24;
let differenceInDays = differenceInMilliseconds / millisecondsPerDay;

// Only count whole days
differenceInDays = Math.trunc(differenceInDays);

console.log(differenceInDays);
```

Even though this calculation should work out to an exact number of days (because neither date has any time information), you still need to use `Math.round()` on the result to deal with the rounding errors inherent to floating-point math (see Recipe 3.4).

Discussion

There are two pitfalls to be aware of when performing date calculations:

- Dates may contain time information. (For example, a new `Date` object created for the current day is accurate up to the millisecond it was created.) Before you count days, use `setHours()` to remove the time component, as explained in Recipe 4.4.

- Calculations with two dates only make sense if the dates are in the same time zone. Ideally, that means you are comparing two local dates or two dates in the UTC standard. It may seem straightforward enough to convert dates from one time zone to another, but often there are unexpected edge cases with daylight saving time.

There is a tentative replacement for the aging `Date` object. The `Temporal` object (*https://oreil.ly/BAbB2*) aims to improve calculations with local dates and different time zones. In the meantime, if your date needs go beyond the `Date` object, you can experiment with a third-party library for manipulating the date. Both *day.js* (*https:// github.com/iamkun/dayjs*) and *date-fns* (*https://date-fns.org*) are popular choices.

And if you want to use tiny time calculations for profiling performance, the `Date` object is not the best choice. Instead, use the `Performance` object, which is available in a browser environment through the built-in `window.performance` property. It lets you capture a high-resolution timestamp that's accurate to *fractions* of a millisecond, if supported by the system. Here's an example:

```
// Get a DOMHighResTimeStamp object that represents the start time
const startTime = window.performance.now();

// (Do a time consuming task here.)

// Get a DOMHighResTimeStamp object that represents the end time
const endTime = window.performance.now();

// Find the elapsed time in milliseconds
const elapsedMilliseconds = endTime - startTime;
```

The result (`elapsedMilliseconds`) is not the nearest whole millisecond, but the most accurate fractional millisecond count that's supported on the current hardware.

Although Node doesn't provide the `Performance` object, it has its own mechanism for retrieving high-resolution time information. You use its global `process` object, which provides the `process.hrtime.bigint()` method. It returns a timing readout in *nanoseconds*, or billionths of a second. Simply subtract one `process.hrtime.bigint()` readout from another to find the time difference in nanoseconds. (Each millisecond is 1,000,000 nanoseconds.)

Because the nanosecond count is obviously going to be a very large number, you need to use the `BigInt` data type to hold it, as described in Recipe 3.9.

See Also

Recipe 4.3 shows how to move a date forward or backward by adding to it or subtracting from it.

4.6 Formatting a Date Value as a String

Problem

You want to create a formatted string based on a `Date` object.

Solution

If you print a date with `console.log()`, you'll get the date's nicely formatted string representation, like "Wed Oct 21 2020 22:17:03 GMT-0400 (Eastern Daylight Time)." This representation is created by the `DateTime.toString()` method. It's a standardized, nonlocale-specific date string that's defined in the JavaScript standard (*https://oreil.ly/S0lMb*).

> Internally, the `Date` object stores its time information as a UTC time, with no additional time zone information. When you convert a `Date` to a string, that UTC time is converted into a locale-specific time for the current time zone, as set on the computer or device where your code is running.

If you want your date string formatted differently, you could call one of the other prebuilt `Date` methods demonstrated here:

```
const date = new Date(2021, 0, 1, 10, 30);

let dateString;
dateString = date.toString();
 // 'Fri Jan 01 2021 10:30:00 GMT-0500 (Eastern Standard Time)'

dateString = date.toTimeString();
 // '10:30:00 GMT-0500 (Eastern Standard Time)'

dateString = date.toUTCString();
 // 'Fri, 01 Jan 2021 15:30:00 GMT'

dateString = date.toDateString();
 // 'Fri Jan 01 2021'

dateString = date.toISOString();
 // '2021-01-01T15:30:00.000Z'

dateString = date.toLocaledateString();
 // '1/1/2021, 10:30:00 AM'

dateString = date.toLocaleTimeString();
// '10:30:00 AM'
```

Keep in mind that if you use `toLocaleString()` or `toLocaleTime()`, your string representation is based on the browser implementation and the settings of the current computer. Do not assume consistency!

Discussion

There are many possible ways to turn date information into a string. For display purposes, the *toXxxString()* methods work well. But if you want something more specific or fine-tuned, you may need to take control of the `Date` object yourself.

If you want to go beyond the standard formatting methods, there are two approaches you can take. You can use the *getXxx()* methods described in Recipe 4.1 to extract individual time components from a date, and then concatenate those into the exact string you need. Here's an example:

```
const date = new Date(2021, 10, 1);

// Ensure date numbers less than 10 are padded with an initial 0.
const day = date.getDate().toString().padStart(2, '0');

// Ensure months are 0-padded and add 1 to convert the month from its
// 0-based JavaScript representation
const month = (date.getMonth()+1).toString().padStart(2, '0');

// The year is always 4-digit
const year = date.getFullYear();

const customDateString = `${year}.${month}.${day}`;
// now customDateString = '2021.11.01'
```

This approach is extremely flexible, but it forces you to write your own date boilerplate, which isn't ideal because it adds complexity and creates room for new bugs.

If you want to use a standard format for a specific locale, life is a bit easier. You can use the `Intl.DateTimeFormat` object to perform the conversion. Here are three examples that use locale strings for the US, the UK, and Japan:

```
const date = new Date(2020, 11, 20, 3, 0, 0);

// Use the standard US date format
console.log(new Intl.DateTimeFormat('en-US').format(date));  // '12/20/2020'

// Use the standard UK date format
console.log(new Intl.DateTimeFormat('en-GB').format(date));  // '20/12/2020'

// Use the standard Japanese date format
console.log(new Intl.DateTimeFormat('ja-JP').format(date));  // '2020/12/20'
```

All of these are date-only strings, but there are many other options you can set when you create the `Intl.DateTimeFormat()` object. Here's just one example that adds the day of the week and month to the string, in German:

```
const date = new Date(2020, 11, 20);

const formatter = new Intl.DateTimeFormat('de-DE',
  { weekday: 'long', year: 'numeric', month: 'long', day: 'numeric' });

const dateString = formatter.format(date);
// now dateString = 'Sonntag, 20. Dezember 2020'
```

These options also give you the ability to add time information to your string with the `hour`, `minute`, and `second` properties, which can be set to:

```
const date = new Date(2022, 11, 20, 9, 30);

const formatter = new Intl.DateTimeFormat('en-US',
  { year: 'numeric', month: 'numeric', day: 'numeric',
    hour: 'numeric', minute: 'numeric' });

const dateString = formatter.format(date);
// now dateString = '12/20/2022, 9:30 AM'
```

See Also

Recipe 2.2 introduced the `Intl` object and the concept of locale strings, which identify different geographic and cultural regions. For a comprehensive explanation of the 21 options the `Intl.DateTimeFormat` object supports, see the MDN reference (*https://oreil.ly/at36f*). It's worth noting that a few of these details are implementation dependent and may not be present on all browsers. (Examples include the `timeStyle`, `dateStyle`, and `timeZone` properties, which we haven't discussed here.) As always, for complex `Date` manipulation, consider a third-party library.

## CHAPTER 5

Arrays

Since its inception, JavaScript has had arrays as a separate, standalone data type. But over the years, the way we interact with arrays has changed considerably.

In the past, manipulating an array involved plenty of loops and iterative logic, along with a small set of underpowered methods. Today, the `Array` object is stocked with much more functionality, including methods that emphasize *functional* approaches. Using these methods, you can filter, sort, copy, and transform data, without stepping through array elements one at a time.

In this chapter, you'll see how to use these functional approaches—and learn when you might need to sidestep them. The focus is on solving problems using the most modern practices that are available today.

 If you're trying these examples out in the browser's developer console, be warned that *lazy evaluation* can fool you. For example, consider what happens if you output an array with `console.log()`, sort it, and then log it again. You expect to see the information for two differently sorted arrays. But you'll actually see the final, sorted array twice. That's because most browsers won't examine the items in your array until you open the console and click to expand the array. One way to avoid this problem is to iterate over the array and log each item separately. For more about the issue, see "Why Chrome's Developer Console Sometimes Lies" (*https://oreil.ly/VDHtm*).

5.1 Checking If an Object Is an Array

Problem

Before you perform an array operation, you want to verify that your object truly is an array.

Solution

Use the static `Array.isArray()` method:

```
const browserNames = ['Firefox', 'Edge', 'Chrome', 'IE', 'Safari'];

if (Array.isArray(browserNames)) {
  // We end up here, because browserNames is a valid array.
}
```

Discussion

The `Array.isArray()` method is an obvious choice. Problems happen when developers are tempted to use the older `instanceOf` operator. For historical reasons, the `instanceOf` operator has weird edge cases with arrays (for example, it returns `false` when you test an array that was created in another execution context, such as a different window). The `isArray()` method was added to patch this gap.

It's also important to understand that `isArray()` specifically checks for instances of the `Array` object. If you call it on a different type of collection (like `Map` or `Set`), it returns `false`. This is true even if these collections have array-like semantics, and even if they have *array* in the name, like `TypedArray` (a low-level wrapper for a buffer of binary data).

5.2 Iterating Over All the Elements in an Array

Problem

You want to use the best approach for looping over every element in an array, in order.

Solution

The traditional approach is a for...of loop, which automatically gets each item:

```
const animals = ['elephant', 'tiger', 'lion', 'zebra', 'cat', 'dog', 'rabbit'];

for (const animal of animals) {
```

```
    console.log(animal);
  }
```

In modern JavaScript, it's becoming increasingly common to favor *functional* approaches in array-processing code. You can iterate over your array in a functional way using the `Array.forEach()` method. You supply a function, and that function is called once for each element in the array, and passed three potentially useful parameters (the element, the element's index, and the original array). Here's an example:

```
const animals = ['elephant', 'tiger', 'lion', 'zebra', 'cat', 'dog', 'rabbit'];

animals.forEach(function(animal, index, array) {
  console.log(animal);
});
```

It's possible to condense this further with arrow syntax (Recipe 6.2):

```
animals.forEach(animal => console.log(animal));
```

Discussion

In long-lived languages like JavaScript, there are often many ways to accomplish the same thing. The `for...of` loop offers a straightforward syntax for iterating over an array. It doesn't allow you to modify the elements in the array you're traversing, which is a safe, sensible approach.

However, there are cases when you'll need to use something different. One of the most flexible choices is a basic `for` loop with a counter:

```
const animals = ['elephant', 'tiger', 'lion', 'zebra', 'cat', 'dog', 'rabbit'];

for (let i = 0; i < animals.length; ++i) {
  console.log(animals[i]);
}
```

This approach can allow off-by-one errors to slip by undetected, which are still a surprisingly common source of mistakes in modern-day programming. However, you'll need to use a `for` loop in some situations, such as when you're moving through more than one array at the same time (see Recipe 5.3).

You can also iterate over an array by passing a function to the `Array.forEach()` method. This function is then called once for each element. Your function can receive three parameters: the current array element, the current array index, and a reference to the original array. Usually, you'll only need the element. (You could use the index to make changes to the element in the original array, but that's considered bad form.)

Instead, if you want to use a functional approach to change or examine your array, consider using a more specific, targeted method. Table 5-1 lists the most useful.

Table 5-1. Methods for functional array processing

Task	Array method	Covered in
Change every array element	map()	Recipe 5.17
See if all elements meet a specific condition	every()	Recipe 5.19
See if at least one element meets a specific condition	some()	Recipe 5.19
Find array elements matching your criteria	filter()	Recipe 5.9
Reorder an array	sort()	Recipe 5.16
Use all the values of an array in one calculation	reduce()	Recipe 5.18

Modern coding practice favors *functional approaches* to array processing over *iterative approaches*. The advantage of a functional approach is that your code can be more concise, often more readable, and less error-prone. Most of the time, the functional approach also enforces *immutability* for your array. It does that by creating a new copy of the array with the changes you want, rather than making direct modifications on the original array object. This approach also makes certain types of errors less likely.

> As a rule of thumb, look at the functional array methods as a *first resort*. If they make your task more difficult (which might happen if you need to write multiple arrays or perform several array operations at once), switch to the iterative approach. And if you're writing performance-intensive code (for example, routines that operate on extremely large arrays), consider the iterative approach, because it tends to perform better. But don't forget to profile both approaches first to see if the difference is truly significant.

5.3 Checking If Two Arrays Are Equal

Problem

You want a simple way to test if two arrays are equivalent (have exactly the same contents).

Solution

The most straightforward approach is actually the old-fashioned approach: use a basic for loop with a counter, step through both arrays at the same time, and compare each element. Of course, there are a couple of checks to make before you start looping, like verifying that each object is an array, isn't null, and so on. Here's a bit of code that packages all these criteria into a single useful function:

```
function areArraysEqual(arrayA, arrayB) {
  if (!Array.isArray(arrayA) || !Array.isArray(arrayB)) {
```

```
      // These objects are null, undeclared, or non-array objects
      return false;
    }
    else if (arrayA === arrayB) {
      // Shortcut: they're two references pointing to the same array
      return true;
    }
    else if (arrayA.length !== arrayB.length) {
      // They can't match if they have a different item count
      return false;
    }
    else {
      // Time to look closer at each item
      for (let i = 0; i < arrayA.length; ++i) {
        // We require items to have the same content and be the same type,
        // but you could use loosely typed equality depending on your task
        if (arrayA[i] !== arrayB[i]) return false;
      }
      return true;
    }
  }
```

Now you can check that two arrays are the same, like this:

```
const fruitNamesA = ['apple', 'kumquat', 'grapefruit', 'kiwi'];
const fruitNamesB = ['apple', 'kumquat', 'grapefruit', 'kiwi'];
const fruitNamesC = ['avocado', 'squash', 'red pepper', 'cucumber'];

console.log(areArraysEqual(fruitNamesA, fruitNamesB));  // true
console.log(areArraysEqual(fruitNamesA, fruitNamesC));  // false
```

In this version of `areArraysEqual()`, arrays with the same items in a different order are considered nonmatching. You can easily sort arrays of strings or numbers using the `Array.sort()` method. However, it doesn't make sense to put this code in the `areArrayEquals()` method, because it may not be appropriate for the data types you want to use, or it may be prohibitively slow if you want to compare huge arrays. Instead, sort your arrays before you test them for equality:

```
const fruitNamesA = ['apple', 'kumquat', 'grapefruit', 'kiwi'];
const fruitNamesB = ['kumquat', 'kiwi', 'grapefruit', 'apple'];

console.log(areArraysEqual(fruitNamesA.sort(), fruitNamesB.sort()));  // true
```

Discussion

Often in programming, it's up to you to decide what equality means. In this example, `areArraysEqual()` performs a *shallow compare*. If two arrays have the same primitives or the same object references, and their elements are in the same order, they match. But if you start comparing more complex *objects*, ambiguities appear.

For example, consider this comparison of two arrays that hold a single, identical Date object:

```
const datesA = [new Date(2021,1,1)];
const datesB = [new Date(2021,1,1)];

console.log(areArraysEqual(datesA, datesB));  // false
```

These arrays don't match because even though the underlying date content is the same, the Date *instances* are different. (Or, to put it another way, there are two separate Date objects that just happen to save the same information in them.)

Of course, you can easily compare the content of two Date objects (just call get Time() to convert them to the millisecond time representation, as explained in Recipe 4.4). But if you want to do that in an array comparison, it's up to you to write a different function. In your function, you can use instanceOf to identify Date objects, and then call getTime() on them:

```
function areArraysEqual(arrayA, arrayB) {
  if (!Array.isArray(arrayA) || !Array.isArray(arrayB)) {
    return false;
  }
  else if (arrayA === arrayB) {
    return true;
  }
  else if (arrayA.length !== arrayB.length) {
    return false;
  }
  else {
    for (let i = 0; i < arrayA.length; ++i) {
      // Check for equal dates
      if (arrayA[i] instanceOf Date && arrayB[i] instanceOf Date) {
        if (arrayA[i].getTime() !== arrayB[i].getTime()) return false;
      }
      else {
        // Use the normal strict equality check
        if (arrayA[i] !== arrayB[i]) return false;
      }
    }
    return true;
  }
}
```

The problem shown in this example applies to arrays that hold any type of JavaScript object. It even applies to arrays that hold nested arrays (because every Array is an object). Your solution will differ, however, because different equality tests make sense for different objects.

Finally, it's worth noting that many popular JavaScript libraries have their own generic solutions for deep array comparison, which may or may not be suitable for your data. If you're already using a library like Lodash or *Underscore.js*, investigate its isEqual() method.

5.4 Breaking Down an Array into Separate Variables

Problem

You need to assign array element values to several variables, but you want a convenient approach that doesn't force you to assign each variable separately.

Solution

Use the array *destructuring syntax* to assign multiple variables at a time. You write an expression that declares several variables (on the left) and grabs the values from an array (on the right). Here's an example:

```
const stateValues = [459, 144, 96, 34, 0, 14];
const [arizona, missouri, idaho, nebraska, texas, minnesota] = stateValues;
console.log(missouri);   // 144
```

When you use array destructuring, the values are copied by position. In this example, that means arizona gets the first value in the array, missouri the second, and so on. If you have more variables than array elements, the extra variables get the value unde fined.

Discussion

When you use array destructuring, you don't need to copy every value that's in the array. You can skip values you don't want by adding extra commas without a variable name:

```
const stateValues = [459, 144, 96, 34, 0, 14];

// Just get three values from the array
const [arizona, , , nebraska, texas] = stateValues;
console.log(nebraska);   // 34
```

You can also use the *rest operator* to stuff all the remaining values (ones you didn't explicitly assign to variables) into a new array. Here's an example that copies the three last array elements into an array named others:

```
const stateValues = [459, 144, 96, 34, 0, 14];
const [arizona, missouri, idaho, ...others] = stateValues;
console.log(others);   // 34, 0, 14
```

JavaScript's rest operator looks just like the spread operator (it's three dots before a variable). They even "feel" similar in your code, although they actually play complementary roles. The rest operator vacuums up extra values and squashes them into a single array. The spread operator *expands* an array (or another type of iterable object) into separate values.

So far you've seen the variable declaration and assignment in one statement, but you can split them, just as you can when you create ordinary variables. Just make sure you keep the square brackets, because they indicate that you're using array destructuring:

```
let arizona, missouri, idaho, nebraska, texas, minnesota;
[arizona, missouri, idaho, nebraska, texas, minnesota] = stateValues;
```

See Also

If you want a way to convert an array into a list of values *without* assigning these values to variables, check out the spread operator described in Recipe 5.5.

5.5 Passing an Array to a Function That Expects a List of Values

Problem

Your array has a list of values that you want to pass to a function. But the function expects a list of argument values, not an array object.

Solution

Use the spread operator to expand your array. Here's an example with the `Math.max()` method:

```
const numbers = [2, 42, 5, 304, 1, 13];

// This syntax is not allowed. The result is NaN.
const maximumFail = Math.max(numbers);

// But this works, thanks to the spread operator. (The answer is 304.)
const maximum = Math.max(...numbers);
```

Discussion

The spread operator unfolds an array into a list of elements. Technically, it works with any iterable object, including other types of collections. You'll see it at work in several recipes in this chapter.

The spread operator doesn't need to supply all the arguments to a function, or even the final arguments. It's perfectly valid to use it like this:

```
const numbers = [2, 42, 5, 304, 1, 13];

// Call max() on the array values, along with three more arguments.
const maximum = Math.max(24, ...numbers, 96, 7);
```

You probably don't want to use this approach if the order of your arguments has any significance. It's just too easy to end up with an array that's a bit bigger or smaller than you thought, which will then displace your other arguments to new positions and change their significance.

See Also

Recipe 5.7 shows an example of how you can use the spread operator to merge different arrays. Recipe 5.15 shows how you can use spread when removing items. Recipe 5.6 shows how you can use spread to copy an array.

5.6 Cloning an Array

Problem

You want to make a copy of an existing array.

Solution

Use the spread operator to expand your array into items and feed it into a new array:

```
const numbers = [2, 42, 5, 304, 1, 13];
const numbersCopy = [...numbers];
```

An equally good approach is to use the `Array.slice()` method with no arguments, which tells it to take a slice of the entire array:

```
const numbers = [2, 42, 5, 304, 1, 13];
const numbersCopy = numbers.slice();
```

Both of these approaches are preferable to looping over array elements and building up a new array by hand.

Discussion

Creating array copies is important because it allows you to perform *nondestructive changes*. For example, you might keep your original array intact while you make changes to a new copy. That way, you reduce the risk of unanticipated side effects (for example, if other parts of your code are still using the original array).

As with all reference objects, arrays cannot be copied by assignment. This code, for example, ends with two variables pointing to the same in-memory Array object:

```
const numbers = [2, 42, 5, 304, 1, 13];
const numbersCopy = numbers;
```

To properly copy an array, you need to duplicate all of its elements. The easiest approach is to use the spread operator, although the Array.slice() method works equally well.

Both approaches shown here create *shallow copies*. If your array consists of primitives (numbers, strings, or Boolean values), the copied array matches exactly. But if your array holds objects, these techniques copy the *reference*, not the entire object. As a result, your new array will have references pointing to the same objects. Change one of the objects in the copied array, and it also affects the original array:

```
const objectsOriginal = [{name: 'Sadie', age: 12}, {name: 'Patrick', age: 18}];
const objectsCopy = [...objectsOriginal];

// Change one of the people objects in objectsCopy
objectsCopy[0].age = 14;

// Investigate the same object in objectsOriginal
console.log(objectsOriginal[0].age);  // 14
```

This may or may not be a problem, depending on how you plan to use your arrays. If you want multiple copies of objects that you can manipulate separately, there are several possible solutions you can use:

- Loop through your array with a for loop, create the new objects you need explicitly, and then add them to the new array.

- Use the Array.map() function. This works well for simple objects, but doesn't do a deep clone all the way down. (For example, if you have objects referencing *other* objects, only the first layer of objects is truly duplicated.)

- Use a helper function from another JavaScript library, like cloneDeep() in Lodash or clone() in Ramda.

Here's an example that demonstrates Array.map(). It works a little bit of magic by first expanding the array element into its properties with the spread operator (...ele ment), then uses them to create a new object ({...element}), which is assigned to the new array:

```
const objectsOriginal = [{name: 'Sadie', age: 12}, {name: 'Patrick', age: 18}];

// Create a new array with copied objects
const objectsCopy = objectsOriginal.map( element => ({...element}) );

// Change one of the people objects in objectsCopy
```

```
objectsCopy[0].age = 14;

// Investigate the same object in objectsOriginal
console.log(objectsOriginal[0].age);  // 12
```

To take a closer look at the map() method, see the full explanation in Recipe 5.17.

 The spread operator (...) does double duty. In the original solution, you saw how the spread operator can expand an array into
separate elements. In the Array.map() example, the spread operator expands an *object* into separate properties. For more about how
the spread operator works on objects, see Recipe 7.6.

See Also

If you want to copy only *some* array items, see Recipe 5.8. To learn more about different ways of making deep copies of an object, see Recipe 7.11.

5.7 Merging Two Arrays

Problem

You want to join two entire arrays together into a new array.

Solution

There are two commonly used approaches for combining two arrays. The time-
honored approach (and likely the most performant option) is to use the Array.con
cat() method. You call concat() on the first array, passing in the second array as an
argument. The result is a third array that contains all the elements of both:

```
const evens = [2, 4, 6, 8];
const odds = [1, 3, 5, 7, 9];

const evensAndOdds = evens.concat(odds);
// now evensAddOdds contains [2, 4, 6, 8, 1, 3, 5, 7, 9]
```

The resulting array has the first array's items first (evens, in this example), followed
by second array's items (odds). Of course, you can follow up your concat() with a
call to the Array.sort() method (Recipe 5.16).

An alternate approach is to use the spread operator (introduced in Recipe 5.5):

```
const evens = [2, 4, 6, 8];
const odds = [1, 3, 5, 7, 9];

const evensAndOdds = [...evens, ...odds];
```

The advantage of this approach is that the code is (arguably) more intuitive and easier to read. The spread operator is also a great tool if you want to combine more than two arrays at a time, or you want to combine arrays with literal values:

```
const evens = [2, 4, 6, 8];
const odds = [1, 3, 5, 7, 9];

const evensAndOdds = [...evens, 10, 12, ...odds, 11];
```

Performance testing suggests that on current implementations, large arrays are merged faster with concat(). But in most scenarios, this performance different won't be significant (or even apparent).

Discussion

After you merge arrays with either of these techniques, you are left with three arrays: the original two, and the new merged result. If your arrays contain primitive values (numbers, strings, Boolean values), these are duplicated in the new array. But if your array holds objects, the object *reference* is copied. For example, if you merge two arrays of Date objects, no new Date objects are created. Instead, the new merged array gets references pointing to the *same* Date objects. If you change a Date object in the merged array, you'll see the modification in the original array as well:

```
const dates2020 = [new Date(2020,1,10), new Date(2020,2,10)];
const dates2021 = [new Date(2021,1,10), new Date(2021,2,10)];

const datesCombined = [...dates2020, ...dates2021];

// Change a date in the new array
datesCombined[0].setYear(2022);

// The same object is in the first array
console.log(dates2020[0]);    // 2022/02/10
```

For more about the difference between shallow and deep copies, see Recipe 7.11.

See Also

When you merge arrays, you have no power to control how the elements are combined. If you want to copy just a portion of an array, or put one array in the *middle* of another, see the slice() method in Recipe 5.8.

5.8 Copying a Portion of an Array by Position

Problem

You want to copy a portion of an array, and keep the original array intact.

Solution

Use the `Array.slice()` method, which makes a *shallow copy* of a portion of an existing array, and returns that as a new array:

```
const animals = ['elephant', 'tiger', 'lion', 'zebra', 'cat', 'dog',
  'rabbit', 'goose'];

// Get the chunk from index 4 to index 7.
const domestic = animals.slice(4, 7);

console.log(domestic); // ['cat', 'dog', 'rabbit']
```

Discussion

The `slice()` method takes two parameters, indicating a starting and ending position. You can omit the second parameter to go from the start index to the end of the array. Calling `slice(0)` on an array copies the whole array.

For example, this code uses slice to get two subsections of the first array, and use them to build a new array:

```
const animals = ['elephant', 'tiger', 'lion', 'zebra', 'cat', 'dog',
  'rabbit', 'goose'];

const firstHalf = animals.slice(0, 3);
const secondHalf = animals.slice(4, 7);

// Put two new animals in the middle
const extraAnimals = [...firstHalf, 'emu', 'platypus', ...secondHalf];
```

This may seem like an arbitrary example, because the index numbers are hard-coded. But you can combine it with array searches and the `findIndex()` method (see Recipe 5.13) to find the place where you should divide an array.

 The `slice()` method is easily confused with the `splice()` method, which is used to replace or delete portions of an array. Unlike `slice()`, the `splice()` method makes in-place changes that affect the original array. In modern practice, it's considered better to lock-down your objects, keep them immutable when possible (hence the use of `const`), and create a new copy with changes. So stick with `slice()` unless you have a strong reason to use `splice()` (for example, there's a difference in performance that's significant in your use case).

See Also

Recipe 5.15 shows how you can use `slice()` to remove sections of an array.

5.9 Extracting Array Items That Meet Specific Criteria

Problem

You want to find all the items in an array that match a certain condition, and copy them to a new array.

Solution

Use the `Array.filter()` method to run a test on every item:

```
function startsWithE(animal) {
  return animal[0].toLowerCase() === 'e';
}

const animals = ['elephant', 'tiger', 'emu', 'zebra', 'cat', 'dog',
 'eel', 'rabbit', 'goose', 'earwig'];
const animalsE = animals.filter(startsWithE);
console.log(animalsE);   // ["elephant", "emu", "eel", "earwig"]
```

This example is intentionally long-winded so you can see the different pieces of the solution. The *filter function* is called for every item in the array. In this case, that means `startsWithE()` is called 10 times, and passed a different string each time. If the filter function returns `true`, that item is added to the new array.

Here's the same example condensed with an arrow function. Now the filter logic is defined in the same place in code where you use it:

```
const animals = ['elephant', 'tiger', 'emu', 'zebra', 'cat', 'dog',
 'eel', 'rabbit', 'goose', 'earwig'];
const animalsE = animals.filter(animal => animal[0].toLowerCase() === 'e');
```

Discussion

In this example, the filter function checks that each item begins with the letter *e*. But you could just as easily grab numbers that fall in a certain range, or objects that have certain property values.

The `filter()` method is one of a new set of modern array methods that replace old-fashioned iterative code with a functional approach. Nothing stops you from using a `for` loop to step through your array, test each item, and insert matches into a new array with `Array.push()`. However, if you can perform the same task with the `filter()` method, you'll usually be rewarded with more compact code and easier testing.

See Also

Several of the recipes in this chapter introduce similar methods for functional array processing. In particular, Recipe 5.17 shows how to transform all the elements in an array, and Recipe 5.18 shows how to perform a calculation that combines all the values in an array into one result.

5.10 Emptying an Array

Problem

You need to remove all the elements from an array, either to reclaim memory or so that your array can be reused.

Solution

Set the `length` property of your array to 0:

```
const numbers = [2, 42, 5, 304, 1, 13];
numbers.length = 0;
```

Discussion

One of the easiest ways to give yourself a new array is to simply assign a new blank array, like this:

```
myArray = [];
```

However, this approach has a couple of limits. First, because it creates a whole new array object, it doesn't work if you've defined your array with the `const` keyword. This is a small detail, but modern practice favors using `const` over `let` to narrow the possibilities for bugs in your code. Second, this assignment doesn't actually destroy the array. If you have another variable pointing to your array, it will stay alive and remain in memory.

An alternate solution is to call the `Array.pop()` method repeatedly. Each time you call `pop()`, you remove the last item from the array, so you can empty an array with a loop that continues calling `pop()` until the array is empty. However, the `length` setting trick has exactly the same effect and requires just a single statement. Developers sometimes overlook this technique, because they expect `length` to be a read-only property (as it is in many other languages). But setting `length` on a JavaScript array allows you to shrink its size and drop the leftover items.

There are other interesting ways to use the `length` property. For example, you can chop off only part of an array by reducing `length`, but not all the way to 0. Or, you can add blank items to the end of an array by increasing `length`:

```
const numbers = [2, 42, 5, 304, 1, 13];
numbers.length = 3;

console.log(numbers);  // [2, 42, 5]
```

```
numbers.length = 5;
console.log(numbers);  // [2, 42, 5, undefined, undefined]
```

5.11 Removing Duplicate Values

Problem

You want to ensure that every value in your array is unique by removing the duplicates.

Solution

Create a new `Set` object and fill it with your array. The `Set` object will discard duplicates automatically. Then, convert the `Set` object back to an array:

```
const numbersWithDuplicates = [2, 42, 5, 42, 304, 1, 13, 2, 13];

// Create a Set with unique values (the duplicate 42, 2, and 13 are discarded)
const uniqueNumbersSet = new Set(numbersWithDuplicates);

// Turn the Set back into an array (now with 6 items)
const uniqueNumbersArray = Array.from(uniqueNumbersSet);
```

Once you understand the idea, you can compress this down to a single statement with the spread operator:

```
const numbersWithDuplicates = [2, 42, 5, 42, 304, 1, 13, 2, 13];

const uniqueNumbers = [...new Set(numbersWithDuplicates)];
```

Discussion

The `Set` object is a special type of collection that ignores duplicate values. It also works as a quick and efficient way to remove duplicates from an array. This technique (switching to a `Set` and then back to an array) is far more efficient than iterating over the array and looking for duplicates with `findIndex()`.

When searching for duplicates, the `Set` uses a test that's similar to the strict equality comparison ===, which means 3 and '3' are not considered duplicates. One special bit of behavior the `Set` implements is that it treats repeated NaN values as duplicates, even though NaN === NaN ordinarily evaluates to `false`.

See Also

This example uses the spread operator described in Recipe 5.5. For more about the `Set` object, see Recipe 5.20.

5.12 Flattening a Two-Dimensional Array

Problem

You want to flatten a two-dimensional array so that it becomes a one-dimensional list.

Solution

Use the `Array.flat()` method:

```
const fruitArray = [];

// Add three elements to fruitArray
// Each element is an array of strings
fruitArray[0] = ['strawberry', 'blueberry', 'raspberry'];
fruitArray[1] = ['lime', 'lemon', 'orange', 'grapefruit'];
fruitArray[2] = ['tangerine', 'apricot', 'peach', 'plum'];

const fruitList = fruitArray.flat();
// Now fruitList has 11 elements, and each one is a string
```

Discussion

Consider a two-dimensional array, like this one:

```
const fruitArray = [];
fruitArray[0] = ['strawberry', 'blueberry', 'raspberry'];
fruitArray[1] = ['lime', 'lemon', 'orange', 'grapefruit'];
fruitArray[2] = ['tangerine', 'apricot', 'peach', 'plum'];
```

Each element in the `fruitArray` holds *another* array. For example, `fruitArray[0]` has three strings, representing different berries. `fruitArray[1]` has citrus fruits, and `fruitArray[2]` has stone fruits.

You could transform `fruitArray` with the help of the `concat()` method. Start with the first nested array, call `concat()`, and pass the other nested arrays, like this:

```
const fruitList =
  fruitArray[0].concat(fruitArray[1],fruitArray[2],fruitArray[3]);
```

If the array has several members, this approach is tedious and error prone. Alternatively, you could use a loop or recursion, but these approaches can be equally tedious. The `flat()` method implements the same logic, and concatenates every row for you.

The `flat()` method takes an optional `depth` argument, with a default value of 1. You can increase this number to flatten more deeply nested arrays. For example, imagine you have an array that contains nested arrays, and those arrays hold *another* layer of nested arrays. In this case, a `depth` of 2 will concatenate both layers, putting everything into a single list:

```
// An array with several levels of nested arrays inside
const threeDimensionalNumbers = [1, [2, [3, 4, 5], 6], 7];

// The default flattening
const flat2D = threeDimensionalNumbers.flat(1);
// now flat2D = [1, 2, [3, 4, 5], 6, 7]

// Flatten two levels
const flat1D = threeDimensionalNumbers.flat(2);
// now flat1D = [1, 2, 3, 4, 5, 6, 7]

// Flatten all levels, no matter how many there are
const flattest = threeDimensionalNumbers.flat(Infinity);
```

The `depth` argument sets the maximum level of flattening that's used, if needed. There's no risk to increasing the `depth` beyond the actual dimensions of your array.

5.13 Searching Through an Array for Exact Matches

Problem

You want to search an array for a specific value. You may want to know if the array contains a match, or the position where that match occurred.

Solution

Use one of the array searching methods: `indexOf()`, `lastIndexOf()`, or `includes()`:

```
const animals = ['dog', 'cat', 'seal', 'elephant', 'walrus', 'lion'];
console.log(animals.indexOf('elephant'));    // 3
console.log(animals.lastIndexOf('walrus'));  // 4
console.log(animals.includes('dog'));        // true
```

This technique only works for primitive values (typically numbers, strings, and Boolean values). If you want to search for objects, you need to use the `Array.find()` method instead (Recipe 5.14).

Discussion

Both `indexOf()` and `lastIndexOf()` take a search value that is then compared to every element in the array. If the value is found, they return the index position of the array element. If the value is not found, they return –1.

The `indexOf()` method returns the first match found searching from lowest to highest index (in other words, starting at the beginning of the array and going forward).

The `lastIndexOf()` method goes in reverse, starting at the end of the array. The difference appears if the same item appears more than once in the array:

```
const animals = ['dog', 'cat', 'seal', 'walrus', 'lion', 'cat'];

console.log(animals.indexOf('cat'));       // 1
console.log(animals.lastIndexOf('cat'));   // 5
```

Both `indexOf()` and `lastIndexOf()` take an optional starting index argument. That sets the position where the search will begin:

```
const animals = ['dog', 'cat', 'seal', 'walrus', 'lion', 'cat'];

console.log(animals.indexOf('cat', 2));       // 5
console.log(animals.lastIndexOf('cat', 4));   // 1
```

It may occur to you that you can use a loop to step through increasingly higher indexes with `indexOf()` until you've found all the matches. But before you write that kind of boilerplate code, consider using the `filter()` method, which quickly and painlessly creates an array with all the matches for a condition you specify (see Recipe 5.9).

Finally, it's important to understand that `indexOf()`, `lastIndexOf()`, and `includes()` all use the `===` operator to test for matches. That means no type conversion is performed (so 3 will not equal `'3'`). Also, if your array contains objects, the references are compared, not the content. If you need to change the meaning of equality or you want to use a different search test, use the `findIndex()` method instead (see Recipe 5.14).

See Also

For customizable searching, see the `find()` and `findIndex()` methods in Recipe 5.14.

5.14 Searching Through an Array for Items That Meet Specific Criteria

Problem

You want to search an array for an item that meets certain criteria. For example, maybe you're looking for an object with a specific property.

Solution

Use one of the functional array searching methods: `find()` or `findIndex()`. Either way, you supply the function that tests each item until a match is found.

Here's an example that finds the first number over 10:

```
const nums = [2, 4, 19, 15, 183, 6, 7, 1, 1];

// Find the first value over 10.
const bigNum = nums.find(element => element > 10);

console.log(bigNum);  // 19 (the first match)
```

If instead of finding the matching element, you would rather know its position, you can use the similar findIndex() method:

```
const nums = [2, 4, 19, 15, 183, 6, 7, 1, 1];

const bigNumIndex = nums.findIndex(element => element > 100);

console.log(bigNumIndex);  // 4 (the index of the first match)
```

If no match is found, find() returns undefined, and findIndex() returns –1.

Discussion

When using find() and findIndex(), you supply a callback function that receives up to three parameters (the current array element in the iteration, its index, and the array itself). Arrow syntax offers a more streamlined approach, allowing you to define the callback function right where you use it.

The find() and findIndex() methods really shine when you need to write more complicated conditions. Consider the following code, which finds the first date in a specific year:

```
// Remember, the Date constructor takes a zero-based month number, so a
// month value of 10 corresponds to the eleventh month, November
const dates = [new Date(2021, 10, 20), new Date(2020, 3, 12),
 new Date(2020, 5, 23), new Date(2022, 3, 18)];

// Find the first date in 2020
const matchingDate = dates.find(date => date.getFullYear() === 2020);

console.log(matchingDate);  // 'Sun Apr 12 2020 ...'
```

This approach isn't possible with the indexOf() method, because it involves examining a *property* of an array item. (In fact, the standard indexOf() method can't even test Date objects for equality, because it only checks if the object references match.)

See Also

If you want to write a finding function and use it to get multiple results, you probably want the filter() function described in Recipe 5.9. For more about the syntax of arrow function, see Recipe 6.2.

5.15 Removing or Replacing Array Elements

Problem

You want to find occurrences of a given value in an array, and either remove the element or replace it.

Solution

First, find the location of the item you want to remove using `indexOf()`. Then, you can use one of two approaches.

For small jobs, the cleanest solution is to construct a new array *around* the item you don't want. You build the new array using `slice()` and the spread operator:

```
const animals = ['dog', 'cat', 'seal', 'walrus', 'lion', 'cat'];

// Find where the 'walrus' item is
const walrusIndex = animals.indexOf('walrus');

// Join the portion before 'walrus' to the portion after 'walrus'
const animalsSliced =
  [...animals.slice(0, walrusIndex), ...animals.slice(walrusIndex+1)];

// now animalsSliced has ['dog', 'cat', 'seal', 'lion', 'cat']
```

Discussion

An alternate approach is to perform an in-place array edit, instead of creating a changed copy. This may perform better for large arrays. However, the more mutability you allow, the more complex your code becomes, which may make it more difficult to manage and debug in the future.

To perform an in-place edit, you use the similarly named but very different `splice()` method. It lets you remove as many items as you want, starting from any position:

```
const animals = ['dog', 'cat', 'seal', 'walrus', 'lion', 'cat'];

// Find where the 'walrus' item is
const walrusIndex = animals.indexOf('walrus');

// Starting at walrusIndex, remove 1 element
animals.splice(walrusIndex, 1);

// now animals = ['dog', 'cat', 'seal', 'lion', 'cat']
```

The first argument to the `splice()` method is the index where the splicing starts. This is the only argument you need to supply. If you leave out the others, all the array elements from the index to the end are removed:

```
const animals = ['cat', 'walrus', 'lion', 'cat'];

// Start at 'lion', and remove the rest of the elements
animals.splice(2);
// now animals = ['cat', 'walrus']
```

The optional second argument is the number of elements to remove. The third argument is an optional set of the replacement elements to *insert* at the same location.

```
const animals = ['cat', 'walrus', 'lion', 'cat'];

// Remove one element and add two new elements
animals.splice(2, 1, 'zebra', 'elephant');
// now animals = ['cat', 'walrus', 'zebra', 'elephant', 'cat']
```

You could use indexOf() in a loop to find and remove a series of matching elements. But if this is your goal, the filter() method usually provides a cleaner approach, letting you define a function that picks the items you want to keep (see Recipe 5.9).

5.16 Sorting an Array of Objects by a Property Value

Problem

You want to sort an array that contains objects, based on one of its properties.

Solution

The Array.sort() method reorders an array. For example, it arranges an array of numbers from smallest to largest, or it puts an array of strings in alphabetical order. But you don't need to stick to the array's standard sorting system. Instead, you can pass a comparison function to the sort() method, and the array will use it to order its items.

The comparison function gets two items (corresponding to two different array elements), compares them, and returns a number that indicates the result. You return *0* if the values should be considered equal, *−1* if the first value is less than the second, or *1* if the first value is greater than the second.

Here's a simple implementation that sorts an array of objects with people information:

```
const people  = [
  { firstName: 'Joe', lastName: 'Khan', age: 21 },
  { firstName: 'Dorian', lastName: 'Khan', age: 15 },
  { firstName: 'Tammy', lastName: 'Smith', age: 41 },
  { firstName: 'Noor', lastName: 'Biles', age: 33 },
  { firstName: 'Sumatva', lastName: 'Chen', age: 19 }
];

// Sort the people from youngest to oldest
```

```
people.sort( function(a, b) {
  if (a.age < b.age) {
    return -1;
  } else if (a.age > b.age) {
    return 1;
  } else {
    return 0;
  }
});
console.log(people);
// Now the order is Dorian, Sumatva, Joe, Noor, Tammy
```

A couple of shortcuts are possible here. Technically, you can return any negative number instead of –1, and any positive number instead of 1. That allows you to write a much shorter comparison function:

```
people.sort(function(a, b) {
  // Subtract the ages to sort from youngest to oldest
  return a.age - b.age;
});
```

Combine that with the compact arrow syntax, and it gets shorter still:

```
people.sort((a,b) => a.age - b.age);
```

Sometimes, when you perform sorting you can make use of existing comparison methods. For example, if you want this example to sort by last name, there's no need to reinvent the wheel. Instead, make good use of the `String.localeCompare()` method, like this:

```
people.sort((a,b) => a.lastName.localeCompare(b.lastName));
console.log(people);
// Now the order is Noor, Sumatva, Joe, Dorian, Tammy
```

Discussion

The `sort()` method alters your array *in place*. This is different than most of the other array methods you'll use, which return changed copies but leave your original array untouched. If this isn't the behavior you want, you can clone your array before you sort it, as detailed in Recipe 5.6.

5.17 Transforming Every Element of an Array

Problem

You want to convert every element in an array using the same transformation, and use the changed values to build a new array.

Solution

Use the `Array.map()` method, and supply a function that performs the change. The `map()` method goes through the entire array, applying your function to each element and building a new array with the return values.

Here's an example that uses this approach to change an array of decimal numbers into a new array with their hexadecimal equivalents (using the conversion technique described in Recipe 3.6):

```
const decArray = [23, 255, 122, 5, 16, 99];

// Use the toString() method to conver to base-16 values
const hexArray = decArray.map( element => element.toString(16) );

console.log(hexArray);  // ['17', 'ff', '7a', '5', '10', '63']
```

Discussion

Usually, the `map()` function is only interested in the array elements. However, your callback function can accept two more parameters: the index and the original array. Using these details, it's technically possible to use `map()` to change your *original* array. This is considered an antipattern. In other words, if you don't plan to use the new array that `map()` returns, you shouldn't use the `map()` method. Consider using the `forEach()` method instead (Recipe 5.2), or just iterate over your array procedurally.

5.18 Combining an Array's Values in a Single Calculation

Problem

You want to use all the values in an array in some sort of aggregate calculation, like computing a sum or average.

Solution

You could iterate over the array in a loop. But for a more streamlined solution, use the `Array.reduce()` method with a callback function. Your function (called the *reducer function*) is called for each element in the array. You build some sort of running total using an *accumulator*, a value that the `reduce()` method maintains until the process is finished.

For example, imagine you want to calculate the sum of an array of numbers. Each time your reducer function is called, it gets the current running total in the accumulator. It then adds the value of the current element and returns the new total:

```
const reducerFunction = function (accumulator, element) {
   // Add the current value to the running total in the accumulator.
```

```
    const newTotal = accumulator + element;
    return newTotal;
}
```

This new total becomes the accumulator when the reducer is called for the *next* item.

Now you can use this function to sum up an array:

```
const numbers = [23, 255, 122, 5, 16, 99];

// The second argument (0) sets the starting value of the accumulator.
// If you don't set a starting value, the accumulator is automatically set
// to the first element.
const total = numbers.reduce(reducerFunction, 0);
console.log(total);  // 520
```

When the reducer function is called on the last item, it makes its final calculation. That return value becomes the result that's returned from reduce().

Once you're comfortable with the way reduce() works, you can make your code shorter and more concise with inline functions and arrow syntax. Here's a demonstration that uses reduce() to calculate the sum of squared values, an average, and the maximum value:

```
const numbers = [23, 255, 122, 5, 16, 99];

// The reducer function adds to the accumulator
const totalSquares = numbers.reduce( (acc, val) => acc + val**2, 0);
// totalSquares = 90520

// The reducer function adds to the accumulator
const average = numbers.reduce( (acc, val) => acc + val, 0) / numbers.length;
// average = 86.66...

// The reducer function returns the higher value (accumulator or current value)
const max = numbers.reduce( (acc, val) => acc > val ? acc: val);
// max = 255
```

Discussion

Using the reduce() method can seem more complicated than other functional-style array processing methods, like map() (Recipe 5.17), filter() (Recipe 5.9), or sort() (Recipe 5.16). The difference is that you need to think carefully about what data you need to store after each function call. Remember that you can use the accumulator to store a custom object with more than one property, allowing you to track as much information as you need. You can also add two more optional parameters to your reducer function: index (the current index number of the element), and array (the entire array that's being reduced). But be careful. Over-enthusiastic code that uses reduce() can quickly get hard for others to understand.

See Also

There's another way to get the maximum out of an array of numbers. You can use the `Math.max()` method in conjunction with the spread operator to turn your array into a list of arguments (see Recipe 5.5).

5.19 Validating Array Contents

Problem

You want to ensure that array contents meet certain criteria.

Solution

Use the `Array.every()` method to check that every element passes a given test. For example, the following code checks to ensure that every element in the array consists of alphabetic characters using a regular expression:

```
// The testing function
function containsLettersOnly(element) {
  const textExp = /^[a-zA-Z]+$/;
  return textExp.test(element);
}

// Test an array
const mysteryItems = ['**', 123, 'aaa', 'abc', '-', 46, 'AAA'];
let result = mysteryItems.every(containsLettersOnly);
console.log(result);  // false

// Test another array
const mysteryItems2 = ['elephant', 'lion', 'cat', 'dog'];
result = mysteryItems2.every(containsLettersOnly);
console.log(result);  // true
```

Or, use the `Array.some()` method to ensure that at least one of the elements passes the test. As an example, the following code checks to ensure that at least one of the array elements is an alphabetical string:

```
const mysteryItems = new Array('**', 123, 'aaa', 'abc', '-', 46, 'AAA');

// testing function
function testValue (element) {
  const textExp = /^[a-zA-Z]+$/;
  return textExp.test(element);
}

// run test
const result = mysteryItems.some(testValue);
console.log(result);  // true
```

Discussion

Unlike many other array methods that use callback functions, the `every()` and `some()` methods do not work against all array elements. Instead, they only process as many array elements as necessary to fulfill their functionality.

The solution demonstrates that the same callback function can be used for both the `every()` and `some()` methods. The difference is that when using `every()`, as soon as the function returns a `false` value, the processing is finished, and the method returns `false`. The `some()` method continues to test against every array element until the callback function returns `true`. At that time, no other elements are validated, and the method returns `true`. However, if the callback function tests against all elements, and doesn't return `true` for any of them, `some()` returns `false`.

See Also

To review regular expression syntax, which is used for the string matching pattern in this example, see Recipe 2.10.

5.20 Creating a Collection of Nonduplicated Values

Problem

You want to create an array-like object that never contains more than one copy of the same value.

Solution

Create a `Set` object. It quietly ignores attempts to add the same item more than once, without generating an error.

The `Set` is not an array, but—like an array—it's an iterable collection of elements. You can add elements to a `Set` one at a time with the `add()` method, or you can pass an array in the `Set` constructor to add multiple items at once:

```
// Start with six elements
const animals = new Set(['elephant', 'tiger', 'lion', 'zebra', 'cat', 'dog']);

// Add two more
animals.add('rabbit');
animals.add('goose');

// Nothing happens, because this item is already in the Set
animals.add('tiger');

// Iterate over the Set, just as you would with an array
for (const animal of animals) {
```

```
        console.log(animal);
    }
```

Discussion

The `Set` object is not an array. Unlike the `Array` class, which is stocked with thirty-some useful methods, the `Set` class offers much less. You can use `add()` to insert an item, `delete()` to remove one, `has()` to check if an item is in the `Set`, and `clear()` to remove all the items at once. There are no methods for sorting, filtering, transforming, or copying.

However, if you need to process your `Set` object like an array, it's easy enough to make the conversion by passing your `Set` to the static `Array.from()` method:

```
// Convert an array to a Set
const animalSet = new Set(['elephant', 'tiger', 'zebra', 'cat', 'dog']);

// Convert a Set to an array
const animalArray = Array.from(animalSet);
```

In fact, you can convert a `Set` to an `Array` object and back as many times as you want, with no cost other than possible performance (if you have a very long list of items).

 To count the number of items in a `Set` or `Map` collection, you use the `size` property. This is different than arrays, which have a `length` property.

5.21 Creating a Key-Indexed Collection of Items

Problem

You want to create a collection where each item is labeled with a unique string key.

Solution

Use the `Map` object. Each object is indexed with a unique key (usually, but not necessarily, a string). To add an item, you call the `set()` method. When you need to retrieve a specific item, you can grab exactly the item you want by using the key:

```
const products = new Map();

// Add three items
products.set('RU007', {name: 'Rain Racer 2000', price: 1499.99});
products.set('STKY1', {name: 'Edible Tape', price: 3.99});
products.set('P38', {name: 'Escape Vehicle (Air)', price: 2999.00});
```

```
// Check for two items using the item code
console.log(products.has('RU007'));  // true
console.log(products.has('RU494'));  // false

// Retrieve an item
const product = products.get('P38');
if (typeof product !== 'undefined') {
  console.log(product.price);  // 2999
}

// Remove the Edible Tape item
products.delete('STKY1');

console.log(products.size);  // 2
```

Discussion

When adding items to a Map object, you must always use the set() method. Don't fall into this trap:

```
const products = new Map();

// Don't do this!
products['RU007'] = {name: 'Rain Racer 2000', price: 1499.99};
```

Although this seems to work at first (and it uses the same kind of syntax that's used with name-value collections in many other programming languages), it actually bypasses the Map collection and sets an ordinary property named RU007 on the Map object. These properties won't appear if you iterate over the Map with a for...of loop, and they won't be visible to the has() or get() methods.

The Map object has a small set of methods for managing its contents: set(), get(), has(), and delete(). If you want to make use of the functionality in the Array object, you can easily convert your Map to an array with the static Array.from() method:

```
const productArray = Array.from(products);

console.log(productArray[0]);
  // ['RU007', {name: 'Rain Racer 2000', price: 1499.99}]
```

You might expect that the productArray in this example will hold a collection of product objects, but that's not quite true. Instead, each element in productsArray is a *separate* array with two elements. The first element is the key (like *RUU07*), and the second element is the value (the product object).

In some situations, you might not need to keep the key name when you convert a Map to an array. Maybe the key isn't important, or it's duplicated by a property of your elements. In this case, you can choose to transform your collection, throwing away the key values as you copy your data out of the Map. Here's how that works:

```
const productArray = Array.from(products, ([name, value]) => value);

console.log(productArray[0]);
 // {name: 'Rain Racer 2000', price: 1499.99}
```

## CHAPTER 6

Functions

Functions are the building blocks that you use to assemble a program out of discrete, reusable code routines. But in JavaScript, that's only part of the story.

JavaScript functions are also genuine *objects*—instances of the Function type. They can be assigned to variables and passed around your code. They can be declared in an expression, without a function name, and optionally using a streamlined *arrow syntax*. You can even wrap one function in another to create a private package that includes the function's state (called a *closure*).

Functions are also at the core of JavaScript's object-oriented support. That's because custom classes are really just a special type of constructor function (as you'll see in Chapter 8). Sooner or later, everything in JavaScript comes back to functions.

6.1 Passing a Function as an Argument to Another Function

Problem

You're calling a function that expects you to provide your own function. What's the best way to pass it?

Solution

Many functions in JavaScript accept, or even require, a function that's passed as an argument. Some operations ask for a callback function that will be triggered when a task is complete. Others need to use your function to complete a broader task. For example, many methods of the Array object ask you to provide a function for sorting, converting, combining, or selecting data. The array then uses your function multiple times, until it has processed every element.

There are several different approaches you can use when supplying a function as an argument. Here are three common patterns:

- Provide a reference to a function that's already declared elsewhere in your code. This approach makes sense if you want to use the function in other parts of your application, or if the function is particularly long or complex.

- Declare the function in a *function expression*, then pass it as an argument. This approach works well for straightforward tasks, and if you don't plan to use the function anywhere else.

- Declare the function inline, at the exact moment it's required—when you pass it as an argument to another function. This is similar to the second approach, but it makes your code even more compact. It works best for very short, straightforward functions (especially one-liners).

Let's start with a simple page that has this button:

```
<button id="runTest">Run Test</button>
```

We attach an event handler as follows:

```
// Attach button event handler.
document.getElementById('runTest').addEventListener("click", buttonClicked);
```

Now consider the built-in setTimeout() function, which schedules a function to run after a certain delay (you supply the function). Here's the first approach to function passing, with a separate function named showMessage():

```
// Runs when a button is clicked
function buttonClicked() {
  // Trigger the function after 2000 milliseconds (2 seconds)
  setTimeout(showMessage, 2000);
}

// Runs when setTimeout() triggers it
function showMessage() {
  alert('You clicked the button 2 seconds ago');
}
```

 When you pass a function reference by name, make sure you don't add a set of empty parentheses. This example passes showMessage to the setTimeout() function. If you accidentally write showMessage(), JavaScript will *run* the showMessage() function immediately, and pass its return value to setTimeout() instead of passing a function reference.

Here's the second approach, which declares the function closer to where it's needed using a function expression:

```
function buttonClicked() {
  // Declare a function expression to use with setTimeout()
  const timeoutCallback = function showMessage() {
    alert('You clicked the button 2 seconds ago');
  }

  // Trigger the function after 2000 milliseconds (2 seconds)
  setTimeout(timeoutCallback, 2000);
}
```

In this case, the scope of showMessage() is limited to the buttonClicked() function. It can't be called from another function elsewhere in your code. Optionally, you could omit the function name (showMessage), making it an *anonymous function*. Either way, timeoutCallback works the same, but a function name can be useful in debugging, because it will appear in a stack trace if an error occurs.

And here's the third approach, which declares the function inline when calling setTimeout():

```
function buttonClicked() {
  // Trigger the function after 2000 milliseconds (2 seconds)
  setTimeout(function showMessage() {
    alert('You clicked the button 2 seconds ago');
  }, 2000);
}
```

Now the showMessage() function is declared and passed to setTimeout() in one statement. There's no way for any other part of code to interact with showMessage(), even inside the buttonClicked() function. Optionally, you can leave out the name showMessage() so that it becomes an anonymous function:

```
setTimeout(function() {
  alert('You clicked the button 2 seconds ago');
}, 2000);
```

You can simplify this approach even further using arrow syntax, as demonstrated in Recipe 6.2. But using a function name is a good practice for long or complex code routines. That's because you'll see the function name in the stack trace if an error occurs inside the function.

Pay attention to your organization's style conventions when you use anonymous functions. One common pattern is to place the `func tion()` declaration and the opening { brace on the same line. Then, put all the code for the anonymous function underneath, with one extra level of indent. Finally, put the closing } brace on a separate line, followed immediately by the rest of the arguments for the function call.

Discussion

These three approaches demonstrate a gradually narrowing scope, from the most accessible function (in the first example) to the least accessible function (in the last example). As a general rule, it's best to use the narrowest scope possible. This reduces ambiguity in your code (making it more understandable for the other developers who follow in your footsteps), and reduces the possibility of unexpected side effects. However, there's a trade-off. As a function becomes longer and more complex, inline declarations become less readable. And if you want to use the function separately, or run unit tests against it, you will need to break it out into a separate function.

If you're in any doubt about how a function *uses* a function reference, here's a simple example with a custom function named `callYouBack()` that accepts a function parameter and then calls it. Inside the `callYouBack()` function, you treat the function reference exactly like an ordinary function, calling it by name and supplying any parameters it needs:

```
function buttonClicked() {
  // Create a function that will handle the callback
  function logTime(time) {
    console.log('Logging at: ' + time.toLocaleTimeString());
  }

  console.log('About to call callYouBack()');
  callYouBack(logTime);
  console.log('All finished');
}

function callYouBack(callbackFunction) {
  console.log('Starting callYouBack()');

  // Call the provided function and supply an argument
  callbackFunction(new Date());

  console.log('Ending callYouBack()');
}
```

If you run this code and click the button, it produces output like this:

```
About to call callYouBack()
Starting callYouBack()
Logging at: 2:20:59 PM
Ending callYouBack()
All finished
```

See Also

See Recipe 6.2 for a syntax that lets you simplify the declaration of anonymous functions, and is especially useful for single-line functions that return a value. See
Table 5-1 for the most important `Array` methods that accept function parameters.

6.2 Using Arrow Functions

Problem

You want to use JavaScript's arrow syntax to declare an inline function in the most
compact way possible.

Solution

In recent years, JavaScript has shifted to emphasize functional programming patterns
—array processing and asynchronous promises are two notable examples. To help,
they've added a new, streamlined function syntax for writing inline functions, called
arrow syntax.

Here's an example of using the `Array.map()` method to transform the contents of an
array using a named function without using arrow syntax. The initial array is a list of
numbers, and the transformed array has the square of each number:

```
const numbers = [1,2,3,4,5,6,7,8,9,10];

function squareNumber(number) {
  return number**2;
}
const squares = numbers.map(squareNumber);

console.log(squares);
// Displays [1, 4, 9, 16, 25, 36, 49, 64, 81, 100]
```

Here's the same example, but with the `squareNumber()` function declared inline using
arrow syntax:

```
const numbers = [1,2,3,4,5,6,7,8,9,10];
const squares = numbers.map( number => number**2 );

console.log(squares);
```

Discussion

This example uses the most compact form of arrow syntax. This works for single-parameter, single-statement functions. Other functions may not be able to use all the simplifications of arrow syntax. To understand why, here's a step-by-step breakdown of how you convert a named function to a function expression that uses arrow syntax:

1. Put the list of parameters first, followed the => symbol. If there are no parameters, use an empty set of parentheses before the => symbol.

   ```
   (number) =>
   ```

2. If there is exactly one parameter (as in this example), you can remove the parentheses around the parameter list.

   ```
   number =>
   ```

3. Put the braces and body of the function on the other side of the arrow.

   ```
   number => {
     return number**2;
   }
   ```

4. If there is just one statement, you can remove the braces and the return keyword. But if you have more than one statement, you must keep both the braces *and* the return keyword.

   ```
   number => number**2;
   ```

Remember, the arrow function is used for declaring inline functions, so you'll always be passing it to a parameter or assigning it to a variable in an expression:

```
const myFunc = number => number**2;

const squaredNumber = myFunc(10);
// squaredNumber = 100
```

Now let's look at converting this slightly more complex function:

```
function raiseToPower(number, power) {
  return number**power;
}
```

You can carry out steps 1, 3, and 4, but step 2 doesn't apply (because this function has two parameters):

```
const myFunc = (number, power) => number**power;
```

Or, consider this more detailed string processing function:

```
function applyTitleCase(inputString) {
  // Split the string into an array of words
  const wordArray = inputString.split(' ');

  // Create a new array that will hold the processed words
  const processedWordArray = [];

  for (const word of wordArray) {
    // Capitalize the first letter of this word
    processedWordArray.push(word[0].toUpperCase() + word.slice(1));
  }

  // Join the words back into a single string
  return processedWordArray.join(' ');
}
```

Here, steps 1, 2, and 3 apply, but step 4 does not. You must keep the braces and `return` statement intact.

```
const myFunc = inputString => {
  // Split the string into an array of words
  const wordArray = inputString.split(' ');

  // Create a new array that will hold the processed words
  const processedWordArray = [];

  for (const word of wordArray) {
    // Capitalize the first letter of this word
    processedWordArray.push(word[0].toUpperCase() + word.slice(1));
  }

  // Join the words back into a single string
  return processedWordArray.join(' ');
}
```

Now the difference between the traditional approach and the arrow syntax is much smaller. Only the function declaration at the beginning has changed, and the overall code savings is minimal.

Here's where the decisions around arrow syntax become murkier. It's often possible to compress a function with several statements into a single expression. In the string processing example, you could use method chaining (as in Recipe 2.8) and the `Array.map()` function (Recipe 5.17) instead of a `for` loop. Applied aggressively, these changes can shorten `applyTitleCase()` down to one long statement. You could then use all the arrow syntax shortcuts. However, in this case the goal of more concise code isn't worth the tradeoff in clarity. As a general rule of thumb, arrow syntax is a benefit only when it helps you write more readable code.

Arrow functions have a different way of binding the `this` keyword. In a declared function, `this` maps to the object that calls the function, which could be the current window, a button, and so on. In an arrow function, `this` simply refers to the code where the arrow function is defined. (In other words, whatever `this` is where you create your arrow function remains `this` when the function runs.) This behavior simplifies many issues, but at a cost. It means that arrow syntax isn't suitable for object methods and constructors, because arrow functions won't be bound to the object on which they're called. Even using `Function.bind()` won't change this behavior.

There are a few smaller restrictions as well. Arrow functions can't be used with `yield` to make a generator function, and don't support the `arguments` object.

See Also

Chapter 5 has numerous examples that use arrow syntax to pass short functions to array-processing methods. See, for instance, Recipes 5.9, 5.14, and 5.16.

6.3 Providing a Default Parameter Value

Problem

You want to specify a default value for a parameter, which will be used if the caller doesn't pass in an argument when calling the function.

Solution

You can directly assign default values to your parameters when you declare a function. Here's an example that sets a default value for the third parameter, `thirdNum`:

```
function addNumbers(firstNum, secondNum, thirdNum=0) {
  return firstNum+secondNum+thirdNum;
}
```

Now it's possible to call this function without specifying all three parameters:

```
console.log(addNumbers(42, 6, 10));  // displays 58
console.log(addNumbers(42, 6));      // displays 48
```

Discussion

Default parameters are a relatively recent invention. However, JavaScript has never forced function callers to supply all the parameters for a function. In this distant past, functions could simply check if a parameter was `undefined` (by testing it with the `typeof` operator, as described in Recipe 7.1).

You can set default values for as many parameters as you want. As a matter of good style, you should put your required parameters first, followed by parameters that have default values. In other words, once you add a default parameter, all the parameters *after* should also become optional and have default values. This convention isn't required, but it makes code clearer.

When calling a function that has multiple default parameters, you can pick and choose which values you supply. Consider this example:

```
function addNumbers(firstNum=10, secondNum=20, thirdNum=30, multiplier=1) {
  return multiplier*(firstNum+secondNum+thirdNum);
}
```

If you want to specify `firstNum`, `secondNum`, and `multiplier`, but omit the `thirdNum` parameter, you need to use `undefined` as a placeholder. This allows you to pass all your parameters in the proper order:

```
const sum = addNumbers(42, 10, undefined, 1);
// sum = 82
```

But `null` won't work as a placeholder. In this example, it's simply converted to the number 0, changing the result:

```
const sum = addNumbers(42, 10, null, 1);
// sum = 52
```

Many other languages have nicer shortcuts for default parameters (such as using commas to indicate order without needing to supply a placeholder value, or setting parameter values by name). JavaScript does not, although you can simulate named parameters using object literal syntax (Recipe 6.5).

6.4 Creating a Function That Accepts Unlimited Arguments

Problem

You want to create a function that accepts as many arguments as the caller wants to supply, without requiring the creation of an array.

Solution

Use a *rest parameter* when you declare your function. The rest parameter is defined with three dots before its name:

```
function sumRounds(...numbers) {
  let sum = 0;
  for(let i = 0; i < numbers.length; i+=1)  {
    sum += Math.round(numbers[i]);
  }
```

```
    return sum;
}

console.log(sumRounds(2.3, 4, 5, 16, 18.1));  // 45
```

Discussion

The rest parameter does not need to be the only parameter, but it must be the last parameter. It collects all the extra arguments that are passed to the function and adds them to a new array.

In the past, JavaScript developers used the `arguments` object for similar functionality. The `arguments` object is available in every function (technically, it's the `Function.arguments` property), and it provides array-like access to all the parameters. However, `arguments` is not a true array, and developers often used boilerplate code to transform it into one. You may still see this approach in the wild, but today rest parameters avoid this hassle.

 The rest parameter looks the same as the spread operator (Recipe 5.4), but the two play complementary roles. The spread operator *expands* an array or the properties of an object into separate values, whereas the rest operator collects separate values and inserts them into a single array object.

See Also

If you have an array of values that you want to pass into a function, but the function expects a rest parameter, you can make the conversion using the spread operator (see Recipe 5.4).

This example uses a loop to process the array of values, but you could achieve the same result more cleanly with the `Array.reduce()` function, as demonstrated in Recipe 5.18.

6.5 Using Named Function Parameters

Problem

You want an easier way to choose the optional parameters you send to a function.

Solution

Bundle all the optional parameters into a single object literal (Recipe 7.2). The caller can then decide what optional parameters to include when they create the object literal. Here's an example of how you call a function that uses this pattern:

```
someFunction(arg1, arg2, {optionalArg1: val1, optionalArg2: val2});
```

In your function, you can use *destructuring assignment* to quickly copy the values out of the object literal and into separate variables. Here's an example of a function that accepts three arguments. The first two (`newerDate` and `olderDate`) are required, but the third parameter is an object literal that can hold three optional values (`discardTime`, `discardYears`, and `precision`):

```
function dateDifferenceInSeconds(
 newerDate, olderDate, {discardTime, discardYears, precision} = {}) {
  if (discardTime) {
    newerDate = newerDate.setHours(0,0,0,0);
    olderDate = newerDate.setHours(0,0,0,0);
  }
  if (discardYears) {
    newerDate.setYear(0);
    olderDate.setYear(0);
  }

  const differenceInSeconds = (newerDate.getTime() - olderDate.getTime())/1000;
  return differenceInSeconds.toFixed(precision);
}
```

You can call `dateDifferenceInSeconds()` with or without the object literal:

```
// Compare the current date to an older date
const newDate = new Date();
const oldDate = new Date(2010, 1, 10);

// Call the function without an object literal
let difference = dateDifferenceInSeconds(newDate, oldDate);
console.log(difference);    // Shows something like 354378086

// Call the function with an object literal, and specify two properties
difference = dateDifferenceInSeconds(
 newDate, oldDate, {discardYears:true, precision:2});
console.log(difference);    // Shows something like 7226485.90
```

Discussion

A common pattern in JavaScript is to use an object literal to transmit optional values. This lets you set only the properties you need, without worrying about the order.

```
// This works
dateDifferenceInSeconds(newDate, oldDate, {precision:2});

// This also works
dateDifferenceInSeconds(newDate, oldDate, {discardYears:true, precision:2});

// This works too
dateDifferenceInSeconds(newDate, oldDate, {precision:2, discardYears:true});
```

In the function, you can retrieve properties from the object literal individually, like this:

```
function dateDifferenceInSeconds(newerDate, olderDate, options) {
  const precision = options.precision;
```

But this solution in this recipe uses a better shortcut. It unpacks the object literal into named variables using destructuring, which maps the properties of an object to individual, named variables. You can use destructuring assignment in a statement:

```
function dateDifferenceInSeconds(newerDate, olderDate, options) {
  const {discardTime, discardYears, precision} = options;
```

or right in the function declaration:

```
function dateDifferenceInSeconds(
  newerDate, olderDate, {discardTime, discardYears, precision})
```

It's a good practice to set an empty object literal as a default value (Recipe 6.3). This empty object is used if the caller doesn't supply the object literal:

```
function dateDifferenceInSeconds(
  newerDate, olderDate, {discardTime, discardYears, precision} = {})
```

It's up to the caller whether they decide to set some, all, or none of the properties in the object literal. Any values that aren't set will evaluate to the special value `unde fined`, which you can test for in your code. Here's a less-optimized example:

```
if (discardTime != undefined || discardTime === true) {
```

Often, you won't need to explicitly check for `undefined` values. For example, `unde fined` evaluates to `false` in conditional logic. The `dateDifferenceInSeconds()` function uses the behavior when it evaluates the `discardYears` and `discardTime` properties, allowing us to shorten the code:

```
if (discardTime) {
```

There's a similar shortcut with the `precision` property. It's safe to call `Number.toPre cision(undefined)`, because that's the same as calling `toPrecision()` with no argument. Either way, the number is rounded to the nearest whole integer.

The only disadvantage to the object literal pattern is that there's no way to prevent property-naming mistakes, like this one:

```
// We want discardYears, but we accidentally set discardYear
dateDifferenceInSeconds(newDate, oldDate, {discardYear:true});
```

See Also

Recipe 7.2 introduces object literals. Recipe 5.4 shows the array destructuring syntax, which is similar to the object destructuring syntax used in this recipe, except it acts on arrays instead of objects (and uses square brackets instead of curly braces).

6.6 Creating a Function That Stores its State with a Closure

Problem

You want to create a function that can remember data, but without having to use global variables and without repeatedly sending the same data with each function call.

Solution

Wrap the function that needs to preserve its state in *another* function. The outer function returns the inner function, following this structure:

```
function outerFunction() {

  function innerFunction() {
    ...
  }

  return innerFunction;
}
```

Both of these functions can accept parameters. But here's the trick. The outer function's parameters live as long as you have a reference to the inner function. You can call the inner function as many times as you want, and the data from the outer function persists. (Conceptually, it's as though the outer function is an object-creation method, and the inner function is an object with state.)

Here's a complete example:

```
function greetingMaker(greeting) {
  function addName(name) {
    return `${greeting} ${name}`;
  }
  return addName;
}

// Use the outer function to create two copies of the inner function,
// each with a different value for greeting
const daytimeGreeting = greetingMaker('Good Day to you');
const nightGreeting = greetingMaker('Good Evening');

console.log(daytimeGreeting('Peter'));    // Shows 'Good Day to you Peter'
console.log(nightGreeting('Sally'));      // Shows 'Good Evening Sally'
```

Discussion

Often, you'll find that you need a way to store data that's used across several function calls. You could use global variables, but that's a technique of last resort. Global variables lead to naming collisions, complicate code, and often lead to hidden inter-dependencies between different functions, limiting the reuse of your code and giving cover for subtle coding bugs to hide.

You could ask the function caller to maintain this information, and send it with each function call, but this can also be awkward. This example shows a different solution—creating a stateful function package called a *closure*.

In this solution, the outer function `greetingMaker()` takes one argument, which is a specific greeting. It also returns an inner function, `addName()`, which itself takes the person's name. The closure encompasses the `addName()` function and its surrounding context, which includes the parameter that was passed to the `greetingMaker()` function. To demonstrate this fact, two copies of `addName()` are created, in two different contexts. One exists in a closure where a daytime message was passed to `greeting Maker()`, and the other exists in a closure where a nighttime message was passed to `greetingMaker()`. Either way, when the `addName()` function is called, it uses the current context to construct its message.

It's worth noting that state isn't limited to parameter values. Any variables that are in the outer function also stay alive as long as the function reference exists. Here's an example that uses a simple counter variable to keep track of how many function calls you've made:

```
function createCounter() {
  // This variable persists as long as the createCounter function reference
  let count = 0;

  function counter() {
    count += 1;
    console.log(count);
  }
  return counter;
}

const counterFunction = createCounter();
counterFunction();  // displays 1
counterFunction();  // displays 2
counterFunction();  // displays 3
```

See Also

To see an another example of a function that uses a closure to store state, see "Extra: Building a Repeatable Pseudorandom Number Generator" on page 133.

It's not an accident that closures and wrapped functions seem to echo object-oriented programming. In the past, JavaScript developers used functions to mimic custom classes (see Recipe 8.4), and JavaScript's `class` keyword extends this approach (see Recipe 8.1).

6.7 Creating a Generator Function That Yields Multiple Values

Problem

You want to create a *generator*, a function that can provide multiple values on-demand. Each time a generator returns a value, it pauses its execution until the caller requests the next value.

Solution

To declare a generator function, start by replacing the function keyword with function*:

```
function* generateValues() {
}
```

Inside the generator function, use the yield keyword each time you want to return a result. Remember, execution stops after you yield (much like when you use the return keyword). However, execution *resumes* when the caller asks for the function's next value. This process continues until your function code ends, or you return a final value with the return keyword.

Here is a naïve implementation of a generator. (It works, but it doesn't solve a useful problem.) This function yields three values, followed by a return value:

```
function* generateValues() {
  yield 895498;
  yield 'This is the second value';
  yield 5;
  return 'This is the end';
}
```

When you call a generator function, you receive a Generator object as a return value. This happens immediately, before the generator function code begins to run. You use the Generator object to run the function and retrieve the values that are yielded. You can also use it to determine when the generator function is finished.

Each time you call Generator.next(), the generator function runs until it reaches the next yield (or the final return). The next() method returns an object with two values. The value property wraps the yielded or returned value from the generator function. The done property is a Boolean that remains false until the generator function has ended.

```
const generator = generateValues();

// Start the generator (it runs from the beginning to the first yield)
console.log(generator.next().value);  // 895498
```

```
// Resume the generator (until the next yield)
console.log(generator.next().value);  // 'This is the second value'

// Get the final two values
console.log(generator.next().value);  // 5
console.log(generator.next().value);  // 'This is the end'
```

Discussion

Generators allow you to create functions that can be paused and resumed. Best of all, JavaScript manages their state automatically, which means you don't need to write any code to preserve values in-between calls to `next()`. (This is different than building a custom iterator, for example.)

Because generators have a lazy-execution model, they're a good choice for time-consuming data creation or retrieval operations. For example, you could use a generator to calculate numbers in a complex sequence, to retrieve chunks of information from a stream of data.

Usually, you won't know how many values a generator will return. You could write a `while` loop that checks the `Generator.done` property and keeps calling `next()` until it's finished. But because the generator object is iterable, a `for...of` loop works even better:

```
// Get all the values from the generator
for (const value of generateValues()) {
  console.log(value);
}

// With spread syntax, you can dump everything into an array in one step
const values = [...generateValues()];
```

Either way, this approach only gets *yielded* results. If your generator has a final return value, it's ignored.

Some generator functions are designed to be *infinite*. As long as you keep calling `next()`, they keep yielding values. If you're calling an infinite generator, you can't dump all its values into an array (your program will hang). Instead, you'll probably use a `while` loop with a condition that turns `false` when you have all the values you need.

See Also

Recipe 9.6 shows how to create generators that run asynchronously.

Extra: Building a Repeatable Pseudorandom Number Generator

Although you've dissected the essential syntax for generator functions, you haven't seen a truly practical example. Here's one that shows how an infinite generator function can provide a useful sequence of values.

As explained in Recipe 3.1, the `Math.random()` method lets you generate pseudorandom numbers, but you can't control the *seed value*. (Instead, `Math.random()` seeds its pseudorandom number generator using a opaque, noncryptographically secure method that may vary from one JavaScript implementation to the next.) This is fine for most applications. But in some scenarios you need a way to generate a *repeatable* sequence of random-seeming numbers. The numbers still need to be statistically random in their distribution; the only difference is that you need to be able to ask your pseudorandom number generator to give you same sequence more than once. Examples where repeatable pseudorandom numbers are important include certain types of simulations or tests that need to be precisely reproducible.

There are several third-party JavaScript libraries that provide seedable (and thus repeatable) pseudorandom number generators. You can find a long list at GitHub (*https://github.com/bryc/code/blob/master/jshash/PRNGs.md*). One of the simplest is Mulberry32. Its JavaScript implementation fits in a single dense block of code:

```
function mulberry32(seed) {
  return function random() {
    let t = seed += 0x6D2B79F5;
    t = Math.imul(t ^ t >>> 15, t | 1);
    t ^= t + Math.imul(t ^ t >>> 7, t | 61);
    return ((t ^ t >>> 14) >>> 0) / 4294967296;
  }
}

// Choose a seed
const seed = 98345;

// Get a version of mulberry32() that uses this seed:
const randomFunction = mulberry32(seed);

// Generate some random numbers
console.log(randomFunction());  // 0.9057375795673579
console.log(randomFunction());  // 0.44091642647981644
console.log(randomFunction());  // 0.7662326360587031
```

The `mulberry32()` function uses the closure technique described in Recipe 6.6. It accepts a seed value that's then locked into the context of the inner `random()` function. That means that whenever you call `random()`, the original seed value will be available in the outer function. This is important, because a different seed means a different sequence of random variables. If you call `mulberry32()` with the same seed value, you're guaranteed to get the same sequence of pseudorandom numbers from random().

 Like most pseudorandom number generators, Mulberry32 returns a fractional value between 0 and 1. To convert this to integer in a given range, use the technique shown in Recipe 3.1.

Closures have been a part of the JavaScript language since time immemorial, but generators are a much newer innovation. You can rewrite this example using a generator function, which more clearly expresses its purpose:

```
function* mulberry32(seed) {
  let t = seed += 0x6D2B79F5;

  // Generate numbers indefinitely
  while(true) {
    t = Math.imul(t ^ t >>> 15, t | 1);
    t ^= t + Math.imul(t ^ t >>> 7, t | 61);
    yield ((t ^ t >>> 14) >>> 0) / 4294967296;
  }
}

// Use the same seed to get the same sequence.
const seed = 98345;

const generator = mulberry32(seed);
console.log(generator.next().value);  // 0.9057375795673579
console.log(generator.next().value);  // 0.7620641703251749
console.log(generator.next().value);  // 0.0211441791616380
```

Because the mulberry32() function is declared with function*, it's immediately obvious that it will return multiple values. Inside, an infinite loop ensures that the generator will always be ready to create a new number. After each pass through the loop, random() yields a new random value and then pauses until a new value is requested with next(). The overall operation of this solution is similar to its original version, but now it follows a familiar pattern that could make its usage easier to discover. (But—as always—the value of a refactoring like this depends on the conventions of your organization, the expectations of the people reading your code, and your own personal taste.)

There's no danger to building an infinite loop in a generator as long as it yields. Yielding pauses the code, ensuring that it won't tie up the JavaScript event loop. Unlike normal functions, there is no expectation that a generator function will run to its final closing brace. As soon as a `Generator` object goes out of scope, that function and its context are made available for garbage collection.

6.8 Reducing Redundancy by Using Partial Application

Problem

You have a function that takes several arguments. You want to wrap this function with one or more specialized versions that require fewer arguments.

Solution

The following `makestring()` function accepts three parameters (in other words, it has an *arity* of 3):

```
function makeString(prefix, str, suffix) {
    return prefix + str + suffix;
}
```

However, the first and last arguments are often repeated based on a specific use case. You want to eliminate the repetition of arguments whenever possible.

You can solve this problem by creating new functions that wrap the previously created `makeString()` function, but with known argument values locked down:

```
function quoteString(str) {
    return makeString('"',str,'"');
}

function barString(str) {
    return makeString('-', str, '-');
}

function namedEntity(str) {
    return makeString('&#', str, ';');
}
```

Now only one argument is needed to call any of these new functions:

```
console.log(quoteString('apple')); // "apple"
console.log(barString('apple'));   // -apple-
console.log(namedEntity(169));     // "&#169; (the copyright symbol in HTML)
```

Discussion

The technique of wrapping one function in another function to lock down one or more argument values is called *partial application* (because the new functions *partially apply* the argument values to the original function). Of course, the tradeoff is that the extra functions you create can also clutter up your code, so don't build wrappers you don't intend to use and reuse.

Advanced: A Partial Function Factory

You can reduce the redundancy of this approach even further by creating a function that can partial-ize *any* other function. In fact, this approach is a fairly common JavaScript design pattern. In the past, you needed to rely on the JavaScript `arguments` object and array manipulation. In modern JavaScript, the rest and spread operators make the job much simpler.

In the implementation shown here, the partial-izing function is named `partial()`. It's capable of reducing any number of arguments for any function.

```
function partial(fn, ...argsToApply) {
  return function(...restArgsToApply) {
    return fn(...argsToApply, ...restArgsToApply);
  }
}
```

This function requires a bit of unpacking. But first, it helps to see a simple example that uses it. Here, the `partial()` function is used to create a new `cubeIt()` function that wraps the more general `raiseToPower()` function. In other words, `cubeIt()` uses partial application to lock down one of the `raiseToPower()` arguments (the exponent, which it sets to 3).

```
// The function you want to partialize
function raiseToPower(exponent, number) {
  return number**exponent;
}

// Using partial(), make a customized function
const cubeIt = partial(raiseToPower, 3);

// Calculate the cube of 9 (9**3)
console.log(cubeIt(9));  // 729
```

Now when you call `cubeIt(9)`, the call is mapped to `raiseToPower(3, 9)`.

So how does it work? The `partial()` function accepts two arguments. First is the function you want to partial-ize (`fn`). Second is a list of all the arguments you want to lock in place (`argsToApply`), which is captured in an array using the rest operator (`...`), as explained in Recipe 6.4.

```
function partial(fn, ...argsToApply) {
```

Now things get interesting. The `partial` function returns a nested inner function (a technique explored in Recipe 6.6). The nested inner function accepts all the arguments that *aren't* locked in place. Once again, these arguments are captured in an array using the rest operator (`...restToApply`):

```
// This returns a new anonymous function
return function(...restArgsToApply) {
```

This newly created function now has three key pieces of information: the underlying function (`fn`), the arguments that are locked in place (`argsToApply`), and the arguments that are set each time the function is called (`restArgsToApply`).

There's only one line of code inside this function, but it packs in a lot. It expands the two arrays into argument lists using the spread operator (which, somewhat confusingly, looks exactly like the rest operator). In other words, `argsToApply` becomes a list or arguments followed by `restToApply`:

```
// This calls the wrapped function
return fn(...argsToApply, ...restArgsToApply);
```

 A common practice in functional programming is writing *higher-order functions* (functions that operate on other functions). The `par tial()` function is a higher-level function that creates a wrapper for another function.

There is one limitation to this implementation of the `partial()` function. Because it puts fixed arguments first, you can't lock down a later argument without locking down all the arguments that occur first. If you wanted to use `partial()` to make a wrapper for the `makeString()` function from the original solution, you need to rearrange its arguments first:

```
function makeString(prefix, suffix, str) {
  return prefix + str + suffix;
}

const namedEntity = partial(makeString, "&#", ";");

console.log(namedEntity(169));
```

Extra: Using bind() to Partially Provide Arguments

You can also create partial applications with the `Function.bind()` method. The `bind()` method returns a new function, setting `this` to whatever is provided as a first argument. All the other arguments are prepended to the argument list for the new function.

Rather than having to use `partial()` to create the named entity function, we can now use `bind()` to provide the same functionality, passing in `undefined` as the first argument:

```
function makeString(prefix, suffix, str) {
  return prefix + str + suffix;
}

const named = makeString.bind(undefined, "&#", ";");

console.log(named(169)); // "&#169;"
```

Now you have two good ways to create multiple versions of a function that use different parameters.

6.9 Fixing this with Function Binding

Problem

Your function is attempting to use the keyword `this`, but it's not bound to the right object.

Solution

Use the `Function.bind()` method to change the context of your function and the meaning of the `this` reference:

```
window.onload = function() {
  window.name = 'window';

  const newObject = {
    name: 'object',

    sayGreeting: function() {
      console.log(`Now this is easy, ${this.name}`);

      const nestedGreeting = function(greeting) {
        console.log(`${greeting} ${this.name}`);
      }.bind(this);

      nestedGreeting('hello');
    }
  };

  newObject.sayGreeting();
};
```

Discussion

The keyword this refers to the owner or parent of a function. The challenge associated with this in JavaScript is that we can't always guarantee what parent object will apply to a function.

In the solution, the object has a method, sayGreeting(), which outputs a message and maps another nested function to its property, nestedGreeting. You'll see this approach if you use the constructor pattern (Recipe 8.4) to create class-like function objects.

Without the Function.bind() method, the first message would say "Now this is easy, object," but the second would say "hello window." The reason the second message has a different name is because the nesting of the function disassociates the inner function from the surrounding object, and all *unscoped* functions automatically become the property of the window object.

The bind() method solves this problem by binding the function to the object you choose. In the example, the bind() method is invoked on the nested function and given a reference to the parent object. Now, when the code inside nestedGreeting() uses this, it points to the parent object you set.

The bind() method is particularly useful for the setTimeout() and setInterval() timer functions. Ordinarily, when these functions trigger your callback, the this reference is lost (it becomes undefined). But with bind(), you can ensure that the callback function keeps the reference you want.

Example 6-1 is a web page that uses setTimeout() to perform a countdown operation from 10 to 0. As the numbers are counted down, they're inserted into the web page. This example also uses the constructor pattern for object creation (as described in Recipe 8.4) to create a class-like Counter function.

Example 6-1. Demonstrating the utility of bind()

```
<!DOCTYPE html>
<html lang="en">
  <head>
    <meta charset="UTF-8" />
    <meta name="viewport" content="width=device-width, initial-scale=1.0" />
    <meta http-equiv="X-UA-Compatible" content="ie=edge" />
    <title>Using Bind with Timers</title>
  </head>
  <body>
    <div id="counterDiv"></div>

    <script>
    // This is the constructor function for the Counter object.
```

```
function Counter(from, to, divElement) {
  this.currentCount = from;
  this.finishCount = to;
  this.element = divElement;

  // The incrementCounter() method updates the page
  this.incrementCounter = function() {
    this.currentCount -= 1;
    this.element.textContent = this.currentCount;

    if (this.currentCount > this.finishCount) {
      // Schedule this function to run again after 1 second.
      setTimeout(this.incrementCounter.bind(this), 1000);
    }
  };

  this.startCounter = function() {
    this.incrementCounter();
  }
}

// Create the counter for this page.
const counter = new Counter(10, 0, document.getElementById('counterDiv'));

// When the page loads, start the counter.
window.onload = function() {
  counter.startCounter();
}
</script>
</body>
</html>
```

If the setTimeout() function in the code sample had been the following:

```
setTimeout(this.incrementCounter, 1000);
```

it would lose this, and the callback function wouldn't be able to access variables like currentCount, even though the incrementCounter() method is part of the same object.

Extra: self = this

An older alternative to using bind(), and one that is still in use, is to assign this to a variable in the outer function, which is then accessible to the inner. Typically this is assigned to a variable named that or self:

```
window.onload = function() {
  window.name = 'window';

  const newObject = {
    name: 'object',
```

```
  sayGreeting: function() {
    const self = this;
    alert('Now this is easy, ' + this.name);
    nestedGreeting = function(greeting) {
      alert(greeting + ' ' + self.name);
    };

    nestedGreeting('hello');
  }
};

newObject.sayGreeting('hello');
};
```

Without the assignment, the second message would once again reference "window," not "object."

6.10 Implementing a Recursive Algorithm

Problem

You want to implement a function that *calls itself* to accomplish a task, which is a technique called recursion. Recursion is useful when dealing with hierarchical data structures (for example, node trees or nested arrays), certain types of algorithms (sorting), and some mathematical calculations (the Fibonacci sequence).

Solution

Recursion is a well-known concept in the field of mathematics, as well as computer science. An example of recursion in mathematics is the *Fibonacci sequence*. A Fibonacci number is the sum of the two previous Fibonacci numbers:

```
f(n)= f(n-1) + f(n-2),
  for n= 2,3,4,...,n and
  f(0) = 0 and f(1) = 1
```

Another example of mathematical recursion is a *factorial*, usually denoted with an exclamation point (4!). A factorial is the product of all integers from 1 to a given number n. If n is 4, then the factorial (4!) would be:

```
4! = 4 x 3 x 2 x 1 = 24
```

These recursions can be coded in JavaScript using a series of loops and conditions, but they can also be coded using functional recursion. Here's a recursive function that finds the nth number in the Fibonacci sequence:

```
function fibonacci(n) {
  return n < 2 ? n : fibonacci(n - 1) + fibonacci(n - 2);
}
```

And here's one that solves a factorial:

```
function factorial(n) {
  return n <= 1 ? 1 : n * factorial(n - 1);
}
```

Discussion

A characteristic that distinguishes recursive functions is a *termination condition* (also known as a *base case*). A recursive function cannot keep calling itself indiscriminately, because that would lead to an infinite loop (until stack space is exhausted and the program fails). Instead, a recursive function examines a condition and then decides to call itself (stepping one level deeper into recursion) or return a value (stepping one level back, to the calling function). When the top-level function returns a value, that becomes the final result and the recursive operation is complete.

In the Fibonacci example, n is tested to see if it's less than 2. If it is, it's returned; otherwise the Fibonacci function is called again with (n-1) and with (n-2), and the sum of both is returned.

In the factorial example, when the function is first called, the value passed as the argument is compared to the number 1. If n is less than or equal to 1 (negative numbers aren't supported in this simple implementation), the function terminates, returning 1. However, if n is greater than 1, what's returned is the value of n times a call to the factorial() function again, this time passing in a value of n-1. The value of n then decreases with each iteration of the function, until the termination condition is reached.

As a factorial is being computed, the interim values of each function call are pushed onto a stack in memory and kept until the termination condition is met. Then the values are popped from memory and returned, in a state similar to the following:

```
return 1;              // 0!
return 1;              // 1!
return 1 * 2;          // 2!
return 1 * 2 * 3;      // 3!
return 1 * 2 * 3 * 4;  // 4!
```

Most recursive functions can be replaced with code that performs the same function linearly, via some kind of loop. And loops may perform better, although the difference is often negligible. The advantage of recursion is that recursive functions can be very terse and minimal. Whether they are clearer is a matter of debate. (They are clearly *shorter*, which makes them easier to digest, but their self-referential nature can make their logic harder to grasp at first glance, particularly for programmers who haven't used recursive functions before.)

If a recursive function calls itself over and over again, it will eventually exhaust the call stack. This condition leads to an error with a message like "Out of stack space," "Too much recursion," or "Maximum call stack size exceeded." The exact message and the number of open function calls that are allowed at once depend on the implementation of the JavaScript engine. However, these error messages usually indicate an incorrectly structured recursive function that is failing to evaluate its termination condition and calling itself in an infinite loop.

## CHAPTER 7

Objects

There are two broad categories of types in JavaScript. On one side is a small set of *primitive* types, like strings and numbers. On the other side are genuine objects, all of which derive from JavaScript's `Object`.

JavaScript's built-in objects are easy to recognize. They have constructors, and you'll usually instantiate them with the `new` keyword. Basic ingredients like arrays, `Date`, error objects, `Map` and `Set` collections, and `RegExp` regular expressions are all objects.

JavaScript objects also differ in important ways from the objects you find in traditional object-oriented programming languages. For example, JavaScript allows you to create instances of the base `Object` type, and attach new properties and functions at runtime. In fact, you can take a live object—any object—and modify its members, with no need to respect a class definition.

In this chapter you'll take a closer look at the functionality and quirks of JavaScript's `Object` type. You'll see how to use the core `Object` features to inspect, extend, and copy objects of all types. And in the next chapter, you'll go one step further and learn the best practices for formalizing your own custom objects.

7.1 Checking if an Object Is a Certain Type

Problem

You have a mystery object and you want to determine its type.

Solution

Use the `instanceof` operator:

```
const mysteryObject = new Date(2021, 2, 1);

if (mysteryObject instanceof Date) {
  // We end up here because mysteryObject is a Date
}
```

You can test if an object is *not* an instance of some type using the not operator (!). But make sure you use parentheses to apply the ! to the entire `instanceof` condition:

```
if (!(mysteryObject instanceof Date)) {
  // You get here if mysteryObject isn't a Date
}

// Don't make this mistake!
if (!mysteryObject instanceof Date) {
  // This code never runs
}
```

There's one gap in the `instanceof` operator. It doesn't work with primitive values, like numbers, strings, Booleans, `BigInt` values, `null`, and `undefined`. Here's a demonstration of the problem:

```
const testNumber = 42;
if (testNumber instanceof Number) {
  // This code never runs
}

const testString = 'Hello';
if (testString instanceof String) {
  // This code never runs
}

// The following two tests work because the primitives are wrapped in objects,
// but that's uncommon in modern JavaScript.
const numberObject = new Number(42);
if (numberObject instanceof Number) {
  // This code runs
}

const stringObject = new String('Hello');
if (stringObject instanceof String) {
  // This code runs
}
```

The solution is to use the `typeof` operator if you're testing a variable that might hold one of the primitive data types. Unlike `instanceof`, `typeof` provides you with one of nine predefined string values (as described in Recipe 2.1). If you get a value of `object`, you can use the `instanceof` operator to dig deeper:

```
const mysteryPrimitive = 42;
const mysteryObject = new Date();
```

```
if (typeof mysteryPrimitive === 'number') {
  // This code runs
}

if (typeof mysteryObject === 'object') {
  // This code runs, because a Date is an object, not a primitive

  if (mysteryObject instanceof Date) {
    // This code also runs
  }
}
```

Discussion

The `instanceof` operator works by inspecting an object's *prototype chain*, a concept explained in "Extra: Prototype Chains" on page 195. Depending on how an object is constructed, there can be several types in the prototype chain (similar to the way an object in a traditional OOP language might inherit from a sequence of classes). For example, every object has the `Object` prototype at the base of its chain, so this is always true:

```
if (mysteryObject instanceof Object) {
  // This is true, unless mysteryObject is a primitive type
}
```

Remember, primitives don't just include numbers, strings, and Booleans. They encompass the specialized `BigInt` and `Symbol`, and the special values `null` and `undefined`. All of these values will return `false` if you use the `instanceof Object` test.

7.2 Using an Object Literal to Bundle Data

Problem

You want to group several variables together to create a basic data package.

Solution

Use the *object literal* syntax to create a new instance of the `Object` type. You don't use the new keyword or even name the `Object` type. Instead, you simply write a set of `{}` braces that encloses a comma-separated list of properties. Each property consists of a property name, followed by a colon, followed by the property value:

```
const employee = {
  employeeId: 402,
  firstName: 'Lisa',
  lastName: 'Stanecki',
  birthDate: new Date(1995, 8, 15)
```

```
};

console.log(employee.firstName);   // 'Lisa'
```

Of course, you can add additional properties after creating the object, as with any JavaScript object:

```
employee.role = 'Manager';
```

This technique works even if you've declared your object with const, because object literals are *reference types*, not values (unlike structs in other languages). Adding a property changes the object, but it doesn't change the reference. (On the other hand, assigning the employee variable to a new object wouldn't be allowed in this example, because that operation would change the reference.)

Discussion

Object literal syntax gives you the cleanest, most compact way to quickly create a simple object. However, it's just a shortcut for explicitly creating a new Object instance and assigning properties, like this:

```
const employee = new Object();
employee.employeeId = 402;
employee.firstName = 'Lisa';
employee.lastName = 'Stanecki';
employee.birthDate = new Date(1995, 8, 15);
```

or you can use key-value syntax:

```
const employee = new Object();
employee['employeeId'] = 402;
employee['firstName'] = 'Lisa';
employee['lastName'] = 'Stanecki';
employee['birthDate'] = new Date(1995, 8, 15);
```

One of the nicer features of object literal syntax is the way it handles nested objects, like birthPlace in this example:

```
const employee = {
  employeeId: 402,
  firstName: 'Lisa',
  lastName: 'Stanecki',
  birthPlace: {country: 'Canada', city: 'Toronto'}
};

console.log(employee.birthPlace.city);   // 'Toronto'
```

In JavaScript's eyes, an object literal is an instance of the base Object type. This simplicity makes it easy to create an object out of any ad hoc grouping of data, but it also has a cost—your object has no meaningful *identity*.

Yes, you can test if an object has a certain property (Recipe 7.3) or enumerate all its properties (Recipe 7.4). But you can't use `instanceof` to test against a custom object type. In other words, there's no contract to program against, and no easy way to validate that your objects are what you expect. If you need to use more durable objects that are passed around your code, model complex entities, and include their own methods, you should consider using formal classes (Recipe 8.1).

 It might occur to you that you could streamline the object creation process by creating a factory function that accepts parameters and builds the corresponding object. While there's nothing inherently wrong with this approach, there's a more powerful and conventional alternative. As soon as you want to build multiple objects with the same structure, consider using classes (Recipe 8.1).

See Also

To find all the properties on an object literal, see Recipe 7.4. To step up to a formal class definition, see Recipe 8.1.

Extra: Computed Property Names

As you know, you can add a new property to any JavaScript object in two ways. You can use dot-syntax with property names:

```
employee.employeeId = 402;
```

Or key-value syntax:

```
employee['employeeId'] = 402;
```

These two approaches aren't equivalent. When you use key-value syntax, the property name is stored as a string, which means you have the opportunity to generate the property name at runtime. This is called a *computed property name*, and it's important in certain extensibility scenarios. (For example, imagine if you're fetching some external data and using that to create a matching object.)

```
const dynamicProperty = 'nickname';
const dynamicPropertyValue = 'The Izz';

employee[dynamicProperty] = dynamicPropertyValue;
// Now employee.nickname = 'The Izz'

const i = 10;
employee['sequence' + i] = 1;
// Now employee.sequence10 = 1
```

Computed property names are always converted to strings. They support characters that wouldn't be allowed in ordinary variable names, like spaces. For example, this is possible (although it's a very bad idea):

```
const employee = {};
const today = new Date();

employee[today] = 42;

// This reveals that 42 is stored in a property that has a long string name like
// "Tue May 04 2021 08:18:16 GMT-0400 (Eastern Daylight Time)"
console.log(employee);
```

Object literal syntax also allows you to created computed properties. But because it doesn't use a format with string key names, you need to enclose each computed property name in square brackets. Here's what that looks like:

```
const dynamicProperty = 'nickname';
const dynamicPropertyValue = 'The Izz';
const i = 10;

const employee = {
  employeeId: 402,
  firstName: 'Lisa',
  lastName: 'Stanecki',
  [dynamicProperty]: dynamicPropertyValue,
  ['sequence' + i]: 1
};
```

 If you're creating property names dynamically, you may run into a situation where you need to ensure your property name is unique. Various homemade workarounds are possible: checking for the property and adding a sequence number until you get something unique, or just using a GUID (globally unique identifer). But JavaScript provides a built-in solution with the Symbol type, which is your best bet (see Recipe 7.12).

7.3 Checking If an Object Has a Property

Problem

You want to check at runtime if an object has a given property.

Solution

Use the in operator to look for a property by name:

```
const address = {
  country: 'Australia',
```

```
    city: 'Sydney',
    streetNum: '412',
    streetName: 'Worcestire Blvd'
};

if ('country' in address) {
  // This code runs, because there is an address.country property
}

if ('zipCode' in address) {
  // This code does not run, because there is no address.zipCode property
}
```

Discussion

If you attempt to read a property that doesn't exist, you get the value undefined. You could test for undefined, but that alone is not an ironclad guarantee that the property doesn't exist. (It's technically possible to have a property and set it to undefined, in which case the property still exists but your test would miss it.) A better approach to finding properties is using the in operator.

The in operator searches an object *and* its prototype chain. That means if you create an object Dog that derives from another object Animal, an in test will return true if a property is defined in Dog or Animal. Alternatively, you can use the hasOwnProp erty() method, which only searches the current object, and ignores inherited properties.

```
const address = {
  country: 'Australia',
  city: 'Sydney',
  streetNum: '412',
  streetName: 'Worcestire Blvd'
};

console.log(address.hasOwnProperty('country'));  // true
console.log(address.hasOwnProperty('zipCode'));  // false
```

For more information about using inheritance, see Recipe 8.8.

See Also

Recipe 7.4 shows how to retrieve all the properties of an object into an array. Recipe 7.5 shows how to test if your object is empty of all data.

7.4 Iterating Over All the Properties of an Object

Problem

You want to examine all the properties in an object.

Solution

Use the static `Object.keys()` method to get an array with the property names for your object. For example, this code:

```
const address = {
  country: 'Australia', city: 'Sydney', streetNum: '412',
  streetName: 'Worcestire Blvd'
};

const properties = Object.keys(address);

// Show every property and its value
for (const property of properties) {
  console.log(`Property: ${property}, Value: ${address[property]}`);
}
```

creates this console output:

```
Property: country, Value: Australia
Property: city, Value: Sydney
Property: streetNum, Value: 412
Property: streetName, Value: Worcestire Blvd
```

This technique—examining an object, finding all its properties, and displaying them —is similar to what the `console.log()` method does when you pass it an object.

Discussion

When using `Object.keys()`, you retrieve all the property names (also known as *keys*). But you still need to look up the corresponding value in the object. You can't use the dot syntax to do that (`object.propertyName`) because you have the property as a string. Instead, you use the array-like indexer syntax (`object['propertyName']`). Properties will typically appear in the order they were defined, but JavaScript doesn't guarantee the order.

The `Object.keys()` method is also commonly used to count the number of properties (or *length*) of an object:

```
const address = {
  country: 'Australia', city: 'Sydney', streetNum: '412',
  streetName: 'Worcestire Blvd'
};

properties = Object.keys(address);
console.log(`The address object has a length of ${properties.length}`);
// (In this example, the length is 4.)
```

The `Object.keys()` method is just one of many possible solutions for reflecting on JavaScript objects. However, it's a good default starting point because it ignores inherited properties and nonenumerable properties, which is the behavior you want in most scenarios.

Another option is to use a `for...in` loop, like this:

```
for (const property in address) {
  console.log(`Property: ${property}, Value: ${address[property]}`);
}
```

The `for...in` loop travels up the prototype chain to find properties that your object has inherited. In this example, with the object literal named `address`, there's no difference. However, if you need to reflect on objects often, inadvertently using `for...in` loops when `Object.keys()` would suffice could adversely affect `performance`.

 Contrary to what you might expect, the `for...in` loop has slightly different coverage than the `in` operator. The `in` operator examines *all* properties, including nonenumerable properties, symbol properties, and inherited properties. The `for...in` loop finds inherited properties but ignores nonenumerable properties and symbol properties.

JavaScript also has other, more specialized functions that find different subsets of properties. For example, the `getOwnPropertyNames()` function ignores inherited properties, and the `getOwnPropertyDescriptors()` function ignores inherited properties but also finds nonenumerable properties and symbol properties, which are often used for extensibility (see Recipe 7.12). Table 7-1 outlines these different approaches. For even more detailed information, the Mozilla Developer Network has a full accounting of the different property searching functions (*https://oreil.ly/rbd7z*).

Table 7-1. Different ways to find object properties

Method	Returns	Gets enumerable properties	Gets non-enumerable properties	Gets symbol properties	Includes inherited properties
`Object.keys()`	An array of property names	Yes	No	No	No
`Object.values()`	An array of property values	Yes	No	No	No
`Object.entries()`	An array of property arrays, each of which holds a property name and the corresponding value	Yes	No	No	No
`Object.getOwnProperty Names()`	An array of property names	Yes	Yes	No	No
`Object.getOwnProperty Symbols()`	An array of property names	No	No	Yes	No
`Object.getOwnProperty Descriptors()`	An array of property descriptor objects, like when you use `defin eProperty()` (Recipe 7.7)	Yes	Yes	Yes	No
`Reflect.ownKeys()`	An array of property names	Yes	Yes	Yes	No
`for...in` loop	Each property name	Yes	No	No	Yes

See Also

Recipe 7.3 explains how to use the `in` operator to check for a single property.

7.5 Testing for an Empty Object

Problem

You want to determine if an object is empty (has no properties).

Solution

Get an array of properties using `Object.keys()`, and check for a `length` of 0:

```
const blankObject = {};

if (Object.keys(blankObject).length === 0) {
  // This code runs because there's nothing in this object
}
```

```
const objectWithProperty = {price: 47.99};
if (Object.keys(objectWithProperty).length === 0) {
  // This code won't run, because objectWithProperty isn't empty
}
```

Discussion

It's possible to create an empty object with object literal syntax:

```
const blankObject = {};
```

or by creating an instance of `Object` with `new`:

```
const blankObject = new Object();
```

Empty objects can also come about from other, less common, methods, such as taking an existing object and removing properties with the `delete` operator:

```
const objectWithProperty = {price: 47.99};
delete objectWithProperty.price;

if (Object.keys(objectWithProperty).length === 0) {
  // This code runs, because objectWithProperty had its only property removed
}
```

Because objects are reference types, you can't just compare one empty object to another. For example, this test won't recognize that your unknown object is empty:

```
const blankObject = {};
const unknownObject = {};

if (unknownObject === blankObject) {
  // We never get here
  // Even though unknownObject is empty, like blankObject, it holds a
  // different reference to a different memory location
}
```

Many JavaScript libraries, like Underscore and Lodash, provide an `isEmpty()` method for checking objects. However, the `Object.keys()` test is just as easy.

7.6 Merging the Properties of Two Objects

Problem

You've created two simple objects with properties, and you want to combine their data into a single object.

Solution

Use the spread operator (`...`) to expand both objects, and assign them to a new object:

```
const address = {
  country: 'Australia', city: 'Sydney', streetNum: '412',
  streetName: 'Worcestire Blvd'
};

const customer = {
  firstName: 'Lisa', lastName: 'Stanecki'
};

const customerWithAddress = {...customer, ...address};
console.log(customerWithAddress);
// The customerWithAddress now has all six properties
```

Discussion

Merging two objects is an easy operation, but not without potential problems. If both objects have properties with the same name, the properties from the second object (that's address in the previous example) will quietly overwrite the properties from the first object. Here's a modified version of the example that demonstrates the problem:

```
const address = {
  country: 'Australia', city: 'Sydney', streetNum: '412',
  streetName: 'Worcestire Blvd'
};

const customer = {
  firstName: 'Lisa', lastName: 'Stanecki', country: 'South Korea'
};

const customerWithAddress = {...customer, ...address};
console.log(customerWithAddress.country);  // Shows 'Australia'
```

In this example, there are two instances of the country property. When the two objects are merged, the customer object is expanded first, followed by the address object. As a result, the address.country property overwrites the customer.country property.

7.7 Customizing the Way a Property Is Defined

Problem

You can easily slap a new property onto an object. But sometimes you need to explicitly customize your property so you have more control of how it's used.

Solution

Instead of creating a property by assigning to it, use the `Object.defineProperty()` method to define it. For example, consider the following object:

```
const data = {};
```

Let's say you want to add the following two properties, with the given characteristics:

type

Initial value set and can't be changed, can't be deleted or modified, but can be enumerated

id

Initial value set, but can be changed, can't be deleted or modified, and can't be enumerated

Use the following JavaScript:

```
const data = {};

Object.defineProperty(data, 'type', {
  value: 'primary',
  enumerable: true
});

// Attempt to change the read-only property
console.log(data.type); // primary
data.type = 'secondary';
console.log(data.type); // nope, still primary

Object.defineProperty(data, 'id', {
  value: 1,
  writable: true
});

// Change this modifiable property
console.log(data.id); // 1
data.id = 300;
console.log(data.id); // 300

// See what properties appear during enumeration
for (prop in data) {
  console.log(prop); // only type displays
}
```

In this example, attempting to change the read-only property fails silently. More commonly, you'll be in strict mode, either because your code is in a module (see Recipe 8.9) or because you've added the `'use strict';` directive to the top of your JavaScript file. In strict mode, trying to set a read-only property interrupts your code with a `TypeError`.

Discussion

The `defineProperty()` is a way of adding a property to an object other than direct assignment that gives you some control over its behavior and state. Even if all you do with `defineProperty()` is set the property name and value, it's not the same as simply setting the property. That's because the properties created with `defineProperty()` are read-only and nonenumerable by default.

The `defineProperty()` method takes three arguments: the object you're setting the property on, the name of the property, and a descriptor object that configures the property. Here's where things get a bit more interesting. There are actually two types of descriptors you can use. The example in the solution uses a *data descriptor*, which has four details you can set:

`configurable`
  Controls whether the property descriptor can be changed. It's `false` by default.

`enumerable`
  Controls whether the property can be enumerated. It's `false` by default.

`value`
  Sets the initial value for the property.

`writable`
  Controls whether the property value can be changed. It's `false` by default.

Instead of using a data descriptor, you can use an *accessor descriptor*, which supports a slightly different set of options:

`configurable`
  Same as for a data descriptor

`enumerable`
  Same as for a data descriptor

`get`
  Sets a function to use as a property getter, which returns the property value

`set`
  Sets a function to use as a property setter, which applies the property value

Here's an example that uses `defineProperty()` with an accessor descriptor:

```
const person = {
  firstName: 'Joe',
  lastName: 'Khan',
  dateOfBirth: new Date(1996, 6, 12)
};
```

```
Object.defineProperty(person, 'age', {
  configurable: true,
  enumerable: true,
  get: function() {
    // Calculate the difference in years
    const today = new Date();
    let age = today.getFullYear() - this.dateOfBirth.getFullYear();

    // Adjust if the bithday hasn't happened yet this year
    const monthDiff = today.getMonth() - this.dateOfBirth.getMonth();
    if (monthDiff < 0 ||
        (monthDiff === 0 && today.getDate() < this.dateOfBirth.getDate())) {
      age -= 1;
    }

    return age;
  }
});

console.log(person.age);
```

Here `defineProperty()` creates a computed property (`age`) that performs a calculation using a different property (`birthdate`). (You'll note that you can refer to other instance properties in a setter or getter using `this`.) At this point, the design of the object is becoming a bit too ambitious for ad hoc creation with object literal syntax. You'll do better using a formal class, which has a more natural way of exposing the same property getter and setter feature (Recipe 8.2).

You can use `defineProperty()` to *change* an existing property rather than add a new one. In fact, the syntax is exactly the same—the only difference is that the property name you specify already exists in the object. However, there's one restriction. If the property is set to be nonconfigurable, you'll get a `TypeError` when you call `define Property()` on it.

See Also

Recipe 8.2 explains how properties are set on classes, which partially overlaps with the `defineProperty()` approach. Recipe 7.8 covers freezing an object to prevent property changes.

7.8 Preventing Any Changes to an Object

Problem

You've defined your object, and now you want to make sure that its properties aren't redefined or edited by other code.

Solution

Use `Object.freeze()` to freeze the object against any and all changes:

```
const customer = {
  firstName: 'Josephine',
  lastName: 'Stanecki'
};

// freeze the object
Object.freeze(customer);

// This statement throws an error in strict mode
customer.firstName = 'Joe';

// So does an attempt to add a property
customer.middleInitial = 'P';

// Or remove one
delete customer.lastName;
```

When you attempt to change a frozen object, one of two things will happen. If strict mode is on, a `TypeError` exception is thrown. If strict mode is off, the operation fails silently—the object is not changed but your code continues to execute. Strict mode is always on in modules (see Recipe 8.9) or if you add the `'use strict';` directive to the top of your JavaScript file.

Discussion

As you know, objects are reference types and JavaScript allows you to change them in any way. You can change property values and add or remove properties, even if you've declared your object variable with `const`.

However, JavaScript also includes some static methods in the `Object` class that you can use to lock down your object. You have three choices, listed here from least to most restrictive:

`Object.preventExtensions()`
> Prevents you from adding new properties. However, you can still set property values. You can also delete properties and configure properties with `Object.getOwnPropertyDescriptor()`.

`Object.seal()`
> Prevents properties from being added, removed, or configured. However, you can still set property values. This is sometimes used to catch assignments to non-existent properties, which is a silent mistake.

```
Object.freeze()
```
Disallows property modifications of any kind. You can't configure properties, add new properties, or set property values. The object becomes immutable.

If you're using strict mode (as you always will be, except when writing test code in the console), attempting to change a frozen object throws a `TypeError` exception. If you're not using strict mode, attempts to change a property will fail silently, leaving the original property values but allowing the code to continue.

You can check if an object is frozen using `Object.isFrozen()`, the companion method:

```
if (Object.isFrozen(obj)) ...
```

7.9 Intercepting and Changing Actions on an Object with a Proxy

Problem

You want to run code when certain actions take place with an object, but you don't want to put your code *inside* the object.

Solution

The `Proxy` class allows you to intercept a variety of different actions on any object. The following example uses a proxy to perform validation on an object named `prod uct`. The proxy ensures that code can use a property that doesn't exist, or use a non-numeric data type to set a number:

```
// This is the object that we'll watch with the proxy
const product = {name: 'banana'};

// This is the handler that the proxy uses to intercept traps
const propertyChecker = {
  set: function(target, property, value) {
    if (property === 'price') {
      if (typeof value !== 'number') {
        throw new TypeError('price is not a number');
      }
      else if (value <= 0) {
        throw new RangeError('price must be greater than zero');
      }
    }
    else if (property !== 'name') {
      throw new ReferenceError(`property '${property}' not valid`);
    }
    target[property] = value;
  }
```

```
};

// Create the proxy
const proxy = new Proxy(product, propertyChecker);

// Now, modify the product object through the proxy object
proxy.name = 'apple';

// This throws a ReferenceError
proxy.type = 'red delicious';

// This throws a TypeError
proxy.price = 'three dollars';

// This throws a RangeError
proxy.price = -1.00;

// This bypasses the proxy and succeeds
product.price = -1.00;
```

 Once you've created a useful proxy that works on one property, you can reuse it to intercept actions on other properties or other objects.

Discussion

The Proxy object wraps an object and can be used to *trap* specific actions, and then provide additional or alternative behaviors based the action and the object's data at the time of the action.

When you create a Proxy, you supply two parameters: the object you want to watch, and the handler that can intercept the operations you choose. In the solution shown here, the handler only intercepts property set operations. Each time it intercepts a property set action, it receives the target object, the property that's being set, and the new property value. The function then tests to see if the property being set is price. If so, it then checks to see if it's a number. If it isn't, a TypeError is thrown. If it is, then the value is checked to make sure it's greater than zero. If it's not, then a RangeError is thrown. Finally, the handler checks to see if the property is name. If it isn't, the final exception, a ReferenceError, is thrown. If none of the error conditions are triggered, then the property is assigned the value, as usual.

The Proxy object supports a considerable number of traps, which are listed in Table 7-2. The table lists each trap, followed by the parameters the handler function expects, expected return value, and how it's triggered.

Table 7-2. Proxy traps

Proxy trap	Function parameters	Expected return value	How the trap is triggered
`getOwnProperty Descriptor`	target, name	desc or undefined	`Object.getOwnPropertyDe scriptor(proxy,name)`
`getOwnPropertyNames`	target	string	`Object.getOwnProperty Names(proxy)`
`getPrototypeOf`	target	any	`Object.getPrototy peOf(proxy)`
`defineProperty`	target, name, desc	Boolean	`Object.defineProp erty(proxy,name,desc)`
`deleteProperty`	target, name	Boolean	`Object.deleteProp erty(proxy,name)`
`freeze`	target	Boolean	`Object.freeze(target)`
`seal`	target	Boolean	`Object.seal(target)`
`preventExtensions`	target	Boolean	`Object.preventExten sions(proxy)`
`isFrozen`	target	Boolean	`Object.isFrozen(proxy)`
`isSealed`	target	Boolean	`Object.isSealed(proxy)`
`isExtensible`	target	Boolean	`Object.isExtensible(proxy)`
`has`	target, name	Boolean	name in proxy
`hasOwn`	target, name	Boolean	`({}).hasOwnProp erty.call(proxy,name)`
`get`	target, name, receiver	any	`receiver[name]`
`set`	target, name, value, receiver	Boolean	`receiver[name] = val`
`enumerator`	target	iterator	for (name in proxy) (iterator should yield all enumerable own and inherited properties)
`keys`	target	string	`Object.keys(proxy)` (return array of enumerable own properties only)
`apply`	target, thisArg, args	any	`proxy(...args)`
`construct`	target, args	any	`new proxy(...args)`

Proxies can also wrap built-in objects, such as the `Array` or `Date` object. In the following code, a proxy is used to redefine the semantics of what happens when the code accesses an array. When a `get` operation takes place, the handler checks the value of the array at the given index. If it's a value of zero (0), a value of `false` is returned; otherwise, a value of `true` is returned:

```
const handler = {
    get: function(array, index) {
```

```
            if (array[index] === 0) {
              return false;
            }
            else {
              return true;
            }
        }
    };

    const numbers = [1,0,6,1,1,0];
    const proxy = new Proxy(numbers, handler);

    console.log(proxy[2]);  // true
    console.log(proxy[0]);  // true
    console.log(proxy[1]);  // false
```

The array value at an index of 2 is not zero, so `true` is returned. The same is true for the value at an index of zero. However, the value at the index of 1 is zero, so `false` is returned. This behavior holds anytime this array proxy is accessed.

7.10 Cloning an Object

Problem

You want to create an exact copy of a custom object.

Solution

Use the spread operator (...) to unpack your object into a collection of properties, and put that property list inside brackets {} to build a new object:

```
    const animal = {
      name: 'Red Fox', class: 'Mammalia', order: 'Carnivora',
      family: 'Canidae', genus: 'Vulpes', species: 'Vulpes vulpes'
    };

    const animalCopy = {...animal};
    console.log(animalCopy.species);  // 'Vulpes vulpes'
```

Discussion

You might expect that this statement would copy an object:

```
    const animalCopy = animal;
```

This works for primitive types, like strings, numbers, and `BigInt`. But objects are reference types, and assigning an object copies the reference. You end up with two variables (`animal` and `animalCopy`) pointing to the same in-memory object.

To properly copy a custom object, you need to create a new object and then iterate over the old one, copying each of its properties. You could do the long way, using the in operator (Recipe 7.4). But the spread operator offers a better approach, because you can compress the work down to a single clean line of code.

When you use the spread operator, you get all the *enumerable* properties of an object. This includes all the properties you create using object literal syntax, or any new property you assign after the fact. However, you can specifically choose to create nonenumerable properties using the Object.defineProperty() method (as introduced in Recipe 7.7). Usually, a nonenumerable property is something extra—for example, a piece of data that another service adds as part of some kind of extensibility system.

 Usually, you don't want to copy nonenumerable properties, so it makes sense that the spread operator ignores them. However, other approaches are possible. JavaScript objects have special built-in plumbing, like the Object.getOwnPropertyDescriptors() method, that let you find nonenumerable properties. Recipe 7.4 explains property enumeration in more detail.

You may also see a slightly older cloning approach that uses the Object.assign() method. This is equivalent to using the spread operator:

```
const animalCopy = Object.assign({}, animal);
```

Either way, these operations perform a *shallow copy*. If your object includes arrays or other objects as properties, these details won't be copied. Instead, they'll be *shared* between the original object and the new object. Here's a demonstration of the issue:

```
const student = {
  firstName: 'Tazie', lastName: 'Yang',
  testScores: [78, 88, 94, 91, 88, 96]
};

const studentCopy = {...student};

// Now there are two objects sharing the same testScores array
// We can see this if we change some details.
// This affects just the copy:
studentCopy.firstName = 'Dori';
// This affects both objects:
studentCopy.testScores[0] = 56;

console.log(student);
// {firstName: "Tazie", lastName: "Yang", testScores: [56, 88, 94, 91, 88, 96]
console.log(studentCopy);
// {firstName: "Dori", lastName: "Yang", testScores: [56, 88, 94, 91, 88, 96]
```

This isn't necessarily a problem, depending on what you're trying to accomplish. But if you want to copy more than one layer deep, you'll need to consider a different cloning approach that can create a *deep copy* (Recipe 7.11).

See Also

Recipe 7.11 shows how to take the same basic structure of data (an student object that holds an array) and create a deep copy of it.

7.11 Making a Deep Copy of an Object

Problem

You want to create an exact copy of a custom object. You want to copy not just the top-level object, but also every object it references.

Solution

There is no single solution for deep copying an object. Instead, there are a variety of techniques that developers use, each with its own trade-offs.

The safest approach is to write your own cloning logic that's specific to the type of object you want to clone. Here's an example that makes a deep copy of the `student` object introduced in Recipe 7.10.

```
const student = {
  firstName: 'Tazie', lastName: 'Yang',
  testScores: [78, 88, 94, 91, 88, 96]
};

function cloneStudent(student) {
  // Start with a shallow copy
  const studentCopy = {...student};

  // Now duplicate the array (by expanding it with spread)
  studentCopy.testScores = [...studentCopy.testScores];

  return studentCopy;
}

// Create a truly independent student copy
const studentCopy = cloneStudent(student);

// Verify the arrays are separate
studentCopy.testScores[0] = 56;

console.log(student.testScores[0]);      // 78
console.log(studentCopy.testScores[0]);  // 56
```

The beauty of this approach is that you know the object, so you know how deep you should go. In this example, we know that the `testScores` array holds numbers. Therefore, you know simple cloning with the spread operator is good enough to duplicate it. But if the array held objects, you'd need to decide whether to duplicate all those objects, a technique demonstrated in Recipe 5.6. Or, if `testScores` was some other type of collection object (like a `Set` or `Map`), you could properly create and fill a new collection of the corresponding type.

If you want a generic solution that can deep copy any arbitrary object, your best bet (by far) is to use a prebuilt, pretested routine from a well-known JavaScript library, like Lodash's `cloneDeep()`, which can be imported separately through the `lodash.clo nedeep` module.

Discussion

There has been discussion about built-in serialization and deep copying support in future versions of JavaScript. But right now, deep cloning is a gap you'll need to patch yourself.

If you're making a full-fledged class (Recipe 8.1), consider making your custom cloning function a method of the class itself:

```
class Student {
  constructor(firstName, lastName, testScores) {
    this.firstName = firstName;
    this.lastName = lastName;
    this.testScores = testScores;
  }

  clone() {
    return new Student(this.firstName, this.lastName,
      [...this.testScores]);
  }
}

const student = new Student('Tazie', 'Yang', [78, 88, 94, 91, 88, 96]);
const studentCopy = student.clone();

// Verif the arrays are separate
studentCopy.testScores[0] = 56;

console.log(student.testScores[0]);      // 78
console.log(studentCopy.testScores[0]);  // 56
```

This example doesn't use the spread operator. Instead, it creates a new `Student` object using the constructor. If you use the spread operator, your copy will be an instance of the base `Object` class, not an instance of `Student`. Your copy will still have the same properties as the original, but it won't appear to be a `Student` if you test it with

instanceof (Recipe 7.1). It also won't be able to use any methods you add to the Stu
dent class. To avoid these issues, you should always create the correct object type for
your copies.

You might wonder whether it's possible to create your own a generic object-copying
routine. The problems are more difficult than they seem, and there are many anti-
patterns that are recommended on the web but are likely to cause serious headaches.

A naïve approach with recursive logic will fail catastrophically (with a stack overflow)
for self-referencing object chains. A simple example is when an object references
another object that references the original object. However, subtler versions are surprisingly common.

Another variation of this problem is if one object has two references to the same
object. For example, consider a ProductCatalog that has an array of Product objects,
some of which refer to the same Supplier object. A naïve approach will create multiple copies of the Supplier, one for each Product. A more sophisticated implementation, like Lodash's cloneDeep(), tracks references as it goes to make sure it doesn't
recreate the same object more than once. (The source for its cloning implementation
(*https://github.com/lodash/lodash/blob/master/.internal/baseClone.js*) is a useful anti-
dote for anyone considering reinventing the wheel.)

Another commonly recommended cloning approach is to use JSON serialization to
convert an object to a string representation and back. This runs into problems with
Date objects (which become strings), special values like Infinity, and custom objects
that include functions (which are discarded). Worst of all, you won't be alerted about
the missing information.

The same considerations come into play if you want to test if two
objects are equal. The === operator will only tell you if the two variables point to the same object. It returns false if you have separate
objects with the same data. You could write a generic routine that
finds and compares all the properties of any two objects. However,
the meaning of equality depends on the type of data you're comparing, so writing your own isEqual() function is always the safest
approach.

7.12 Creating Absolutely Unique Object Property Keys

Problem

You want to add a uniquely named property to an object, and you want to be guaranteed that it won't clash with any other property name.

Solution

Create a new property name using the Symbol type. Then, use that name to set the property, using key-value syntax:

```
const newObj = {};

// Set a unique property that will never clash with anything else
const uniqueId = Symbol();
newObj[uniqueId] = 'No two alike';

// Set another one
const anotherUniqueId = Symbol();
newObj[anotherUniqueId] = 'This will not clash, either';

console.log(newObj);
```

Interestingly, you never actually see the unique identifier that the Symbol type uses. In this example, here's the output you'll get in the console:

```
{Symbol(): 'No two alike', Symbol(): 'This will not clash, either'}
```

To access a property created with Symbol, you need to keep track of the variable that has the property name. You use that to retrieve your value at will:

```
console.log(newObj[uniqueID]);  // 'No two alike'
```

Discussion

Property name collisions are not a common event, but they are more common in JavaScript than many other languages. Part of the problem is that properties are always public. That means that if you're inheriting from another class (see Recipe 8.8), you need to be aware of every inherited property and make sure not to use the same name yourself. But the most common cause of naming clashes is if you're creating some kind of extensibility system or service that needs you to add properties to other people's objects. In this situation, you won't know if your properties will conflict with the properties already in that object, because you don't own the design of that object.

There are various workarounds you can use to check for properties and generate random names. But the Symbol type gives you a quick and effective solution. Every Symbol is guaranteed to be unique. You create it by calling the Symbol() method. (You don't call a constructor with new, because Symbol is a primitive type, not an object.)

Optionally, you can give your symbol a description, which is useful for debugging:

```
newObj = {};
const propertyName = Symbol('Log Status');
newObj[propertyName] = 'logged';
```

However, the description is not used to create the Symbol. If you create two Symbol instances with the same description, there will be two completely separate unique identifiers, which JavaScript stores internally in a global registry of Symbol values.

7.13 Creating Enums with Symbol

Problem

You want to store a small, related group of constants, so you can refer to them by name in your code.

Solution

Use the Symbol() to set the value for each constant:

```
// Create three constants to use as an enum
const TrafficLight = {
  Green: Symbol('green'),
  Red: Symbol('red'),
  Yellow: Symbol('yellow')
}

// This function uses the light enum
function switchLight(newLight) {
  if (newLight === TrafficLight.Green) {
    console.log('Turning light green');
  }
  else if (newLight === TrafficLight.Yellow) {
    console.log('Get ready to stop');
  }
  else {
    console.log('Turning light red');
  }
  return newLight;
}

let light = TrafficLight.Green;
light = switchLight(TrafficLight.Yellow);
light = switchLight(TrafficLight.Red);

console.log(light);   // shows "Symbol('red')"
```

Discussion

An enum (or *enumerated identifier*) is a group of named constants. Enums are useful anytime you have a variable that can only take a small set of allowed values. By using the enum values, you make your code clearer. You also reduce the chance of mistakes (versus using magic numbers), because you won't forget what each number means and you can't accidentally use a number that doesn't have a constant defined for it.

 There's some debate about the proper convention for the capitalization of constants. The Math class puts read-only properties like Math.PI and Math.E in uppercase. The solution in this example uses initial capitalization for enum constants and the object that wraps them, as in TrafficLight.Red.

Often constants are created with numeric values or string values. That's a particularly good approach if the constant maps to some other useful bit of information, like the unit conversion values shown here:

```
const Units = {
  Meters: 100,
  Centimeters: 1,
  Kilometers: 100000,
  Yards: 91.44,
  Feet: 30.48,
  Miles: 160934,
  Furlongs: 20116.8,
  Elephants: 625,
  Boeing747s: 7100
};
```

If you don't have a natural unique value to use for your enum constants, consider using a Symbol. This saves you from needing to pick your own arbitrary numbers, and the guaranteed uniqueness of every Symbol ensures that you can't substitute any other value. (It also removes the chance that you'll accidentally use a hard-coded number in some places and a const variable in other places, which can lead to bug-causing inconsistencies when you make changes.) The TrafficLight example in this recipe uses a Symbol for each of its three values.

The drawback to using Symbol is that the underlying value is completely opaque. That's why the solution in this recipe gives each Symbol a descriptive name, like Symbol('red'). That's the text you'll see when you log the Symbol to the console or convert it to a string. If you don't supply a descriptive name when you create your Symbol, you'll only see the generic text "Symbol()".

See Also

To look closer at the Symbol data type, see Recipe 7.12.

## CHAPTER 8

Classes

Is JavaScript an object-oriented programming language? The answer depends on who you ask (and how you phrase the question). But the general consensus is *yes*, with some caveats.

Outside of academic circles, object-oriented programming languages usually revolve around concepts like classes, interfaces, and inheritance. But until recently, JavaScript was an outlier—an object-oriented programming language built on functions and *prototypes*. Then, along came ES6, and all of sudden classes were available as a native language construct, muddying the waters. Was it just syntactic sugar or a major language evolution?

The answer lies somewhere in between. Overall, ES6 classes are a higher-level language feature built on the familiar foundation of JavaScript prototypes. But the mapping isn't exact, and the class model introduces some new subtleties that aren't completely captured in the prototype model. Furthermore, it's likely that classes will support new object-oriented features in the future, pushing the two overlapping models farther apart.

The bottom line is this: today new development favors using classes, but prototype-based code is still common (and far from obsolete). This chapter focuses on common patterns using classes, but also explores prototypes.

8.1 Creating a Reusable Class

Problem

You want to create a reusable template for custom objects.

Solution

Use the `class` keyword, and give your class a name. Inside, add a constructor function that initializes your object. Here's a complete `Person` class example:

```
class Person {
  constructor(firstName, lastName) {
    this.firstName = firstName;
    this.lastName = lastName;
  }
}

// Test the Person class by creating an object
// The constructor is invoked when you use the new keyword with the class
const newPerson = new Person('Luke', 'Takei');
console.log(newPerson.firstName);  // 'Luke'
```

In this example, the `Person` class is a simple package that bundles together two public fields (`firstName` and `lastName`). But it's easy enough to add methods to your class, which work like functions but don't include the `function` keyword. Here's how you would code a `Person.swapNames()` method:

```
class Person {
  constructor(firstName, lastName, dateOfBirth) {
    this.firstName = firstName;
    this.lastName = lastName;
    this.dateOfBirth = dateOfBirth;
  }

  // This is a method
  swapNames() {
    // Use a handy shortcut (destructuring assignment) to assign both
    // properties at once
    [this.firstName, this.lastName] = [this.lastName, this.firstName];
  }
}

// Test the Person class
const newPerson = new Person('Luke', 'Takei', new Date(1990, 5, 22));
newPerson.swapNames();
console.log(newPerson.firstName);  // 'Takei'
```

Discussion

In essence of a JavaScript class is the constructor function. In fact, behind the scenes a JavaScript class *is* a constructor function, and all methods are attached to that function's *prototype*. That means that a method like `Person.swapNames()` is shared between all the instances of the `Person` class, because they share the same prototype. (To dig deeper into this behind-the-scenes reality, check out the constructor pattern in Recipe 8.4.)

Classes have their own syntax requirements that you must follow:

- Constructor functions are always named `constructor`.
- Neither constructors nor methods use the keyword `function`, although they are declared like functions in every other respect.

When you write a constructor, you use `this` to create new public fields on the current object. You can then refer to these fields wherever you need them in your class methods, as long as you remember to always prefix the variable name with `this`. You can also access these fields outside of the class code, using the familiar dot syntax.

You might wonder how you can change this accessibility—say, make your fields private and wrap them with public properties. The answer is that currently you can't—at least, not without a home brew solution that introduces complications of its own. For a full discussion of the subject, see Recipe 8.2.

As with functions, JavaScript allows you to create classes in an *expression*. Here's an example:

```
const personExpression = class Person {
  constructor(firstName, lastName) {
    this.firstName = firstName;
    this.lastName = lastName;
  }
}

// This won't work, because there is no Person class to be found in scope
const newPerson = new Person('Luke', 'Takei');

// This works because you can create a new instance of the variable that holds
// the class expression
const newPerson = new personExpression('Luke', 'Takei');
```

This is a specialized—but not rare—technique. It allows you to avoid adding a class to the current scope. For example, that might be useful in this example if you were worried that there might already be a definition for another `Person` class. (Another way to solve the problem of name collisions is by using modules, as described in Recipe 8.9.)

See Also

For the old-fashioned constructor pattern for object creation, see Recipe 8.4. To see how to create class properties, refer to Recipe 8.2. To learn how to connect classes in an inheritance relationship, see Recipe 8.8.

Extra: Multiple Constructors

In most object-oriented languages it's possible to create multiple constructors, so the code that creates the class has a choice of what parameters to specify. But JavaScript doesn't support constructor overloading or method overloading.

This isn't quite as limiting as it seems, because JavaScript is notoriously loose with function arguments and never forces you to supply them. So even though `Person` has a single three-argument constructor, these are all valid ways to create an instance without supplying every argument:

```
const noDatePerson = new Person('Luke', 'Takei');
const firstNamePerson = new Person('Luke');
const noDataPerson = new Person();
```

Every class has exactly one constructor, and it always runs. Even if you don't specify any arguments when you create a `Person` object, the three-argument constructor still runs and sets `this.firstName`, `this.lastName`, and `this.birthDate` (all of which will be set to `undefined`). If this isn't acceptable, you can set default parameter values, just as you do with ordinary functions (see Recipe 6.3).

> If you create a class without a constructor, JavaScript automatically gives it a blank no-argument constructor. This detail becomes significant if you decide to use class inheritance (Recipe 8.8).

Another way to deal with optional arguments is using an object literal that gets passed to the constructor. That way the caller can choose to set only the named properties they want to use:

```
const partialInfoPerson1 = new Person({
  lastName: "Takei",
  birthDate: new Date(1990, 04, 23)
});
const partialInfoPerson2 = new Person({firstName: 'Luke', lastName: 'Takei'});
```

This is a common JavaScript design pattern that's described in detail in Recipe 6.5. One advantage it provides is that you don't need to worry about the order of properties in the object literal. A disadvantage is that there's nothing to prevent you from accidentally creating incorrectly named parameters that will be silently ignored:

```
// The Person class will look for a firstName property in this object literal
// It will quietly ignore the firstname property
const partialInfoPerson2 = new Person({firstname: 'Luke'});
```

Another possible approach is to create a single constructor for your class, but add static methods that create differently configured instances of the object. Depending

---

on the implementation, this is sometimes called the *builder pattern* or *factory pattern*. It's described in Recipe 8.7.

8.2 Adding Properties to a Class

Problem

You want to add property getters and setters to wrap your class data.

Solution

First, consider if properties are the best solution for your use case. (As explained in the discussion, they have well-known limitations and are slightly controversial.) If you decide to use properties, you can create get and set methods for each one. Here's an example with a computed property, called age, which is calculated from the date stored in this.dateOfBirth:

```
class Person {
  constructor(firstName, lastName, dateOfBirth) {
    this.firstName = firstName;
    this.lastName = lastName;
    this.dateOfBirth = dateOfBirth;
  }

  // This is a getter for the age property
  get age() {
    if (this.dateOfBirth instanceof Date) {
      // Calculate the difference in years
      const today = new Date();
      let age = today.getFullYear() - this.dateOfBirth.getFullYear();

      // Adjust if the bithday hasn't happened yet this year
      const monthDiff = today.getMonth() - this.dateOfBirth.getMonth();
      if (monthDiff < 0 ||
        (monthDiff === 0 && today.getDate() < this.dateOfBirth.getDate())) {
        age -= 1;
      }

      return age;
    }
  }
}

// Test the Person class
const newPerson = new Person('Luke', 'Takei', new Date(1990, 5, 22));
console.log(newPerson.age);
```

It's up to you whether you include only a getter, only a setter, or both. Here's an example that uses the property pattern to apply basic validation to the date of birth:

```
class Person {
  constructor(firstName, lastName, date) {
    this.firstName = firstName;
    this.lastName = lastName;

    // Set the date using the property setter so a Person
    // can't be created in an invalid state
    this.dateOfBirth = date;
  }

  // Just return the date with no extra processing
  get dateOfBirth() {
    return this._dateOfBirth;
  }

  // Don't allow dates in the future
  set dateOfBirth(value) {
    if (value instanceof Date && value < Date.now()) {
      // This is a valid date
      this._dateOfBirth = value;
    }
    else {
      throw new TypeError('Birthdate needs to be a valid date in the past');
    }
  }
}

// Test the date restrictions
const newPerson = new Person('Luke', 'Takei', new Date(1990, 5, 22));
console.log(newPerson.dateOfBirth);

// This change is allowed
newPerson.dateOfBirth = new Date(2010, 10, 10);
console.log(newPerson.dateOfBirth);

// This change causes an error
newPerson.dateOfBirth = new Date(2035, 10, 10);
```

This example throws an exception (Recipe 10.5) to notify the caller when they attempt to set an invalid value. This is a reasonable design decision, but it's not always the best choice. Having an error occur when setting a property (or even worse, when attempting to create a Person with an invalid date) is not expected behavior in JavaScript, and the potential error may not be anticipated by the calling code. (The alternative—silently ignoring the offending error —is also risky.) In the end, a better approach may be to use methods to supply potentially problematic data instead of properties.

Discussion

There are many reasons you might consider creating property procedures. Some examples include:

- To calculate a value (like `Person.age`)
- To transform a field into another representation
- To perform validation before updating a field
- To add hooks for some other service (like logging or testing) that should happen every time a field is read or set
- To use some kind of lazy initialization, which only creates or calculates a property value when it's needed
- To expose a single property of an object that's stored in a field

This recipe presents two examples. The `Person.age` property is a read-only computed property. The `Person.dateOfBirth` property is a settable property with validation.

When you use properties, you must be careful to avoid name collisions. The field that stores the value cannot have the same name as the property or the constructor parameter. To understand why, let's take a closer look at the `dateOfBirth` example. The constructor accepts a `date` parameter, which it sets like this:

```
this.dateOfBirth = date;
```

At first glance, you might assume this statement stores the date in a public field named `this.dateOfBirth` (which is the usual pattern). But in this case, `this.dateOfBirth` refers to the `dateOfBirth` property. Its setter takes over:

```
set dateOfBirth(value) {
if (value instanceof Date && value < Date.now()) {
  // This is a valid date
  this._dateOfBirth = value;
}
else {
  throw new TypeError('Birthdate needs to be a valid date in the past');
}
```

If the new value passes the test, it's stored in a public field named `this._dateOfBirth`. The awkward naming is necessary, because both `this.dateOfBirth` (the property) and `this._dateOfBirth` (the field) have the same scope. If you use the same name for both, you'll end up calling the wrong one (and triggering an infinite sequences of calls that will eventually overflow the stack).

The leading underscore in a variable name like `_dateOfBirth` has another purpose. Currently, JavaScript doesn't have any way to create private fields. But the underscore signals that a field is *supposed* to be private to the class. Then, you trust that the calling code will avoid using this field. If you don't follow this convention, you're almost certain to run into a problem where the calling code accidentally uses the field instead of the property. And even if you *do* observe this pattern, there's no guarantee that the calling code will follow it.

Many JavaScript developers argue that a more natural pattern in JavaScript is to use setXxx() and getXxx() methods:

```
class Person {
  constructor(firstName, lastName, date) {
    this.firstName = firstName;
    this.lastName = lastName;
    this.setDateOfBirth(date);
  }

  getDateOfBirth() {
    return this._dateOfBirth;
  }

  setDateOfBirth(value) {
    if (value instanceof Date && value < Date.now()) {
      // This is a valid date
      this._dateOfBirth = value;
    }
    else {
      throw new TypeError('Birthdate cannot be in the future');
    }
  }
}

const newPerson = new Person('Luke', 'Takei', new Date(1990, 5, 22));
console.log(newPerson.getDateOfBirth());

// This change is allowed
newPerson.setDateOfBirth (new Date(2010, 10, 10));
console.log(newPerson.getDateOfBirth());

// This change causes an error
newPerson.setDateOfBirth (new Date(2035, 10, 10));
```

This approach is a bit more cumbersome, but it has some advantages. It makes it obvious that you're calling a method and running code, not simply setting a variable. As a result, the calling code can expect exceptions from type-checking or other side effects. Methods also prevent problems like this:

```
// This isn't the property you want (that's dateOfBirth) but JavaScript
//  creates it anyway, and you won't notice the mistake
person.DateOfBirth = new Date(2035, 10, 10);

// You can't call a function that doesn't exist, so this typo
```

```
// ("Data" instead of "Date") always fails and won't be ignored
person.setDataOfBirth(new Date(2035, 10, 10));
```

 Both the Google JavaScript Style Guide (*https://google.github.io/ styleguide/jsguide.html*) and the often-consulted Airbnb JavaScript Style Guide (*https://github.com/airbnb/javascript*) discourage the usage of property getters and setters but allow setXxx() and getXxx() methods.

There's one more wrinkle to consider with properties. Behind the scenes, JavaScript uses the Object.defineProperty() method to implement your property getters and setters. Most of the time, that works perfectly well. However, there are specialized cases when you may decide to use defineProperty() because it allows you to configure metadata details you can't otherwise set. For example, if you want to make a property nonconfigurable (so its implementation can't be altered) or nonenumerable (so it won't show up in a for...in loop), you need to explicitly call defineProperty(). In this situation, the usual approach is to call defineProperty in the constructor.

See Also

If you want to use property procedures to react to property changes and trigger other actions (like logging), consider using proxies instead (Recipe 7.9). For more about creating properties with Object.defineProperty(), see Recipe 7.7.

Extra: Private Fields

Currently, JavaScript does not have a way to make member variables (those created with this) private. Many workarounds are used, and many of them are dangerously creative. The most popular implementation uses a WeakMap to store internal data. It works, but it adds a dangerous layer of extra homemade complexity.

A better approach is to use the underscore convention (like _firstName) to name fields that should not be accessed outside a class. In the future, JavaScript will patch this gap and adopt some version of the *private class fields* proposal (*https:// github.com/tc39/proposal-class-fields*). Right now, the private field syntax uses a # to identify private fields, which can be declared at the beginning of your class block, making your class self documenting. Here's what that looks like:

```
// A likely implementation of private field syntax in the near future
class Person {
  #firstName;
  #lastName;

  constructor(firstName, lastName) {
    this.#firstName = firstName;
    this.#lastName = lastName;
```

```
  }

  // Wrap the fields in properties
      get firstName() {
    return this.#firstName;
  }
  set firstName(name) {
    this.#firstName = name;
  }

  get lastName() {
    return this.#lastName;
  }
  set lastName(name) {
    this.#lastName = name;
  }
}
```

If you want to experiment with these features today, you can use Babel (*https://babeljs.io*) to transpile your code, although be aware that the syntax may change.

Interestingly, this is one case where JavaScript classes have *less* functionality than the old-fashioned constructor pattern (Recipe 8.4). That's because the constructor pattern can use closures to store private variables, as explained in Recipe 6.6.

8.3 Giving a Class a Better String Representation

Problem

You want to choose a suitable text representation that will be used for your object when it's converted to a string.

Solution

Add a method named toString() to your class and return the string you want to use:

```
class Person {
  constructor(firstName, lastName) {
    this.firstName = firstName;
    this.lastName = lastName;
  }

  toString() {
    return `${this.lastName}, ${this.firstName}`;
  }
}

const newPerson = new Person('Luke', 'Takei');
console.log(newPerson.toString());   // 'Takei, Luke'
```

Discussion

The default implementation of `toString()` for all objects displays the unhelpful text `[object Object]`. You can set your own text by adding a `toString()` method.

The `toString()` method can be called explicitly (as in this example), or it can be called implicitly when your object is converted to a string. For example, if you concatenate your object with a string, `toString()` is called automatically:

```
const newPerson = new Person('Luke', 'Takei');
const message = 'The name is ' + newPerson;

// Now message = 'The name is Takei, Luke'
// which is much better than 'The name is [object Object]'
```

However, calling `console.log()` on an object, on its own, does not trigger your `toString()`. That's because `console.log()` has an extra bit of logic that iterates over the properties of your object and uses that to build its own custom string. You can get around this by calling `toString()` yourself, or using a template literal (Recipe 2.5). Here's a comparison:

```
const newPerson = new Person('Luke', 'Takei');

console.log(newPerson);        // 'Person {firstName: "Luke", lastName: "Takei"}'
console.log(`${newPerson}`);   // 'Takei, Luke'
console.log(newPerson+'');     // 'Takei, Luke'
```

8.4 Using the Constructor Pattern to Make a Custom Class

Problem

You want to create a reusable, class-like entity in your code. You want to use the traditional constructor pattern because it matches your existing code.

Solution

The constructor pattern is a slightly dated but still acceptable pattern for object creation. Even if you plan to use formal classes (Recipe 8.1), it's worth knowing the constructor pattern, because you're likely to encounter it out in the wild. It can also help you understand how JavaScript classes work.

Here's one of the `Person` class examples from Recipe 8.1, but written as a function with the constructor pattern:

```
function Person(firstName, lastName) {
  // Store public data using 'this'
  this.firstName = firstName;
  this.lastName = lastName;
```

```
  // Add a nested function to represent a method
  this.swapNames = function() {
    [this.firstName, this.lastName] = [this.lastName, this.firstName];
  }
}

// Create a Person object
const newPerson = new Person('Luke', 'Takei');
console.log(newPerson.firstName);  // 'Luke'

newPerson.swapNames();
console.log(newPerson.firstName);  // 'Takei'
```

Notice that the code for using a function-based object is the same as the code for using a class-based with an identical constructor. As a result, you can usually migrate code from the constructor pattern to formal classes without disrupting the rest of your application.

Discussion

Classes were a relative latecomer to the JavaScript language. Before they existed, developers used functions in their place. This works because JavaScript allows you to create new *instances* of a function (function objects) using the new keyword. Every function gets its own scope, with its own local data.

The constructor pattern exists in several variants. The most common approach is to create a function with the name of your "class" and accept all the constructor parameters you need to create an instance. Inside your function, you use this to create public fields. You can also create ordinary variables, which won't be visible to outside code, and are only usable by the constructor and any nested functions.

There are two common ways to create method-like functions. The approach shown here creates each method using a function expression, and makes them publicly accessible with this. Because the method functions are wrapped inside the constructor function, they have the same scope as the constructor, and they have access to all the same variables and local variables. (Technically, the constructor function creates a closure, as explained in Recipe 6.6.)

The other way to create methods is to explicitly add them to the *prototype* of your constructor function. If you haven't encountered prototypes yet, they're a basic (but mostly hidden) ingredient that allows objects to share functionality. When you attempt to call a method (like Person.swapNames()), JavaScript looks for the swap Names() function in the Person constructor. If it doesn't find it, JavaScript looks for a swapNames() function in the prototype. The process gets a bit more involved when inheritance is involved, because JavaScript will search an entire *prototype chain* looking for a function, as explained in Recipe 8.8.

So how do you add a function to a prototype? You can do it directly, using the proto type property:

```
function Person(firstName, lastName) {
  this.firstName = firstName;
  this.lastName = lastName;
}

// Add function to the Person prototype to represent a method
Person.prototype.swapNames = function() {
  [this.firstName, this.lastName] = [this.lastName, this.firstName];
}

const newPerson = new Person('Luke', 'Takei');
newPerson.swapNames();
console.log(newPerson.firstName);  // 'Takei'
```

This example behaves mostly the same as the version with the nested constructor functions. But there is a difference. Before, the swapNames() existed independently in each Person object. Now, there is a single swapNames() function set in the prototype and shared among all Person instances. This is important if you plan to create an inheritance relationship linking prototypes together (see "Extra: Prototype Chains" on page 195). It's also significant if you attempt to use private variables with a closure (Recipe 6.6), because functions attached to the prototype don't exist in the same context as the constructor function, and won't have access to private variables defined in the constructor.

 Using prototypes, you can alter the behavior of built-in JavaScript objects. For example, you can add functionality to the base Array or String types. This sounds like a nifty feature, but it's rife with complications and is strongly discouraged (except perhaps for building frameworks). Blurring the distinction between standard and custom code invites confusion, and creates the possibility for nonstandard patterns, poorly optimized code, and hidden mistakes. It can also fail outright if more than one person attempts to extend a built-in object with the same name.

It's interesting to compare the constructor pattern to the class keyword shown in Recipe 8.1. Most of the code is exactly the same in both examples:

- You write a constructor function that accepts parameters and initializes your object.

- You use the this keyword to create publicly accessible fields.

- You use the new keyword when creating the object (only now it's technically an instance of a function, not a class).

But there are also some subtle differences, most obviously in syntax. In the constructor pattern there are no dedicated properties, and methods are declared separately, not nested in the constructor or explicitly attached to the constructor's prototype (although that's exactly what happens at runtime).

See Also

Recipe 8.1 demonstrates the preferred way to create a custom object template in modern JavaScript, which is using the class keyword.

8.5 Supporting Method Chaining in Your Class

Problem

You want to define your class methods in such a way that several methods can be called in quick succession, in a single statement.

Solution

Make sure to return the current object at the end of each method that should support method chaining. In a custom class, this is usually as simple as adding a return this statement.

Here's an example of a custom Book object with two methods, raisePrice() and releaseNewEdition(), both of which use method chaining:

```
class Book {
  constructor(title, author, price, publishedDate) {
    this.title = title;
    this.author = author;
    this.price = price;
    this.publishedDate = publishedDate;
  }

  raisePrice(percent) {
    const increase = this.price*percent;
    this.price += Math.round(increase)/100;
    return this;
  }

  releaseNewEdition() {
    // Set the pulishedDate to today
    this.publishedDate = new Date();
    return this;
  }
}
```

```
    }

    const book = new Book('I Love Mathematics', 'Adam Up', 15.99,
      new Date(2010, 2, 2));

    // Raise the price 15% and then change the edition, using method chaining
    console.log(book.raisePrice(15).releaseNewEdition());
```

Discussion

The ability to directly call one method on the result of another method, in a single code statement, is known as *method chaining*. Here's an example with a string and the replaceAll() method. Because replaceAll() returns a new string, you can call replaceAll() again on that string, and get a *third* string:

```
    const safePieceOfHtml =
      originalPieceOfHtml.replaceAll('<', '&lt;').replaceAll('>', '&gt;');
```

Method chaining doesn't have to be with the same method. It works with any method that returns an object. Consider how this code joins two arrays and then sorts the resulting array by chaining a call to concat() with one to sort():

```
    const evens = [2, 4, 6, 8];
    const odds = [1, 3, 5, 7, 9];

    const evensAndOdds = evens.concat(odds).sort();
    console.log(evensAndOdds);  // [1, 2, 3, 4, 5, 6, 7, 8, 9]
```

Chaining is used extensively in built-in JavaScript objects and in many JavaScript libraries and frameworks. To use this pattern in your own classes, you simply return a reference to this at the end of your method. The calling code can then ignore this reference, or use it to perform method chaining.

In the current example, calling a method on Book changes the object and returns a reference to the changed object. The caller can ignore the return value, because they already have a reference to the Book object. However, many functional programming purists do something different. They write methods that return a changed object *copy*, while keeping the original object unchanged. Here's how you'd implement this pattern:

```
    class Book {
      constructor(title, author, price, publishedDate) {
        this.title = title;
        this.author = author;
        this.price = price;
        this.publishedDate = publishedDate;
      }

      getRaisedPriceBook(percent) {
        const increase = this.price*percent;
```

```
      return new Book(this.title, this.author, Math.round(increase)/100,
        this.publishedDate);
    }

    getNewEdition() {
      return new Book(this.title, this.author, this.price, new Date());
    }
  }
```

This pattern doesn't affect the way method chaining works, but it does mean the caller needs to take the return value, or they won't see the changes.

8.6 Adding Static Methods to a Class

Problem

You want to create a utility method that's tied to your class, but can be called without creating an object.

Solution

Place the static keyword before the method. Make sure your method doesn't attempt to use any instance fields, properties, or methods. Here's an example with a static method named Book.isEqual():

```
class Book {
  constructor(isbn, title, author, publishedDate) {
    this.isbn = isbn;
    this.title = title;
    this.author = author;
    this.publishedDate = publishedDate;
  }

  static isEqual(book, otherBook) {
    if (book instanceof Book && otherBook instanceof Book) {
      // Books are deemed equal if their ISBNs match,
      // irrespective of dashes
      return (book.isbn.replaceAll('-','') === otherBook.isbn.replaceAll('-',''));
    }
    else {
      return false;
    }
  }
}
```

You access a static method through the class name (as in Book.isEqual()). You can't access it through an object variable.

```
const firstPrinting = new Book('978-3-16-148410-0', 'A.I. Is Not a Threat',
  'Anne Droid', new Date(2019, 2, 2));
```

```
const secondPrinting = new Book('978-3-16-148410-0', 'A.I. Is Not a Threat',
 'A. Droid', new Date(2021, 2, 10));

// Compare the books with the static method
const sameBook = Book.isEqual(firstPrinting, secondPrinting);
// sameBook = true

// This doesn't work, because isEqual isn't available in Book instances
sameBook = firstPrinting.isEqual(firstPrinting, secondPrinting);
```

Discussion

Static methods have functionality that's logically related to a class, but not tied to a specific instance. The `Array.isArray()` method is a good example—it lets you test whether any object is an array, without forcing you to create an array object first. Occasionally, classes are made up entirely of static methods. JavaScript's `Math` class is a good example.

In the current example, you might want to give the `Book` class static methods related to processing or verifying ISBNs. You can also use static methods to make decisions about how objects of a certain class should be copied or compared. The solution demonstrates this principle with a static `isEqual()` method. You could also add a `compare()` method that would let you sort your objects in array (as shown in Recipe 5.16).

In a static method, `this` refers to the current class, not an object instance. This can lead to problems, because your code will still be allowed to store data in `this` (or retrieve it). It just might not have the effect you expect. Essentially, everything in the static `this` acts like a class-scoped global variable, which is best avoided.

 If you want one static method to call another static method, you can use the `this` keyword. For example, if you want to call the static `isEqual()` from another static method in the `Book` class, you can refer to it as `Book.isEqual()` or `this.isEqual()`, which may be clearer.

Property `set` and `get` methods can also be static, although their usage is sometimes controversial. For example, you can use a static getter to store a constant, like this:

```
class Book {
  constructor(isbn, title, author, publishedDate) {
    this.isbn = isbn;
    this.title = title;
    this.author = author;
    this.publishedDate = publishedDate;
  }
```

```
    // Create a static, read-only Books.isnbnPrefix property
    static get isbnPrefix() {
      return '978-1';
    }
  }
```

You can write a static setter, which acts like a global variable in your application. However, because there's no static constructor, you'll be forced to run code somewhere to assign the initial value. This isn't particularly clear, so a new static property syntax is under development (*https://oreil.ly/7O28H*), and currently supported by more modern browser versions. It allows you to set a public static property using a variable-like syntax:

```
class Book {
  // Create a static Book.isbnPrefix property
  static isbnPrefix = '978-1';

  constructor(isbn, title, author, publishedDate) {
    this.isbn = isbn;
    this.title = title;
    this.author = author;
    this.publishedDate = publishedDate;
  }
}
```

However, it's best to avoid this language feature altogether—or at least until some future data when its use in JavaScript is more normative.

8.7 Using a Static Method to Create Objects

Problem

You want to create a method that generates a preconfigured object, possibly to get around JavaScript's single-constructor limitation.

Solution

Add a static method to your class that creates and returns the object you want. Here's an example with a Book class that you can create through the constructor or through the static Book.createSequel() method:

```
class Book {
  constructor(title, firstName, lastName) {
    this.title = title;
    this.firstName = firstName;
    this.lastName = lastName;
  }

  static createSequel(prevBook, title) {
```

```
      return new Book(title, prevBook.firstName, prevBook.lastName);
  }
}
```

Here's how you use the static method:

```
// Create a Book with the usual constructor
const book = new Book('Good Design', 'Polly', 'Morfissim');

// Create a sequel with the static method
const sequel = Book.createSequel(book, 'Even Gooder Design');
console.log(sequel);
```

Discussion

Using static methods, you can implement different types of *creational* patterns—basically, patterns that help you create preconfigured instances of a class. For example, the JavaScript Date class has a now() property that returns a new Date object that's automatically set to the current date and time.

This approach is particularly suited to creating more complex combinations of objects. For example, you could extend the previous example with a Book.create Trilogy() method to get an array of three Book objects. In this example, the Book objects share a single Author object, which means that if you update the Author object, all the Book instances that link to it see the change:

```
class Author {
  constructor(firstName, lastName) {
    this.firstName = firstName;
    this.lastName = lastName;
  }
}

class Book {
  constructor(title, author) {
    this.title = title;
    this.author = author;
  }

  static createSequel(prevBook, title) {
    return new Book(title, prevBook.author);
  }

  static createTrilogy(author, title1, title2, title3) {
    return [new Book(title1, author),
      new Book(title2, author),
      new Book(title3, author)];
  }
}

// Create a trilogy of three books with a factory method
```

```
const author = new Author('Koh','Der');
const books = Book.createTrilogy(author, 'A Sea of Fire', 'A Sea of Ice',
 'A Sea of Water');
console.log(books);
```

Unlike constructors, there's no limit to how many static methods you can add to support different object-creation scenarios.

 Sometimes these static methods are called *factory methods*, although that description isn't technically precise. In object-oriented design theory, the factory pattern is used when you don't know the exact type of object you're creating. For example, you might write a createBook() method that examines the arguments you supply and returns an instance of either the TechBook class or the FictionBook class, both of which inherit from a base Book class. It's possible to implement this design in JavaScript, too, but opinions are mixed about how well the language handles the heavier weight of this sort of classical OOP abstraction.

8.8 Inheriting Functionality from Another Class

Problem

You want to create a custom class that inherits the functionality of another class.

Solution

With inheritance, one or more *child* classes derive from a *parent* class. To model this in code, you use the extends keyword when you declare the child class:

```
public class SomeChild extends SomeParent {

}
```

Here's an example with a Triangle class that inherits from a more basic parent class named Shape:

```
// This is the parent class
class Shape {
  getArea() {
    return null;
  }
}

// This is a child class
class Triangle extends Shape {
  constructor(base, height) {
    // Call the base class constructor
    super();
```

```
    this.base = base;
    this.height = height;
  }

  getArea() {
    return this.base * this.height/2;
  }
}
```

In this example, the parent class (Shape) doesn't have any useful functionality. The getArea() method is only there as a placeholder. But in other cases, base classes may be useful on their own. For example, you could use inheritance with the Book class to create an EBook child or with the Person class to create a Customer.

It may seem that there's no point to build a Triangle that derives from a Shape if you only plan to use the Triangle. And in a loosely typed language like JavaScript, this is often true! But the potential value appears when you use a single parent class to standardize more child classes:

```
class Circle extends Shape {
  constructor(radius) {
    super();
    this.radius = radius;
  }

  getArea() {
    return Math.PI * this.radius**2;
  }
}

class Square extends Shape {
  constructor(length) {
    super();
    this.length = length;
  }

  getArea() {
    return this.length**2;
  }
}
```

Now it becomes possible to write code like this:

```
// Create an array of different shapes
const shapes = [new Triangle(15, 8), new Circle(8), new Square(7)];

// Sort them by area from smallest to largest
shapes.sort( (a,b) => a.getArea()-b.getArea() );

console.log(shapes);
// New order: Square, Triangle, Circle
```

Of course, JavaScript is a loosely typed language, and you could call `getArea()` on `Triangle` and `Circle` and `Square` objects even if they didn't share a parent class that defined the method. But formalizing this interface with inheritance can help make these requirements explicit. It's also important if you need to test objects using `instanceof` (Recipe 7.1):

```
const triangle = new Triangle(15, 8);

if (triangle instanceof Shape) {
  // We end up here, because triangle is a Triangle which is a Shape
}
```

Discussion

If you don't write a constructor for a child class, JavaScript creates one automatically. That constructor calls the base class constructor (but provides no arguments).

If you write a constructor for your child class, you *must* call the parent class constructor. Otherwise, you'll receive a `ReferenceError` when you try to create an instance. To call the parent class constructor, you use the `super()` keyword:

```
constructor(length) {
  super();
}
```

If the parent class constructor accepts arguments, you should pass them to `super()` like you would when creating the object. Here's an example with an `EBook` class that extends `Book`:

```
class Book {
  constructor(title, author, publishedDate) {
    this.title = title;
    this.author = author;
    this.publishedDate = publishedDate;
  }
}

class EBook extends Book {
  constructor(title, author, publishedDate, format) {
    super(title, author, publishedDate);
    this.format = format;
  }
}
```

You can also use `super()` to call other methods or properties in the parent class. For example, if a child class wants to call the parent class implementation of `format String()`, it would call `super.formatString()`.

Classes are a relatively late introduction to JavaScript. Although they support inheritance, many of the other tools you might be used to in traditional object-oriented languages, like abstract base classes, virtual methods, and interfaces, have no analog in JavaScript. Some developers enjoy the lightweight nature of JavaScript and its emphasis on prototypes, while others feel they are missing vital tools for building large, complex applications. (If you're in the latter camp, your best better is to consider TypeScript, a more rigorous superset of JavaScript.)

But inheritance isn't without its own tradeoffs. It can encourage you to write tightly coupled classes that are dependent on one another and difficult to adapt to future changes. Even worse, it's often difficult to identify these dependencies, and developers become reluctant to make changes to the parent class (a situation called the *fragile base class* problem). Because of problems like these, modern development often prefers aggregating groups of objects instead of using inheritance relationships. For example, instead of building an Employee class that extends Person, you might create an Employee object that includes a Person property, along with all the other details it needs. This pattern is called *composition*:

```
class Person {
  constructor(firstName, lastName) {
    this.firstName = firstName;
    this.lastName = lastName;
  }
}

class Employee {
  constructor(person, department, hireDate) {
    // person is a full-fledged Person object
    this.person = person;

    // These properties hold the extra, nonperson information
    this.department = department;
    this.hireDate = hireDate;
  }
}

// Create an Employee object that's composed of a Person object
// and some extra details
const employee = new Employee(new Person('Mike', 'Scott'), 'Sales', new Date());
```

Extra: Prototype Chains

You may remember that the JavaScript class feature creates a prototype for an object. This prototype holds the implementation of all its methods and properties, and is shared between all instances of that class. Prototypes are also the secret to inheritance. When one class extends another, they are linked in a *prototype chain*.

For example, consider the relationship of Shape and Triangle. The Triangle class has a prototype that holds whatever you've defined for the child class. However, that prototype has *its own* prototype, which is the prototype for Shape class, with all its members. The Shape prototype has its own prototype, too: the base Object.proto type, which ends the prototype chain.

Inheritance can go as many levels deep as you want, so a prototype chain can become much longer. When you call a method like Triangle.getArea(), JavaScript searches the prototype chain. It looks for a method in the Triangle prototype, then the Shape prototype, and then the Object prototype (at which point it fails with an error if it can't find a matching method).

Of course, JavaScript classes are relatively new, and prototypes have been around since the first version of the language. So it's no surprise that you can create inheritance-like relationships using prototypes even if you aren't using JavaScript classes. Sometimes this is paired with the old-fashioned constructor pattern (Recipe 8.4), which results in some decidedly inelegant code:

```
// This will be the parent class
function Person(firstName, lastName) {
  this.firstName = firstName;
  this.lastName = lastName;
}

// Add the methods you want to the Person class
Person.prototype.greet = function() {
  console.log('I am ' + this.firstName + ' ' + this.lastName);
}

// This will be the child class
function Employee(firstName, lastName, department) {
  // The Object.call() method allows you to chain constructor functions
  // It binds the Person constructor to this object's context
  Person.call(this, firstName, lastName);

  // Add extra details
  this.department = department;
}

// Link the Person prototype to the Employee function
// This establishes the inheritance relationship
Employee.prototype = Object.create(Person.prototype);
Employee.prototype.constructor = Employee;

// Now add the methods you want to the Employee class
Employee.prototype.introduceJob = function() {
  console.log('I work in ' + this.department);
}

// When you create an instance of the Employee function, its prototype
// is chained back to the Person prototype
const newEmployee = new Employee('Luke', 'Takei', 'Tech Support');
```

```
// You can call Person methods and Employee methods
newEmployee.greet();          // 'I am Luke Takei'
newEmployee.introduceJob();   // 'I work in Tech Support'
```

This pattern *should* be mostly obsolete now, because classes give you a cleaner method to create inheritance relationships. But it still lingers in plenty of long-lived codebases.

8.9 Organizing Your JavaScript Classes with Modules

Problem

You want to encapsulate your classes in a separate namespace to facilitate reuse and prevent naming conflicts with other libraries.

Solution

Use the module system introduced with ES6. There are three steps:

1. Decide which functionality represents a complete module. Put the code for those classes, functions, and global variables in a separate script file.

2. Choose which code details you want to *export* (make available to other scripts in other files).

3. In another script, *import* the features you want to use.

Here's an example of a module; we'll store it in a file named *lengthConverterModule.js*:

```
const Units = {
  Meters: 100,
  Centimeters: 1,
  Kilometers: 100000,
  Yards: 91.44,
  Feet: 30.48,
  Miles: 160934,
  Furlongs: 20116.8,
  Elephants: 625,
  Boeing747s: 7100
};

class InvisibleLogger {
  static log() {
    console.log('Greetings from the invisible logger');
  }
}

class LengthConverter {
  static Convert(value, fromUnit, toUnit) {
    InvisibleLogger.log();
```

```
    return value*fromUnit/toUnit;
  }
}

export {Units, LengthConverter}
```

The important line is the `export` statement at the end. It lists all the functions, variables, and classes that will be made accessible to other code files. In this example, the `Units` constant (really just an enum) and the `LengthConverter` class are made available, while the `InvisibleLogger` class is not.

 When you create module files, the extension *.mjs* is sometimes recommended. The *.mjs* extension clearly signals that you're using an ES6 module, and it helps tools like Node and Babel recognize these files automatically. However, the *.mjs* extension can also cause problems if your web server isn't configured to serve *.mjs* files with the right MIME type (`text/javascript`), like ordinary *.js* files. For that reason, we don't use it in this example.

Now you can import the functionality you need into another module. You can write this module as a separate file, or use a `<script>` block in a web page as we do here. But either way, your `<script>` tag must include the `type="module"` attribute.

Here's the complete page, including a button that triggers a `doSampleConversion()` test:

```
<!DOCTYPE html>
<html lang="en">
  <head>
    <meta charset="UTF-8" />
    <meta name="viewport" content="width=device-width, initial-scale=1.0" />
    <meta http-equiv="X-UA-Compatible" content="ie=edge" />
    <title>Module Test</title>
  </head>
  <body>
    <h1>Module Test</h1>
    <button id="convertButton">Do Sample Conversion</button>

<script type="module">
  import {Units, LengthConverter} from './lengthConverterModule.js';

  function doSampleConversion() {
    const lengthInMiles = 495;

    // This works because you have access to LengthConverter and Units
    const lengthInElephants =
     LengthConverter.Convert(lengthInMiles, Units.Feet, Units.Yards);
    alert(lengthInElephants);
```

```
    // This wouldn't work, because you don't have access to InvisibleLogger
    //InvisibleLogger.log();
  }

  // Connect the button
  document.getElementById('convertButton').addEventListener('click',
    doSampleConversion);
</script>

  </body>
</html>
```

Discussion

JavaScript has used a number of module systems over the years, most notably with Node and npm. But since ES6, JavaScript has had its own module standard, which is supported natively in all modern browsers.

Before you create a solution with modules, there are a few considerations you should know:

- Browser security restrictions mean that you can't run a module example from the local filesystem. Instead, you need to host your example on a development web server (as described in Recipe 1.9).

- Modules are locked into their own distinct "module" scope. You can't access a module from a normal nonmodule script. Similarly, you can't access modules from the developer console.

- You can't access modules from the HTML of your page. That means you can't wire up an event handler using an HTML attribute like onclick, for example, because the page won't be able to access an event handler that's inside a module. Instead, your module code needs to reach *out* to the surrounding browser context using window or document.

- Modules are automatically executed in strict mode (Recipe 1.4).

Module features can only be imported into another module. If you want to create a <script> block for a module in a web page, make sure you set the type attribute to module, or the module importing feature won't work:

```
<script type="module">
```

When you import functionality from a module, you must specify the file path of the module in the from part of the import statement. Modules support a convenient shortcut that lets you start relative paths with ./, so ./lengthConverterModule.js points to the *lengthConverterModule.js* file in the current folder:

```
import {Units, LengthConverter} from './lengthConverterModule.js';
```

There's quite a bit of flexibility in the naming you use when you import module features. You can wrap your imports in a *module object*, which is a special sort of container that namespaces everything. Here's an example that imports every exported type into a module object named LConvert:

```
import * as LConvert from './lengthConverterModule.js';

// Now you can access LengthConverter as LConvert.LengthConverter
```

Notice that no curly brackets are required when using module objects.

You can also set a *default* export in your module:

```
export default LengthConverter
```

And then you can import it using any name:

```
import LConvert from './lengthConverterModule.js';
```

The default export feature matches similar functionality in other module systems. That makes it easier for those modules to be migrated into the ES6 modules standard.

It's likely that ES6 modules will eventually become the dominant module standard in JavaScript. But today, the implementation of ES modules in npm is still a bit rough around the edges. For the foreseeable future, that means developers will be juggling at least two module standards: the ES6 standard that's recognized natively by modern browsers, and the older CommonJS standard that's mature and well-established in the Node and npm ecosystem.

See Also

For information on using CommonJS modules with Node and npm, see Chapter 18.

## CHAPTER 9

Asynchronous Programming

JavaScript was built as a single-threaded programming language, with one call stack, one memory heap, and able to execute just one code routine at a time. But over the years, JavaScript has grown. It's acquired the ability to send network messages, read files, and wait for user confirmation—all operations that might take time and could lock up the user interface. To handle these operations safely, JavaScript has introduced its own asynchronous programming patterns.

In the early days, JavaScript's asynchronous support revolved around *callbacks*. With a callback, you request an operation (say, fetching an image from the web) and the browser does the work on another thread, outside of your application code. When the image has finished downloading and your application is idle, JavaScript triggers your callback and passes the data back to your code. The end result is that your application code is still single-threaded, but you have the ability to launch asynchronous work through a set of standardized web APIs.

Callbacks are still found all over JavaScript, but in recent years they've been wrapped with more polished language features, like *promises* and the `async` and `await` keywords. The underlying plumbing is the same, but now it's possible to create sophisticated applications that manage concurrent asynchronous tasks, handle sequences of asynchronous calls, and deal gracefully with unexpected errors.

In this chapter, you'll use callback and promises to manage asynchronous tasks. You'll also see how you can break out of JavaScript's single-threaded model and perform continuous background work with the Web Worker API.

9.1 Updating the Page During a Loop

Problem

You want to update the page during a long, CPU-intensive operation, but the browser won't repaint the window while it's busy.

Solution

Use the `setTimeout()` function periodically to queue your work. Contrary to the name, you don't need to set a delay with `setTimeout()`. Instead, use a timeout value of 0 to schedule the next step in your operation to execute immediately, as soon as the UI thread is idle.

For example, consider this loop, which increments a counter for 10 seconds (10,000 milliseconds). After each pass through the loop, it attempts to change the text in a `<p>` element named `status`:

```
function doWork() {
  // Get the <p> element to change
  const statusElement = document.getElementById('status');

  // Track the time and the number of passes through the loop
  const startTime = Date.now();
  let counter = 0;

  statusElement.innerText = 'Processing started';

  while ((Date.now() - startTime < 10000)) {
    counter += 1;
    statusElement.innerText = `Just generated number ${counter}`;
  }

  statusElement.innerText = 'Processing completed';
}
```

If you run this code, you won't see any of the "Just generated number" messages. Instead, the page will become unresponsive for 10 seconds, then display "Processing completed."

To fix the problem, you move the work (in this case, incrementing the counter and showing a message) to a separate function. Then, instead of calling this function over and over again in a loop, you call it with `setTimeout()`. Each time, the function increments the counter, updates the page, and then calls `setTimeout()` for *another* pass, until the 10-second time limit has finished:

```
function doWorkInChunks() {
  // Get the <p> element to change
  const statusElement = document.getElementById("status");
```

```
// Track the time and the number of passes through the loop
const startTime = Date.now();
let counter = 0;

statusElement.innerText = 'Processing started';

// Create an anonymous function that does one chunk of work
const doChunkedTask = () => {
  if (Date.now() - startTime < 10000) {
    counter += 1;
    statusElement.innerText = `Just generated number ${counter}`;

    // Call the function again, for the next chunk
    setTimeout(doChunkedTask, 0);
  }
  else {
    statusElement.innerText = 'Processing completed';
  }
};

// Start the process by calling the function for the first time
doChunkedTask();
}
```

Here, the doChunkedTask variable holds an anonymous function that's defined with arrow function syntax (Recipe 6.2). You don't need to use an anonymous function or arrow syntax, but it simplifies the code. The doChunkedTask function gets access to everything that's in scope when you create it, including the startTime and statusEle ment variables. As a result, you don't need to worry about passing this information to the function, which would be necessary if you declared it separately.

When you run this code, you'll see the numbers quickly flash by in the paragraph on the web page, and then be replaced with the completion message after 10 seconds.

Discussion

JavaScript has a mature solution for asynchronous work with the *web workers* feature (see Recipe 9.7). However, you don't always need this level of sophistication. Web workers are great if you have a long-running task, an asynchronous operation that needs to accept chunks of data as it works, or an asynchronous operation that needs support for cancellation. But if you're dealing with a relatively short task and you have more modest requirements—for example, you just want to update the page during a brief burst of CPU-intensive work—the setTimeout() approach works perfectly well.

In the example presented here, the setTimeout() method is called repeatedly. Each time, the page relinquishes control and waits for the browser to schedule the requested function, which it does as soon as the main application thread is idle (in this case, almost instantaneously). To understand how this works, it's important to realize that `setTimeout()` does not set *exactly* when a function will run. Instead, it sets a *minimum* time interval. When the `setTimeout()` timer ends, it asks the browser to execute the function, but it's up to the browser to schedule this request. If the browser is busy, the request will be delayed. (In fact, even if the browser isn't busy, modern browsers throttle a sequence of requests so it is never triggered more frequently than once every 4 milliseconds.) But in practice these delays are very small, and calling `setTimeout()` with a value of 0 milliseconds causes your code to be triggered almost immediately.

The `setTimeout()` method isn't the only method JavaScript has for scheduling work with a timer. There's also the `window.setInterval()` method, which calls a function repeatedly, with a fixed wait time before each subsequent call. And if you want to use a timer to create an animation (for example, by redrawing objects in a `<canvas>`), it's better to use `requestAnimationFrame()`, which synchronizes itself with the browser's repainting operations to make sure you don't waste resources calculating an animation more frequently that it can be shown.

 Both the `setTimeout()` and the `setInterval()` methods are ancient parts of JavaScript. However, they are not obsolete or deprecated. For more complex scenarios, you should web workers rather than roll your own custom solutions built on `setTimeout()` or `setInterval()`. However, both methods are still acceptable.

See Also

Recipe 9.7 describes how to carry out more ambitious operations in the background using web workers.

9.2 Using a Function That Returns a Promise

Problem

You want to run code when an asynchronous task completes (successfully or unsuccessfully). You want to be notified about task completion through a `Promise` object.

Solution

A `Promise` is an object that helps you manage an asynchronous task. It tracks the status of the task and—most importantly—handles the callbacks that notify your code when the task succeeds or fails. Technically, promises don't add new functionality to JavaScript, but they do make it easier to cleanly coordinate a sequence of asynchronous operations.

In order to use promises, the API you're calling must support them. There's rarely any ambiguity about this, because APIs that support promises have methods that return Promise objects. Older APIs that *don't* use promises will ask you to supply one or more callback functions or handle a specific event. (If you want to use a promise with a callback-based API, see Recipe 9.3 instead.)

To specify what should happen after a promise finishes, you call Promise.then() and supply a function. To specify what should happen in the case of an error, you call Promise.catch() and supply a different function. To add some clean-up code that should run after the promise has succeeded *or* failed, you call Promise.finally() with a third function.

Here's a naïve implementation of promises, using the Fetch API:

```
// Create the promise
const promise = fetch(
  'https://upload.wikimedia.org/wikipedia/commons/b/b2/Eagle_nebula_pillars.jpg');

// Supply a function that logs successful requests
promise.then( function onSuccess(response) {
  console.log(`HTTP status: ${response.status}`);
});

// Supply a function that logs errors
promise.catch( function onError(error) {
  console.error(`Error: ${error}`);
});

// Supply a function that runs either way
promise.finally( function onFinally() {
  console.log('All done');
});
```

If the call succeeds, you'll see the HTTP status appear in the console window, followed by the "All done" message.

This example shows the structure of a basic promise call, but it isn't the way we typically write promise-based code, for two reasons. First, for more compact and readable code, we favor declaring the functions with arrow function syntax (Recipe 6.2). Second, the then(), catch(), and finally() methods are usually chained into one statement. This is possible because these methods all return the same Promise object.

Here's the more compact and more typical way to write this code:

```
fetch(
  'https://upload.wikimedia.org/wikipedia/commons/b/b2/Eagle_nebula_pillars.jpg')
.then(response => {
  console.log(`HTTP status: ${response.status}`);
})
.catch(error => {
```

```
    console.error(`Error: ${error}`);
})
.finally(() => {
  console.log('All done');
});
```

 This promise-based example uses just a single statement, and you're able to break the line wherever you like. One common convention, which we've used here, is to break the statement just *before* the dot operator, so the next line begins with `.then` or `.catch`. This way, the code is easy to follow and has an error-handling layout that's similar to synchronous code. This is also the structure applied by the Prettier code formatter (Recipe 1.11).

Discussion

A `Promise` object is not a result, but a *placeholder* for a result that will be available in the future.

As soon as you create a `Promise` object, its code begins to execute. It's even possible that the `Promise` may finish its work before you call `then()` or `catch()`. This won't change how your code works. If you call `then()` on a promise that's already resolved (successfully), or `catch()` on a promise that's already rejected (with an error), your code runs right away.

The simple solution shown here uses chaining to attach a success function (with `then()`) and a failure function (with `catch()`). However, it's also common to use chaining to tie multiple asynchronous tasks together, so they run one after the other. The `fetch()` function provides a good example. It returns a promise that resolves once the server responds. However, if you want to read the body of this message, you need to start a second asynchronous operation. (This sounds needlessly painful, but it makes perfect sense, because the amount of data being sent could be huge, so you don't want to risk blocking your code while you retrieve it. In JavaScript, I/O operations are always asynchronous.)

Here's an example that performs an asynchronous `fetch` request, then reads the results as a binary stream using `response.blob()`, which returns a second `Promise` object. Now `then()` is called on that object to add a third step—turning the binary data into a Base64-encoded string that can be shown in an `<img>` element:

```
fetch(
  'https://upload.wikimedia.org/wikipedia/commons/b/b2/Eagle_nebula_pillars.jpg')
.then(response => response.blob())
.then(blob => {
  const img = document.getElementById('imgDownload');
  img.src = URL.createObjectURL(blob);
});
```

Good code formatting is important, because a promise chain can become quite long. But if organized consistently, your asynchronous calls can look similar to a linear block of code, which is a significant improvement over the past, when developers coined the term *callback hell* to describe nested pyramids of consecutive callback functions.

When chaining multiple promises, you call `catch()` and `finally()` at the end of the chain, if you decide to use them. That gives you one place to collect unhandled errors that occur during any stage of the promise chain. You can even throw your own exceptions in a `then()` function to signify failure and end the chain:

```
fetch(
 'https://upload.wikimedia.org/wikipedia/commons/b/b2/Eagle_nebula_pillars.jpg')
.then(response => {
  if (!response.ok) {
    // Ordinarily, it's not an error if the server responds to our request
    // Now, let's treat any response other than HTTP 200 OK as an error
    throw new Error(`HTTP code: ${response.status}`);
  }
  else {
    return response.blob();
  }
})
.then(blob => {
  const img = document.getElementById('imgDownload');
  img.src = URL.createObjectURL(blob);
})
.catch(error => {
  console.log('An error occurred in the first or second promise');
});
```

As soon as an unhandled error occurs, the entire promise chain is derailed. You can react to this error to perform logging or some other diagnostic task, but you can't resume the promises that were abandoned further down the chain. If you don't catch an error in a promise, it's eventually raised as the `window.unhandledrejection` event and, if not canceled there, it's logged to the console.

See Also

Chapter 13 explains the Fetch API in more detail. Recipe 9.4 shows how to link concurrent tasks with a promise. Recipe 9.5 shows how to use `fetch()` with the `await` keyword.

9.3 Promisifying an Asynchronous Function That Uses a Callback

Problem

You want to change a callback-based asynchronous function to use a promise.

Solution

Create another function to wrap your asynchronous function. This function creates and returns a new Promise object. When the asynchronous task finishes, the function calls either Promise.resolve() if it succeeded or Promise.reject() if it failed.

Here's an example of a function that acts like a traditional, callback-based asynchronous function. It uses a timer to perform its asynchronous work:

```
function factorializeNumber(number, successCallback, failureCallback) {
  if (number < 0) {
    failureCallback(
      new Error('Factorials are only defined for positive numbers'));
  }
  else if (number !== Math.trunc(number)) {
    failureCallback(new Error('Factorials are only defined for integers'));
  }
  else {
    setTimeout( () => {
      if (number === 0 || number === 1) {
        successCallback(1);
      }
      else {
        let result = number;
        while (number > 1) {
          number -= 1;
          result *= number;
        }
        successCallback(result);
      }
    }, 5000);  // This hard-coded 5-second delay simulates a long async process
  }
}
```

There's no benefit to calculating factorials asynchronously or to using a timer. This example is just a stand-in for any older API that uses callbacks.

Right now, you can use the factorializeNumber() function like this:

```
function logResult(result) {
  console.log(`5! = ${result}`);
}
```

```
function logError(error) {
  console.log(`Error: ${error.message}`);
}

factorializeNumber(5, logResult, logError);
```

The easiest way to promisify the `factorializeNumber()` function is to create a new function that wraps it:

```
function factorializeNumberPromise(number) {
  return new Promise((resolve, reject) => {
    factorializeNumber(number,
      result => {
        resolve(result);
      },
      error => {
        reject(error);
      });
  });
}
```

Now you can call `factorializeNumberPromise()`, receive a `Promise` object, and handle the result with `Promise.then()`:

```
factorializeNumberPromise(5)
.then( result => {
  console.log(`5! = ${result}`);
});
```

You can also catch potential errors, and even create a whole chain of asynchronous operations.

```
factorializeNumberPromise('Bad value')
.then( result => {
  console.log(`6! = ${result}`);
})
.catch( error => {
  console.log(error);
});
```

Discussion

Before going deeper into this solution, it's important to address one possible misconception right away. It's easy to create a function that returns a `Promise` object. However, this does *not* make your code asynchronous. Your code will run synchronously on the UI thread, as usual. (It's similar to calling `setTimeout()` with a delay of 0.)

To get around this limitation, the `factorializeNumber()` example uses a timer to simulate an asynchronous API. If you really want to run your own code in the background on another thread, you need to use the Web Workers API (Recipe 9.7).

In JavaScript you'll use promises often, but you'll create them rarely. The most common reason for creating a Promise object is because you're wrapping older callback-based code, as in this example.

To make a promisified version of a function, you need a function that creates a Promise object and returns it. That's the main job of the factorializeNumberPro mise() function. And although creating a Promise is easy, it can look complex at first because there are two layers of nested functions at work. t its heart, the Promise object wraps a function that has this structure:

```
function(resolve, reject) {
  ...
}
```

The promise function receives two parameters, which are essentially callback functions. You use these functions to signal the completion of the promise. Call resolve() (with your return value) to successfully end the promise, or reject() (with an error object) to indicate a failure. Alternately, if an unhandled error occurs anywhere in your promise function, the Promise object will catch it and automatically call reject(), passing the error along.

Inside the promise function, you launch your asynchronous task. Or, in the factoria lizeNumberPromise() example, you call the existing factorializeNumber() function that starts the timer. You still need to use the callback functions to interface with the old factorializeNumber() function. The difference is that now you will forward them through the promise by calling resolve() or reject(). For example, here's the function for the successCallback, which calls resolve():

```
function(resolve, reject) {
  factorializeNumber(number,
    function successCallback(result) {
      resolve(result);
    },
    ...
  );
}
```

And here's the failure callback that calls reject():

```
function(resolve, reject) {
  factorializeNumber(number,
    function successCallback(result) {
      resolve(result);
    },
    function failureCallback(error) {
      reject(error);
    });
```

```
  );
}
```

 The `Promise.reject()` method takes one argument, which represents the reason for the failure. This reason can be any type of object, but it's strongly recommended that you use an instance of the `Error` object or a custom object that derives from `Error` (Recipe 10.6). In the current example, the failure callback already sends an `Error` object, so we can simply pass that to `reject()`.

The full solution makes the code more compact by declaring the `successCallback`, the `failureCallback`, and the promise function that holds them with arrow syntax (Recipe 6.2).

It is possible to write a generic promisifying function that can promisify any callback-based function. In fact, some libraries, like BlueBird.js, provide this functionality. However, in most cases it's simpler and less confusing to use promisification judiciously—for example, when you want to unify one asynchronous task with another one that already uses promises—rather than attempt to wrap every old asynchronous API.

See Also

If you're developing for the Node runtime environment, you can use the `promisify` utility to wrap a function with a promise, as described in Recipe 19.2.

9.4 Executing Multiple Promises Concurrently

Problem

You want to execute multiple promises at the same time, and react once all the promises have finished their work.

Solution

Use the static `Promise.all()` method to combine multiple promises into a single promise and wait for them all to resolve successfully (or for any one of them to fail).

To demonstrate how this works, imagine you have a function that returns a promise that resolves after a wait of roughly 0 to 10 seconds. Here's a `randomWaitPromise()` function that does exactly that using `setTimeout()`. Treat it as a stand-in for any asynchronous operation:

```
function randomWaitPromise() {
  return new Promise((resolve, reject) => {
```

```
  // Decide how long to wait
  const waitMilliseconds = Math.round(Math.random() * 10000);

  // Simulate an asynchronous task with setTimeout()
  setTimeout(() => {
    console.log(`Resolved after ${waitMilliseconds}`);

    // Return the number of seconds waited
    resolve(waitMilliseconds);
  }, waitMilliseconds);
 });
}
```

Now you can use `randomWaitPromise()` to quickly create any number of new promises. To wait for several promises to finish, you need to place all the `Promise` objects in an array, and pass that array to the `Promise.all()` method. `Promise.all()` returns a new promise that represents the completion of all your promises. Using that, you can call `then()` and `catch()` to build a promise chain, like usual:

```
// Create three promises
const promise1 = randomWaitPromise();
const promise2 = randomWaitPromise();
const promise3 = randomWaitPromise();
const promises = [promise1, promise2, promise3];

// Wait for all of them, then log the result
Promise.all(promises).then(values => {
  console.log(`All done with: ${values}`);
});
```

There's no `Promise.catch()` in this chain, because it's impossible for this code to fail.

When you run this example, each promise will write to the console as it finishes. When the last, slowest promise resolves, you'll get the final "All done" message:

```
Resolved after 790
Resolved after 4329
Resolved after 6238
All done with: 790,6238,4329
```

 When you're using several promises at a time, it's common to pass an object with some sort of identifier to your promise (like a URL or an ID). Then, when the promise resolves it can pass back an object that includes this identifying detail. This way, you can determine which result goes with which promise. This tracking is convenient, but it isn't necessary, because you can tell which result is which by their order. The order of the results that you receive in the results array matches the order of the promises that you submitted originally in the promises array.

Discussion

One advantage of asynchronous programming is being able to collapse your wait time. In other words, rather than wait for one task to complete, and then another, and then another, you can start all three at once. In real life, this is somewhat of a specialized scenario. It's far more common to have an asynchronous task that depends on the results from another asynchronous task, in which case you need to chain one task after the other. But if this isn't the case, you can save considerable time by running multiple promises at once and waiting for them with `Promise.all()`.

`Promise.all()` uses a *fail-fast* behavior. As soon as one of the promises is rejected (either deliberately by calling `Promise.reject()` or with an unhandled error), the combined promise you created with `Promise.all()` is also rejected, triggering whatever function you attached to the promise chain with `Promise.catch()`. The other promises will still run, and you can get their results from the corresponding `Promise` objects. For example, if `promise1` rejects, nothing stops you from calling `promise2.then()` to get its result. But in practice, when you use `Promise.all()` you will probably treat a failure in one promise as the end of your combined operation. Otherwise, it would be easier to keep your promises separate, or use one of the alternative `Promise` methods listed below.

There are other static `Promise` methods besides `all()` that accept multiple promises and return a single combined promise. They all have slightly different behavior:

`Promise.allSettled()`
: Resolves when every promise has been resolved *or* rejected. (This is unlike `Promise.all()`, which only resolves if *all* the promises are successful.) The function you attach with `Promise.then()` receives an array of result objects, one for each promise. Each result object has two properties: `status` indicates if the promise was fulfilled or rejected, and `value` has the returned value or error object.

`Promise.any()`
: Resolves as soon as one promise has resolved successfully. It provides the value for that promise only.

`Promise.race()`
: Resolves as soon as one promise has resolved successfully or been rejected. It's the most specialized of all the `Promise` methods, but it can be used to build some sort of custom scheduling system that queues up new asynchronous tasks as existing ones are finished.

9.5 Waiting for a Promise to Finish with Await and Async

Problem

Instead of creating a promise chain, you want to write linear logic that's easier to read and looks more like synchronous code.

Solution

Don't call `Promise.then()`. Instead, use the `await` keyword on your promise:

```
console.log('taskPromise is working asynchronously');
await taskPromise;
console.log('taskPromise has finished');
```

The code after `await` doesn't run until the awaited promise has been resolved or rejected. The execution of your code pauses, but without blocking the thread, locking up the UI, or preventing other timers and events from triggering.

But there's a catch. The `await` keyword is only useable inside an `async` function. That means you may need some rearranging to use `await`. Consider the `fetch()` example from Recipe 9.2. With promises, it looks like this:

```
const url =
 'https://upload.wikimedia.org/wikipedia/commons/b/b2/Eagle_nebula_pillars.jpg';

fetch(url)
.then(response => {
  // The fetch operation has completed
  console.log(`HTTP status: ${response.status}`);
  console.log('All asynchronous steps completed');
})
```

With the `async` and `await` keywords, you can structure it like this:

```
async function getImage() {
  const url =
'https://upload.wikimedia.org/wikipedia/commons/b/b2/Eagle_nebula_pillars.jpg';

  const response = await fetch(url);

  // The fetch operation has completed and the promise is resolved or rejected
  console.log(`HTTP status: ${response.status}`);
}

getImage().then(() => {
  console.log('All asynchronous steps completed');
});
```

You can also use traditional exception-catching blocks around awaited operations, instead of the `Promise.catch()` method:

```
async function getImage() {
  const url =
'https://upload.wikimedia.org/wikipedia/commons/b/b2/Eagle_nebula_pillars.jpg';

  try {
    const response = await fetch(url);
    console.log(`HTTP status: ${response.status}`);
  }
  catch(err) {
    console.error(`Error: ${error}`);
  }
  finally {
    console.log('All done');
  }
}
```

The advantage of using `await` for just one call is relatively small. However, `await` can make your code considerably cleaner if you have a whole sequence of asynchronous operations that need to occur one after the other. Ordinarily, you would handle this with a promise chain that calls `Promise.then()` multiple times. But with `await`, the code looks like ordinary synchronous code. Here's an example that duplicates the image-reading example from Recipe 9.2 to send an asynchronous web request, and then asynchronously read the image data that's returned:

```
async function getImage() {
  const url =
    'https://upload.wikimedia.org/wikipedia/commons/b/b2/Eagle_nebula_pillars.jpg';

  // Wait (asynchronously) for the response
  const response = await fetch(url);

  if (response.ok) {
    // Wait (asynchronously) for the blob to be read
    const blob = await response.blob();

    // Now show the image
    const img = document.getElementById('imgDownload');
    img.src = URL.createObjectURL(blob);
  }
}
```

Discussion

The `await` keyword handles promises in a way that looks like synchronous code, but doesn't lock up your application. Consider a statement like this:

```
const response = await fetch(url);
```

From the point of view of your code, it's as though execution stops and the `fetch()` function becomes synchronous. But in reality, JavaScript takes the remainder of your function and attaches it to the promise returned by `fetch()`, just as if you passed it to

Promise.then(). As a result, the rest of your code is *scheduled* and the UI thread isn't blocked. Your application is free to handle other events and timers while it waits for the fetch operation to finish.

The await keyword only works in an async function. You can't use await in the top level of web page code. Instead, you need to create a new async function to hold it, like the getImage() function in this example:

```
async function getImage() {
  ...
}
```

Now that getImage() is an async function, it will automatically return a Promise object. You attach the code that runs when getImage() finishes using Promise.then(), as you would with any promise chain.

If you forget that getImage() is an asynchronous function, you might call it but forget to use the promise. This is a common mistake by developers who are new to async and await:

```
// This probably isn't right, because you're discarding the Promise object
getImage();
```

Instead, you need to accept the Promise object returned by getImage(), and call then() and catch() to attach the code that should run next, and your error-handling code, respectively:

```
getImage()
.then(response => {
  console.log('Image download finished');
})
.catch(error => {
  console.error(`Error: ${error}`);
});
```

You might wonder why you're dealing with a promise when the async and await keywords are supposed to save you from that effort. The answer is that you always need to manage the root-level Promise object that starts your asynchronous operation.

 There's one relatively recent exception. You can use await in the top-level code of a module (see Recipe 8.9). If you use this ability, make sure you place the statement that uses await inside a try...catch exception-handling block to catch any unhandled errors.

The await keyword becomes more useful when you need to perform multiple asynchronous operations and make decisions along the way. For example, imagine you need to write code that waits for an asynchronous task to finish, evaluates its result, and then decides what task to launch next. You can implement this pattern with promises, but the logic is harder to follow. With `await`, it's organized like traditional synchronous code:

```
const step1 = await someAsyncTask();

if (step1 === someResult) {
  const step2 = await differentAsyncTask();
  ...
}
else {
  const step2 = await anotherAsyncTask();
  ...
}
```

Given that this code looks so clean and straightforward, you might wonder why you *wouldn't* use `await`. Like all abstractions, `await` hides some details of the underlying `Promise` object and makes certain situations more difficult. For example, it's a common mistake with `await` to wait for a series of actions to complete one after another with separate `await` statements, when what you really want is to launch all of them at once. Here's a demonstration of the problem:

```
const response1 = await slowFunction(dataObject1);
const response2 = await slowFunction(dataObject2);
const response3 = await slowFunction(dataObject3);
```

You could solve this situation with `Promise.all()` (as described in Recipe 9.4). But that's not necessary. You can still use `await`, as long as you make sure all the promises are started first. Here's a correction:

```
const promise1 = slowFunction(dataObject1);
const promise2 = slowFunction(dataObject2);
const promise3 = slowFunction(dataObject3);

const response1 = await promise1;
const response2 = await promise2;
const response3 = await promise3;
```

This works because a promise starts running code as soon as it is created. By the time the code has assigned `promise1`, `promise2`, and `promise3`, all three asynchronous processes are underway. And although `await` is often used with a function that returns a promise, it works on any `Promise` object.

It also doesn't matter which promise you wait for first, because you can safely use `await` on a promise that's already completed. No matter what you do, you won't get past this section of your code until each promise is resolved or rejected. (Technically, that means this code follows the same behavior as `Promise.allSettled()` rather than `Promise.all()`, because the code keeps waiting for *all* the promises to be dealt with, even if one of them has failed.)

9.6 Creating an Asynchronous Generator Function

Problem

You want to create a generator for an operation that returns values asynchronously.

Solution

Use the `async` keyword with the specialized generator function syntax shown in Recipe 6.7.

Consider this exceedingly simple generator that yields a never-ending sequence of random numbers:

```
function* getRandomIntegers(max) {
  while (true) {
    yield Math.floor(Math.random() * Math.floor(max) + 1);
  }
}
```

Which you call like this:

```
const randomGenerator = getRandomIntegers(6);

// Get 10 random values between 1 and 6
for (let i=0; i<10; i++) {
  console.log(randomGenerator.next());
}
```

To make the generator asynchronous, you simply add the `async` keyword, exactly as you do with an ordinary function:

```
async function* getRandomIntegers(max) {
  while (true) {
    yield Math.floor(Math.random() * Math.floor(max) + 1);
  }
}
```

And as with any other `async` function, an asynchronous generator function will not yield direct results. Instead, it will yield `Promise` objects that wrap the results. You can call `Promise.then()` to get the result, when it's ready. Here's an example that shows what's happening:

```
const randomGenerator = getRandomIntegers(6);

// Get 10 random values between 1 and 6
for (let i=0; i<10; i++) {
  const promise = randomGenerator.next();
  console.log('Received promise.');
  promise.then(result => console.log(`Received result: ${result.value}`));
}
```

When you run this, you'll see a list of "Received promise" messages, immediately followed by the list of results.

Often, asynchronous generators are combined with the await keyword. A common shortcut is the for await loop, which waits to request new values from the generator until the previous promise has resolved. Here's an example that uses this technique to search for random numbers, one number at a time:

```
// This function uses a for await loop to perform consecutive awaits
async function searchRandomNumbers(searchNumber, generator) {
  for await (const value of generator) {
    console.log(value);
    if (value === searchNumber) return;
  }
}

// Use the searchRandomNumbers() function to generate random numbers
// from 1 to 100, asynchronously, until we find 42
const randomGenerator = getRandomIntegers(100);
searchRandomNumbers(42, randomGenerator).then(result => {
  console.log('Number found');
});
```

You'll notice that the code that uses the asynchronous iterator is now itself wrapped in an async function. This is because you can't use await in top-level code (as explained in Recipe 9.5).

Discussion

Generator functions provide a streamlined way to return on-demand values. After each yield statement, JavaScript pauses the generator function. But the context around it (all the local variables and passed-in arguments) is preserved until the next value is requested by the calling code.

The example in the solution doesn't do any real asynchronous work, and the random numbers are available immediately. You could simulate an asynchronous process in this example by adding a timeout. But it's more interesting to consider an example that shows asynchronous generators using a true asynchronous API.

Asynchronous generators are most useful for tasks that access an external resource and have some latency. For example, you might see them in web request or filestream APIs. Here's a generator that uses the Fetch API to retrieve its list of random numbers from a web service:

```
async function* getRandomWebIntegers(max) {
  // Construct a URL to get a random number in the requested range
  const url = https://www.random.org/integers/?num=1&min=1&max=' + max +
  '&col=1&base=10&format=plain&rnd=new';
```

```
    while (true) {
      // Start the request (and wait asynchronously for the response)
      const response = await fetch(url);

      // Start reading the text asynchronously
      const text = await response.text();

      // Yield the result and wait for the next request
      yield Number(text);
    }
  }
```

Now, each time the calling code requests a value, the generator starts an asynchronous `fetch()` operation and returns a promise. When `fetch()` finishes, the promise resolves. The calling code could start several asynchronous calls at once by calling `next()` multiple times on the generator. But it's much more common to use a `for await` loop to go one-by-one. Either way, there's no need to change the code from what was used in the original solution. If you run this version of the example, you'll see that each random number takes a short but measurable delay before it appears in the developer console.

See Also

Recipe 6.7 explains how to create nonasynchronous generators. Recipe 9.5 explains how to create ordinary asynchronous functions.

9.7 Using a Web Worker to Perform a Background Task

Problem

You want long-running code to execute on a separate thread, so it doesn't block the user interface.

Solution

Use the Web Worker API. You create a `Worker` object, which runs all its code on a background thread. Although the `Worker` object is isolated from the rest of your code (it can't access the DOM, the page, or any global variables, for instance), you can communicate with it by sending messages back and forth.

Figure 9-1 shows an example page that calculates all the prime numbers in a given range. Because the page uses web workers, the interface remains responsive while the job is underway. For example, it's still possible to type in the text boxes or click the Cancel button.

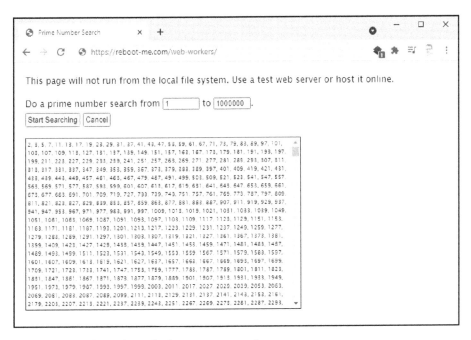

Figure 9-1. A web worker calculates prime numbers

The Start button triggers a function called `startSearch()`. It creates a new worker, attaches functions to handle the `Worker.error` and `Worker.message` events, and finally starts the operation by calling `Worker.postMessage()`. Here's the relevant code in the script for the web page:

```
// Keep a reference to the worker so we can cancel it, if needed
let worker;

function startSearch() {
  // Create the worker
  worker = new Worker('prime-worker.js');

  const statusDisplay = document.getElementById('status');
  statusDisplay.textContent = 'Search started.';

  // Report error message on the page
  worker.onerror = error => {
    statusDisplay.textContent = error.message;
  };

  // Respond to messages from the worker, and display the final result
  // (the list of primes) on the page when it's received
  worker.onmessage = event => {
    const primes = event.data;
```

```
      document.getElementById('primeContainer').textContent = primes.join(', ');
    };

    // Get the search range and tell the worker to start
    const fromNumber = document.getElementById('from').value;
    const toNumber = document.getElementById('to').value;
    worker.postMessage({from: fromNumber, to: toNumber});
  }
```

The `prime-worker.js` file contains the code that the web worker runs. That includes a `findPrimes()` function (not shown here) which holds the logic for finding prime numbers using the Sieve of Eratosthenes (*https://oreil.ly/6CyO9*). The prime-worker.js file also handles the `Worker.message` event, which is triggered whenever the page calls `Worker.postMessage()`. In this example, the page calls `postMessage()` to send the range of numbers to the worker and begin the search:

```
// This is the code the worker uses to handle messages from the page
onmessage = (event) => {
  // Get the sent object from event.data and call the time-consuming
  // findPrimes() method to do the search
  const primes = findPrimes(Number(event.data.from), Number(event.data.to));

  // Send back the result
  postMessage(primes);
};
```

The only remaining ingredient is the event handler for the Cancel button, which shuts down the web worker, even if it's in the middle of its search:

```
function cancelSearch() {
  // Cancel the worker, provided the page has created it
  if (worker) worker.terminate();
}
```

Discussion

Ordinarily, the JavaScript code you write runs on a single application thread. JavaScript uses a scheduling system that's based on an event loop. It continually watches for events, listens to timer ticks, and waits for callbacks from asynchronous APIs. When it receives functions to run, it queues them up in the order they arrive. If you decide to write CPU-intensive code (like performing time-consuming calculations), you'll tie up the main thread and prevent other functions from running until your work is finished.

You may be confused about how ordinary JavaScript code is single-threaded, but JavaScript provides certain APIs (like fetch) that are able to work asynchronously. This is because these APIs are provided by services in the browser and, ultimately, the operating system. They go outside of the JavaScript environment. For example, web requests made with fetch() are made on a separate thread, not the main application thread used for your application.

The Web Worker API gives you a way to escape JavaScript's single-threaded execution model. With web workers, you are able to run code concurrently, on a separate thread from the main application user interface. To ensure that you don't have to deal with messy problems like thread safety, race conditions, and locks, web workers are kept in a separate execution context. They can't interact with a web page, the browser window, or the rest of your code. To emphasize this fact, the Worker object asks that you put your web worker code in a separate file, which you then supply when you create the worker:

```
worker = new Worker('prime-worker.js');
```

Once you understand this limitation, the rest of the web worker model is quite intuitive. All the communication between the application and a worker happens through message passing. To send a message, you call postMessage(). In the prime number example, the page sends an object literal with two properties, to and from, to represent the search range:

```
worker.postMessage({from: fromNumber, to: toNumber});
```

When the worker responds, it calls postMessage() to send array of prime numbers:

```
postMessage(primes);
```

There's no limit to how often you can send messages. For example, you could create a worker, call postMessage() to send it some work, leave it idle for a while, and then call postMessage() to send it more work. Web workers can also use the setTime out() and setInterval() functions to schedule periodic work.

There are two ways to stop a worker. First, a worker can stop itself by calling close(). More commonly, the page that created the worker will shut it down by calling worker.terminate(). Once a worker is stopped in this way, it can't be resurrected.

See Also

To see the full code, including the prime number search routine, refer to the book's sample code (*https://github.com/javascripteverywhere/cookbook*). For a revised version of this example that uses more sophisticated message passing, see Recipe 9.8.

9.8 Adding Progress Support to a Web Worker

Problem

You want your web worker to report progress while it's running a task.

Solution

You can use the standard message-passing behavior of your worker. Use a property of your message object to distinguish between different types of messages.

For example, consider a version of the prime number example (from Recipe 9.8) that sends two types of messages: progress notifications (while the work is underway) and the prime number list (when the work is finished).

To allow the application to tell the difference between these two types of messages, it adds a string `messageType` property, which it sets to either `"Progress"` or `"PrimeList"`. Here's the rewritten code to return the result:

```
onmessage = function(event) {
  // Perform the prime number search.
  const primes = findPrimes(Number(event.data.from), Number(event.data.to));

  // Send back the results.
  postMessage(
    {messageType: "PrimeList", data: primes}
  );
};
```

Now the prime-number calculation code also needs to use `postMessage()` to report on its progress. It uses a rate-limiting check to round the progress to the nearest percent, and to make sure it doesn't notify about the same progress more than once:

```
function findPrimes(fromNumber, toNumber) {
  // Prepare the prime number search range
  ...

  // This is the loop that searches for primes
  for (let i = 0; i < list.length; i+=1) {

    // Check if the current number is prime
    ...

    // Calculate and report the progress
    var progress = Math.round(i/list.length*100);

    // Only send a progress update if the progress has changed at least 1%
    if (progress !== previousProgress) {
      postMessage(
        {messageType: 'Progress', data: progress}
```

```
      );
      previousProgress = progress;
    }

  }

  // Clean up and return the list of prime numbers
  ...
}
```

When the page receives a message, it checks the `messageType` property to determine the type of message and then acts accordingly. If it's a prime list, it shows the results in the page. If it's a progress notification, it updates the progress text, as shown in Figure 9-2.

```
worker.onmessage = event => {
  const message = event.data;

  if (message.messageType === 'PrimeList') {
    const primes = message.data;
    document.getElementById('primeContainer').textContent = primes.join(', ');
  }
  else if (message.messageType === 'Progress') {
    statusDisplay.textContent = `${message.data} % done ...`;
  }
};
```

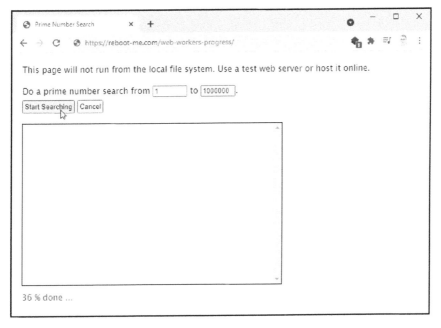

Figure 9-2. A web worker reports progress as it works

Discussion

To enforce thread safety, there's no way for an application and a web worker to interact except by passing messages. You can send any object you want as a message, as long as it can be serialized to JSON. It's much the same as when you're sending a message to a remote website.

You might decide to create your own custom class for messages to formalize the structure you're using. However, keep in mind that once the object is sent between threads, it will look exactly like an ordinary object literal. It won't have a custom prototype or any methods, and you won't be able to test its type with `instanceof`. Similarly, you might think of using the enumerated values trick from Recipe 7.13, but it won't work because the application and the worker can't share their symbols.

See Also

JavaScript also has two specialized APIs that build on the Web Worker API. You can used *shared workers* (*https://oreil.ly/jGV06*) if you want to interact with the same worker from different windows. And you can use more advanced *service workers* (*https://oreil.ly/vh3L3*) to create workers that, once installed, stay alive even when your page isn't open. The idea behind this API is to help you build caching, synchronization, and notification services that make a website behave more like a native app.

## CHAPTER 10

Errors and Testing

To write code is to write errors. Often, an error can be anticipated. Risky activities include actions that interact with outside resources (like files, databases, or web server APIs). Information that comes from outside your code—whether you're reading it from a web page form or receiving it from another library—may arrive with errors, or in a different form than you expect. But to modify a well-worn cliché, it's not so much the error as what you do with it that matters.

What should we do with our errors, then? JavaScript's default behavior is to die at the point of the error, quietly logging a stack trace to the console. However, better options are available. You can capture an error, react to it, modify it, rethrow it, and even hide it if you choose. Compared to many other languages, JavaScript's error-handling features are relatively underdeveloped. But basic error handling is still just as important, and many of the recipes in this chapter focus on that task.

Defending against errors is essential practice, but it's equally important to *prevent* them wherever possible. To that end, there are many testing frameworks that work with JavaScript, including Jest, Mocha, Jasmine, and Karma. With their help, you can write unit tests that guarantee your code is executing as expected. You'll take a quick look at Jest in this chapter.

10.1 Catching and Neutralizing an Error

Problem

You are performing a task that may not succeed, and you don't want an error to interrupt your code or appear in the developer console.

Solution

Wrap the section of your code in a `try...catch` block, like this one:

```
try {
  // This is guaranteed to fail with a URIError
  const uri = decodeURI('http%test');

  // We never get here
  console.log('Success!');
}
catch (error) {
  console.log(error);
}
```

When the `decodeURI()` function fails and an error occurs, execution jumps to the `catch` block. The catch block receives an error object (also known as an *exception*), which provides the following properties:

name
> A string that usually reflects the error subtype (as in "URIError"), but it may just be "Error."

message
> A string that gives you a human-language description of the problem, like "URI malformed."

stack
> A string that lists the currently open functions on the stack, in order, from the most recent calls to the earlier ones. Depending on the browser, the `stack` property may include information about the location of the function (such as line number and filename) and the arguments the functions were called with.

 Be careful. There are a few other properties defined on the error object (like `description` and `lineNumber`) that only work in specific browsers. Don't rely on these nonstandard properties when writing error-handling code, because they won't work on all browsers.

If you pass the error object directly to the `console.log()` method (as in this example), you'll get the information extracted from all three of these properties. It will look something like this, depending on the browser:

```
URIError: URI malformed
    at decodeURI (<anonymous>)
    at runTest (<anonymous>):14:15
    at <anonymous>:20:1
```

Here, a piece of top-level code written in the developer console (represented by the bottom `<anonymous>` in the call stack list) called a function named `runTest()`, which then used the code shown above to call `decodeURI()` with a bad URI, triggering the error that was then logged.

Solution

Before you test your error-handling code, you need a routine that can cause an error to occur. For this example, we don't want to consider syntax errors or any logical mistake that should realistically be caught when you're writing your code (perhaps using a linter, as described in Recipe 1.10). Instead, we want an operation that is *risky* because it relies on an outside resource and could fail due to no fault of your code.

JavaScript is unusually tolerant of usage that would be considered an error in many other programming languages. Attempting to access a property that doesn't exist gets an error-free value of `undefined`. The same is true if you go beyond the bounds of an array. JavaScript's error tolerance is particularly apparent with math, where nonsensical calculations like multiplying a number by a string returns an error-free value of `NaN` (not a number), and dividing by zero returns the special value `Infinity`. Attempting to use the `decodeURI()` function is an example of an operation that can fail, in this case with a `UriError`.

 The `decodeURI()` and `encodeURI()` methods are designed to replace characters that aren't allowed in web URLs with escape sequences that are acceptable, which is an important technique if you're storing arbitrary data in the *query string* (the portion of the URL that follows the ?). Attempting to reverse this encoding on a string that has not been properly encoded can fail—for example, if it includes a % character that should begin an escape sequence.

The act of catching an error prevents it from being an unhandled error. This means your code can continue (and in the case of a Node application, prevents your application from ending altogether). However, you should only catch errors that you understand and are prepared to deal with. You never use error-handling simply to suppress and ignore potential problems. Recipe 10.4 has more about the effect of unhandled errors.

Although a `try...catch` block is the most common structure for error handling, you can optional add a `finally` section to the end. The code in the `finally` block always runs. It runs after the `try` block if no errors occurred, or after the `catch` block if an error was caught. It's most commonly used as a place to put cleanup code that should run regardless of whether your code succeeded or failed.

```
try {
  const uri = decodeURI('http%test');

  // We never get here
  console.log('Success!');
}
catch (error) {
  console.log(error);
}
finally {
  console.log('The operation (and any error handling) is complete');
}
```

See Also

Recipe 10.2 shows how to selectively catch different error types. Recipe 10.3 shows how to catch errors that happen during asynchronous operations.

10.2 Catching Different Types of Errors

Problem

You want to distinguish between different types of errors and handle them differently, or handle only specific types.

Solution

Unlike many languages, JavaScript does not allow you to catch errors by type. Instead, you must catch all errors (as usual), and then investigate the error with the `instanceof` operator:

```
try {
  // Some code that will raise an error
}
catch (error) {
  if (error instanceof RangeError) {
    // Do something about the value being out of range
  }
  else if (error instanceof TypeError) {
    // Do something about the value being the wrong type
  }
  else {
    // Rethrow the error
    throw error;
  }
}
```

Finally, if the error is not a type that you can handle, you should rethrow the error.

Discussion

JavaScript has eight error types, which are represented by different error objects (see Table 10-1). You can check an error's type to determine the kind of problem that occurred. This may indicate what actions you should take, or if you can carry out alternate code, retry an operation, or recover. It may also provide more information about exactly what went wrong.

Table 10-1. Error objects

Error Type	Description
RangeError	Occurs when a numeric value is outside of its allowed range.
ReferenceError	Occurs when trying to assign a nonexistent object to a variable.
SyntaxError	Occurs when code has a clear syntactical error, like an extra (or missing }.
TypeError	Occurs when a value is not the right data type for a given operation.
URIError	Raised by problems escaping URLs with decodeURI() and other related functions.
AggregateError	Is a wrapper for multiple errors, which is useful for errors that occur asynchronously. An array of error objects is provided in the errors property.
EvalError	Meant to represent problems that occur with the built-in eval(), but it's no longer used. Now, using eval() on syntactically invalid code will cause a SyntaxError to be thrown.
InternalError	Occurs for a variety of nonstandard cases, and is browser specific. For example, on Firefox an InternalError occurs if you exceed the recursion limit (by having a function call itself over and over again), while in Chrome the same condition is represented by a RangeError.

In addition to these error types, you can also throw and catch your own custom error objects, as described in Recipe 10.6.

JavaScript only allows one catch block for every try block, which prevents you from catching errors by type. However, you can catch the standard Error object, examine its type with instanceof, and write conditional code to deal with it accordingly. When you use this approach, you must be careful not to accidentally suppress errors you can't deal with.

In the current example, the code explicitly handles the RangeError and TypeError type. If the error is something else, we assume there's nothing practical we can do to resolve the problem. The error is then rethrown with the throw statement. When you use throw, it's as if the same error occurred again. If your code is in a function, this allows the error to continue to bubble up the stack until it reaches some error-handling code that can deal with it appropriately. If there is no other error-handling that catches this error, it becomes an unhandled error, just as it would have if you hadn't caught it in the first place. (See Recipe 10.4 for more about that.)

In other words, rethrowing unknown errors gives you the same behavior you would have if you caught only specific exception types—which is the approach you would probably take if the JavaScript language supported it.

See Also

Recipe 10.6 shows how to create your own error class to indicate a custom error condition and pass along extra information about the error.

10.3 Catching Asynchronous Errors

Problem

You want to add error handling but the risky operation is performed on a background thread.

Solution

JavaScript APIs have more than one model of asynchronicity, and the way you handle errors depends on the function you're using.

If you're using an older API, you may need to supply a callback function that will be called in the event of an error, or attach an event handler. The XMLHttpRequest object provides an error event to notify you about failed requests, for example:

```
const request = new XMLHttpRequest();

request.onerror = function errorHander(error) {
  console.log(error);
}

request.open('GET', 'http://noserver');
request.send();
```

Here the call to send() triggers the asynchronous operation that leads to the error, but the actual error occurs on a separate thread. Adding a try...catch block around this statement won't catch the problem. The best you can do is receive a notification through the error event.

If you're using a promise-based API, you attach your error-handling function by calling Promise.catch(). Here's an example with the Fetch API:

```
fetch('http://noserver')
.then((response) => {
  console.log('We did it, fam.');
})
.catch((error) => {
```

```
    console.log(error);
  });
```

The code you write here will be triggered in the event of an unhandled error or a rejected promise. If you don't catch an error that occurs in a promise, it will bubble up to your main application thread and trigger the `window.unhandledrejection` event, which is the promise-based equivalent to the `window.error` event (see Recipe 10.4).

Finally, if you're using promises with the higher-level `async` and `await` model, you can use a traditional error-handling block. The `catch` section will be attached to the promise automatically with `Promise.catch()`. Here's an example:

```
async function doWork() {
  try {
    const response = await fetch('http://noserver');
  }
  catch (error) {
    console.log(error);
  }
}

doWork().then(() => {
  console.log('All done');
});
```

Discussion

Putting error-handling code in the wrong place is a common mistake. Unfortunately, it's not always obvious that your error-handling code is ineffective or will never run, although a linting tool (Recipe 1.10) may alert you to the problem. The best solution is to test actual error conditions in your application, and verify that your error-handling code runs and mitigates them.

See Also

Recipe 9.2 shows a complete example with the Fetch API and promise-based error handling. Recipe 9.5 shows a complete example with the Fetch API and `async` and `await` error handling.

10.4 Detecting Unhandled Errors

Problem

You want to catch errors that have not been handled in your code, possibly to create a diagnostic log.

Solution

Handle the `window.error` event. Your event-handling function receives five parameters with error information. Along with an error object that represents the actual error, you also get a separate `message` parameter and location information (`source` with the URL of the script file, `lineno` with the line number where the error occurred, and `colno` with the column number).

Here's an example that tests this event:

```
// Attach the event handler
window.onerror = (message, url, lineNo, columnNo, error) => {
  console.log(`An unhandled error occurred in ${url}`);
}

// Cause an unhandled error
console.log(null.length);
```

Note that to test this example, you need to use a sample test page. You can't attach a function to the `window.error` event handler using the developer console.

 In some cases, the browser's cross-origin security policy will prevent your JavaScript code from having access to the error details. One example is if you're running your test page from the local filesystem instead of using a test server. In this situation, the `message` parameter will have the generic text "Script error," and the `url`, `lineNo`, `columnNo`, and `error` properties will be blank. For more information, see the `onerror` notes (*https://oreil.ly/9MbGP*).

Discussion

Unhandled errors that occur on the main thread of your application bubble up the stack until they reach the top level of your code and—if it's not handled there—trigger the `window.error` event in the browser.

The `window.error` event is unusual in that it allows you to *cancel* the error, effectively suppressing it. To do that, you return `true` from the event-handling function. If you don't suppress an error, the browser's default error-handler springs into action. It displays the error information in the developer console in bright red lettering, just as when you log it with the `console.error()` method. But if you return `true` from `window.error`, the error vanishes, and no trace of it will appear in the developer console.

Other than that, there's no practical difference between suppressing or allowing an error in your `window.error` event handler. By the time an error has triggered the `window.error` event, your code has already been halted and the stack has been unwound. However, this doesn't stop your web page from working. As soon as another event occurs (for example, you click a button), JavaScript begins executing your code again.

 Modern practice discourages us from hiding errors, even from the developer console, unless there's a very good reason. One possibility might be you're replacing the default error display with something that's fine-tuned to your application, and provides more useful information or removes information you don't want to make visible to users.

You can use your window.error event handler to execute any type of JavaScript code. For example, you could log the error to a local data store or even send it to a web server using the Fetch API. If an error occurs *during* the window.error event handler, the event handler won't be triggered again. It will simply pass straight to the browser's default error handler and show up in the developer console.

For asynchronous code, errors are handled differently. For older callback-based APIs, there usually are no errors. Instead, these APIs use callbacks to notify your code about error conditions (see Recipe 10.3). But for promise-based APIs, unhandled errors bubble up and will trigger the window.unhandledrejection event:

```
// Attach the event handler
window.onunhandledrejection = (e) => {
  console.log(e.reason);
}

// Create a promise that will cause an unhandled asynchronous error
const faultyPromise = new Promise(() => {
  throw new Error('Disaster strikes!');
});

// Create a promise that rejects (also triggers window.onunhandledrejection)
const rejectedPromise = new Promise((resolve, reject) => {
  reject(new Error('Another disaster strikes!'));
});
```

The unhandledrejection event passes a single object with event properties to your event handler. The reason property (used in the example above) has the unhandled error object, or whatever object was passed to Promise.reject() if the promise was manually rejected. You can also get the underlying Promise object from the promise property.

Like window.error, window.unhandledrejection is a cancellable event. However, it uses a different, more modern convention for cancellation. Instead of returning true, you can use the preventDefault() method of the object with the event arguments. Here's an example that shows a message when an unhanded promise error occurs, but hides the automatic error logging:

```
window.onunhandledrejection = (e) => {
  console.log('An error occurred, but we won\'t tell you what it was');

  // Cancel the default error handling
  e.preventDefault();
}
```

 You might think that the unhandled exception events are a good place to put your logging code. Sometimes they are. But usually, you'll want to catch errors closer to where they occur, log them there, and rethrow them if necessary. However, the unhandled exception events are always a good way to find risky bits of code that need exception-handling logic but don't have it.

Extra: Logging Tools

Broadly speaking, there are two times you catch errors: when you're testing your code and you're able to fix them, and when your application is in production and you want to know what went wrong. In the first case, logging is simple—your goal is to detect the problem and fix it. Often your logging simply involves calling `console.log()`. In the latter case, you need to investigate a problem that may be occurring sporadically, in a specific environment, and in front of an end user. Now you need a way to detect the problem and report the details back to you.

You could handle the `window.error` and `window.unhandledrejection` events, and then write the details to some sort of storage. For example, you could save error information in the `localStorage` object so it persists for longer than the current browser session. You could use `fetch()` to send the details to a web API on your server. If you're building a Node application, you could write the details to a file or database on the server. You could add extra contextual information, like system details, a priority level, and a timestamp. But as your logging needs grow, you may want to consider using an open source logging tool rather than roll your own solution.

A good logging tool gives you an *abstraction layer* over your logging. That means you'll log messages (in much the same way you call the usual `console.log()` method), without thinking about where that log is or how it's implemented. While you're testing, the logging layer might just output your messages to the console. But when your application is deployed, the logging layer might ignore low-level messages entirely while sending the important ones somewhere else, such as to a remote web server. The logging tool can implement advanced features, like batching, which improves performance when multiple messages are logged to a remote site in quick succession.

There's a dizzying array of logging libraries for JavaScript applications, including Winston, Bunyan, Log4js, Loglevel, Debug, Pino, and many more. Some are designed specifically for Node applications, but many can also work with web page code in a browser.

10.5 Throwing a Standard Error

Problem

You want to indicate an error condition by throwing an error object.

Solution

Create an instance of the Error object, passing a short description of the problem to the constructor, which is used for the message property. Throw the Error object with the throw statement. Your code can then catch this Error object just like it catches any other type of JavaScript error:

```
function strictDivision(number, divisor) {
  if (divisor == 0) {
    throw new Error('Dividing by zero is not allowed');
  }
  else {
    return number/divisor;
  }
}

// Catch the error
try {
  const result = strictDivision(42, 0);
}
catch (error) {
  // Shows the custom error message
  console.log(`Error: ${error.message}`);
}
```

Discussion

There are two ways to create an Error object. You can use the new keyword to create it, as in the solution. Or (less commonly), you can call Error() like a function, which has the same result:

```
// Standard error-throwing
throw new Error(`Dividing by zero is not allowed`);

// An equivalent approach
throw Error(`Dividing by zero is not allowed`);
```

The `Error` object has the standard error properties, including the `message` you set, a `name` (unhelpfully set to "Error"), and `stack` (the stack trace that pinpoints where the error occurred).

 JavaScript also allows code to use `throw` with nonerror objects (like strings). This usage is nonstandard and can cause problems in exception-handling code that expects properties like `name` and `message`. As a rule of thumb, do not throw nonexception objects.

Sometimes, you may be able to repurpose a more specific error subtype. Most of JavaScript's built-in error types (listed in Table 10-1) are for specialized cases and are not suitable for custom code. But a couple are potentially useful. You can use `RangeError` if a function receives a value that falls outside of the acceptable numeric range. Make sure to include an informative error message that includes the given value and the expected range:

```
function setAge(age) {
  const upper = 125;
  const lower = 18;
  if (age > 125 || age < 18) {
    throw new RangeError(
      `Age [${age}] is out of the acceptable range of ${lower} to ${upper}.`);
  }
}
```

`RangeError` is specifically intended for numeric values. However, you might use `TypeError` to indicate errors where the supplied value was of the wrong type. It's up to you to decide what constitutes a "wrong" type; perhaps a string when you expect a number (test that with `typeof`), or the wrong sort of object (test that with `instanceof`).

```
function calculateValue(num) {
  if (typeof num !== 'number') {
    throw new TypeError(`Value [${num}] is not a number.`);
  }
}
```

Less useful error subtypes that you might consider include `ReferenceError` (if you receive a `null` reference or `undefined` value when you expect an object) or `SyntaxError` (for instance, if you're parsing some type of string content that doesn't follow the rules you've established). To get more specific about other error conditions, consider making your own error class (Recipe 10.6).

Compared to many stricter languages, JavaScript uses errors sparingly. When designing your own libraries, it's usually best to follow that convention. Don't use exceptions for cases that JavaScript would ordinarily tolerate (like implicit type conversions). Don't use errors to notify the calling code about nonexceptional cases—in other words, things that are likely to happen during normal operation, like invalid user input. *Do* use exceptions to prevent code from continuing with an operation that will fail because something hasn't been initialized correctly.

See Also

Recipe 10.6 explains how to create your own error object.

10.6 Throwing a Custom Error

Problem

You want to indicate a specific error condition by throwing a custom error object.

Solution

Create a class that inherits from the standard `Error` class. The constructor should accept the descriptive text for the `message` property, and use `super()` to call the base `Error` class constructor with the message. Here's a bare minimum custom error, with the code that throws it:

```
class CustomError extends Error {
  constructor(message) {
    super(message);
    this.name = 'CustomError';

    // Optional improvement: clean up the stack trace, if supported
    if (Error.captureStackTrace) {
      Error.captureStackTrace(this, CustomError);
    }
  }
}

// Try raising this error
throw new CustomError('An application-specific problem occurred');
```

There's one more recommended, but optional, refinement. You can use the static `Error.captureStackTrace()` method to clean up the stack trace slightly. (Technically, `captureStackTrace()` ensures that the call to the error constructor doesn't appear in the stack trace that's stored in the `Error.stack` property.)

You can also add custom properties to pass extra information about the error condition. Here's an example that stores a `productID` after a failed lookup:

```
class ProductNotFound extends Error {
  constructor(missingProductID) {
    super(`Product ${missingProductID} does not exist in the catalog`);

    this.name = 'ProductNotFound';
    this.productID = missingProductID;
```

```
    if (Error.captureStackTrace) {
      Error.captureStackTrace(this, ProductNotFound);
    }
  }
}

try {
  throw new ProductNotFound(420);
}
catch (error) {
  console.log(`An error occured with the message: ${error.message}`);

  if (error instanceof ProductNotFound) {
    console.log(`Missing: ${error.productID}`);
  }
}
```

Discussion

When creating custom Error classes, we should keep in mind two possibly compet-
ing concerns: staying within the bounds of a typical JavaScript error, and expressing
enough information for our customized error condition. In the former case, do not
attempt to recreate the errors or exceptions of your second favorite language. Do not
overextend JavaScript's Error type with unnecessary methods and extra functionality.

When you create a custom error, there are a few conventions to keep in mind:

- Use the class name to indicate the error type, and set the name property to match.
  This is important if any code checks the name to determine the type of error
  (rather than using instanceof). It also persists even if the error object is serialized to JSON, and it appears in the error's default string representation and the
  developer console.

- In the constructor, put your custom properties first in the parameter list. If you
  include a message parameter, it should be the last parameter.

- In the constructor, call super() and pass the message to the base class
  constructor.

- As a nicety, properly set the stack trace. Check for the captureStackTrace()
  method, and, if present, call it, passing a reference to the current instance (as
  this) and your custom error class.

See Also

To learn more about inheritance and the extends keyword, see Recipe 8.8.

10.7 Writing Unit Tests for Your Code

Problem

You want to use automated tests to ensure your code matches your design criteria now and in the future.

Solution

Use a tool like Jest to write unit tests for your code at the earliest possible stage.

The easiest way to install Jest is with npm (Recipe 1.7). Open a terminal window in your project folder, and create the *package.json* configuration file if you don't already have it with npm init:

```
$ npm init -y
```

Next, install Jest using the --save-dev parameter so that it's only included in development builds:

```
$ npm install --save-dev jest
```

Now you need to find some code to test. Let's say you have a file named *factorialize.js*, with the factorialize() function shown here:

```
function factorialize(number) {
  if (number < 0) {
    throw new RangeError('Factorials are only defined for positive numbers');
  }
  else if (number != Math.trunc(number)) {
    throw new RangeError('Factorials are only defined for integers');
  }
  else {
    if (number == 0 || number == 1) {
      return 1;
    }
    else {
      let result = number;
      while (number > 1) {
        number--;
        result *= number;
      }
      return result;
    }
  }
}
```

To make this function accessible to Jest, you need to export the factorialze() function by adding this line to the end of the file:

```
export {factorialize}
```

Jest assumes you're using the Node module standard (CommonJS). If you're already using the newer ES6 module standard, you need to use Babel, a JavaScript transpilation tool, to convert your module references before Jest processes your code. This sounds complicated, but the `plugin-transform-modules-commonjs` module will take care of most of the work. To see the completely configured solution both ways (with CommonJS modules or ES6 modules), refer to the sample code. For more about CommonJS modules, see Recipe 18.2. For more about ES6 modules, see Recipe 8.9.

Now you need to create your test file. In Jest, test files have the extension *.test.js*. In this case, that means you need to create a new file named *factorialize.test.js*. This file then imports the function you want to test:

```
import {factorialize} from './factorialize.js';
```

The rest of your test file defines the test you want to run. The simplest approach to testing is to start by verifying that your function works the way you expect. For example, you can write a Jest test that verifies that `factorialize()` returns the correct information for a few representative cases. Here's an example that checks that 10! is 3,628,800:

```
test('10! is 3628800', () => {
  expect(factorialize(10)).toBe(3628800);
});
```

Jest's `test()` function creates a named test. The name allows you to identify tests in the test report, so you know exactly which tests succeeded and which ones failed. The test in this example uses Jest's `expect()` function, which calls your code (in this case, the `factorialize()` function) and then evaluates the result with `toBe()`. Technically, `toBe()` is one of several Jest *matcher functions*. It determines whether the code passes or fails the test.

To run this test, you need to use Jest. You can run it from the command line, with your test file and the help of npm's package runner, npx. In this example, you would use this command in the terminal:

```
$ npx jest factorialize.test.js
```

which runs the single test you've written and generates a report like this:

```
PASS  ./factorialize.test.js
 √ 10! is 3628800 (4 ms)

Test Suites: 1 passed, 1 total
Tests:       1 passed, 1 total
Snapshots:   0 total
Time:        2.725 s, estimated 3 s
```

```
Ran all test suites matching /factorialize.test.js
```

More commonly, you'll add Jest to the `scripts` section of your *package.json* file so it can run all your tests automatically:

```
{
  "scripts": {
    "test": "jest"
  }
}
```

Now you can ask Jest to run all the tests (the *.test.js* files) in your project folder.

Discussion

There are multiple types of tests, such as tests for security, usability, and performance, but the most basic form of testing is *unit testing*. Unit testing consists of performing tests of discrete source code units, and verifying that those units behave as expected. In JavaScript, the most common unit for unit testing is a function.

Although there are many possible testing frameworks (Jest, Mocha, Jasmine, Karma, and more), most of them use a similar syntax. In Jest, everything revolves around a `test()` function that takes two arguments. The first argument is a label for the test, which appears in the test report. The second argument is a function that includes one or more test assertions—claims that will either be successfully proved true (a pass) or false (a fail):

```
test('Some test name', () => {
  // Test assertions go here
});
```

To create test assertions, you use the `expect()` function, which is the lynchpin of Jest. It works in conjunction with a matching function like `toBe()` that evaluates the results from your test call:

```
test('10! is 3628800', () => {
  expect(factorialize(10)).toBe(3628800);
});
```

This example demonstrates a single test of the `factorialize()` function. But the goal of the test writer is broader. You need to choose a representative group of tests—ones that check multiple values and capture boundary conditions where possible. For example, with the `factorialize()` function test, it makes sense to test how the function deals with nonnumeric input, negative values, 0, very large values, and so on.

The following code shows a more complete test suite. It checks the results of five different calls to `factorialize()`. These calls are all grouped into one test suite using `describe()`. The `describe()` function simply lets you label a collection of related test calls. In this example, describe() is grouping calls to the same function, but you might also use it to group calls that use the same set of sample data:

```
describe('factorialize() function tests', () => {
  test('0! is 1', () => {
    expect(factorialize(0)).toBe(1);
  });
  test('1! is 1', () => {
    expect(factorialize(1)).toBe(1);
  });
  test('10! is 3628800', () => {
    expect(factorialize(10)).toBe(3628800);
  });
  test('"5"! is 120', () => {
    expect(factorialize('5')).toBe(120);
  });
  test('NaN is 0', () => {
    expect(factorialize(NaN)).toBe(0);
  });
});
```

When you run this test, you'll find that the final test fails. It expects the call factori alize(NaN) to return 0, but it actually throws an error, as the test log makes clear:

```
FAIL   ./factorialize.test.js
 factorialize() function tests
   √ 0! is 1 (3 ms)
   √ 1! is 1
   √ 10! is 3628800
   √ "5"! is 120
   × NaN is 0 (3 ms)

 • factorialize() function tests › NaN is 0

   RangeError: Factorials are only defined for integers

      4 |   }
      5 |   if (number != Math.trunc(number)) {
    > 6 |     throw new RangeError('Factorials are only defined for integers');
        |     ^
      7 |   }
      8 |   else {
      9 |     if (number == 0 || number == 1) {

      at factorialize (factorialize.js:6:11)
      at Object.<anonymous> (factorialize.test.js:17:12)

Test Suites: 1 failed, 1 total
Tests:       1 failed, 4 passed, 5 total
Snapshots:   0 total
Time:        2.833 s
Ran all test suites.
```

Right now, every test you've seen uses the `toBe()` matching function to check for an exact value. But Jest, like all testing frameworks, lets you use different types of rules. For example, you could check that a number falls in a specific range, that text matches a certain pattern, or that a value isn't null. Table 10-2 outlines some of the most useful matching functions you can use with `expect()`. For a comprehensive list, consult the Jest documentation for the `expect()` method (*https://oreil.ly/hnbiy*).

Table 10-2. Jest matchers

Function	Description
`arrayContaining()`	Searches an array for a given value.
`not()`	Allows you to reverse any condition. For example, using `expect(...).not.toBe(5)`` passes if the value is *not 5*.
`stringContaining()`	Searches a string for a substring.
`stringMatching()`	Attempts to match a string to a regular expression.
`toBe()`	Tests for standard JavaScript equality, just as if you used the == operator.
`toBeCloseTo()`	Tests that two numbers are equal or *very* close. Intended to avoid minute rounding errors with floating-point numbers (an issue detailed in Recipe 3.4).
`toBeGreaterThan()`	Checks if a numeric value is greater than the value you specify. There's a small set of similar matchers for different comparisons, including `toBeGreaterThanOrEqual()`, `toBeLessThan()`, and `toBeLessThanOrEqual()`.
`toBeInstanceOf()`	Checks if a returned object is an instance of a specified class, just as if you used the `instanceof` operator.
`toBeNull()`	Checks if a value is `null`. You can also test for NaN values with `toBeNaN()` and undefined values with `toBeUndefined()`.
`toBeTruthy()`	Tests if a number is *truthy*, which means it will be coerced to `true` in an `if` statement. In JavaScript, everything is truthy except `null`, `undefined`, empty strings, NaN, 0, and `false`.
`toEqual()`	Performs a *deep comparison* that checks if one object has the same content as another. This is in contrast to `toBe()`, which tests reference equality for objects. As a general rule of thumb, `toBe()` works for primitive types, but `toEqual()` is what you need to compare object instances. (Recipe 7.11 explains more about object equality in JavaScript.)
`toHaveProperty()`	Checks if a returned object has a specific property and (optionally) if that property matches a certain value.
`toStrictEqual()`	Similar to `toEqual()` but requires the objects to match exactly. For example, objects with the same properties and property values won't match if they are instances of different classes, or if one is a class instance and the other an object literal.
`toThrow`	Tests if the function throws an exception. You can optionally require the exception to be a specific error object.

To fix the current example, you can indicate that you expect a value of NaN to throw an exception with the `toThrow()` matcher. However, `toThrow()` requires an extra step. You need to wrap the code inside `expect()` inside *another* anonymous function.

Otherwise, the exception won't be caught and the test will still fail. Here's the correct code:

```
test('NaN causes error', () => {
  expect(() => {
    factorialize(NaN);
  }).toThrow();
});
```

See Also

This example gives a good overview of Jest's core functionality, but there are many additional features you may want to consider. For example, Jest has additional support for using mock data, handling asynchronous results from promises, simulating timers, and snapshot testing (which verifies that the UI of a page hasn't changed). For more information about all these features, refer to the Jest documentation (*https://oreil.ly/aeu1l*).

Extra: Writing Tests First

Modern development practices have embraced the idea of writing the tests before much of the functionality for the application (and libraries) is written. This test-driven development (TDD) is a component of the Agile development paradigm.

TDD takes some getting used to. Rather than a more formal *structured programming* or *waterfall* project design, which delays testing until you have reasonably complete code, TDD mandates that you write tests before your write anything else. Here's how it unfolds:

1. *Define the tests.* For example, if you were planning to write the `factorialize()` function shown in the previous example, you would begin by defining a representative set of tests that capture its expected inputs: for example, the largest number it can factorialize, boundary values like 0, and potential edge cases (like an implicitly coerced string or `BigInt` value). You would also write tests to check that failure cases are treated appropriately—in this case, by throwing the expected error.

2. *Make it fail.* Once you've written your tests, you write the code. Some TDD practitioners suggest that the first step is to make your code compile and your tests fail. By achieving this step, you ensure that your tests are running, your test requirements are meaningful, and you aren't accidentally passing code before it's complete.

3. *Make it pass.* The next step is sometimes described as "make the tests pass any way possible." In other words, you don't worry about creating the best possible solution, but simply making all the tests pass. Do not write more code than dictated by the test requirements.

4. *Refactor.* After you successfully pass your tests, you start the work of refining the code. This is the time when you refactor, remove duplicate code, and introduce improvements, repeating your tests all the while to make sure they continue to pass. You'll probably also discover cases you haven't covered, and end up writing more tests.

One obvious advantage in TDD is that it makes you focus on the problem at hand. You don't need to interpret design requirements to decide how you should code a solution. Instead, you code to the exacting specifications that are formalized in tests. But TDD development also helps as an application evolves, because it diminishes the fear of change. As long as your code continues to pass the tests you've set out, and as long as your tests are truly representative (a bigger "if"), it's safe to commit new revisions to your codebase.

The cost for this protection is that creating proper tests takes significantly more time to complete and significant experience to get right. One metric that can help you evaluate your testing regimen is *test code coverage* (Recipe 10.8).

10.8 Tracking Test Code Coverage

Problem

You want to assess how well your test cases cover all the possibilities in your code.

Solution

Get a code coverage report from your testing tool. In Jest, you use the `--collect-coverage` option:

```
$ npx jest --collect-coverage
```

Now Jest will run all the tests in all the *test.js* files (as usual), followed by a more detailed report that analyzes the code coverage of your tests. Here's the report with the tests for the `factorialize()` function shown in Recipe 10.7:

```
-----------------|---------|----------|---------|---------|-------------------
File             | % Stmts | % Branch | % Funcs | % Lines | Uncovered Line #s
-----------------|---------|----------|---------|---------|-------------------
All files        |   82.61 |    66.67 |     100 |   82.61 |
 factorialize.js |   82.61 |    66.67 |     100 |   82.61 | 3-4,6-7
-----------------|---------|----------|---------|---------|-------------------
Test Suites: 1 passed, 1 total
Tests:       4 passed, 4 total
Snapshots:   0 total
Time:        2.741 s
```

Discussion

Determining test code coverage requires a multifaceted approach. To be successful, it should include techniques such as code reviews and walkthroughs with peers. However, all testing tools also include automated code analysis features that can help you size up how successful your tests are at evaluating your code.

In Jest, the `--collect-coverage` parameter triggers this analysis. You can use this parameter at the command line or add it to the `jest` command in the *package.json* configuration file for your application.

The code coverage report assesses how much of your code is tested using several percentages, which appear in separate columns:

Functions
> Shows how many of your functions are tested. This is a good starting point for evaluating your test coverage, but it's also the least fine-grained statistic. In the `factorialize()` test, all the functions are tested. That doesn't mean that all the code in these functions is executed!

Statements
> Shows the percentage of code statements that are executed during your tests. In the `factorialize()` test, roughly 83% of all the code written is covered by at least one test.

Branch
> Shows how many different branches (through conditional logic, like `if` statements) are reached. In the `factorialize()` test, the tests travel down 67% of the separate conditional branches.

Additionally, the code report can point you to lines that don't have code coverage. For example, the `factorialize()` example highlights lines 3–4 in your source code file, which rejects negative numbers, and lines 6–7, which rejects noninteger numbers. To improve your test code coverage, you could write a test assertion that uses `toThrow()` to ensure that both these cases are rejected properly.

The command-line report gives you a quick review of your coverage, but Jest also generates a more comprehensive HTML-formatted report, which it stores in the *coverage* folder. Open *index.html* to see a list of all the tested files with the top-line statistics in slightly more detail (see Figure 10-1). For example, rather than just giving you percentages, the report tells you the exact number of statements, branches, and functions. Click on any file in the list to go to another page that shows the code, with a twist: uncovered statements are highlighted for quick reference (see Figure 10-2).

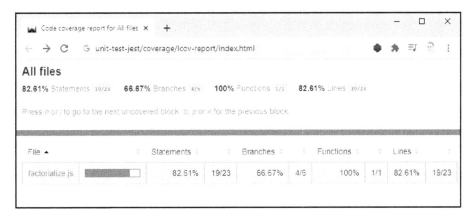

Figure 10-1. Code coverage report

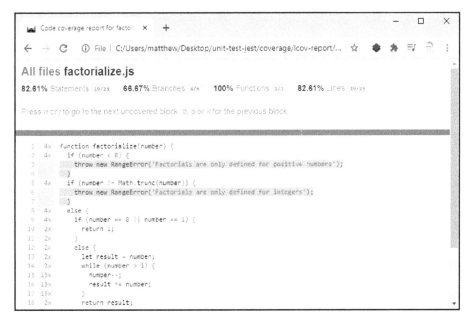

Figure 10-2. Highlighted code without test coverage

The appropriate test coverage goal is much-debated. Some developers advocate for getting as close to 100% as possible, while others argue that 70%–80% is more practical and achieves the best return for your test-writing investment. However, the honest answer is that test coverage is not a definitive metric. Not only does the percentage differ based on how you measure it (functions, statements, or branches), but testing tools have no way to identify the riskiest or most vulnerable paths in your codebase.

## PART II

JavaScript in the Browser

## CHAPTER 11

Browser Tools

As a web developer, the browser is the window through which the world accesses your creations. It also provides helpful tooling for developing and testing your sites. It is a worthwhile investment to learn how to use your browser's development tools so that you may better and more easily debug your code. In this chapter we'll cover several useful features for debugging, profiling, and analyzing JavaScript.

For simplicity, all of the examples in this book will make use of Google Chrome's Developer Tools (DevTools). At the time of writing, Chrome's usage makes up over 65% (*https://oreil.ly/QFZD9*) of the global browser share. Most other browsers offer similar functionality. Mozilla's Firefox Developer Edition (*https://oreil.ly/lJSel*) is an excellent alternative with useful developer features.

11.1 Debugging JavaScript

Problem

You need to know the value of a variable at a specific point in your JavaScript code's execution.

Solution

Use a breakpoint to inspect code values and types. When setting a breakpoint, the browser's debugger will stop at the point of the breakpoint's code execution and display each of the current values in scope. It is then possible to step through the code or allow the JavaScript to finish executing. Figure 11-1 shows a screenshot of code paused on a breakpoint.

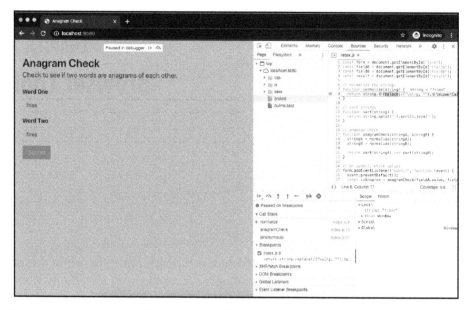

Figure 11-1. A screenshot of the Chrome debugger with a breakpoint set

To set a breakpoint on a specific line of JavaScript code in Chrome's Developer Tools:

1. Open Chrome's Developer Tools using Command-Option-C (Macintosh) or Control+Shift+C (Windows or Linux).

2. Click the DevTools **Sources** tab.

3. Select the JavaScript file from the file list.

4. Click the line number where you would like to set the breakpoint.

5. Execute the code by either interacting with the page or refreshing the browser window.

Discussion

It is common practice to use `console.log` statements to identify values at specific points in code, but breakpoints offer more information and greater flexibility. As you become familiar with debugging in this manner, you'll be able to more easily trouble-shoot your browser-based JavaScript code.

In addition to setting breakpoints in the browser's user interface, it is also possible to set them with code by adding a `debugger` statement. Doing so will pause code execution at the point of the `debugger` statement.

```
function normalize(string) {
  const normalized = string.replace(/[^\w]/g, "").toLowerCase();
  debugger;
  return normalized;
}
```

Once the breakpoint has been reached, you are given several options as to how the JavaScript should be executed:

Resume script execution
> Continue executing the code in full.

Step over
> Execute a function without "stepping into it" to debug.

Step into
> Step into a function to debug it further.

Step out of
> Execute the rest of the current function's code.

Step
> Step to the next line of code.

These line-based breakpoints are only one type of breakpoint that can be set. In addition, it is possible to set breakpoints based on DOM changes, conditional values, event listeners, exceptions, and fetch/XHR requests. The use of breakpoints provides greater control over the JavaScript debugging experience.

11.2 Analyzing Runtime Performance

Problem

The execution of your JavaScript code seems slow or buggy, but you are unsure of the source of the problem.

Solution

Use the browser developer tool's Performance analysis to look for bottlenecks and CPU-intensive tasks in your code (Figure 11-2).

To analyze JavaScript code performance in Chrome's Developer Tools:

1. Open Chrome's Developer Tools using Command-Option-C (Macintosh) or Control+Shift+C (Windows or Linux).

2. Click the DevTools **Performance** tab.

3. Either click the **Record** button to interact with the page, or click the **Reload** button to see the performance metrics related to a new page load.

Once Chrome completes the profile of the page, you will be presented with information that allows you to review potential performance bottlenecks.

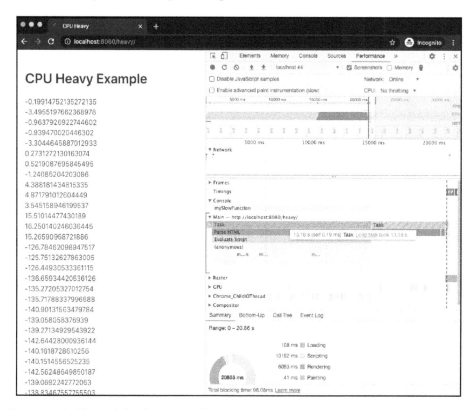

Figure 11-2. Chrome's Performance tab

Discussion

The Chrome Performance tooling breaks down the browser's rendering process for a page and presents it using a visual timeline, screenshots, and a summary chart (see Figure 11-3). Using this information allows you to look for places where performance is negatively affected.

As a developer, you may have a high-end machine and a fast internet connection. One of the most useful features of browser performance tools is the ability to simulate a throttled CPU or internet connection. Doing so may allow you to spot performance issues that users will encounter, but may not be apparent to you.

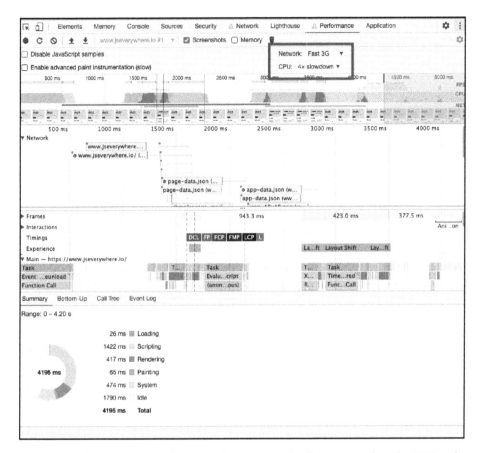

Figure 11-3. The Chrome Developer Performance tools allow you to throttle CPU and network connections

Reviewing performance data is an important step in ensuring a positive user experience. Good site performance has been shown to improve user retention rates and sales conversions. In Recipe 11.4, we'll cover how to further review potential performance issues.

11.3 Identifying Unused JavaScript

Problem

Your application's performance is impacted by large JavaScript files.

Solution

Use the Chrome Developer Tool's Coverage feature to identify unused JavaScript (Figure 11-4).

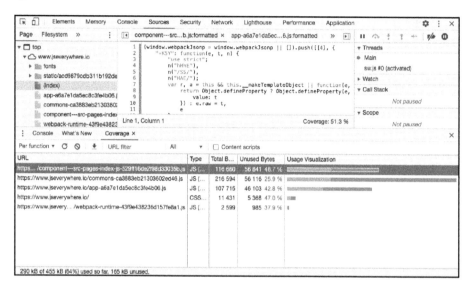

Figure 11-4. Chrome's Coverage tool

To view unused JavaScript, access the Coverage tab:

1. Open Chrome's Developer Tools using Command-Option-C (Macintosh) or Control+Shift+C (Windows or Linux).

2. Open the Command Menu using Command-Shift-P (Macintosh) or Control +Shift+P (Windows or Linux) and type **coverage**.

3. Select **Show Coverage** and press Enter.

4. Either click the **Record** button to interact with the page, or click the **Reload** button to record the coverage results related to a new page load.

5. Click **Stop Instrumenting Coverage And Show Results** when you want to stop recording the results.

The results will display a report with the following information:

- File URL
- File type
- Total bytes
- Unused bytes
- Usage visualization

You can then use this information to aid in refactoring code to reduce the total amount of unused bytes on a page.

Discussion

Viewing code usage is helpful for getting a sense of the percentage of unused Java-Script you are serving your users. The task of reducing this unused code is then often left to manual refactoring. However, a JavaScript bundling tool, such as Webpack, can also be used to split code into multiple bundles and perform "tree shaking" to automatically eliminate dead code. These methods are covered in Recipe 16.2.

11.4 Using Lighthouse to Measure Best Practices

Problem

You want to measure your web application's adherence to best practices.

Solution

Use Google's Lighthouse tool, which is built into the Chrome Developer Tools (Figure 11-5).

1. Open Chrome's Developer Tools using Command-Option-C (Macintosh) or Control+Shift+C (Windows or Linux).
2. Click the DevTools **Lighthouse** tab.
3. Select the categories you would like to profile and the device type (mobile or desktop).
4. Click **Generate Report**.

Lighthouse will then create a report, with a score for each category and specific recommendations for improvement.

Figure 11-5. The results of a Google Lighthouse report within Chrome's Developer Tools

Discussion

Lighthouse is an open source tool, created by Google, to measure the performance and best practices of a website. The tool is built into Chrome's Developer Tools, but it can also be run as a standalone browser extension, a Node module, or from the command line. The Lighthouse report can be generated in a desktop or mobile view, allowing you to quickly get a sense of mobile performance. Lighthouse generates reports and recommendations for each of the following areas:

- Performance
- Progressive Web Application
- Best Practices
- Accessibility
- SEO

The report output provides actionable feedback with specific problems, and links to documentation and recommended improvements. In Figure 11-6, you can see performance recommendations for a profiled website, including removing unused JavaScript and reducing the impact of third-party code. Expanding each of these diagnostics will provide additional details and file specifics.

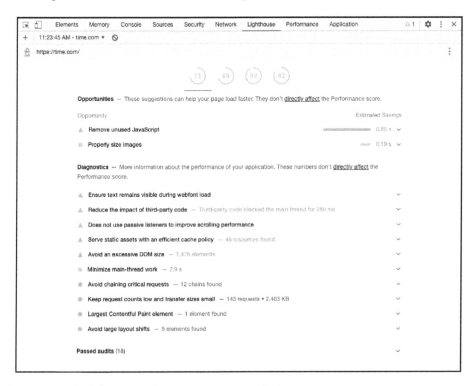

Figure 11-6. Lighthouse performance recommendations

Google's Lighthouse is a useful tool for gauging the overall health and performance of the websites and applications that you develop. Accessing Lighthouse through the browser Developer Tools provides a quick and efficient way to profile a site during development. In addition to the developer tools user interface, the open source (*https://github.com/GoogleChrome/lighthouse*) command-line tooling and Node module make it possible to build Lighthouse reports into continuous integration and delivery pipelines.

CHAPTER 12

Working with HTML

In 1995 Netscape tasked software developer Brendan Eich with creating a programming language designed to add interactivity to pages in the Netscape Navigator browser. In response, Eich infamously developed the first version of JavaScript in 10 days. A few years later, JavaScript became a cross-browser standard through the adoption of the ECMAScript standardization.

Despite the early attempt at standardization, web developers battled for years with browsers that had different JavaScript engine interpretations or features. Popular libraries, such as jQuery, effectively allowed us to write simple cross-browser JavaScript. Thankfully, today's browsers share a near uniform implementation of the language, allowing web developers to write "vanilla" (library-free) JavaScript to interact with an HTML page.

When working with HTML, we are working with the Document Object Model (DOM), which is the data representation of the HTML page. The recipes in this chapter will review how to interact with the DOM of an HTML page by selecting, updating, and removing elements from the page.

12.1 Accessing a Given Element and Finding Its Parent and Child Elements

Problem

You want to access a specific web page element, and then find its parent and child elements.

Solution

Give the element a unique identifier:

```
<div id="demodiv">
  <p>
    This is text.
  </p>
</div>
```

Use `document.getElementById()` to get a reference to the specific element:

```
const demodiv = document.getElementById("demodiv");
```

Find its parent via the `parentNode` property:

```
const parent = demodiv.parentNode;
```

Find its children via the `childNodes` property:

```
const children = demodiv.childNodes;
```

Discussion

A web document is organized like an upside-down tree, with the topmost element at the root and all other elements branching out beneath. Except for the root element (HTML), each element has a parent node, and all of the elements are accessible via the document.

There are several different techniques available for accessing these document elements, or *nodes* as they're called in the DOM. Today, we access these nodes through standardized versions of the DOM, such as DOM Levels 2 and 3. Originally, though, a de facto technique was to access the elements through the browser object model, sometimes referred to as DOM Level 0. DOM Level 0 was invented by the leading browser company of the time, Netscape, and its use has been supported (more or less) in most browsers since. The key object for accessing web page elements in the DOM Level 0 is the document object.

The most commonly used DOM method is `document.getElementById()`. It takes one parameter: a case-sensitive string with the element's identifier. It returns an element object, which is referenced to the element if it exists; otherwise, it returns null.

 There are numerous ways to get one specific web page element, including the use of selectors, covered later in the chapter. But you'll always want to use the most restrictive method possible, and you can't get more restrictive than `document.getElementById()`.

The returned element object has a set of methods and properties, including several inherited from the node object. The node methods are primarily associated with traversing the document tree. For instance, to find the parent node for the element, use the following:

```
const parent = document.getElementById("demodiv").parentNode;
```

You can find out the type of element for each node through the nodeName property:

```
const type = parent.nodeName;
```

If you want to find out what children an element has, you can traverse a collection of them via a NodeList, obtained using the childNodes property:

```
let outputString = '';

if (demodiv.hasChildNodes()) {
  const children = demodiv.childNodes;
  children.forEach(child => {
    outputString += `has child ${child.nodeName} `;
  });
}
console.log(outputString);
```

Given the element in the solution, the output would be:

```
"has child #text has child P has child #text "
```

You might be surprised by what appeared as a child node. In this example, whitespace before and after the paragraph element is itself a child node with a nodeName of #text. For the following div element:

```
<div id="demodiv" class="demo">
  <p>Some text</p>
  <p>Some more text</p>
</div>
```

the demodiv element (node) has five children, not two:

```
has child #text
has child P
has child #text
has child P
has child #text
```

The best way to see how messy the DOM can be is to use a debugger such as the Firefox or Chrome developer tools, access a web page, and then utilize whatever DOM inspection tool the debugger provides. I opened a simple page in Chrome and used the developer tools to display the element tree, as shown in Figure 12-1.

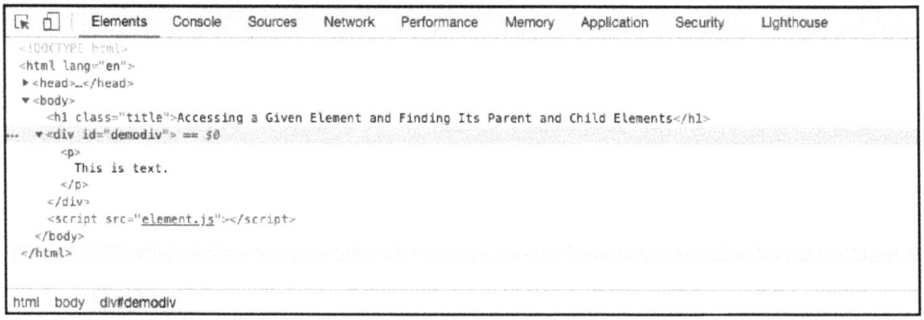

Figure 12-1. Examining the element tree of a web page using Chrome's Developer Tools

12.2 Traversing the Results from querySelectorAll() with forEach()

Problem

You want to loop over the `nodeList` returned from a call to `querySelectorAll()`.

Solution

In modern browsers, you can use `forEach()` when working with a `NodeList` (the collection returned by `querySelectorAll()`):

```
// use querySelectorAll to find all list items on a page
const items = document.querySelectorAll('li');

items.forEach(item => {
  console.log(item.firstChild.data);
});
```

Discussion

`forEach()` is an array method, but `querySelectorAll()` produces a `NodeList` which is a different type of object than an array. Thankfully, modern browsers have built-in support for `forEach`, allowing us to iterate over a `NodeList` as though it is an array.

Unfortunately, Internet Explorer (IE) does not support using `forEach` in this way. If you'd like to support IE, the recommended approach is to include a polyfill that uses a standard `for` loop under the hood:

```
if (window.NodeList && !NodeList.prototype.forEach) {
  NodeList.prototype.forEach = function(callback, thisArg) {
    thisArg = thisArg || window;
    for (var i = 0; i < this.length; i++) {
      callback.call(thisArg, this[i], i, this);
    }
  };
}
```

In the polyfill, we check for the existence of NodeList.prototype.forEach. If it does not exist, a forEach method is added to the NodeList prototype that uses a for loop to iterate over the results of a DOM query. By doing so, you can use the forEach syntax freely across your codebase.

12.3 Adding Click Functionality to an Element

Problem

You need to add JavaScript functionality when a user clicks a button, link, or element on the page.

Solution

Add a click event listener for the element:

```
// define an event handler function
const clickHandler = (event) => {
  window.alert('The element has been clicked!');
};

// select element
const btn = document.getElementById('click-button');
// add the event listener to the element and call 'clickHandler' function
btn.addEventListener('click', clickHandler);
```

Discussion

The addEventListener() method allows our JavaScript to listen for a specific type of event and define a function that will be called when the event is triggered. In the previous example, I have added a click listener to a button element. When the button is clicked, the clickHandler function will be called, which fires an alert.

By default, you should use a button element for clickable event handlers, as it is the most accessible solution for handling click events. The button element can be styled to appear as a link if necessary for the application's design. However, it is appropriate to use an element when the fallback behavior of linking to a page, should the

JavaScript fail to load, is the desired behavior. When doing so, the `preventDefault` event method allows you to override the default link behavior:

```
const clickHandler = (event) => {
  event.preventDefault();
  window.alert(`The ${event.currentTarget.nodeName} element has been clicked!`);
};

const href = document.getElementById('click-link');
href.addEventListener('click', clickHandler);
```

 In traditional JavaScript functions, the `this` keyword would be bound to the item being clicked. However, when using JavaScript's newer arrow function syntax, such as in this example, the value of `this` is inherited from the parent function, which by default is `window`. This can be confusing if you are accustomed to nonarrow syntax functions. If you are interested in reading more, I recommend Joe Cardillo's article on the topic (*https://oreil.ly/wK7Ik*).

On rare instances, it may be desirable to make a block element, such as a `div` clickable. I'd recommend doing so sparingly, in favor of the `button` element whenever possible. However, for these occasions, you will need to ensure that the functionality is accessible for those using screen readers and keyboard navigation. First, in your markup apply a `role` of `button` and a `tabindex` value. The `role` property will inform screen reader users that this is a clickable element, while the `tabindex` will make the element keyboard navigable:

```
<div tabindex="0" role="button" id="click-div">Click me</div>
```

In this instance, we use a `keydown` event handler. This will allow keyboard users to interact with the element:

```
const clickHandler = (event) => {
  window.alert(`The ${event.currentTarget.nodeName} element has been clicked!`);
};

const clickableDiv = document.getElementById('click-link');
clickableDiv.addEventListener('click', clickHandler);

// when using a div add a keydown event listener for keyboard users
clickableDiv.addEventListener('keydown', (event) => {
  if (event.code === 'Space' || event.code === 'Enter') {
    clickableDiv.click();
  }
});
```

12.4 Finding All Elements That Share an Attribute

Problem

You want to find all elements in a web document that share the same attribute.

Solution

Use the *universal selector* (*) in combination with the attribute selector to find all elements that have an attribute, regardless of its value:

```
const elems = document.querySelectorAll('*[class]');
```

The universal selector can also be used to find all elements with an attribute that's assigned the same value:

```
const reds = document.querySelectorAll('*[class="red"]');
```

Discussion

The solution demonstrates a rather elegant query selector, the *universal selector* (*). The universal selector evaluates all elements, so it's the one you want to use when you need to verify *something* about each element. In the solution, we want to find all of the elements with a given attribute.

To test whether an attribute exists, all you need to do is list the attribute name within square brackets (*[attrname]*). In the solution, we're first testing whether the element contains the class attribute. If it does, it's returned with the element collection:

```
var elems = document.querySelectorAll('*[class]');
```

Next, we're getting all elements with a class attribute value of red. If you're not sure of the class name, you can use the substring-matching query selector:

```
const reds = document.querySelectorAll('*[class="red"]');
```

Now any class name that contains the substring red matches.

You could also modify the syntax to find all elements that don't have a certain value. For instance, to find all div elements that don't have the target class name, use the :not negation operator:

```
const notRed = document.querySelectorAll('div:not(.red)');
```

12.5 Accessing All Elements of a Specific Type

Problem

You want to access all img elements in a given document.

Solution

Use the `document.getElementsByTagName()` method, passing in `img` as the parameter:

```
const imgElements = document.getElementsByTagName('img');
```

Discussion

The `document.getElementsByTagName()` method returns a collection of nodes (a `NodeList`) of a given element type, such as the `img` tag in the solution. The collection can be traversed like an array, and the order of nodes is based on the order of the elements within the document (the first `img` element in the page is accessible at index 0, etc.):

```
const imgElements = document.getElementsByTagName('img');
for (let i = 0; i < imgElements.length; i += 1) {
  const img = imgElements[i];
  ...
}
```

As discussed in Recipe 12.2, a `NodeList` collection can be traversed like an array, but it isn't an `Array` object. You can't use `Array` object methods, such as `push()` and `reverse()`, with a `NodeList`. Its only property is `length`, and its only method is `item()`, returning the element at the position given by an index passed in as a parameter:

```
const img = imgElements.item(1); // second image
```

`NodeList` is an intriguing object because it's a live collection, which means changes made to the document after the `NodeList` is retrieved are reflected in the collection. Example 12-1 demonstrates the `NodeList` live collection functionality, as well as `getElementsByTagName`.

In the example, three images in the web page are accessed as a `NodeList` collection using the `getElementsByTagName` method. The `length` property, with a value of 3, is output to the console. Immediately after, a new paragraph and `img` elements are created, and the `img` is appended to the paragraph. To append the paragraph following the others in the page, `getElementsByTagName` is used again, this time with the paragraph tags (p). We're not really interested in the paragraphs, but in the paragraphs' parent elements, found via the `parentNode` property on each paragraph.

The new paragraph element is appended to the paragraph's parent element, and the previously accessed `NodeList` collection's length property is again printed out. Now, the value is 4, reflecting the addition of the new `img` element.

Example 12-1. Demonstrating `getElementsByTagName` and the `NodeList` live collection property

```
<!DOCTYPE html>
<html>
<head>
<title>NodeList</title>
</head>
<body>
  <p><img src="firstimage.jpg" alt="image description" /></p>
  <p><img src="secondimage.jpg" alt="image description" /></p>
  <p><img src="thirdimage.jpg" alt="image description" /></p>

<script>
  const imgs = document.getElementsByTagName('img');
  console.log(imgs.length);
  const p = document.createElement('p');
  const img = document.createElement('img');
  img.src = './img/someimg.jpg';
  p.appendChild(img);

  const paras = document.getElementsByTagName('p');
  paras[0].parentNode.appendChild(p);

  console.log(imgs.length);
</script>

</body>
</html>
```

Example 12-1 will log the following output to the browser console:

```
<img src="img/firstimage.jpg" alt="image description">
<img src="img/secondimage.jpg" alt="image description">
<img src="img/thirdimage.jpg" alt="image description">
3
4
```

In addition to using `getElementsByTagName()` with a specific element type, you can also pass the universal selector (*) as a parameter to the method to get all elements:

```
const allElems = document.getElementsByTagName('*');
```

See Also

In the code demonstrated in the discussion, the children nodes are traversed using a traditional `for` loop. In modern browsers, the `forEach()` method can be used directly with a `NodeList`, as demonstrated in Recipe 12.2.

12.6 Discovering Child Elements Using the Selectors API

Problem

You want to get a list of all instances of a child element, such as img elements, that are descendants of a parent element, such as article elements, without having to traverse an entire collection of elements.

Solution

Use the Selectors API and access the img elements contained within article elements using CSS-style selector strings:

```
const imgs = document.querySelectorAll('article img');
```

Discussion

There are two selector query API methods. The first, querySelectorAll(), is demonstrated in the solution; the second is querySelector(). The difference between the two is that querySelectorAll() returns all elements that match the selector criteria, while querySelector() only returns the first found result.

The selector syntax is derived from CSS selector syntax, except that rather than style the selected elements, they're returned to the application. In the example, all img elements that are descendants of article elements are returned. To access all img elements regardless of parent element, use:

```
const imgs = document.querySelectorAll('img');
```

In the solution, you'll get all img elements that are direct or indirect descendants of an article element. This means that if the img element is contained within a div that's within an article, the img element will be among those returned:

```
<article>
  <div>
     <img src="..." />
  </div>
</article>
```

If you want only those img elements that are direct children of an article element, use the following:

```
const imgs = document.querySelectorAll('article > img');
```

If you're interested in accessing all img elements that are immediately followed by a paragraph, use:

```
const imgs = document.querySelectorAll('img + p');
```

If you're interested in an img element that has an empty alt attribute, use the following:

```
const imgs = document.querySelectorAll('img[alt=""]');
```

If you're only interested in img elements that don't have an empty alt attribute, use:

```
const imgs = document.querySelectorAll('img:not([alt=""])');
```

The negation pseudoselector (:not) is used to find all img elements with alt attributes that are not empty.

Unlike the collection returned with getElementsByTagName() covered earlier, the collection of elements returned from querySelectorAll() is *not* a "live" collection. Updates to the page are not reflected in the collection if the updates occur after the collection is retrieved.

 Though the Selectors API is a wonderful creation, it shouldn't be used for every document query. To keep your applications performant, I recommend always using the most restrictive query possible when accessing elements. For example, it's more efficient (meaning faster for the browser) to use getElementById() to get a specific element given an identifier than using querySelector All() for the same element.

See Also

There are three different CSS selector specifications, labeled as Selectors Level 1, Level 2, and Level 3. CSS Selectors Level 3 (*https://oreil.ly/rGfxD*) contains links to the documents defining the other levels. These documents provide the definitions of, and examples for, the different types of selectors.

12.7 Changing an Element's Class Value

Problem

You want to update the CSS rules applied to an element by changing its class value.

Solution

Use the classList property of an element to add, remove, and toggle class values:

```
const element = document.getElementById('example-element');
// add a new class
element.classList.add('new-class');
// remove an existing class
element.classList.remove('existing-class');
```

```
// if toggle-me is present it is removed, if not it is added
element.classList.toggle('toggle-me');
```

Discussion

Using `classList` allows you to easily manipulate the class properties of a selected element. This can come in handy for updating or swapping styles without using inline CSS. At times, it may be helpful to check if an element already has a class value applied, which can be accomplished with the `contains` method:

```
if (element.classList.contains('new-class')) {
  element.classList.remove('new-class');
}
```

It is also possible to add, remove, or toggle multiple classes, either by passing them each as individual properties or using a spread operator:

```
// add multiple classes
.classList.add("my-class", "another-class");

// remove multiple classes with a spread operator
const classes = ["my-class", "another-class"];
div.classList.remove(...classes);
```

12.8 Setting an Element's Style Attribute

Problem

You want to directly add or replace an inline style on a specific element.

Solution

To change one CSS property as an inline style, modify the property value via the element's `style` property:

```
elem.style.backgroundColor = 'red';
```

To modify one or more CSS properties for a single element, you can use `setAttribute()` and create an entire CSS style rule:

```
elem.setAttribute('style',
  'background-color: red; color: white; border: 1px solid black');
```

These techniques set an inline style value for the HTML element, which will appear within the HTML itself. To demonstrate further, the following JavaScript sets a style attribute on an element with an ID of `card`:

```
const card = document.getElementById('card');
card.setAttribute(
  'style',
```

```
    'background-color: #ecf0f1; color: #2c3e50;'
);
```

The resulting HTML output includes the inline style value:

```
<div id="card" style="background-color: #ecf0f1; color: #2c3e50;">
...
</div>
```

Discussion

An element's CSS properties can be modified in JavaScript using one of three approaches. As the solution demonstrates, the simplest approach is to set the property's value directly using the element's `style` property:

```
elem.style.width = '500px';
```

If the CSS property contains a hyphen, such as `font-family` or `background-color`, use the *CamelCase notation* for the property:

```
elem.style.fontFamily = 'Courier';
elem.style.backgroundColor = 'rgb(255,0,0)';
```

The CamelCase notation removes the dash and capitalizes the first letter following the dash.

You can also use `setAttribute()` or `cssText` to set the `style` property. This is useful when adding multiple styles:

```
// using setAttribute
elem.setAttribute('style','font-family: Courier; background-color: yellow');

// alternately apply a value to style.cssText
elem.style.cssText = 'font-family: Courier; background-color: yellow';
```

The `setAttribute()` method is a way of adding an attribute or replacing the value of an existing attribute for a web page element. The first argument to the method is the attribute name (automatically lowercased if the element is an HTML element) and the new attribute value.

When setting the `style` attribute, all CSS properties that are changed must be specified at the same time, as setting the attribute erases any previously set values. However, setting the `style` attribute using `setAttribute()` does not erase any settings made in a stylesheet, or set by default by the browser.

Extra: Accessing an Existing Style Setting

For the most part, accessing existing attribute values is as easy as setting them. Instead of using `setAttribute()`, use `getAttribute()`. For example, to get the value of the class:

```
const className = elem.getAttribute('class');
```

Getting access to a style setting, though, is much trickier, because a specific element's style settings at any one time is a composite of all settings merged into a whole. This *computed style* for an element is what you're most likely interested in when you want to see specific style settings for the element at any point in time. Happily, there is a method for that, `window.getComputedStyle()`, which will return the current computed styles applied to the element:

```
const style = window.getComputedStyle(elem);
```

Advanced

Rather than using `setAttribute()` to add or modify the attribute, you can create an attribute and attach it to the element using `createAttribute()` to create an `Attr` node, set its value using the `nodeValue` property, and then use `setAttribute()` to add the attribute to the element:

```
const styleAttr = document.createAttribute('style');
styleAttr.nodeValue = 'background-color: red';
someElement.setAttribute(styleAttr);
```

You can add any number of attributes to an element using either `createAttribute()` and `setAttribute()`, or `setAttribute()` directly. Both approaches are equally efficient, so unless there's a real need, you'll most likely want to use the simpler approach of setting the attribute name and value directly using `setAttribute()`.

When would you use `createAttribute()`? If the attribute value is going to be another entity reference, as is allowed with XML, you'll need to use `createAttribute()` to create an `Attr` node, as `setAttribute()` only supports simple strings.

12.9 Adding Text to a New Paragraph

Problem

You want to create a new paragraph with text and insert it into the document.

Solution

Use the `createTextNode` method to add text to an element:

```
const newPara = document.createElement('p');
const text = document.createTextNode('New paragraph content');
newPara.appendChild(text);
```

Discussion

The text within an element is, itself, an object within the DOM. Its type is a `Text` node, and it is created using a specialized method, `createTextNode()`. The method takes one parameter: the string containing the text.

Example 12-2 shows a web page with a `div` element containing four paragraphs. The JavaScript creates a new paragraph from text provided by the user via a prompt. The text could just as easily have come from a server communication or other process.

The provided text is used to create a text node, which is then appended as a child node to the new paragraph. The `paragraph` element is inserted in the web page before the first paragraph.

Example 12-2. Demonstrating various methods for adding content to a web page

```
<!DOCTYPE html>
<html>
<head>
<title>Adding Paragraphs</title>
</head>
<body>
<div id="target">
  <p>
    There is a language 'little known,'<br />
    Lovers claim it as their own.
  </p>
  <p>
    Its symbols smile upon the land, <br />
    Wrought by nature's wondrous hand;
  </p>
  <p>
    And in their silent beauty speak,<br />
    Of life and joy, to those who seek.
  </p>
  <p>
    For Love Divine and sunny hours <br />
    In the language of the flowers.
  </p>
</div>
<script>
  // use getElementById to access the div element
  const div = document.getElementById('target');

  // get paragraph text
  const txt = prompt('Enter new paragraph text', '');

  // use getElementsByTagName and the collection index
  // to access the first paragraph
  const oldPara = div.getElementsByTagName('p')[0];
```

```
  // create a text node
  const txtNode = document.createTextNode(txt);

  // create a new paragraph
  const para = document.createElement('p');

  // append the text to the paragraph, and insert the new para
  para.appendChild(txtNode);
  div.insertBefore(para, oldPara);
</script>
</body>
</html>
```

 Inserting user-supplied text directly into a web page without scrub-
bing the text first is not a good idea. When you leave a door open,
all sorts of nasty things can crawl in. Example 12-2 is for demonstration purposes only.

12.10 Inserting a New Element in a Specific DOM Location

Problem

You want to insert a new paragraph just before the third paragraph within a div
element.

Solution

Use some method to access the third paragraph, such as getElementsByTagName(), to
get all of the paragraphs for a div element. Then use the createElement() and
insertBefore() DOM methods to add the new paragraph just before the existing
third paragraph:

```
// get the target div
const div = document.getElementById('target');

// retrieve a collection of paragraphs
const paras = div.getElementsByTagName('p');

// create the element and append text to it
const newPara = document.createElement('p');
const text = document.createTextNode('New paragraph content');
newPara.appendChild(text);

// if a third para exists, insert the new element before
// otherwise, append the paragraph to the end of the div
if (paras[2]) {
  div.insertBefore(newPara, paras[2]);
```

```
} else {
  div.appendChild(newPara);
}
```

Discussion

The document.createElement() method creates any HTML element, which then can be inserted or appended into the page. In the solution, the new paragraph element is inserted before an existing paragraph using insertBefore().

Because we're interested in inserting the new paragraph before the existing third paragraph, we need to retrieve a collection of the div element's paragraphs, check to make sure a third paragraph exists, and then use insertBefore() to insert the new paragraph before the existing one. If the third paragraph doesn't exist, we can append the element to the end of the div element using appendChild().

12.11 Checking If a Checkbox Is Checked

Problem

You need to verify that a user has checked a checkbox in your application.

Solution

Select the checkbox element and validate the status with the checked property. In this example, I am selecting an HTML input checkbox element with an id of check and listening for a click event. When the event is fired, the validate function is run, which looks at the checked property of the element and logs its status to the console:

```
const checkBox = document.getElementById('check');

const validate = () => {
  if (checkBox.checked) {
    console.log('Checkbox is checked')
  } else {
    console.log('Checkbox is not checked')
  }
}

checkBox.addEventListener('click', validate);
```

Discussion

A common pattern is for a user to be presented with a checkbox to make some sort of acknowledgement, such as accepting terms of service. In these instances, it is common to disable a button unless the user has checked the checkbox. We can modify the previous example to add this functionality:

```
const checkBox = document.getElementById('check');
const acceptButton = document.getElementById('accept');

const validate = () => {
  if (checkBox.checked) {
    acceptButton.disabled = false;
  } else {
    acceptButton.disabled = true;
  }
}

checkBox.addEventListener('click', validate);
```

12.12 Adding Up Values in an HTML Table

Problem

You want to sum all numbers in a table column.

Solution

Traverse the table column containing numeric string values, convert the values to numbers, and sum the numbers:

```
let sum = 0;

// use querySelectorAll to find all second table cells
const cells = document.querySelectorAll('td:nth-of-type(2)');

// iterate over each
cells.forEach(cell => {
  sum += Number.parseFloat(cell.firstChild.data);
});
```

Discussion

The :nth-of-type(n) selector matches the specific child (n) of an element. By using td:nth-of-type(2) we are selecting the second td child element. In the example HTML markup, the second td element in the table is a numeric value:

```
<td>Washington</td><td>145</td>
```

The parseInt() and parseFloat() methods convert strings to numbers, but parse Float() is more adaptable when it comes to handling numbers in an HTML table. Unless you're absolutely certain all of the numbers will be integers, parseFloat() can work with both integers and floating-point numbers.

Example 12-3 demonstrates how to convert and sum up numeric values in an HTML table, and then how to insert a table row with this sum, at the end. The code uses document.querySelectorAll(), which uses a different variation on the CSS selector, td + td, to access the data this time. This selector finds all table cells that are preceded by another table cell.

Example 12-3. Converting table values to numbers and summing the results

```html
<!DOCTYPE html>
<html lang="en">
<head>
  <meta charset="UTF-8">
  <meta name="viewport" content="width=device-width, initial-scale=1.0">
  <meta http-equiv="X-UA-Compatible" content="ie=edge">
  <title>Adding Up Values in an HTML Table</title>
</head>
<body>
  <h1>Adding Up Values in an HTML Table</h1>
    <table>
      <tbody id="table1">
        <tr>
            <td>Washington</td><td>145</td>
        </tr>
        <tr>
            <td>Oregon</td><td>233</td>
        </tr>
        <tr>
            <td>Missouri</td><td>833</td>
        </tr>
      <tbody>
    </table>

    <script>
      let sum = 0;

      // use querySelector to find all second table cells
      const cells = document.querySelectorAll('td:nth-of-type(2)');

      // iterate over each
      cells.forEach(cell => {
        sum += Number.parseFloat(cell.firstChild.data);
      });

      // now add sum to end of table
      const newRow = document.createElement('tr');

      // first cell
      const firstCell = document.createElement('td');
      const firstCellText = document.createTextNode('Sum:');
      firstCell.appendChild(firstCellText);
      newRow.appendChild(firstCell);

      // second cell with sum
```

```
        const secondCell = document.createElement('td');
        const secondCellText = document.createTextNode(sum);
        secondCell.appendChild(secondCellText);
        newRow.appendChild(secondCell);

        // add row to table
        document.getElementById('table1').appendChild(newRow);
    </script>
</body>
</html>
```

Being able to provide a sum or other operation on table data is helpful if you're working with dynamic updates, such as accessing rows of data from a database. The fetched data may not be able to provide summary values, or you may not want to provide summary data until a web page reader chooses to do so. The users may want to manipulate the table results, and then push a button to perform the summing operation.

Adding rows to a table is straightforward, as long as you remember the steps:

1. Create a new table row using `document.createElement("tr")`.

2. Create each table row cell using `document.createElement("td")`.

3. Create each table row cell's data using `document.createTextNode()`, passing in the text of the node (including numbers, which are automatically converted to a string).

4. Append the text node to the table cell.

5. Append the table cell to the table row.

6. Append the table row to the table. Rinse, repeat.

Extra: forEach and querySelectorAll

In the preceding example, I'm using the `forEach()` method to iterate over the results of `querySelectorAll()`, which returns a `NodeList`, not an array. Though `forEach()` is an array method, modern browsers have implemented `NodeList.prototype.forEach()`, which enables it iterating over a `NodeList` with the `forEach()` syntax, as discussed in Recipe 12.2. The alternative would be a loop:

```
let sum = 0;

// use querySelector to find all second table cells
let cells = document.querySelectorAll("td:nth-of-type(2)");

for (var i = 0; i < cells.length; i++) {
  sum+=parseFloat(cells[i].firstChild.data);
}
```

Extra: Modularization of Globals

As part of a growing effort to *modularize* JavaScript, the parseFloat() and par
seInt() methods are now attached to the Number object, as new *static* methods, as of
ECMAScript 2015:

```
// modular method
const modular = Number.parseInt('123');
// global method
const global = parseInt('123');
```

These modules have reached widespread browser adoption, but can be polyfilled for
older browser support, using a tool like Babel or on their own:

```
if (Number.parseInt === undefined) {
  Number.parseInt = window.parseInt
}
```

12.13 Deleting Rows from an HTML Table

Problem

You want to remove one or more rows from an HTML table.

Solution

Use the removeChild() method on an HTML table row, and all of the child elements,
including the row cells, are also removed:

```
const parent = row.parentNode;
const oldrow = parent.removeChild(parent);
```

Discussion

When you remove an element from the web document, you're not only removing the
element, you're removing all of its child elements. In this *DOM pruning* you get a reference to the removed element if you want to process its contents before it's completely discarded. The latter is helpful if you want to provide some kind of *undo*
method in case you accidentally select the wrong table row.

To demonstrate the nature of DOM pruning, in Example 12-4, DOM methods crea
teElement() and createTextNode() are used to create table rows and cells, as well as
the text inserted into the cells. As each table row is created, an event handler is
attached to the row's *click* event. If any of the new table rows is clicked, a function is
called that removes the row from the table. The removed table row element is then
traversed, and the data in its cells is extracted and concatenated to a string, which is
printed out.

Example 12-4. Adding and removing table rows and associated table cells and data

```
<!DOCTYPE html>
<html lang="en">
  <head>
    <meta charset="UTF-8" />
    <meta name="viewport" content="width=device-width, initial-scale=1.0" />
    <meta http-equiv="X-UA-Compatible" content="ie=edge" />
    <title>Deleting Rows from an HTML Table</title>
    <style>
      table {
        border-collapse: collapse;
      }
      td,
      th {
        padding: 5px;
        border: 1px solid #ccc;
      }
      tr:nth-child(2n + 1) {
        background-color: #eeffee;
      }
    </style>
  </head>
  <body>
    <h1>Deleting Rows from an HTML Table</h1>
    <table id="mixed">
      <tr>
        <th>Value One</th>
        <th>Value two</th>
        <th>Value three</th>
      </tr>
    </table>

    <div id="result"></div>
    <script>
    // table values
    const values = new Array(3);
    values[0] = [123.45, 'apple', true];
    values[1] = [65, 'banana', false];
    values[2] = [1034.99, 'cherry', false];

    const mixed = document.getElementById('mixed');
    const tbody = document.createElement('tbody');

    function pruneRow() {
    // remove row
    const parent = this.parentNode;
    const oldRow = parent.removeChild(this);

    // dataString from removed row data
    let dataString = '';
    oldRow.childNodes.forEach(row => {
```

```
      dataString += `${row.firstChild.data} `;
    });

    // output message
    const msg = document.createTextNode(`removed ${dataString}`);
    const p = document.createElement('p');
    p.appendChild(msg);
    document.getElementById('result').appendChild(p);
    }

    // for each outer array row
    values.forEach(value => {
      const tr = document.createElement('tr');

      // for each inner array cell
      // create td then text, append
      value.forEach(cell => {
        const td = document.createElement('td');
        const txt = document.createTextNode(cell);
        td.appendChild(txt);
        tr.appendChild(td);
      });

      // attache event handler
      tr.onclick = pruneRow;

      // append row to table
      tbody.appendChild(tr);
      mixed.appendChild(tbody);
    });
    </script>
  </body>
</html>
```

12.14 Hiding Page Sections

Problem

You want to hide an existing page element and its children until needed.

Solution

You can set the CSS `visibility` property to hide and show the element:

```
msg.style.hidden = 'visible'; // to display
msg.style.hidden = 'hidden'; // to hide
```

Or you can use the CSS `display` property:

```
msg.style.display = 'block'; // to display
msg.style.display = 'none'; // to remove from display
```

Discussion

Both the CSS `visibility` and `display` properties can be used to hide and show elements. There is one major difference between the two that impacts which one you'll use.

The `visibility` property controls the element's visual rendering, but its presence also affects other elements. When an element is hidden, it still takes up page space. The `display` property, on the other hand, removes the element completely from the page layout.

The `display` property can be set to several different values, but four are of particular interest to us:

none
> When display is set to `none`, the element is removed completely from display.

block
> When display is set to `block`, the element is treated like a `block` element, with a line break before and after.

inline-block
> When display is set to `inline-block`, the contents are formatted like a `block` element, which is then flowed like inline content.

inherit
> This is the default display, and specifies that the `display` property is inherited from the element's parent.

There are other values, but these are the ones we're most likely to use within JavaScript applications.

Unless you're using absolute positioning with the hidden element, you'll want to use the CSS `display` property. Otherwise, the element will affect the page layout, pushing any elements that follow down and to the right, depending on the type of hidden element.

There is another approach to removing an element out of page view, and that is to move it totally offscreen using a negative left value. This could work, especially if you're creating a slider element that will slide in from the left. It's also an approach that the accessibility community has suggested using when you have content that you want rendered by assistive technology (AT) devices, but not visually rendered.

12.15 Creating Hover-Based Pop-Up Info Windows

Problem

You want to create an interaction where a user mouses over a thumbnail image and additional information is displayed.

Solution

This interaction is based on four different functionalities.

First, you need to capture the `mouseover` and `mouseout` events for each image thumbnail in order to display or remove the pop-up window, respectively. In the following code, the cross-browser event handlers are attached to all images in the page:

```
window.onload = () => {
  const imgs = document.querySelectorAll('img');
  imgs.forEach(img => {
    img.addEventListener(
      'mouseover',
      () => {
        getInfo(img.id);
      },
      false
    );

    img.addEventListener(
      'mouseout',
      () => {
        removeWindow();
      },
      false
    );
  });
};
```

Second, you need to access something about the item you're hovering over in order to know what to use to populate the pop-up bubble. The information can be in the page, or you can use web server communication to get the information:

```
function getInfo(id) {
  // get the data
}
```

Third, you need to either show the pop-up window, if it already exists and is not displayed, or create the window. In the following code, the pop-up window is created just below the object, and just to the right when the web server call returns with the information about the item. The `getBoundingClientRect()` method is used to determine the location where the pop-up should be placed, and `createElement()` and `createTextNode()` are used to create the pop-up:

```
// compute position for pop-up
function compPos(obj) {
  const rect = obj.getBoundingClientRect();
  let height;
  if (rect.height) {
    height = rect.height;
  } else {
    height = rect.bottom - rect.top;
  }
  const top = rect.top + height + 10;
  return [rect.left, top];
}

function showWindow(id, response) {
  const img = document.getElementById(id);

  console.log(img);
  // derive location for pop-up
  const loc = compPos(img);
  const left = `${loc[0]}px`;
  const top = `${loc[1]}px`;

  // create pop-up
  const div = document.createElement('popup');
  div.id = 'popup';
  const txt = document.createTextNode(response);
  div.appendChild(txt);

  // style pop-up
  div.setAttribute('class', 'popup');
  div.setAttribute('style', `position: fixed; left: ${left}; top: ${top}`);
  document.body.appendChild(div);
}
```

Lastly, when the `mouseover` event fires, you need to either hide the pop-up window or remove it—whichever makes sense in your setup. Since the application created a new pop-up window in the `mouseover` event, it removes the pop-up in the `mouseout` event handler:

```
function removeWindow() {
  const popup = document.getElementById('popup');
  if (popup) popup.parentNode.removeChild(popup);
}
```

Discussion

Creating a pop-up information or help window doesn't have to be complicated if you keep the action simple and follow the four steps outlined in the solution. If the

---

pop-up provides help for `form` elements, then you might want to cache the information within the page, and just show and hide pop-up elements as needed. However, if you have pages with hundreds of items, you'll have better performance if you get the pop-up window information on demand via a web service call.

When I positioned the pop-up in the example, I didn't place it directly over the object. The reason is that I'm not capturing the mouse position to have the pop-up follow the cursor around, ensuring that I don't move the cursor directly over the pop-up. But if I statically position the pop-up partially over the object, the web page readers could move their mouse over the pop-up, which triggers the event to hide the pop-up…which then triggers the event to show the pop-up, and so on. This creates a flicker effect, not to mention a lot of network activity.

If, instead, I allowed the mouse events to continue by returning `true` from either event handler function, when the web page readers move their mouse over the pop-up, the pop-up won't go away. However, if they move the mouse from the image to the pop-up, and then to the rest of the page, the event to trigger the pop-up event removal won't fire, and the pop-up is left on the page.

The best approach is to place the pop-up directly under (or to the side, or a specific location in the page) rather than directly over the object.

12.16 Validating Form Data

Problem

Your web application gathers data from the users using HTML forms. Before you send that data to the server, though, you want to make sure it's well formed, complete, and valid while providing feedback to the user.

Solution

Use the HTML5's built-in form validation attributes, which can be extended with an external library for string validation:

```
<form id="example" name="example" action="" method="post">
  <fieldset>
    <legend>Example Form</legend>
    <div>
      <label for="email">Email (required):</label>
      <input type="email" id="email" name="email" value="" required />
    </div>
    <div>
      <label for="postal">Postal Code:</label>
      <input type="text" pattern="[0-9]*" id="postal" name="url" value="" />
    </div>
    <div id="error"></div>
```

```
    <div>
      <input type="submit" value="Submit" />
    </div>
  </fieldset>
</form>
```

You can use a standalone library, such as validator.js (*https://github.com/validatorjs/ validator.js*), to check for validity as a user types:

```
<script type="text/javascript">
  function inputValidator(id, value) {
    // check email validity
    if (id === 'email') {
     return validator.isEmail(value);
    }

    // check US postal code validity
    if (id === 'postal') {
     return validator.isPostalCode(value, 'US');
    }

    return false;
  }

  const inputs = document.querySelectorAll('#example input');

  inputs.forEach(input => {
    // fire an event each time an input value changes
    input.addEventListener('input', () => {
     // pass the input value to the validation function
     const valid = inputValidator(input.id, input.value);
     // if not valid set the aria-invalid attribute to true
     if (!valid && input.value.length > 0) {
       this.setAttribute('aria-invalid', 'true');
     }
    });
  });
</script>
```

Discussion

By now, we should not be writing our own forms validation routines. Not unless we're dealing with some really bizarre form behavior and/or data. And by bizarre, I mean so far outside the ordinary that trying to incorporate a JavaScript library would actually be harder than doing it ourselves—a "the form field value must be a string except on Thursdays, when it must be a number—but reverse that in even months" type of validation.

You have a lot of options for libraries, and I've only demonstrated one. The *validator.js* library is a nice, simple, easy-to-use library that provides validation for many different types of strings. It doesn't require that you modify the form fields, either, which means it's easier to just drop it in, instead of reworking the form. Any and all styling and placement of error messages is developer dependent, too.

In the solution, the code adds an event listener to each `input` element. When a user makes any change to the field, the `input` event listener is fired and calls the `inputValidator` function, which checks the value against the *validator.js* library. If the value is invalid, minimal CSS styling is used to add a red border to the input field. When the value is valid, no style is added.

Sometimes you need a smaller library specifically for one type of data validation. Credit cards are tricky things, and though you can ensure a correct format, the values contained in them must meet specific rules in order to be considered valid credit card submissions.

In addition to the other validation libraries, you can also incorporate a credit card validation library, such as Payment (*https://github.com/jessepollak/payment*), which provides a straightforward validation API. As an example, specify that a field is a credit card number after the form loads:

```
const cardInput = document.querySelector('input.cc-num');

Payment.formatCardNumber(cardInput);
```

And then when the form is submitted, validate the credit card number:

```
var valid = Payment.fns.validateCardNumber(cardInput.value);

if (!valid) {
  message.innerHTML = 'You entered an invalid credit card number';
  return false;
}
```

The library doesn't just check format; it also ensures that the value meets a valid card number for all of the major card companies. Depending on how you are processing credit cards, the payment processor may provide similar functionality in the client-side code. For example, the payment processor Stripe's Stripe.js (*https://oreil.ly/GqPVh*) includes a credit card validation API.

Lastly, you can pair client and server validation, using the same library or different ones. In the example, we are using *validator.js* in the browser, but it can also be used to validate inputs on the backend in a Node application.

Extra: HTML5 Form Validation Techniques

HTML5 offers fairly extensive built-in form validation, which does not require JavaScript, including:

min *and* max
> The minimum and maximum values of numeric inputs

minlength *and* maxlength
> The minimum and maximum length of string inputs

pattern
> A regular expression pattern that the entered input must follow

required
> Required inputs must be completed before the form can be submitted

type
> Allows developers to specify a content type for an input, such as date, email address, number, password, URL, or some other specific preset type

Additionally, CSS pseudoselectors can be used to match :valid and :invalid inputs.

Because of this, for simple forms you may not need JavaScript at all. If you need finite control over the appearance and behavior of form validation, you're better off using a JavaScript library than depending on the HTML5 and CSS forms validation specifications. If you do, though, make sure to incorporate accessibility features into your forms. I recommend reading WebAIM's "Creating Accessible Forms" (*https://oreil.ly/5oL3E*).

12.17 Highlighting Form Errors and Accessibility

Problem

You want to highlight form field entries that have incorrect data, and you want to ensure the highlighting is effective for all web page users.

Solution

Use CSS to highlight the incorrectly entered form field, and use WAI-ARIA (Web Accessibility Initiative-Accessible Rich Internet Applications) markup to ensure the highlighting is apparent to all users:

```
[aria-invalid] {
  background-color: #f5b2b2;
}
```

For the fields that need to be validated, assign a function to the form field's oninput event handler that checks whether the field value is valid. If the value is invalid, display information to the user about the error at the same time that you highlight the field:

```
function validateField() {
  // check for number
  if (typeof this.value !== 'number') {
    this.setAttribute('aria-invalid', 'true');
```

```
      generateAlert(
        'You entered an invalid value. Only numeric values are allowed'
      );
    }
  }

  document.getElementById('number').oninput = validateField;
```

For the fields that need a required value, assign a function to the field's onblur event handler that checks whether a value has been entered:

```
function checkMandatory() {
  // check for data
  if (this.value.length === 0) {
    this.setAttribute('aria-invalid', 'true');
    generateAlert('A value is required in this field');
  }
}

document.getElementById('required-field').onblur = checkMandatory;
```

If any of the validation checks are performed as part of the form submission, make sure to cancel the submission event if the validation fails.

Discussion

The WAI-ARIA provides a way of marking certain fields and behaviors so that assistive devices do whatever is the equivalent behavior for people who need these devices. If a person is using a screen reader, setting the aria-invalid attribute to true (or adding it to the element) should trigger an audible warning in the screen reader—comparable to a color indicator doing the same for people who aren't using assistive technologies.

 Read more on WAI-ARIA at the Web Accessibility Initiative at the W3C (*https://oreil.ly/8wGnc*). On Windows, I recommend using NVDA (*http://www.nvaccess.org*), an open source, freely available screen reader, for testing whether your application is responding as you think it should with a screen reader. For macOS, I recommend using the built-in VoiceOver tool with the Safari browser.

In addition, the role attribute can be set to several values of which one, "alert," triggers a comparable behavior in screen readers (typically saying out the field contents).

Providing these cues are essential when you're validating form elements. You can validate a form before submission and provide a text description of everything that's wrong. A better approach, though, is to validate data for each field as the user finishes, so they're not left with a lot of irritating error messages at the end.

As you validate the field, you can ensure your users know exactly which field has failed by using a visual indicator. It shouldn't be the only method used to mark an error, but it is an extra courtesy.

If you highlight an incorrect form field entry with colors, avoid those that are hard to differentiate from the background. If the form background is white, and you use a dark yellow, gray, red, blue, green, or other color, there's enough contrast that it doesn't matter if the person viewing the page is color-blind or not. In the example, I used a darker pink in the form field.

I could have set the color directly, but it makes more sense to handle both updates—setting `aria-invalid` and changing the color—with one CSS setting. Luckily, CSS *attribute selectors* simplify our task in this regard.

In addition to using color, you also need to provide a text description of the error, so there's no question in the user's mind about what the problem is.

How you display the information is also an important consideration. None of us really like to use alert boxes, if we can avoid them. Alert boxes can obscure the form, and the only way to access the form element is to dismiss the alert with its error message. A better approach is to embed the information in the page, near the form. We also want to ensure the error message is available to people who are using assistive technologies, such as a screen reader. This is easily accomplished by assigning an ARIA `alert` `role` to the element containing the alert for those using screen readers or other AT devices.

One final bonus to using `aria-invalid` is it can be used to discover all incorrect fields when the form is submitted. Just search on all elements where the attribute is present and if any are discovered, you know there's still an invalid form field value that needs correcting.

Example 12-5 demonstrates how to highlight an invalid entry on one of the form elements, and highlight missing data in another. The example also traps the form submit, and checks whether any invalid form field flags are still set. Only if everything is clear is the form submission allowed to proceed.

Example 12-5. Providing visual and other cues when validating form fields

```
<!DOCTYPE html>
<head>
<title>Validating Forms</title>
<style>
[aria-invalid] {
    background-color: #ffeeee;
}

[role="alert"] {
```

```
    background-color: #ffcccc;
    font-weight: bold;
    padding: 5px;
    border: 1px dashed #000;
}

div {
    margin: 10px 0;
    padding: 5px;
    width: 400px;
    background-color: #ffffff;
}
</style>
</head>
<body>

<form id="testform">
    <div><label for="firstfield">*First Field:</label><br />
        <input id="firstfield" name="firstfield" type="text" aria-required="true"
        required />
    </div>
    <div><label for="secondfield">Second Field:</label><br />
        <input id="secondfield" name="secondfield" type="text" />
    </div>
    <div><label for="thirdfield">Third Field (numeric):</label><br />
        <input id="thirdfield" name="thirdfield" type="text" />
    </div>
    <div><label for="fourthfield">Fourth Field:</label><br />
        <input id="fourthfield" name="fourthfield" type="text" />
    </div>

    <input type="submit" value="Send Data" />
</form>

<script>

  document.getElementById("thirdfield").onchange=validateField;
  document.getElementById("firstfield").onblur=mandatoryField;
  document.getElementById("testform").onsubmit=finalCheck;

  function removeAlert() {

    var msg = document.getElementById("msg");
    if (msg) {
      document.body.removeChild(msg);
    }
  }

  function resetField(elem) {
    elem.parentNode.setAttribute("style","background-color: #ffffff");
    var valid = elem.getAttribute("aria-invalid");
    if (valid) elem.removeAttribute("aria-invalid");
```

```
}

function badField(elem) {
  elem.parentNode.setAttribute("style", "background-color: #ffeeee");
  elem.setAttribute("aria-invalid","true");
}

function generateAlert(txt) {

  // create new text and div elements and set
  // Aria and class values and id
  var txtNd = document.createTextNode(txt);
  msg = document.createElement("div");
  msg.setAttribute("role","alert");
  msg.setAttribute("id","msg");
  msg.setAttribute("class","alert");

  // append text to div, div to document
  msg.appendChild(txtNd);
  document.body.appendChild(msg);
}

function validateField() {

  // remove any existing alert regardless of value
  removeAlert();

  // check for number
  if (!isNaN(this.value)) {
    resetField(this);
  } else {
    badField(this);
    generateAlert("You entered an invalid value in Third Field. " +
                  "Only numeric values such as 105 or 3.54 are allowed");
  }
}

function mandatoryField() {

  // remove any existing alert
  removeAlert();

  // check for value
  if (this.value.length > 0) {
    resetField(this);
  } else {
    badField(this);
    generateAlert("You must enter a value into First Field");
  }
}

function finalCheck() {
```

```
    removeAlert();
    var fields = document.querySelectorAll("[aria-invalid='true']");
    if (fields.length > 0) {
      generateAlert("You have incorrect field entries that must be fixed " +
                    "before you can submit this form");
      return false;
    }
  }
}
```

```
</script>
```

```
</body>
```

If either of the validated fields is incorrect in the application, the `aria-invalid` attribute is set to `true` in the field, and an ARIA `role` is set to `alert` on the error message, as shown in Figure 12-2. When the error is corrected, the `aria-invalid` attribute is removed, as is the alert message. Both have the effect of changing the background color for the form field.

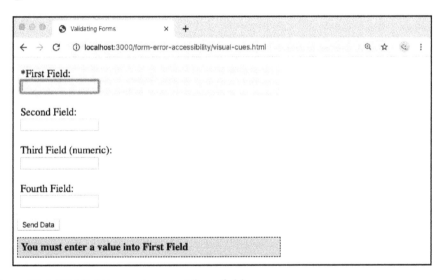

Figure 12-2. Highlighting an incorrect form field

Notice in the code that the element wrapping the targeted form field is set to its correct state when the data entered is correct, so that when a field is corrected it doesn't show up as inaccurate or missing on the next go-round. I remove the existing message alert regardless of the previous event, as it's no longer valid with the new event.

You can also disable or even hide the correctly entered form elements as a way to accentuate those with incorrect or missing data. However, I don't recommend this approach. Your users may find as they fill in the missing information that their answers in other fields are incorrect. If you make it difficult for them to correct the fields, they're not going to be happy with the experience—or the company, person, or organization providing the form.

Another approach you can take is to only do validation when the form is submitted. Many built-in libraries operate this way. Rather than check each field for mandatory or correct values as your users tab through, you only apply the validation rules when the form is submitted. This allows users who want to fill out the form in a different order to do so without getting irritating validation messages as they tab through.

Using JavaScript to highlight a form field with incorrect and missing data is only one part of the form submission process. You'll also have to account for JavaScript being turned off, which means you have to provide the same level of feedback when processing the form information on the server, and providing the result on a separate page.

It's also important to mark if a form field is required ahead of time. Use an asterisk in the form field label, with a note that all form fields with an asterisk are required. Use the `aria-required` and attribute to ensure this information is communicated to those using assistive devices. I also recommend using the HTML5 `required` attribute when using `aria-required`, which provides built-in browser validation.

See Also

In Recipe 12.16 I cover form validation libraries and modules to simplify form validation. I also touch on using the HTML5 declarative form validation techniques.

12.18 Creating an Accessible Automatically Updated Region

Problem

You have a section of a web page that is updated periodically, such as a section that lists recent updates to a file, or one that reflects recent Twitter activity on a subject. You want to ensure that when the page updates, those using a screen reader are notified of the new information.

Solution

Use WAI-ARIA *region* attributes on the element being updated:

```
<div id="update" role="log" aria-live="polite" aria-atomic="true"
aria-relevant="additions">
</div>
```

Discussion

A section of the web page that can be updated after the page is loaded, and without direct user intervention, calls for WAI-ARIA Live Regions. These are probably the simplest ARIA functionality to implement, and they provide immediate, positive results. And there's no code involved, other than the JavaScript you need to create the page updates.

```
<div id="update" role="log" aria-live="polite" aria-atomic="true"
aria-relevant="additions"></div>
```

From left to right, the `role` is set to `log`, which would be used when polling for log updates from a file. Other options include `status`, for a status update, and a more general `region` value, for an undetermined purpose.

The `aria-live` region attribute is set to `polite`, because the update isn't a critical update. The `polite` setting tells the screen reader to voice the update, but not interrupt a current task to do so. If I had used a value of `assertive`, the screen reader would interrupt whatever it is doing and voice the content. Always use `polite`, unless the information is critical.

The `aria-atomic` is set to `false`, so that the screen reader only voices new additions, based on whatever is set with `aria-relevant`. It could get very annoying to have the screen reader voice the entire set with each new addition, as would happen if this value is set to `true`.

Lastly, the `aria-relevant` is set to `additions`, as we don't care about the entries being removed from the top. This setting is actually the default setting for this attribute, so, technically, it isn't needed. In addition, assistive technology devices don't have to support this attribute. Still, I'd rather list it than not. Other values are `removals`, `text`, and `all` (for all events). You can specify more than one, separated by a space.

This WAI-ARIA–enabled functionality was probably the one that impressed me the most. One of my first uses for fetching remote data, years ago, was to update a web page with information. It was frustrating to test the page with a screen reader (JAWS, at the time) and hear nothing but silence every time the page was updated. I can't even imagine how frustrating it was for those who needed the functionality.

Now we have it, and it's so easy to use. It's a win-win.

## CHAPTER 13

Fetching Remote Data

The ability to receive and process data in the browser, without refreshing a page, is one of JavaScript's super powers. Real-time data trackers, chat applications, social media feed updates, and much more, are all made possible through JavaScript's ability to make a request to a server and update content on the page. In this chapter, we'll cover how to make and process those requests.

 You may also hear the term "AJAX," which is an abbreviation for Asynchronous JavaScript and XML. Although originally coined in reference to retrieving XML, AJAX has become a generalized term for retrieving and sending data to a remote server from a web browser.

13.1 Requesting Remote Data with Fetch

Problem

You need to request remote data from a server.

Solution

Use the Fetch API, which allows you to make requests and manipulate the response. To make a simple request, pass a URL as a `fetch` parameter, which returns the response as a promise. The following example requests the URL, parses the JSON response, and logs the response to the console:

```
const url = 'https://api.nasa.gov/planetary/apod?api_key=DEMO_KEY';
fetch(url)
  .then(response => response.json())
  .then(data => console.log(data));
```

Alternately, use the `async`/`await` syntax with `fetch`:

```
const url = 'https://api.nasa.gov/planetary/apod?api_key=DEMO_KEY';

async function fetchRequest() {
  const response = await fetch(url);
  const data = await response.json();
  console.log(data);
}

fetchRequest();
```

Discussion

The Fetch API provides a means for sending and retrieving data from a remote source. When working in a web browser environment, this means that data can be retrieved without refreshing the page. As a web user, you may experience these types of requests frequently. The Fetch API can be used to:

- Load additional items in a social media feed
- Form autocomplete suggestions
- "Like" a social media post
- Update form field values based on a previous response
- Submit a form without navigating away from the page
- Add an item to a shopping cart

As you may imagine, the list can go on and on.

The `fetch()` method accepts two parameters:

url *(mandatory)*
: The URL to which you are making a request

options
: An object of options when making the request

The possible `options` include:

body
: The body content of a request

cache
: The cache mode of the request (`default`, `no-store`, `reload`, `no-cache`, `force-cache`, or `only-if-cached`)

credentials
: The request credentials of the request (`omit`, `same-origin`, or `include`)

headers
> Headers included with the request

`integrity`
> A subresource integrity value, used for verify resources

`keepalive`
> Set to `true` for the request to outlive the page

`method`
> The request method (GET, POST, PUT, or DELETE)

`mode`
> The mode of the request (`cors`, `no-cors`, or `same-origin`)

`redirect`
> Sets behavior for redirects (`follow`, `error`, or `manual`)

`referrer`
> Sets the value of the referrer header (about:client, the current URL, or an empty string)

`referrerPolicy`
> Specifies the referrer policy (`no-referrer`, `no-referrer-when-downgrade`, `same-origin`, `origin`, `strict-origin`, `origin-when-cross-origin`, `strict-origin-when-cross-origin`, or `unsafe-url`)

`signal`
> `AbortController` object to abort request

As shown in the previous example, only the `url` parameter is required. When passed only a URL, the `fetch` method will perform a GET request. The following example demonstrates how to use the options object:

```
const response = await fetch(url, {
  method: 'GET',
  mode: 'cors',
  credentials: 'omit',
  redirect: 'follow',
  referrerPolicy: 'no-referrer'
});
```

`fetch` makes use of JavaScript promises. The initial promise returns a `Response` object, which contains the full HTTP response, including the body, headers, status code, redirect information, cors type, and URL. With the response returned, you can then use an additional parsing method to parse the body of the request. In the example, I'm using the `json()` method to parse the body as JSON. Here are the possible parsing methods:

`arrayBuffer()`
Parse the body as an `ArrayBuffer`

`blob()`
Parse the body as a `Blob`

`json()`
Parse the body as JSON

`text()`
Parse the body as a UTF-8 string

`formData()`
Parse the body as a `FormData()` object

When using `fetch`, you can handle errors based on the server's status response. In async/await:

```
async function fetchRequestWithError() {
  const response = await fetch(url);
  if (response.status >= 200 && response.status < 400) {
    const data = await response.json();
    console.log(data);
  } else {
    // Handle server error
    // example: INTERNAL SERVER ERROR: 500 error
    console.log(`${response.statusText}: ${response.status} error`);
  }
}
```

For more robust error handling, you can wrap the entire `fetch` request in a try/catch block, which will allow you to handle any additional errors:

```
async function fetchRequestWithError() {
  try {
    const response = await fetch(url);
    if (response.status >= 200 && response.status < 400) {
      const data = await response.json();
      console.log(data);
    } else {
      // Handle server error
      // example: INTERNAL SERVER ERROR: 500 error
      console.log(`${response.statusText}: ${response.status} error`);
    }
  } catch (error) {
    // Generic error handler
    console.log(error);
  }
}
```

Errors can be handled similarly when using the the JavaScript then promise syntax:

```
fetch(url)
  .then((response) => {
    if (response.status >= 200 && response.status < 400) {
      return response.json();
    } else {
      // Handle server error
      // example: INTERNAL SERVER ERROR: 500 error
      console.log(`${response.statusText}: ${response.status} error`);
    }
  })
  .then((data) => {
    console.log(data)
  }).catch(error) => {
    // Generic error handler
    console.log(error);
  };
```

If you've worked with AJAX requests in the past, you may have used the XMLHttpRe
quest (XHR) method (covered in Recipe 13.2). Due to its promise-based syntax, simpler syntax, and broad browser support, the Fetch API is now the recommended
method for making these requests. fetch is supported in all modern browsers
(Chrome, Edge, Firefox, Safari), however it is not supported in Internet Explorer. If
your application needs to support older versions of Internet Explorer, you may
choose to use XHR (XMLHttpRequest) or make use of a fetch polyfill (*https://
github.com/github/fetch*) alongside a promise polyfill (*https://github.com/taylorhakes/
promise-polyfill*).

13.2 Using XMLHttpRequest

Problem

Your application needs to request remote data while supporting older browsers.

Solution

Use XMLHttpRequest (XHR) in place of fetch. The following is an XHR GET request,
which mirrors the example demonstrated in Recipe 13.1:

```
const url = 'https://api.nasa.gov/planetary/apod?api_key=DEMO_KEY';
const request = new XMLHttpRequest();
request.open('GET', url);
request.send();

request.onload = () => {
  if (request.status >= 200 && request.status < 400) {
    // successful request logs the returned JSON data
    const data = JSON.parse(request.response);
    console.log(data);
  } else {
```

```
      // server error
      // example: INTERNAL SERVER ERROR: 500 error
      console.log(`${request.statusText}: ${request.status} error`);
    }
  };

  // request error
  request.onerror = () => console.log(request.statusText);
```

Discussion

XMLHttpRequest is the original syntax for making remote data requests. Though XML is in the name, it can be used to request all sorts of data. In the previous example, I'm making a request for JSON data. So how does XMLHttpRequest differ from fetch?

- fetch makes heavy use of JavaScript promises, while XMLHttpRequest is based around the XMLHttpRequest() constructor function.

- XMLHttpRequest is supported in all browsers, including older versions of Internet Explorer. fetch will not work without a polyfill (which is based on XMLHttpRequest) in Internet Explorer 11 or older, as well as some versions of modern auto-updating browsers from 2017 or earlier.

- XMLHttpRequest defaults to sending cookies to the server with each request, while fetch requires that the credentials option be explicitly set.

- XMLHttpRequest supports tracking upload progress, while, at the time of writing, fetch only supports download progress.

- fetch does not support timeouts, leaving the length of the request up to the user's browser.

Though the rest of this chapter will make use of the modern fetch syntax, XMLHttpRequest continues to be a reasonable choice due to its browser support and differentiating features, particularly when working with legacy applications.

13.3 Submitting a Form

Problem

You want to submit a form from the client.

Solution

Make a POST request of a FormData object, using fetch:

```
const myForm = document.getElementById('my-form');
const url = 'http://localhost:8080/';

myForm.addEventListener('submit', async event => {
  event.preventDefault();

  const formData = new FormData(myForm);
  const response = await fetch(url, {
    method: 'post',
    body: formData
  });

  const result = await response.text();
  alert(result);
});
```

Discussion

In the example code, I am selecting an HTML form element using `getElementById` and storing the URL to POST the form to as a variable. In this case, I am POSTing the form to a local development server, as shown in Example 13-1. I've then added an event listener to the form and prevented the default form submission behavior, so that I can instead perform a JavaScript POST request using `fetch`.

The complete HTML Markup and JavaScript is as follows:

```
<!DOCTYPE html>
<html lang="en">
  <head>
    <meta charset="UTF-8" />
    <meta name="viewport" content="width=device-width, initial-scale=1.0" />
    <meta http-equiv="X-UA-Compatible" content="ie=edge" />
    <title>Form POST</title>
  </head>
  <body>
    <h1>Form POST HTML</h1>

    <form id="my-form">
      <label for="name">Name:</label>
      <input type="text" id="name" name="name" />

      <label for="mail">E-mail:</label>
      <input type="email" id="mail" name="email" />

      <label for="msg">Message:</label>
      <textarea id="message" name="message"></textarea>

      <button>Submit</button>
    </form>

    <script>
```

```
const myForm = document.getElementById('my-form');
const url = 'http://localhost:8080/';

myForm.addEventListener('submit', async event => {
event.preventDefault();

const formData = new FormData(myForm);
const response = await fetch(url, {
method: 'post',
body: formData
});

const result = await response.text();
alert(result);
});

  </script>
 </body>
</html>
```

JavaScript's FormData provides a means for easily creating key/value pairs of all the form data. This works with text-based form elements, as demonstrated in the example, as well as with file uploads. First, use the FormData constructor:

```
const myForm = document.getElementById('my-form');
const formData = new FormData(myForm);
```

You may also manipulate the data contained in the FormData with some helpful methods:

FormData.append(key, value) *or* FormData.append(key, blob, filename)
    Appends new data to the form

FormData.delete(key)
    Deletes a field

FormData.set(key, value)
    Appends new data, removing a duplicate key, if present

Here is how you would add an additional field to the previous example:

```
const myForm = document.getElementById('my-form');
const url = 'http://localhost:8080/';

myForm.addEventListener('submit', async event => {
  event.preventDefault();

  const formData = new FormData(myForm);
  // add a new field using FormData.append
  formData.append('user', true);

  const response = await fetch(url, {
```

```
    method: 'post',
    body: formData
  });

  const result = await response.text();
  console.log(result);
});
```

The body of the POST request will now be:

```
{
  name: 'Adam',
  email: 'adam@example.com',
  message: 'Hello',
  user: 'true'
}
```

It is also possible to work with the form values, using the get and has methods:

FormData.get(key)
    Gets the value of a specific key

FormData.has(key)
    Checks for a value with a given key and returns a Boolean

While FormData is incredibly useful, it is not the only value type of a POST body. The following types can be sent in a POST request:

- A string

- An encoded string, such as JSON or XML

- A URLSearchParams object

- A Blob or BufferSource of binary data

In Recipe 13.4 I will demonstrate how to send a JSON POST request with fetch.

Finally, Example 13-1 is an example Node.js Express server that processes the request:

Example 13-1. Express form server example

```
const express = require('express');
const formidable = require('formidable');
const cors = require('cors');

const app = express();
const port = 8080;

app.use(cors());

app.get('/', (req, res) =>
  res.send('Example server for receiving JS POST requests')
```

```
);

app.post('/', (req, res) => {
  const form = formidable();

  form.parse(req, (err, fields) => {
    if (err) {
      return;
    }
    console.log('POST body:', fields);
    res.sendStatus(200);
  });
});

app.listen(port, () =>
  console.log(`Example app listening at http://localhost:${port}`)
);
```

 We cover Express in detail in Chapter 21.

13.4 Populating a Selection List from the Server

Problem

Based on a user's actions with another form element, you want to populate a selection list with values.

Solution

Capture the change event for the form element:

```
const niceThings = document.getElementById('nice-thing');
niceThings.addEventListener('change', async () => {
  // GET request and events go here
});
```

In the event handler function, make a fetch request as a POST with the form data as JSON:

```
const niceThings = document.getElementById('nice-thing');
const url = 'http://localhost:8080/select';

// perform GET request when select value changes
niceThings.addEventListener('change', async () => {
  // object containing select value
  const selection = {
```

```
      niceThing: niceThings.value
    };

    // GET request to server
    const response = await fetch(url, {
      method: 'post',
      headers: {
        'Content-Type': 'application/json;charset=utf-8'
      },
      body: JSON.stringify(selection)
    });

  });
```

Populate the selection list with the result:

```
    const select = document.getElementById('nicestuff');

    if (response.ok) {
      const result = await response.json();
      // empty the select element
      select.length = 0;
      // add a default display option with text and no value
      select.options[0] = new Option('--Please choose an option--', '');
      // populate the select with the returned values
      for (let i = 0; i < result.length; i += 1) {
        select.options[select.length] = new Option(result[i], result[i]);
      }
      // display the select element
      select.style.display = 'block';
    } else {
      // if there's a problem fetching the data, display an error
      alert('Error');
    }
```

Discussion

Populating a select or other form element based on a choice made by the user is a common user interface interaction. Instead of populating a select element with many options, or building a set of 10 or 20 radio buttons, you can capture the user's choice in another form element, query a server application based on the value, and build the other form elements based on the value—all without leaving the page.

Example 13-2 demonstrates a simple page that captures the change event for a select element, makes a fetch request with the value of the selected value, and populates a new selection list by parsing the returned data. In the example, the data is returned as an array, and new options are created with the returned text having both an option label and option value. Before populating the select element, its length is set to 0. This is a quick and easy way to truncate the select element—removing all existing options and starting fresh.

Example 13-2. Creating an on-demand `select` *list*

```
<!DOCTYPE html>
<html lang="en">
  <head>
    <meta charset="UTF-8" />
    <meta name="viewport" content="width=device-width, initial-scale=1.0" />
    <meta http-equiv="X-UA-Compatible" content="ie=edge" />
    <title>Select List</title>
    <style>
      #nicestuff {
        display: none;
        margin: 10px 0;
      }

      label,
      legend {
        display: block;
        font-size: 1.6rem;
        font-weight: 700;
        margin-bottom: 0.5rem;
      }
    </style>
  </head>
  <body>
    <h1>Select List</h1>

    <form id="my-form">
      <label for="pet-select">Select a nice thing:</label>

      <select name="nicething" id="nice-thing">
        <option value="">--Please choose an option--</option>
        <option value="birds">Birds</option>
        <option value="flowers">Flowers</option>
        <option value="sweets">Sweets</option>
        <option value="critters">Cute Critters</option>
      </select>
      <select id="nicestuff">
        <option value="">--Please choose an option--</option>
      </select>
    </form>
    <script>
    const niceThings = document.getElementById('nice-thing');
    const select = document.getElementById('nicestuff');
    const url = 'http://localhost:8080/select';

    // perform GET request when select value changes
    niceThings.addEventListener('change', async () => {
    // object containing select value
    const selection = {
      niceThing: niceThings.value
    };
```

```
      // GET request to server
      const response = await fetch(url, {
        method: 'post',
        headers: {
          'Content-Type': 'application/json;charset=utf-8'
        },
        body: JSON.stringify(selection)
      });

      // if fetch is successful
      if (response.ok) {
        const result = await response.json();
        // empty the select element
        select.length = 0;
        // add a default display option with text and no value
        select.options[0] = new Option('--Please choose an option--', '');
        // populate the select with the returned values
        for (let i = 0; i < result.length; i += 1) {
          select.options[select.length] = new Option(result[i], result[i]);
        }
        // display the select element
        select.style.display = 'block';
      } else {
        // if there's a problem fetching the data, display an error
        alert('Error');
      }
    });

    </script>
  </body>
</html>
```

The example uses a Node application to populate the selection list, but could be written in any server-side programming language. Node is covered in detail in Part III.

```
const express = require('express');
const formidable = require('formidable');
const cors = require('cors');

const app = express();
const port = 8080;

app.use(cors());

app.get('/', (req, res) =>
  res.send('Example server for receiving JS POST requests')
);

app.post('/select', (req, res) => {
  const form = formidable();
```

```
    form.parse(req, (err, fields) => {
      if (err) {
        return;
      }
      if (fields.niceThing === 'critters') {
        res.send(['puppies', 'kittens', 'guinea pigs']);
      } else if (fields.niceThing === 'sweets') {
        res.send(['licorice', 'cake', 'cookies', 'custard']);
      } else if (fields.niceThing === 'birds') {
        res.send(['robin', 'mockingbird', 'finch', 'dove']);
      } else if (fields.niceThing === 'flowers') {
        res.send(['roses', 'lilys', 'daffodils', 'pansies']);
      } else {
        res.send(['No Nice Things Found']);
      }
    });
  });

  app.listen(port, () =>
    console.log(`Example app listening at http://localhost:${port}`)
  );
```

Progressively building form elements isn't necessary in all applications, but it is a great way to ensure a more effective form in cases where the data can change, or the form is complex.

13.5 Parsing Returned JSON

Problem

You want to safely create a JavaScript object from JSON. You also want to replace the numeric representation of true and false (1 and 0, respectively) with their Boolean counterparts (true and false).

Solution

Parse the object with the JSON.parse capability. To transform the numeric values to their Boolean counterparts, create a *reviver* function:

```
  const jsonobj = '{"test" : "value1", "test2" : 3.44, "test3" : 0}';
  const obj = JSON.parse(jsonobj, (key, value) => {
    if (typeof value === 'number') {
      if (value === 0) {
        value = false;
      } else if (value === 1) {
        value = true;
      }
    }
    return value;
  });
```

```
console.log(obj.test3); // false
```

Discussion

To figure out how to create JSON, think about how you create an object literal and just translate it into a string (with some caveats).

If the object is an array:

```
const arr = new Array("one","two","three");
```

the JSON notation would be equivalent to the literal notation for the array:

```
["one","two","three"];
```

Note the use of double quotes ("") rather than single, which are not allowed in JSON.

If you're working with an object:

```
const obj3 = {
    prop1 : "test",
    result : true,
    num : 5.44,
    name : "Joe",
    cts : [45,62,13]
};
```

the JSON notation would be:

```
{"prop1":"test","result":true,"num":5.44,"name":"Joe","cts":[45,62,13]}
```

Notice in JSON how the property names are in quotes, but the values are only quoted when they're strings. In addition, if the object contains other objects, such as an array, it's also transformed into its JSON equivalent. However, the object *cannot* contain methods. If it does, an error is thrown. JSON works with data only.

The JSON static object isn't complex, as it only provides two methods: `stringify()` and `parse()`. The `parse()` method takes two arguments: a JSON-formatted string and an optional `reviver` function. This function takes a key/value pair as parameters, and returns either the original value or a modified result.

In the solution, the JSON-formatted string is an object with three properties: a string, a numeric, and a third property, which has a numeric value but is really a Boolean with a numeric representation—0 is false, 1 is true.

To transform all 0, 1 values into `false`, `true`, a function is provided as the second argument to `JSON.parse()`. It checks each property of the object to see if it is a numeric. If it is, the function checks to see if the value is 0 or 1. If the value is 0, the return value is set to `false`; if 1, the return value is set to `true`; otherwise, the original value is returned.

The ability to transform incoming JSON-formatted data is essential, especially if you're processing the result of an AJAX request or JSONP response. You can't always control the structure of the data you get from a service.

 There are restrictions on the JSON: strings must be double quoted, and there are no hexadecimal values and no tabs in strings.

13.6 Fetching and Parsing XML

Problem

You need to retrieve a remote XML file and parse its contents.

Solution

Use `fetch` along with the `DomParser` API, which provides the ability to parse XML from a string.

First, you will need to use `fetch` to request the XML file. In this example I'm requesting the XML feed of the *New York Times'* home page:

```
const url = 'https://rss.nytimes.com/services/xml/rss/nyt/HomePage.xml';

async function fetchAndParse() {
  const response = await fetch(url);
  const data = await response.text();
  console.log(data);
}

fetchAndParse();
```

Next, use `DOMParser` to parse the returned XML string, and then use the DOM methods to query the document for data:

```
const url = 'https://rss.nytimes.com/services/xml/rss/nyt/HomePage.xml';

async function fetchAndParse() {
  const response = await fetch(url);
  const data = await response.text();
  const parser = new DOMParser();
  const XMLDocument = parser.parseFromString(data, 'text/xml');
  console.log(XMLDocument);
}

fetchAndParse();
```

Discussion

When using fetch to retrieve XML, the document is returned as plain text. You can then use the DOMParser API to enable DOM methods to query the document and process the results.

DOMParser enables you to interact with the XML content using DOM querying methods such as getElementsByTagName. DOMParser requires two arguments. The first argument is the string to be parsed. The second argument is a mimeType, which specifies the document type. The mimeType options are:

- text/html
- text/xml
- application/xml
- applicatiom/xhtml+html
- image/svg+xml

The following example extends the XML parser to use DOM query selectors to output the names of the latest articles to a web page:

```
(async () => {
  const url = 'https://rss.nytimes.com/services/xml/rss/nyt/HomePage.xml';

  // fetch and parse the XML document
  async function fetchAndParse() {
    const response = await fetch(url);
    const data = await response.text();
    const parser = new DOMParser();
    const XMLDocument = parser.parseFromString(data, 'text/xml');
    return XMLDocument;
  }

  function displayTitles(xml) {
    // HTML element where the results will be displayed
    // the markup contains a ul with an id of "results"
    const listElem = document.getElementById('results');
    // get the article titles
    // each is wrapped in a <title> tag within an <item> tag
    const titles = xml.querySelectorAll('item title');
    // loop over each title in the XML; append its text content to the HTML list
    titles.forEach(title => {
      const listItem = document.createElement('li');
      listItem.innerText = title.textContent;
      listElem.appendChild(listItem);
    });
  }

  const xml = await fetchAndParse();
```

```
      displayTitles(xml);
  })();
```

13.7 Sending Binary Data and Loading into an Image

Problem

You want to request a server-side image as binary data.

Solution

Getting binary data via a `fetch` request is a matter of setting the response type to *blob* and then manipulating the data when returned. In the solution, the data is then converted and loaded into an `img` element:

```
<!DOCTYPE html>
<html lang="en">
  <head>
    <meta charset="UTF-8" />
    <meta name="viewport" content="width=device-width, initial-scale=1.0" />
    <meta http-equiv="X-UA-Compatible" content="ie=edge" />
    <title>Binary Data</title>
  </head>
  <body>
    <h1>Binary Data</h1>

    <img id="result" />
    <script>
      async function fetchImage() {
      const url = 'logo.png';
      const response = await fetch(url);
      const blob = await response.blob();

      // add returned url to image element
      const img = document.getElementById('result');
      img.src = URL.createObjectURL(blob);
      }

      fetchImage();
    </script>
  </body>
</html>
```

Discussion

A benefit of the CORS specification is support for binary data (also known as *typed arrays*) in fetch requests. The key requirement to a binary request is to set the response type to one of the following:

```
arraybuffer
```
Fixed-length raw binary data buffer

```
blob
```
File-like immutable raw data

In the solution, I used the `URL.createObjectURL()` method to convert the `blob` to a DOMString (generally mapped to JavaScript String) with the URL of the passed object. The URL is assigned to the `img` element's `src` property.

Of course, it would be just as simple to assign the URL of the PNG file to the `src` attribute in the first place. However, the ability to manipulate binary data is a necessity with various technologies, such as Web Workers and WebGL.

13.8 Sharing HTTP Cookies Across Domains

Problem

You want to access a resource from another domain as a *credentialed* request, including HTTP cookies and any authentication information.

Solution

Changes have to be made in both the client and the server applications to support credentialed requests. In the following example, the client application is served at *somedomain.com* while the server is at *api.example.com*. Because these are different domains, by default credentialed requests would not be shared from the client to the server.

In the client, we have to test the `credentials` property on the `fetch` request:

```
fetch('https://api.example.com', {
  credentials: "include"
})
```

In the server, the `Access-Control-Allow-Controls` header value must be set to `true`:

```
const http = require('http');
const Cookies = require('cookies');

const server = http.createServer((req,res) => {
  // Set CORS headers
  res.setHeader('Content-type', 'text/plain');
  res.setHeader('Access-Control-Allow-Origin', 'https://somedomain.com');
  res.setHeader('Access-Control-Allow-Credentials', true);

  const cookies = new Cookies (req, res);
  cookies.set("apple","red");
```

```
        res.writeHead(200);
        res.end("Hello cross-domain");

});

server.listen(8080);
```

 When using Express, I recommend using the CORS middleware (*https://oreil.ly/vNPPC*). We cover Express in detail in Chapter 21.

Discussion

Sharing information across domains is referred to as Cross-Origin Resource Sharing or CORS. For security reasons, browsers restrict information shared across domains, such as cookies and credential headers. Being able to send HTTP cookies or send authentication headers across domains is possible by configuring CORS extension, as long as both the client and the server signal agreement.

If using XMLHttpRequest on the client in place of fetch, set the withCredentials property:

```
const request = new XMLHttpRequest();

request.onreadystatechange = function() {
    if (this.readyState == 4) {
        console.log(this.status);
        if (this.status == 200) {
            document.getElementById('result').innerHTML = this.responseText;
        }
    }
};
request.open('GET','http://localhost:8080/');
request.withCredentials = true;
request.send(null);
```

13.9 Using Websockets to Establish a Two-Way Communication Between Client and Server

Problem

You want to initiate two-way, real-time communication between a server and web page client.

Solution

WebSockets allows you to support bidirectional communication between the client and server. The client creates a new WebSockets object, passing in the URI for the WebSockets server. Notice that the `ws:` protocol is used in place of `http` or `https`. When the client gets a message, it converts the message text to an object, retrieves the number counter, increments it, and then uses it in the object's string member.

In the following example, the client print outs every other number, starting with 2. State is maintained between the client and server by passing the string to be printed out within the message:

```
<!DOCTYPE html>
<html lang="en">
  <head>
    <meta charset="UTF-8" />
    <meta name="viewport" content="width=device-width, initial-scale=1.0" />
    <meta http-equiv="X-UA-Compatible" content="ie=edge" />
    <title>Using Websockets</title>
  </head>
  <body>
    <h1>Using Websockets</h1>

    <div id="output"></div>
    <script type="text/javascript">
      const socket = new WebSocket('ws://localhost:8080');
      socket.onmessage = event => {
        const msg = JSON.parse(event.data);
        msg.counter = Number(msg.counter) + 1;
        msg.strng += `${msg.counter}-`;
        const html = `<p> ${msg.strng} </p>`;
        document.getElementById('output').innerHTML = html;
        socket.send(JSON.stringify(msg));
      };
    </script>
  </body>
</html>
```

For the server, I'm using the `ws` Node module. Once the server is created, it starts the communication with the client by sending through a JavaScript object with two members: a number counter and a string. The object must first be converted to string. The code listens for both an incoming message and a `close` event. When it gets an incoming message, it increments the counter and sends the object:

```
var wsServer = require('ws').Server;
var wss = new wsServer({port:8001});
wss.on('connection', (function (conn) {

    // object being passed back and forth between
    // client and server
    var counter = {counter: 1, strng: ''};
```

```
        // send first communication to client
        conn.send(JSON.stringify(counter));

        // on response back
        conn.on('message', function(message) {
            var ct = JSON.parse(message);
            ct.counter = parseInt(ct.counter) + 1;
            if (ct.counter < 100) {
                conn.send(JSON.stringify(ct));
            }
        });
    }));
```

Discussion

Bidirectional communication, also known as *full-duplex* communication, is two-way communication that can occur at the same time. Think of it as a two-way road, with traffic going both ways. All modern browsers support the WebSockets specification, and as you can see, it's extremely easy to use.

The advantage to WebSockets, other than being unbelievably easy to work with in browsers, is its ability to traverse both proxies and firewalls, something that isn't trivial or even possible with other bidirectional communication techniques, such as long polling. And to ensure that applications are secure, user agents such as Chrome and Firefox prohibit mixed content (i.e., using both HTTP and HTTPS).

WebSockets supports binary data, as well as text. And as the examples demonstrated, you can transmit JSON by calling `JSON.stringify()` on the object before sending, and `JSON.parse()` on the string in the receiving end.

See Also

See the website for more information on WebSockets (*https://www.websocket.org*).

13.10 Long Polling a Remote Data Source

Problem

You would like to keep a connection open with a server so that the client is immediately updated with new information, but the server does not use WebSockets.

Solution

Use long polling, a technique where the client maintains a connection to the server by using an asynchronous `fetch` function that calls itself after a response. At its most basic, client-side long polling looks like this:

```
const url = 'http://localhost:8080/';

async function longPoll() {
  const response = await fetch(url);
  // if message received, log response to console and call polling function
  const message = await response.text();
  console.log(message);
  await longPoll();
}

longPoll();
```

This can be improved by adding some error handling, which when an error is received will wait a specified amount of time and then attempt to poll the server:

```
const url = 'http://localhost:8080/';

async function longPoll() {
  try {
    // if message received, log response to console and call polling function
    const response = await fetch(url);
    const message = await response.text();
    console.log(message);
    await longPoll();
  } catch (error) {
    // if fetch returns an error, wait 1 second and try again
    console.log(`Request failed ${error}`);
    await new Promise(resolve => setTimeout(resolve, 1000));
    await longPoll();
  }
}

longPoll();
```

Discussion

Long polling a server involves making a request and maintaining a connection to that server until a response is sent. Once the client receives the response, it immediately reconnects to the server and waits for a new response. The process can be broken down in this way:

1. Client sends request to the server.

2. Client stays connected to server while it waits for a response.

3. Server sends a response to the client.

4. Client reconnects to the server and the process repeats itself.

I find that a chat program is a helpful way to think about long polling. Imagine a chat program where we have two users who are chatting with each other, Riley and Harlow. Each of them is connected to a the server. When Riley sends a message, the server sends a response to Harlow's browser, which immediately reconnects and waits for the next message.

The limitation of long polling is in the number of open connections that the server can maintain. Node was designed to handle many concurrent connections, while some languages have limitations. All languages are limited by the hardware of the server itself. Though long polling is a simple and effective method maintaining a connection, WebSockets (as covered in Recipe 13.9) is a more efficient means of two-way communication between the client and server.

## CHAPTER 14

Data Persistence

We can animate and interact, stream, play, and render, but we always come back to the data. Data is the foundation on which we build the majority of our JavaScript applications. In the first part of the book we worked with the JavaScript languages standards for data types, in Chapter 13 we fetched data from a remote source, and in Chapter 20 we'll work with data on the server, manipulating data using APIs and data sources. Data and JavaScript, friends forever.

In this chapter, we're going to look at ways we can persist data with JavaScript in the browser using cookies, sessionStorage, localStorage, and IndexedDB.

14.1 Persisting Information with Cookies

Problem

You need to read or set the value of a browser cookie.

Solution

Use document.cookie to set and retrieve cookie values:

```
document.cookie = 'author=Adam';
console.log(document.cookie);
```

To encode strings, use encodeURIComponent, which will remove any commas, semi-colons, or whitespace:

```
const book = encodeURIComponent('JavaScript Cookbook');
document.cookie = `title=${book}`;
console.log(document.cookie);

// logs title=JavaScript%20Cookbook
```

Options can be added to the end of the cookie value and should be separated with a semicolon:

```
document.cookie = 'user=Abigail;  max-age=86400; path=/';
```

To delete a cookie, set an expiration date for the cookie that has already occurred:

```
function eraseCookie(key) {
  const cookie = `${key}=;expires=Thu, 01 Jan 1970 00:00:00 UTC`;
  document.cookie = cookie;
}
```

Discussion

Cookies are small bits of data that are stored in the browser. They are often set from the server application and sent to the server with nearly every request. In a browser they are accessed via the `document.cookie` object.

Cookies accept the following options, each separated with a semicolon:

domain
> The domain where the cookie is accessible. If not set, this defaults to the current host location. Specifying a domain allows the cookie to be accessed at subdomains.

expires
> Sets a time at which the cookie expires. Accepts a date in GMTString format.

max-age
> Sets the length of time that the cookie is valid. Accepts a value in seconds.

path
> The path at which the cookie is accessible (such as / or /app). If not specified, the cookie defaults to the current path.

secure
> If set to `true`, the cookie will only be transmitted over `https`.

samesite
> Defaults to `strict`. If set to `strict`, the cookie will not be sent in cross-site browsing. Alternatively, `lax` will send cookies on top-level GET requests.

In the following example, the user can enter a value which is stored as a cookie. They can then retrieve the value of a specified key and delete the value.

In an HTML file:

```
<!DOCTYPE html>
<html lang="en">
  <head>
```

```html
    <meta charset="UTF-8" />
    <meta name="viewport" content="width=device-width, initial-scale=1.0" />
    <meta http-equiv="X-UA-Compatible" content="ie=edge" />
    <style>
      div {
        margin: 10px;
      }

      .data {
        width: 200px;
        background-color: yellow;
        padding: 5px;
      }
    </style>
    <title>Store, retrieve, and delete a cookie</title>
  </head>
  <body>
    <h1>Store, retrieve, and delete a cookie</h1>

    <form>
      <div>
        <label for="key"> Enter key:</label>
        <input type="text" id="key" />
      </div>
      <div>
        <label for="value">Enter value:</label>
        <input type="text" id="value" />
      </div>
    </form>
    <button id="set">Set data</button>
    <button id="get">Get data</button>
    <button id="erase">Erase data</button>

    <p>Cookie value:</p>
    <div id="cookiestr" class="data"></div>

    <script src="cookie.js"></script>
  </body>
</html>
```

And the associated *cookie.js* file:

```javascript
// set the cookie
function setData() {
  const formKey = document.getElementById('key').value;
  const formValue = document.getElementById('value').value;

  const cookieVal = `${formKey}=${encodeURIComponent(formValue)}`;
  document.cookie = cookieVal;
}

// retrieve the cookie value for a specified key
function getData() {
```

```
    const key = document.getElementById('key').value;
    const cookie = document.getElementById('cookiestr');
    cookie.innerHTML = '';

    const keyValue = key.replace(/([.*+?^=!:${}()|[\]/\\])/g, '\\$1');
    const regex = new RegExp(`(?:^|;)\\s?${keyValue}=(.*?)(?:;|$)`, 'i');
    const match = document.cookie.match(regex);
    const value = (match && decodeURIComponent(match[1])) || '';
    cookie.innerHTML = `<p>${value}</p>`;
}

// remove the cookie for a specified key
function removeData() {
    const key = document.getElementById('key').value;
    document.getElementById('cookiestr').innerHTML = '';

    const cookie = `${key}=; expires=Thu, 01 Jan 1970 00:00:00 UTC`;
    document.cookie = cookie;
}

document.getElementById('set').onclick = setData;
document.getElementById('get').onclick = getData;
document.getElementById('erase').onclick = removeData;
```

Notice that I am using regular expressions to match the cookie values, which have been encoded using encodeURIComponent. This is because document.cookie returns a string with all of the cookie values. Using regular expressions in this way allows me to extract the information that I need. Regular expressions are covered in more detail in Chapter 2.

14.2 Using sessionStorage for Client-Side Storage

Problem

You want to easily store information for a single session, without running into the size and cross-page contamination problems associated with cookies.

Solution

Use the DOM Storage sessionStorage functionality:

```
sessionStorage.setItem('name', 'Franco');
sessionStorage.city = 'Pittsburgh';

// returns 2
console.log(sessionStorage.length);

// retrieve individual values
const name = sessionStorage.getItem('name');
const city = sessionStorage.getItem('city');
```

```
    console.log(`The stored name is ${name}`);
    console.log(`The stored city is ${city}`);

    // remove an individual item from storage
    sessionStorage.removeItem('name');

    // remove all items from storage
    sessionStorage.clear();

    // returns 0
    console.log(sessionStorage.length);
```

Discussion

sessionStorage allows us to easily store information in the user's browser for a single session. A session lasts for as long as a single browser tab is open. Once the user closes the browser or tab, the session ends. Opening a new tab of the same page will start a new browser session.

By comparison, the default behavior of both cookies and localStorage (discussed in Recipe 14.3) is to persist across sessions. As an example of the differences between these storage methods, Example 14-1 stores information from a form in a cookie, localStorage, and sessionStorage.

Example 14-1. Comparing sessionStorage and cookies

```
<!DOCTYPE html>
<html lang="en">
  <head>
    <meta charset="UTF-8" />
    <meta name="viewport" content="width=device-width, initial-scale=1.0" />
    <meta http-equiv="X-UA-Compatible" content="ie=edge" />
    <style>
      div {
        margin: 10px;
      }

      .data {
        width: 100px;
        background-color: yellow;
        padding: 5px;
      }
    </style>
    <title>Comparing Cookies, localStorage, and sessionStorage</title>
  </head>
  <body>
    <h1>Comparing Cookies, localStorage, and sessionStorage</h1>

    <form>
```

```
    <div>
      <label for="key"> Enter key:</label>
      <input type="text" id="key" />
    </div>
    <div>
      <label for="value">Enter value:</label>
      <input type="text" id="value" />
    </div>
  </form>
  <button id="set">Set data</button>
  <button id="get">Get data</button>
  <button id="erase">Erase data</button>

  <p>Session:</p>
  <div id="sessionstr" class="data"></div>
  <p>Local:</p>
  <div id="localstr" class="data"></div>
  <p>Cookie:</p>
  <div id="cookiestr" class="data"></div>

  <script src="cookie.js"></script>
  <script src="app.js"></script>
  </body>
</html>
```

The *cookies.js* file contains the code necessary to set, retrieve, and erase a given cookie:

```
// set session cookie
function setCookie(cookie, value) {
  const cookieVal = `${cookie}=${encodeURIComponent(value)};path=/`;
  document.cookie = cookieVal;
  console.log(cookieVal);
}

// each cookie separated by semicolon;
function getCookie(key) {
  const keyValue = key.replace(/([.*+?^=!:${}()|[\]/\\])/g, '\\$1');
  const { cookie } = document;
  const regex = new RegExp(`(?:^|;)\\s?${keyValue}=(.*?)(?:;|$)`, 'i');
  const match = cookie.match(regex);

  return match && decodeURIComponent(match[1]);
}

// set cookie date to the past to erase
function eraseCookie(key) {
  const cookie = `${key}=;path=/; expires=Thu, 01 Jan 1970 00:00:00 UTC`;
  document.cookie = cookie;
  console.log(cookie);
}
```

And the *app.js* file contains the rest of the program functionality:

```javascript
// set data for both session and cookie
function setData() {
  const key = document.getElementById('key').value;
  const { value } = document.getElementById('value');

  // set sessionStorage
  sessionStorage.setItem(key, value);

  // set localStorage
  localStorage.setItem(key, value);

  // set cookie
  setCookie(key, value);
}

function getData() {
  try {
    const key = document.getElementById('key').value;
    const session = document.getElementById('sessionstr');
    const local = document.getElementById('localstr');
    const cookie = document.getElementById('cookiestr');

    // reset display
    session.innerHTML = '';
    local.innerHTML = '';
    cookie.innerHTML = '';

    // sessionStorage
    let value = sessionStorage.getItem(key) || '';
    if (value) session.innerHTML = `<p>${value}</p>`;

    // localStorage
    value = localStorage.getItem(key) || '';
    if (value) local.innerHTML = `<p>${value}</p>`;

    // cookie
    value = getCookie(key) || '';
    if (value) cookie.innerHTML = `<p>${value}</p>`;
  } catch (e) {
    console.log(e);
  }
}

function removeData() {
  const key = document.getElementById('key').value;

  // sessionStorage
  sessionStorage.removeItem(key);

  // localStorage
  localStorage.removeItem(key);
```

```
  // cookie
  eraseCookie(key);

  // reset display
  getData();
}

document.getElementById('set').onclick = setData;
document.getElementById('get').onclick = getData;
document.getElementById('erase').onclick = removeData;
```

You can get and set the data from sessionStorage, accessing it directly, as demonstrated in the solution, but a better approach is to use the getItem() and setItem() functions.

Load the example page, add one or more values for the same key, and then click the "Get data" button. The result is displayed in Figure 14-1. No surprises here. The data has been stored in cookies, localStorage, and sessionStorage. Now, open the same page in a new tab window, enter the value into the key form field, and click the "Get data" button. The activity results in a page like that shown in Figure 14-2.

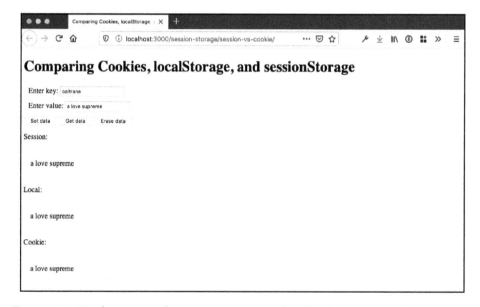

Figure 14-1. Displaying stored sessionStorage and cookie data in original tab

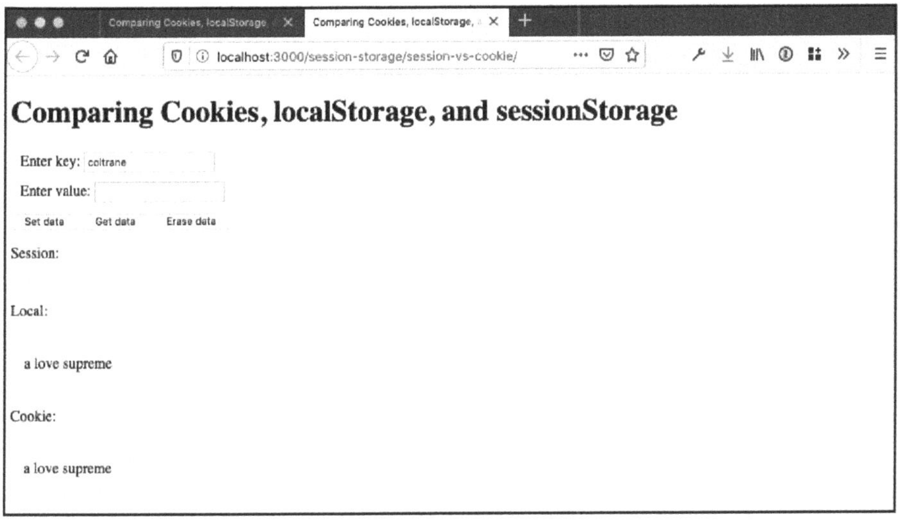

Figure 14-2. Displaying stored `sessionStorage` and cookie data in second tab

In the new tab window, the `cookie` and `localStorage` values persist because the `cookie` is session specific, but the `sessionStorage`, which is specific to the tab window, does not.

The screenshots illustrate the difference in cross-tab persistence, one of the key differences between `sessionStorage` and cookies, aside from how they're set and accessed in JavaScript. Hopefully, the images and the example also demonstrate the potential hazards involved when using `sessionStorage`, especially in circumstances where cookies have normally been used.

If your website or application users are familiar with the cookie persistence across tabbed windows, `sessionStorage` can be an unpleasant surprise. Along with the different behavior, there's also the fact that browser menu options to delete cookies probably won't have an impact on `sessionStorage`, which could also be an unwelcome surprise for your users. On the other hand, `sessionStorage` is incredibly clean to use, and provides a welcome storage option when we want to link storage to a specific tab window only.

One last note on `sessionStorage` related to its implementation: both `sessionStorage` and `localStorage`, covered in the next recipe, are part of the W3C DOM Storage specification. Both are `window` object properties, which means they can be accessed globally. Both are implementations of the `Storage` object, and changes to the `prototype` for `Storage` result in changes to both the `sessionStorage` and `localStorage` objects:

```
Storage.prototype.someMethod = function (param) { ...};
...
localStorage.someMethod(param);
...
sessionStorage.someMethod(param);
```

Aside from the differences covered in this recipe and the next, another major difference is that the Storage objects don't make a round trip to the server—they're purely client-side storage techniques.

See Also

For more information on the Storage object, sessionStorage, localStorage, or the Storage DOM, consult the specification (*https://oreil.ly/PgBUt*). See Recipe 14.3 for a different look at how sessionStorage and localStorage can be set and retrieved.

14.3 Creating a localStorage Client-Side Data Storage Item

Problem

You want to persist form element entries (or any data) in such a way that users can continue where they left off if the browser crashes, the user accidentally closes the browser, or the internet connection is lost.

Solution

You could use cookies if the data is small enough, but that strategy doesn't work in an offline situation. Another, better approach, especially when you're persisting larger amounts of data or if you have to support functionality when no internet connection is present, is to use localStorage:

```
const formValue = document.getElementById('formelem').value;
if (formValue) {
  localStorage.formelem = formValue;
}

// recover
const storedValue = localStorage.formelem;
if (storedValue) {
  document.getElementById('formelem').value = storedValue;
}
```

Discussion

Recipe 14.2 covered `sessionStorage`, one of the DOM Storage techniques. The `localStorage` object interface is the same, with the same approaches to setting the data:

```
// use item methods
sessionStorage.setItem('key', 'value');
localStorage.setItem('key', 'value');

// use property names directly
sessionStorage.keyName = 'value';
localStorage.keyName = 'value';

// use the key method
sessionStorage.key(0) = 'value';
localStorage.key(0) = 'value';
```

and for getting the data:

```
// use item methods
value = sessionStorage.getItem('key');
value = localStorage.getItem('key');

// use property names directly
value = sessionStorage.keyName;
value = localStorage.keyName;

// use the key method
value = sessionStorage.key(0);
value = localStorage.key(0);
```

Again, as with `sessionStorage`, though you can access and set data on `localStorage` directly, you should use `getItem()` and `setItem()`, instead.

Both of the storage objects support the `length` property, which provides a count of stored item pairs, and the `clear` method (no parameters), which clears out all storage. In addition, both are scoped to the HTML5 origin, which means that the data storage is shared across all pages in a domain, but not across protocols (e.g., `http` is not the same as `https`) or ports.

The difference between the two is how long data is stored. The `sessionStorage` object only stores data for the session, but the `localStorage` object stores data on the client forever, or until specifically removed.

The `sessionStorage` and `localStorage` objects also support one event: the `storage` event. This is an interesting event, in that it fires on all pages when changes are made to a `localStorage` item. It is also an area of low compatibility among browsers: you can capture the event on the body or document elements for Firefox, on the body for IE, or on the document for Safari.

Example 14-2 demonstrates a more comprehensive implementation than the use case covered in the solution for this recipe. In the example, all elements of a small form have their onchange event handler method assigned to a function that captures the change element name and value, and stores the values in the local storage via local Storage. When the form is submitted, all of the stored form data is cleared.

When the page is loaded, the form elements onchange event handler is assigned to the function to store the values, and if the value is already stored, it is restored to the form element. To test the application, enter data into a couple of the form fields—but, before clicking the Submit button, refresh the page. Without localStorage, you'd lose the data. Now, when you reload the page, the form is restored to the state it was in before the page was reloaded.

Example 14-2. Using localStorage to back up form entries in case of page reload or browser crash

```
<!DOCTYPE html>
<html lang="en">
  <head>
    <meta charset="UTF-8" />
    <meta name="viewport" content="width=device-width, initial-scale=1.0" />
    <meta http-equiv="X-UA-Compatible" content="ie=edge" />
    <title>Creating a localStorage Client-Side Data Storage Item</title>
  </head>
  <body>
    <h1>Creating a localStorage Client-Side Data Storage Item</h1>

    <form id="inputform">
      <div>
        <label for="field1">Enter field1:</label>
        <input type="text" id="field1" />
      </div>
      <div>
        <label for="field2">Enter field2:</label>
        <input type="text" id="field2" />
      </div>
      <div>
        <label for="field3">Enter field1:</label>
        <input type="text" id="field3" />
      </div>
      <div>
        <label for="field4">Enter field1:</label>
        <input type="text" id="field4" />
      </div>
      <input type="submit" value="Clear Storage" />
    </form>

    <script src="localstorage.js"></script>
```

```
  </body>
</html>
```

In the JavaScript file:

```
// store the form input elements as a variable
const elems = document.querySelectorAll('input');

// store field values
function processField() {
  localStorage.setItem(window.location.href, 'true');
  localStorage.setItem(this.id, this.value);
}

// clear individual fields
function clearStored() {
  elems.forEach(elem => {
    if (elem.type === 'text') {
      localStorage.removeItem(elem.id);
    }
  });
}

// capture submit button to clear storage when clicked
document.getElementById('inputform').onsubmit = clearStored;

// on form element change, store the value in localStorage
elems.forEach(elem => {
  if (elem.type === 'text') {
    const value = localStorage.getItem(elem.id);
    if (value) elem.value = value;

    // change event
    elem.onchange = processField;
  }
});
```

The size allotted for localStorage varies by browser, but most are in the 5 mb to 10 mb range. You can use a try/catch block to test to ensure you have not exceeded the limit in the user's browser:

```
try {
  localStorage.setItem('key', 'value');
} catch (domException) {
  if (
    ['QuotaExceededError', 'NS_ERROR_DOM_QUOTA_REACHED'].includes(
      domException.name
    )
  ) {
    // handle file size exceeded error
  } else {
    // handle any other error
```

```
      }
   }
```

The `localStorage` object can be used for offline work. For the form example, you can store the data in the `localStorage` and provide a button to click when connected to the internet, in order to sync the data from `localStorage` to server-side storage.

See Also

See Recipe 14.2 for more on the `Storage` object, and on `sessionStorage` and `local Storage`.

14.4 Persisting Larger Chunks of Data on the Client Using IndexedDB

Problem

You need more sophisticated data storage on the client than what's provided with other persistent storage methods, such as `localStorage`.

Solution

In modern browsers, use IndexedDB.

The JavaScript file in Example 14-3 uses IndexedDB to create a database and a data object. Once created, it adds data and then retrieves the first object. A more detailed description of what's happening is in the discussion.

Example 14-3. Example of using IndexedDB to create a datastore, add data, and then retreive a data object

```
const data = [
  { name: 'Joe Brown', age: 53, experience: 5 },
  { name: 'Cindy Johnson', age: 44, experience: 5 },
  { name: 'Some Reader', age: 30, experience: 3 }
];

// delete the 'Cookbook' database, so the example can be run more than once
const delReq = indexedDB.deleteDatabase('Cookbook');
delReq.onerror = event => {
  console.log('delete error', event);
};

// open the 'Cookbook' database with a version of '1'
// or create it if it does not exist
const request = indexedDB.open('Cookbook', 1);
```

```javascript
// upgradeneeded event is fired when a db is opened
// with a version number higher than the currently stored version (in this case none)
request.onupgradeneeded = event => {
  const db = event.target.result;
  const { transaction } = event.target;

  // create a new object store named 'reader' in the database
  const objectStore = db.createObjectStore('reader', {
    keyPath: 'id',
    autoIncrement: true
  });

  // create new keys in the object store
  objectStore.createIndex('experience', 'experience', { unique: false });
  objectStore.createIndex('name', 'name', { unique: true });

  // when all data loaded, log to the console
  transaction.oncomplete = () => {
    console.log('data finished');
  };

  const readerObjectStore = transaction.objectStore('reader');

  // add each value from the data object to the indexedDB database
  data.forEach(value => {
    const req = readerObjectStore.add(value);
    // console log a message when successfully added
    req.onsuccess = () => {
      console.log('data added');
    };
  });

  // if the request throws an error, log it to the console
  request.onerror = () => {
    console.log(event.target.errorCode);
  };

  // when the data store is successfully created, log to the console
  request.onsuccess = () => {
    console.log('datastore created');
  };

  // on page click, get a random value from the database and log it to the console
  document.onclick = () => {
    const randomNum = Math.floor(Math.random() * 3) + 1;
    const dataRequest = db
      .transaction(['reader'])
      .objectStore('reader')
      .get(randomNum);
    dataRequest.onsuccess = () => {
      console.log(`Name : ${dataRequest.result.name}`);
    };
```

```
  };
};
```

Discussion

IndexedDB is the specification the W3C and others agreed to when exploring solutions to large data management on the client. Though it is transaction based, and supports the concept of a *cursor*, it isn't a relational database system. It works with JavaScript objects, each of which is indexed by a given *key*, whatever you decide the key to be.

IndexedDB can be both asynchronous and synchronous. It can be used for larger chunks of data in a traditional server or cloud application, but is also helpful for offline web application use.

Most implementations of IndexedDB don't restrict data storage size, but if you store more than 50 MB in Firefox, the user will need to provide permission. Chrome creates a pool of temporary storage, and each application can have up to 20% of it. Other agents have similar limitations. All of the main browsers support IndexedDB, except Opera Mini, though the overall support may not be identical.

As the solution demonstrates, the IndexedDB API methods trigger both success and error callback functions, which you can capture using traditional event handling, or as callback, or assign to a function. Mozilla describes the pattern of use with IndexedDB:

1. Open a database.
2. Create an object store in upgrading database.
3. Start a transaction and make a request to do some database operation, like adding or retrieving data.
4. Wait for the operation to complete by listening to the right kind of DOM event.
5. Do something with the results (which can be found on the request object).

Starting from the top in the solution, a data object is created with three values to add to the datastore. The database is deleted if it exists, so that the example can be run multiple times. Following, a call to open() opens the database, if it exists, or creates it, if not. Because the database is deleted before the example is run, it's recreated. The name and version are both necessary, because the database can be altered only if a new version of the database is opened.

A request object (IDBOpenDBRequest) is returned from the open() method, and whether the operation succeeds or not is triggered as events on this object. In the code, the onsuccess event handler for the object is captured to provide a message to the console about the success. You can also assign the database handle to a global variable in this event handler, but the code assigns this in the next event handled, the `upgradeneeded` event.

The `upgradeneeded` event handler is only invoked when a database doesn't exist for a given database name and version. The event object also gives us a way to access the IDBDatabase reference, which is assigned to the global variable, db. The existing transaction can also be accessed via the event object passed as an argument to the event handler, and it's accessed and assigned to a local variable.

The event handler for this event is the only time you'll be able to create the object store and its associated indexes. In the solution, a datastore named `reader` is created, with its key set to an autoincrementing `id`. Two other indexes are for the datastore's `name` and `experience` fields. The data is also added to the datastore in the event, though it could have been added at a separate time, say when a person submits an HTML form.

Following the `upgradeneeded` event handler, the `success` and `error` handlers are coded, just to provide feedback. Last but not least, the `document.onclick` event handler is used to trigger a database access. In the solution, a random data instance is accessed via the database handler, its transaction, the object store, and eventually, for a given key. When the query is successful, the `name` field is accessed and the value is printed to the console. Rather than accessing a single value, we can also use a cursor, but I'll leave that for your own experimentation.

The resulting printouts to the console are, in order:

```
data added
data finished
datastore created
Name : Cindy Johnson
```

14.5 Simplifying IndexedDB with a Library

Problem

You'd like to work with IndexedDB in an asynchronous fashion, using JavaScript promises.

Solution

Use the IDB library (*https://github.com/jakearchibald/idb*), which offers usability improvements to the IndexedDB API as well as a wrapper for using promises.

The following file imports the IDB library, creates an IndexedDB data store, and adds data to it:

```
import { openDB, deleteDB } from 'https://unpkg.com/idb?module';

const data = [
  { name: 'Riley Harrison', age: 57, experience: 1 },
  { name: 'Harlow Everly', age: 29, experience: 5 },
  { name: 'Abigail McCullough', age: 38, experience: 10 }
];

(async () => {
  // for demo purposes, delete existing db on page load
  try {
    await deleteDB('CookbookIDB');
  } catch (err) {
    console.log('delete error', err);
  }

  // open the database and create the data store
  const database = await openDB('CookbookIDB', 1, {
    upgrade(db) {
      // Create a store of objects
      const store = db.createObjectStore('reader', {
        keyPath: 'id',
        autoIncrement: true
      });

      // create new keys in the object store
      store.createIndex('experience', 'experience', { unique: false });
      store.createIndex('name', 'name', { unique: true });
    }
  });

  // add all of the reader data to the store
  data.forEach(async value => {
    await database.add('reader', value);
  });
})();
```

 In the example, I am loading the idb module from UNPKG
(*https://unpkg.com*), which allows me to directly access the module
from a URL, rather than locally installing it. This works well for
demo purposes, but in an application you will want to install the
module via npm and bundle it with your code.

Discussion

IDB bills itself as "a tiny library that mostly mirrors the IndexedDB API, but with
small improvements that make a big difference to usability." Using idb simplifies
some of the syntax of IndexedDB, along with enabling support for asynchronous
code execution with promises.

The openDB method opens a database and returns a promise:

```
const db = await openDB(name, version, {
  // ...
});
```

In the following example, a user can add data to the database and retrieve all of the data to be displayed on the page. In an HTML file:

```
<!DOCTYPE html>
<html lang="en">
  <head>
    <meta charset="UTF-8" />
    <meta name="viewport" content="width=device-width, initial-scale=1.0" />
    <meta http-equiv="X-UA-Compatible" content="ie=edge" />
    <title>IDB Discussion Example</title>
    <style>
      div {
        margin: 10px;
      }

      .data {
        width: 200px;
        background-color: yellow;
        padding: 5px;
      }
    </style>
  </head>
  <body>
    <h1>IDB Discussion Example</h1>

    <form>
      <div>
        <label for="name"> Enter name:</label>
        <input type="text" id="name" />
      </div>
      <div>
        <label for="age">Enter age:</label>
        <input type="text" id="age" />
      </div>
    </form>
    <button id="set">Set data</button>
    <button id="get">Get data</button>

    <p>Data:</p>
    <div class="data">
      <ul id="data-list"></ul>
    </div>

    <script type="module" src="idb-discussion.js"></script>
  </body>
</html>
```

And the *idb-discussion.js* file:

```
import { openDB } from 'https://unpkg.com/idb?module';

(async () => {
  // open the database and create the data store
  const database = await openDB('ReaderNames', 1, {
    upgrade(db) {
      // Create a store of objects
      const store = db.createObjectStore('reader', {
        keyPath: 'id',
        autoIncrement: true
      });

      // create new keys in the object store
      store.createIndex('age', 'age', { unique: false });
      store.createIndex('name', 'name', { unique: true });
    }
  });

  async function setData() {
    const name = document.getElementById('name').value;
    const age = document.getElementById('age').value;

    await database.add('reader', {
      name,
      age
    });
  }

  async function getData() {
    // get the reader data from the database
    const readers = await database.getAll('reader');

    const dataDisplay = document.getElementById('data-list');

    // add the name and age of each reader in the db to the page
    readers.forEach(reader => {
      const value = `${reader.name}: ${reader.age}`;
      const li = document.createElement('li');
      li.appendChild(document.createTextNode(value));
      dataDisplay.appendChild(li);
    });
  }

  document.getElementById('set').onclick = setData;
  document.getElementById('get').onclick = getData;
})();
```

I won't go into the full API, but highly recommend consulting the library's documentation (*https://github.com/jakearchibald/idb/blob/master/README.md*) and using IDB whenever working with IndexedDB.

## CHAPTER 15

Working with Media

Pretty pictures. Animations. Cool videos. Sound!

The web is a richer place through the availability of many media types. Our old friends SVG and Canvas can be used for complex animations, charts, and graphs. Added to them are the video and audio elements included in HTML5, and the near-future potential of 3D graphics.

Best of all, none of these require any kind of proprietary plug-in—they're all integrated with all your browser clients, including those on your smartphones, tablets, and computers.

15.1 Adding JavaScript to SVG

Problem

You want to add JavaScript to an SVG file or element.

Solution

JavaScript in SVG is included in `script` elements, just as with HTML, except with the addition of CDATA markup surrounding the script (Example 15-1). DOM methods are also available for working with the SVG elements.

Example 15-1. Demonstration of JavaScript within an SVG file

```
<?xml version="1.0" encoding="UTF-8" standalone="no"?>
<svg xmlns="http://www.w3.org/2000/svg"
xmlns:xlink="http://www.w3.org/1999/xlink" width="600" height="600">
  <script type="text/ecmascript">
    <![CDATA[
```

```
      // set element onclick event handler
      window.onload = function() {
        const square = document.getElementById('square');

        // onclick event handler, change circle radius
        square.onclick = function click() {
          const color = this.getAttribute('fill');
          if (color === '#ff0000') {
            this.setAttribute('fill', '#0000ff');
          } else {
            this.setAttribute('fill', '#ff0000');
          }
        };
      };
    ]]>
  </script>
  <rect id="square" width="400" height="400" fill="#ff0000"
   x="10" y="10" />
</svg>
```

Discussion

As the solution demonstrates, SVG is XML, and the rules for embedding script into XML must be adhered to. This means providing the script `type` within the `script` tag, as well as wrapping the script contents in a CDATA block. If you don't have the CDATA section, and your script uses characters such as < or &, your page will have errors, because the XML parser treats them as XML characters, not script.

 There is some drive to treat SVG as HTML, especially when the SVG is inline in HTML documents. That's what Chrome does. Still, it's better to be safe than sorry, and follow XML requirements.

The DOM methods, such as `document.getElementById()`, aren't HTML specific; they're usable with any XML document, including SVG. What's new is the SVG-specific `fill` attribute, an attribute unique to SVG elements, such as `rect`.

 If namespaces were used with any of the elements in the file, then the namespace version of the DOM methods would have to be used.

The code in the solution is a standalone SVG file, with a *.svg* extension. If we were to embed the SVG within an HTML file, as shown in Example 15-2, the color-changing animation would work the same. The CDATA section is removed because all modern browsers understand the SVG is now in an HTML context. If the file is XHTML, though, add them back.

Example 15-2. SVG element from Example 15-1, embedded into an HTML page

```
<!DOCTYPE html>
<html>
<head>
<title>Accessing Inline SVG</title>
<meta charset="utf-8">
</head>
<body>
<svg width="600" height="600">
  <script>
    // set element onclick event handler
    window.onload = function() {
      const square = document.getElementById('square');

      // onclick event handler, change circle radius
      square.onclick = function click() {
        const color = this.getAttribute('fill');
        if (color === '#ff0000') {
          this.setAttribute('fill', '#0000ff');
        } else {
          this.setAttribute('fill', '#ff0000');
        }
      };
    };
  </script>
  <rect id="square" width="400" height="400" fill="#ff0000"
 x="10" y="10" />
</svg>
</body>
</html>
```

The above example embeds the SVG directly into the HTML page. You can also embed a JavaScript-containing SVG file on the page by using the <object> tag with a fallback <img> tag:

```
<object type="image/svg+xml" data="demo.svg">
    <img src="demo.svg" />
</object>
```

All modern browsers support SVG, including SVG in HTML. IE supports SVG after version 9.

To learn more about SVG, I recommend *SVG Animations* by Sarah Drasner (O'Reilly).

Extra: Using SVG Libraries

There aren't quite as many libraries for working with SVG as there are for working with Canvas, but the ones that exist are very handy. One of the most popular is the D3 library, covered in Recipe 15.3. A few other popular libraries include Raphaël (*http://raphaeljs.com*), GreenSock (*https://greensock.com*), Snap.svg (*http://snapsvg.io*), and SVG.js (*https://svgjs.dev/docs/3.0*). All of these can simplify SVG creation and animation. The following code snippet shows an example of using Raphaël:

```
// Creates canvas 320 × 400 at 10, 50
const paper = Raphael(10, 50, 320, 400);
// Creates circle at x = 150, y = 140, with radius 100
const circle = paper.circle(150, 140, 100);
// Sets the fill attribute of the circle to red (#f00)
circle.attr("fill", "#f0f");
// Sets the stroke attribute of the circle to white
circle.attr("stroke", "#ff0");
```

15.2 Accessing SVG from a Web Page Script

Problem

You want to modify the contents of an SVG element from script within the web page.

Solution

If the SVG is embedded directly in the web page, access the element and its attributes using the same functionality you would use with any other web page element:

```
const square = document.getElementById("square");
square.setAttribute("width", "500");
```

However, if the SVG is in an external SVG file embedded into the page via an `object` element, you have to get the document for the external SVG file in order to access the elements. The technique requires object detection because the process differs by browser:

```
window.onload = function onLoad() {
  const object = document.getElementById('object');
  let svgdoc;

  try {
    svgdoc = object.contentDocument;
```

```
    } catch (e) {
      try {
        svgdoc = object.getSVGDocument();
      } catch (err) {
        console.log(err, 'SVG in object not supported in this environment');
      }
    }

    if (!svgdoc) return;

    const square = svgdoc.getElementById('square');
    square.setAttribute('width', '900');
  };
```

Discussion

The first option listed in the solution accesses SVG embedded in an HTML file. You can access SVG elements using the same methods you've used to access HTML elements.

The second option is a little more involved, and depends on retrieving the document object for the SVG document. The first approach tries to access the contentDocument property on the object. If this fails, the application then tries to access the SVG document using getSVGDocument(). Once you have access to the SVG document object, you can use the same DOM methods you would use with elements native to the web page.

Example 15-3 shows the second way to add SVG to a web page, and how to access the SVG element(s) from script in HTML.

Example 15-3. Accessing SVG in an object element from script

```
<!DOCTYPE html>
<head>
  <title>SVG in Object</title>
  <meta charset="utf-8" />
</head>
<body>
  <object id="object" type="image/svg+xml" data="../demo1.svg">
    <p>No SVG support</p>
  </object>
  <script type="text/javascript">
    const object = document.getElementById('object');
    object.onload = function() {
      let svgdoc;

      // get access to the SVG document object
      try {
        svgdoc = object.contentDocument;
      } catch (e) {
```

```
    try {
      svgdoc = object.getSVGDocument();
    } catch (err) {
      console.log(err, 'SVG in object not supported in this environment');
    }
  }

  if (!svgdoc) return;

  // get SVG element and modify
  const square = svgdoc.getElementById('square');
  square.onclick = function() {
    let width = parseFloat(square.getAttribute('width'));
    width -= 50;
    square.setAttribute('width', width);
    const color = square.getAttribute('fill');
    if (color == 'blue') {
      square.setAttribute('fill', 'yellow');
      square.setAttribute('stroke', 'green');
    } else {
      square.setAttribute('fill', 'blue');
      square.setAttribute('stroke', 'red');
    }
  };
};
</script>
</body>
```

In the example code, the object is accessed after it has loaded; the `object.onload`
event handler is then accessed to get the SVG document and assign the function to
the `onclick` event handler.

15.3 Creating an SVG Bar Chart with D3

Problem

You want to create a scalable bar chart, but you're hoping to avoid having to create
every last bit of the graphics.

Solution

Use D3 and SVG to create a chart bound to a set of data that your application provides. Example 15-4 shows a vertical bar chart created using D3 with a given set of
data representing the height of each bar.

Example 15-4. SVG bar chart created using D3

```
<!DOCTYPE html>
<html>
  <head>
    <meta charset="utf-8" />
    <title>SVG Bar Chart using D3</title>
    <script src="https://cdnjs.cloudflare.com/ajax/libs/d3/5.15.0/d3.min.js"></script>
  </head>
  <body>
    <script type="text/javascript">
      const data = [56, 99, 14, 12, 46, 33, 22, 100, 87, 6, 55, 44, 27, 28, 34];

      const height = 400;
      const barWidth = 25;

      const x = d3
        .scaleLinear()
        .domain([0, d3.max(data)])
        .range([0, height]);

      const svg = d3
        .select('body')
        .append('svg')
        .attr('width', data.length * (barWidth + 1))
        .attr('height', height);

      svg
        .selectAll('rect')
        .data(data)
        .enter()
        .append('rect')
        .attr('fill', '#008b8b')
        .attr('x', function(d, i) {
          return i * (barWidth + 1);
        })
        .attr('y', function(d) {
          return height - x(d);
        })
        .attr('width', barWidth)
        .attr('height', x);
    </script>
  </body>
</html>
```

Discussion

D3 isn't a standard graphics tool that creates the shape based on the dimensions you provide. With D3, you give it a set of data, the objects used to visualize the data, and then stand back and let it do its thing. It sounds simple, but to get this data visualization goodness, you do have to properly set it up, and that can be challenging when you first start using the library.

First of all, be aware that D3 makes use of *method chaining* to a maximum degree. Yes, you can invoke methods separately, but it's clearer, cleaner, and more efficient to use the library's chaining support.

In the solution, the first line is the creation of a data set as an array. D3 expects data points to be in an array, though each element can be an object, as well as a simple value, as shown in the solution. Next, the maximum height of the bar chart is defined, as is the width of each bar. Next, we get into the first use of D3.

 D3 (*http://d3js.org*), created by Mike Bostock, is a powerful data visualization tool that isn't necessarily something you can pick up and master in a lazy afternoon. However, it is a tool well worth learning, so consider the example in this recipe more of a teaser to get you interested, rather than a definitive introduction.

For a more in-depth primer, I recommend *D3 for the Impatient* by Philipp Janert (O'Reilly).

I could have added a static SVG element to the web page, but I wanted to demonstrate how D3 creates an element. By creating the SVG element, we're also getting a reference to it for future work, though we could have used D3 to get a reference to an existing element. In the code, a reference to the body element is obtained using D3's select() method. Once this happens, a new SVG element is appended to the body element via append(), and attributes are given to it via the attr() function. The height of the element is already predefined, but the width is equal to multiplying the number of data elements by the bar width (+1, to provide necessary spacing).

Once the SVG element is created, the code uses D3's *scale* functionality to determine the necessary ratio between the element's height and each bar's height, in such a way that the bar chart fills the SVG element, but each bar's height is proportional. It does this by using scale.linear() to create a linear scale. According to the D3 documentation, "The mapping is linear in that the output range value y can be expressed as a linear function of the input domain value x: $y = mx + b$."

The domain() function sets the input domain for the scale, while the range() sets the output range. In the solution, the value given for the domain is zero to the maximum value in the data set, determined via a call to max(). The value given for the range is zero to the height of the SVG element. A function is then returned to a variable that will normalize any data passed to it when called. If the function is given a value equal to the height of the largest data value, the returned value is equal to the height of the element (in this case, the largest data value of 100 returns a scaled value of 400).

The last portion of the code is the part that creates the bars. We need something to work with, so the code calls selectAll() with rect. There aren't any rect elements in the SVG block yet, but we'll be adding them. The data is passed to D3 via the data() method, and then the enter() function is called. What enter() does is process the data and return placeholders for all the missing elements. In the solution, placeholders for all 15 rect elements, one for each bar, are created.

A rect element is then appended to the SVG element with append(), and the attributes for each are set with attr(). In the solution, the fill and stroke are given, though these could have been defined in the page's stylesheet. Following, the position for the x attribute, or the lower-left attribute for the bar, is provided as a function, where d is the current datum (data value) and i is the current index. For the x attribute, the index is multiplied by the barWidth, plus one (1), to account for spacing.

For the y attribute, we have to get a little tricky. SVG's point of origin is the top-left corner, which means increasing values of y go down the chart, not up. To reverse this, we need to subtract the value of y from the height. However, we can't just do this directly. If the code used the datum passed to it directly, then we'd have a proportional chart with very small, scrunched-down bars. Instead we need to use the newly created scale function, x, passing the datum to it.

The width of each bar is a constant value given in barWidth, and the height is just the scale function variable, which is equivalent to calling the scale function and passing in the datum. All of this creates the chart shown in Figure 15-1.

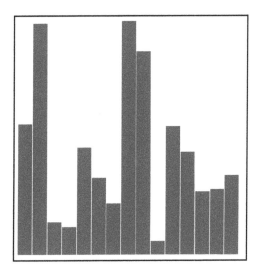

Figure 15-1. Example of a bar chart with each bar's height normalized to fill the given space

15.4 Integrating SVG and the Canvas Element in HTML

Problem

You want to use the canvas element and SVG together within a web page.

Solution

One option is to embed both the SVG and the canvas element directly into the HTML page, and then access the canvas element from script within SVG:

```
<!DOCTYPE html>
<html lang="en">
  <head>
    <meta charset="UTF-8" />
    <meta name="viewport" content="width=device-width, initial-scale=1.0" />
    <meta http-equiv="X-UA-Compatible" content="ie=edge" />
    <title>Integrating SVG and the Canvas Element in HTML</title>
  </head>
  <body>
    <canvas id="myCanvas" width="400px" height="100px">
      <p>canvas item alternative content</p>
    </canvas>

    <svg id="svgelem" height="400">
      <title>SVG Circle</title>
      <script type="text/javascript">
      window.onload = function () {
        var context = document.getElementById("myCanvas").getContext('2d');
        context.fillStyle = 'rgba(0,200,0,0.7)';
        context.fillRect(0,0,100,100);
      }
      </script>
      <circle id="redcircle" cx="100" cy="100" r="100" fill="red" stroke="#000" />
    </svg>
  </body>
</html>
```

Or you can embed the canvas element as a foreign object directly in the SVG:

```
<!DOCTYPE html>
<html>
<head>
<title>Accessing Inline SVG</title>
<meta charset="utf-8">
</head>
<body>
<svg id="svgelem" height="400" width="600">
  <script type="text/javascript">
    window.onload = function () {
      var context2 = document.getElementById("thisCanvas").getContext('2d');
```

```
        context2.fillStyle = "#ff0000";
        context2.fillRect(0,0,200,200);
      };
  </script>

  <foreignObject width="300" height="150">
     <canvas width="300" height="150" id="thisCanvas">
        alternate content for browsers that do not support Canvas
     </canvas>
  </foreignObject>
  <circle id="redcircle" cx="300" cy="100" r="100" fill="red" stroke="#000" />
  </svg>
</body>
</html>
```

Discussion

When the SVG element is embedded into the current web page, you can access HTML elements from within the SVG. However, you can also embed elements directly in SVG, using the SVG foreignObject element. This element allows us to embed XHTML, MathML, RDF, or any other XML-based syntax.

In both solutions, I was able to use getElementById(). However, if I want to manipulate the elements using other methods, such as getElementsByTagName(), I have to be careful about which version of the method I use. For instance, I can use getElements ByTagName() for the outer canvas element, but I would need to use the namespace version of the method, getElementsByTagNameNS, if the contained object is XML, such as RDF/XML. Because the embedded object in the solution is HTML5, a namespace wasn't necessary.

Once you have the canvas context, use the element like you would from script within HTML: add rectangles, draw paths, create arcs, and so on.

Extra: Canvas? Or SVG?

Why would you use Canvas over SVG, or SVG over Canvas? The canvas element is faster in frame-type animations. With each animation, the browser only needs to redraw the changed pixels, not recreate the entire scene. However, the advantage you get with the canvas element animation lessens when you have to support a variety of screen sizes, from smartphone to large monitor. SVG scales beautifully.

Another advantage to SVG is that it figures in rich data visualizations with the assistance of powerful libraries. But then, Canvas is used with 3D systems, such as WebGL.

One use of SVG and Canvas together is to provide a fallback for the canvas element: the SVG writes to the DOM and persists even if JavaScript is turned off, while the canvas element does not.

15.5 Running a Routine When an Audio File Begins Playing

Problem

You want to provide an audio file and then share additional information when the audio file begins or ends playing.

Solution

Use the HTML5 audio element:

```
<audio id="meadow" controls>
  <source src="meadow.wav" type="audio/wav" />
  <p><a href="meadow.wav">Meadow sounds</a></p>
</audio>
```

and capture either its play event (playback has begun) or ended event (playback has finished):

```
const meadow = document.getElementById('meadow');
meadow.addEventListener('play', aboutAudio);
```

then display the information:

```
function aboutAudio() {
  const info = 'A summer field near a lake in July.';
  const txt = document.createTextNode(info);
  const div = document.createElement('div');
  div.appendChild(txt);
  document.body.appendChild(div);
}
```

Discussion

HTML5 added two media elements: audio and video. These simple-to-use controls provide a way to play audio and video files.

In the solution, the audio element's controls Boolean attribute is set, so the controls are displayed. The element has a src of a WAV audio file for in-browser playback. Additionally, a link to the WAV file is provided as a fallback, which means people using browsers that don't support audio can still access the sound file. I could have also provided an object element, or other fallback content.

WAV is a widely supported audio format, but different browsers support various formats and filetypes. The Mozilla Developer Network has a comprehensive table (*http://mzl.la/1DS3rPL*) with audio and video codec support for the various browsers, and Wikipedia maintains a simple browser support table (*https://oreil.ly/55EwV*) for audio coding formats.

The media elements come with a set of methods to control the playback, as well as events that can be triggered when the event occurs. In the solution, the ended event is captured and assigned the event handler aboutAudio(), which displays a message about the file after the playback is finished. Notice that though the code is using a DOM Level 0 event handler with the window load event, it's using DOM Level 2 event handling with the audio element. Browser support is erratic with this event handler, so I strongly recommend you use addEventListener(). However, onended does seem to work without problems when used directly in the element:

```
<audio id="meadow" src="meadow.wav" controls onended="alert('All done')">
  <p><a href="meadow.wav">Meadow sounds</a></p>
</audio>
```

It's interesting to see the appearance of the elements in all of the browsers that currently support them. There is no standard look, so each browser provides its own interpretation. You can control the appearance by providing your own playback controls and using your own elements/CSS/SVG/Canvas to supply the decoration.

15.6 Controlling Video from JavaScript with the video Element

Problem

You want to embed video in your web page along with a consistent look for the video controls, regardless of browser and operating system.

Solution

Use the HTML5 video element:

```
<video id="meadow" poster="purples.jpg" >
   <source src="meadow.m4v" type="video/mp4"/>
   <source src="meadow.ogv" type="video/ogg" />
</video>
```

You can provide controls for it via JavaScript, as shown in Example 15-5. Buttons are used to provide the video control, and text in a div element is used to provide feedback on time during the playback.

Example 15-5. Providing a custom control for the HTML5 video element

```
<!DOCTYPE html>
<html lang="en">
  <head>
    <meta charset="UTF-8" />
    <meta name="viewport" content="width=device-width, initial-scale=1.0" />
    <meta http-equiv="X-UA-Compatible" content="ie=edge" />
    <title>Controlling Video from JavaScript with the video Element</title>
    <style>
      video {
        border: 1px solid black;
        max-width: 600px;
      }
    </style>
  </head>
  <body>
    <h1>Controlling Video from JavaScript with the video Element</h1>

    <video id="meadow" controls>
      <source src="meadow.mp4" type="video/mp4" />
      <source src="meadow.webm" type="video/webm" />
    </video>
    <div id="feedback"></div>
    <div id="controls">
      <button id="start">Play</button>
      <button id="stop">Stop</button>
      <button id="pause">Pause</button>
    </div>

    <script src="video.js"></script>
  </body>
</html>
```

And in `video.js`:

```
// dom elements
const meadow = document.getElementById('meadow');
const start = document.getElementById('start');
const pause = document.getElementById('pause');
const stop = document.getElementById('stop');

// start video, enable stop and pause
// disable play
function startPlayback() {
  meadow.play();
  pause.disabled = false;
  stop.disabled = false;
  this.disabled = true;
}

// pause video, enable start, disable stop
// disable pause
```

```
function pausePlayback() {
  meadow.pause();
  pause.disabled = true;
  start.disabled = false;
  stop.disabled = true;
}

// stop video, return to zero time
// enable play, disable pause and stop
function stopPlayback() {
  meadow.pause();
  meadow.currentTime = 0;
  start.disabled = false;
  pause.disabled = true;
  this.disabled = true;
}

// for every time divisible by 5, output feedback
function reportProgress() {
  const time = Math.round(this.currentTime);
  const div = document.getElementById('feedback');
  div.innerHTML = `${time} seconds`;
}

// event listeners
document.getElementById('start').addEventListener('click', startPlayback);
document.getElementById('stop').addEventListener('click', stopPlayback);
document.getElementById('pause').addEventListener('click', pausePlayback);
meadow.addEventListener('timeupdate', reportProgress);
```

Discussion

The HTML5 `video` element, as with the HTML5 `audio` element, can be controlled with its own built-in controls, or you can provide your own. The media elements support the following methods:

play
    Starts playing the video

pause
    Pauses the video

load
    Preloads the video without starting play

canPlayType
    Tests if the user agent supports the video type

The media elements don't support a stop method, so the code emulates one by pausing video play and then setting the video's `currentTime` attribute to 0, which basically resets the play start time. I also used `currentTime` to print out the video time, using `Math.round` to round the time to the nearest second.

The video control is providing two different video codecs: H.264 (*.mp4*) and VP8 (*.webm*). Nearly all modern browsers support the WebM file format, but including the MP4 provides a fallback for older browsers that support the `video` element.

The video and audio controls are inherently keyboard accessible. If you replace the controls, you'll want to provide accessibility information with your replacements.

 The video playback functionality demonstrated in the solution works, as is, with video that isn't encrypted. If the video (or audio) file is encrypted, considerably more effort is necessary so that the video plays, making use of the HTML 5.1 W3C Encrypted Media Extensions (EME).

The W3C EME working draft (*https://oreil.ly/mMu7q*) has been implemented in Internet Explorer 11 (*http://bit.ly/1DS5umQ*), Chrome, Firefox, Microsoft Edge, and Safari.

## CHAPTER 16

Writing Web Applications

While JavaScript was once used to add simple interactivity to web pages, today it can be used to build complicated and fully featured software applications that run in a web browser. The possibilities include mapping, email clients, streaming video sites, real-time chat applications, and much more. The line between "website" and "application" can be fuzzy, but one way to think about it is that an application is any site that takes user input and returns something as a result.

As a developer, you can develop these applications and deploy them instantly across the world, but this ability comes with unique challenges. As an application code base grows, you will need to split your codebase into smaller modules and ensure that users are receiving optimized code bundles. You will need to create features and experiences that compete with those of native mobile applications, such as offline functionality, notifications, and application icons. Thankfully, modern JavaScript and browser APIs enable these feature-rich experiences.

16.1 Bundling JavaScript

Problem

You want to make use of JavaScript modules in a browser environment.

Solution

Make use of native JavaScript modules or a bundling tool, such as Webpack (*https://webpack.js.org*).

Native JavaScript is supported in all modern browsers (*https://oreil.ly/FhPq9*). If we have a simple module that exports a value, named `mod.js`:

```
export const name = 'Riley';
```

we can use the module natively in an HTML file:

```
<script type='module'>
  import {name} from './mod.js';
  console.log(name);
</script>
```

For more advanced applications and sites, you may benefit from using a bundling tool that can optimize your modules. To use Webpack as a bundling tool, first install its dependencies with npm:

```
$ npm install webpack webpack-cli --save-dev
```

 Before you are able to install packages from npm, your project will need a *package.json* file. To generate this file, make sure you are in the root of your project's directory and type `npm init`. The command-line interface will then guide you through a series of prompts. Additional information about installing and using npm is in Chapter 1.

We can then create a file named *webpack.config.js* in the root of the project directory, where we specify the entry file and output directory:

```
const path = require('path');

module.exports = {
  entry: './src/index.js',
  output: {
    filename: 'bundle.js',
    path: path.resolve(__dirname, 'dist')
  }
};
```

Finally, add a script to the *package.json* to run the Webpack build:

```
"scripts": {
  ...
  "build": "webpack"
}
```

Discussion

JavaScript modules are now widely available and supported by browsers. This allows us to break our code into smaller, more maintainble pieces.

Webpack is a popular tool for compiling JavaScript modules. The power of Webpack lies in the configuration file.

In the previous configuration file, we are instructing Webpack to look at the *src* directory for a file named *index.js*. This file will be the entry file for our project's JavaScript:

```
import foo from './foo.js';
import bar from './bar.js';

foo();
bar();
```

The *index.js* file is importing two additional files, *foo.js* and *bar.js*.

When the `build` script is run, Webpack will output a new minified file named *bundle.js* in the *dist* directory.

Compiling simple import statements is only the tip of the iceberg. Webpack can be used for hot module reloading, code splitting, browser support shims, and even as a development server. In Recipe 16.2, we'll explore how Webpack can be used to reduce the size of a JavaScript bundle.

Extra: Using npm Modules

In addition to using your own modules, Webpack enables you to download and utilize modules directly from npm (*https://www.npmjs.com*). To do so, first install the module and save it as a dependency to the project:

```
$ npm install some-module --save
```

You can then require the module directly in your code, without needing to specify the path to the module:

```
import some-code from 'some-module'
```

16.2 JavaScript and the Mobile Web

Problem

Your website or application makes use of JavaScript, which can noticeably increase the time to load on mobile and slow connections.

Solution

For sites using a small amount of JavaScript in a single file, use a tool such as UglifyJS (*https://github.com/mishoo/UglifyJS*) to minify your JavaScript. Minification will reduce the size of a JavaScript file by removing unnecessary characters (such as whitespace).

To use UglifyJS, first install it with npm:

```
$ npm install uglify-js
```

Then, add a script to your *package.json* file, specifying the input JavaScript file and a name for the minified file:

```
"scripts": {
  "minify": "uglifyjs index.js --output index.min.js"
}
```

For larger sites and applications with multiple JavaScript files, use a bundling tool, such as Webpack (*https://webpack.js.org*), to perform a combination of minification, code splitting, tree shaking, and lazy loading.

Webpack automatically minifies its output in production mode, meaning that no specific configuration or minification tool is needed.

Code splitting is the process of generating multiple bundles, so that HTML pages or templates only load the code they need. The following *webpack.config.js* file will output two JavaScript files (*index.bundle.js* and *secondary.bundle.js*) to the *dist* directory:

```
const path = require('path');

module.exports = {
  entry: {
    index: './src/index.js',
    secondary: './src/secondary.js',
  },
  output: {
    filename: '[name].bundle.js',
    path: path.resolve(__dirname, 'dist'),
  },
};
```

Bundles can balloon in size, particularly when importing third-party libraries with functionality that may not be needed. *Tree shaking* is the concept of eliminating dead or unused code. Webpack can be configured to eliminate dead code with the `optimi zation` setting:

```
module.exports = {
  mode: 'development',
  entry: {
    index: './src/index.js',
    secondary: './src/secondary.js'
  },
  output: {
    filename: '[name].bundle.js',
    path: path.resolve(__dirname, 'dist')
  },
  optimization: {
    usedExports: true
  }
};
```

The final step for code splitting is to add a `sideEffects` field to the project's *package.json* file. According to the Webpack documentation, "a *side effect* is defined as code that performs a special behavior when imported, other than exposing one or more exports." An example of a side effect would be a global polyfill, which does not expose any `export` statements.

If no such file is present, we can set the following in *package.json*:

```
"sideEffects": false
```

If your project does have JavaScript files that would fall under the "side effect" category, we can provide them as an array:

```
"sideEffects": [
  "./src/file-with-side-effect.js"
]
```

Finally, we can utilize Webpack to enable the lazy loading of JavaScript modules, only loading them when they are needed by a browser interaction. Webpack makes this straightforward with a dynamic `import` statements. With a file named *button.js* in the *src* directory, the contents of the file can be loaded when a user clicks a button. In *index.js*:

```
const buttonElement = document.getElementById('button');
buttonElement.onclick = e =>
  import(/* webpackChunkName: "button" */ './button').then(module => {
    const button = module.default;
    button();
  });
```

Discussion

The fastest JavaScript is no JavaScript; however, the interactive demands of modern web applications often rely on client-side JavaScript. With that in mind, our goal is to limit the amount and file size of the JavaScript being downloaded by a user's browser. Utilizing strategies such as minification, code splitting, tree shaking, and lazy loading allows you finer control over size and amount of JavaScript being loaded in a user's browser.

See Also

Webpack's Getting Started guide (*https://oreil.ly/TAnYG*) is a useful introduction to code bundling and Webpack configuration files.

16.3 Writing a Progressive Web Application

Problem

You'd like your web application to take advantage of native application features such as fast load times, offline functionality, and app launching icons.

Solution

Turn your web application into a Progressive Web Application (PWA). The phrase "Progressive Web Applications" was coined to describe a set of technologies that, when combined, enable web applications to use native-like features, such as offline functionality and user-installed app icons, while being built with standard web technologies and deployed to the web.

All PWAs are required to include two features that extend beyond that of a typical web page:

Application manifest
    Defines application specific features for the browser.

Service worker
    Enables the application's offline functionality.

The first step in creating a progressive web application is to add the web app manifest file. This file enables developers to control things like application icons, splash screens, browser display style, and view orientation. In a file named *manifest.json*:

```
{
  "name": "JavaScript Everywhere",
  "short_name": "JavaScript",
  "start_url": "/index.html",
  "display": "standalone",
  "background_color": "#ffc40d",
  "theme_color": "#ffc40d",
  "icons": [
    {
      "src": "/images/icons/icon-192x192.png",
      "sizes": "192x192",
      "type": "image/png"
    },
    {
      "src": "/images/icons/icon-512x512.png",
      "sizes": "512x512",
      "type": "image/png"
    }
  ]
}
```

Now, in your HTML files or templates, add a reference to the manifest file and appropriate application icons in the document's <head>.

Example 16-1. PWA Metatags

```
<!-- link to manifest.json file -->
<link rel="manifest" href="manifest.json" />
<!-- link to iOS icons -->
<link rel="apple-touch-icon" sizes="180x180" href="images/icons/apple-touch-icon.png" />
<!-- Microsoft application tile icons and color settings -->
<meta name="msapplication-TileColor" content="#ffc40d" />
<meta name="msapplication-TileImage" content="/img/icons/mstile-310x310.png" />
<!-- set theme color -->
<meta name="theme-color" content="#ffc40d" />
```

The PWA install prompt is automatically triggered in Chrome when a website meets the PWA criteria (see Figure 16-1). Once installed, the PWA's icon appears on the user's device, much like a native application (Figure 16-2).

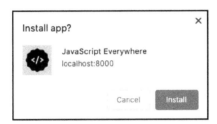

Figure 16-1. PWA install prompt

Figure 16-2. The application can be saved to a mobile device

The second step is to create a service worker. A service worker is a script that runs separately from the page, providing us with a way to make our sites work offline, run faster, and add capabilities for background features. With the limits of mobile connectivity, service workers provide us with a means to build offline-first capable applications, which will load content for our users after an initial site visit, regardless of network conditions. Best of all, service workers are truly a progressive enhancement, layering on an additional feature to supporting browsers without changing the functionality of our site for users of nonsupporting browsers.

When introducing a service worker, the initial step is to register the script that will contain our service worker code with the user's browser. To accomplish this, add the script registration to the bottom of the page just before the closing </body> tag:

```
<!-- initiate the service worker -->
<script>
  if ('serviceWorker' in navigator) {
    window.addEventListener('load', function() {
      navigator.serviceWorker
        .register('service-worker.js')
        .then(reg => {
          console.log('Service worker registered!', reg);
        })
        .catch(err => {
          console.log('Service worker registration failed: ', err);
        });
    });
  }
</script>
```

This script checks for service worker support, and if the support is available, points the browser to a service worker script (in this case *service-worker.js*). For debugging purposes, the script also catches errors and logs them to the console.

In *service-worker.js*, begin by specifying a cache version and listing the files that the browser should cache:

```
var cacheVersion = 'v1';

filesToCache = [
  'index.html',
  '/styles/main.css',
  '/js/main.js',
  '/images/logo.svg'
]
```

For changes to the site, the cacheVersion needs to be updated, or users risk being served content from the cache.

Now, in the *service-worker.js* file, set up the install, fetch, and activate event listeners. The install event provides the browser with instructions for installing our cached files. The fetch event provides the browser with guidelines for handling fetch events by instructing the browser to either load the cached files or those received over the network. Finally, the `activate` event, which fires when the service worker is activated, can be used to check for existing items in the cache and remove them if an updated `cacheVersion` is present and the file is no longer in the `filestoCache` list (see Figure 16-3).

```
const cacheVersion = 'v1';

const filesToCache = ['index.html', '/styles/main.css', '/js/main.js'];

self.addEventListener('install', event => {
  console.log('Service worker install event fired');
  event.waitUntil(
    caches.open(cacheVersion).then(cache => {
      return cache.addAll(filesToCache);
    })
  );
});

self.addEventListener('fetch', event => {
  console.log('Fetch intercepted for:', event.request.url);
  event.respondWith(
    caches.match(event.request).then(cachedResponse => {
      if (cachedResponse) {
        return cachedResponse;
      }
      return fetch(event.request);
    })
  );
});

self.addEventListener('activate', event => {
  event.waitUntil(
    caches.keys().then(keyList => {
      return Promise.all(
        keyList.map(key => {
          if (key !== cacheVersion) {
            return caches.delete(key);
          }
        })
      );
    })
  );
});
```

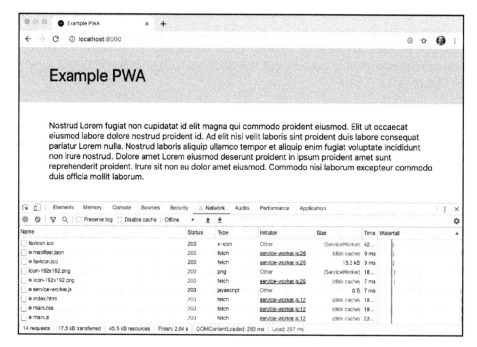

Figure 16-3. With the service worker installed, the application can load files when offline

Discussion

A Progressive Web Application is a user-installable web application with some form of offline functionality. These features allow web applications to closely mimic the best features of native applications while providing the benefits of the open web.

The web app manifest is a JSON file that provides information about the application. The full list of key values that it can contain are as follows:

`background_color`
A color code for a placeholder launch screen background.

`categories`
An array of strings of categories that the application belongs to.

`description`
A string description of the application.

`dir`
The direction in which to display characters. This can be `auto`, `ltr` (left to right), or `rtl` (right to left).

display
> The preferred display mode. This can be either `browser`, for default browser behavior, or `fullscreen`, which will reduce the browser chrome on some devices.

iarc_rating_id
> An International Age Rating value.

icons
> An array of objects linking to icon images and descriptions.

lang
> Identifies the primary language of the application.

name
> The application name.

orientation
> Allows the developer to set the default orientation of the application.

prefer_related_applications
> If set to `true`, allows the developer to specify related applications that should be installed instead of the web application.

related_applications
> An array of objects containing a list of related native applications.

scope
> A string that contains the navigation scope of the app. Specifying a scope restricts navigation in application mode to that directory.

screenshots
> An array of application screenshots.

short_name
> A shortened version of the application name to be used in contexts where the full name is too long to display.

start_url
> The URL that should open when a user launches the application.

theme_color
> A string that defines the default theme color for the application.

The W3C provides an example (*https://oreil.ly/zlk9P*) of a robust manifest file for a web-based game:

```
{
  "lang": "en",
  "dir": "ltr",
```

```
  "name": "Super Racer 3000",
  "description": "The ultimate futuristic racing game from the future!",
  "short_name": "Racer3K",
  "icons": [{
    "src": "icon/lowres.webp",
    "sizes": "64x64",
    "type": "image/webp"
  },{
    "src": "icon/lowres.png",
    "sizes": "64x64"
  }, {
    "src": "icon/hd_hi",
    "sizes": "128x128"
  }],
  "scope": "/racer/",
  "start_url": "/racer/start.html",
  "display": "fullscreen",
  "orientation": "landscape",
  "theme_color": "aliceblue",
  "background_color": "red",
  "screenshots": [{
    "src": "screenshots/in-game-1x.jpg",
    "sizes": "640x480",
    "type": "image/jpeg"
  },{
    "src": "screenshots/in-game-2x.jpg",
    "sizes": "1280x920",
    "type": "image/jpeg"
  }]
}
```

In addition to the web app manifest file, some platforms, such as iOS and Windows, require additional information which can be provided in the form of HTML meta-tags. In Example 16-1, metatags are used to define a theme color, the iOS icon, and Windows tile settings.

 Generating icons for all of the different device types and resolutions can be a tedious affair, so I recommend using RealFavicon-Generator (*https://oreil.ly/ALsQe*).

A service worker is a script that the browser runs in the background, parallel to the rendering and execution of the page. Because it is a "worker," the service worker cannot access the DOM directly, however this parallel script enables all sorts of new use cases. One of the most exciting of these use cases is the ability to cache bits of our application for offline use. In the above example, I'm caching an HTML, JavaScript, and CSS file to provide a full-featured (if minimal) site experience when offline.

Other use cases may include creating a separate offline experience or caching the shared template markup and styles, often referred to as the "application shell."

When utilizing service workers, there are a few limitations to be aware of:

- Sites using a service worker must be served over HTTPS.
- Service workers do not work when a user is in private browsing mode.
- Since service workers run as a separate thread in the browser, they do not have access to the DOM.
- Service workers are scoped, meaning that they should be placed in the root of your application.
- Cache storage sizes can vary by browser and available space on a user's hard drive.

Though I've created a service worker by hand in the above example, that can quickly become unmanageable for larger applications. The Workbox (*https://oreil.ly/Gu3Z6*) library, created by Google, is a package for managing service workers and offline functionality in web applications. Workbox takes much of the pain out of versioning and managing the cache, as well as advanced capabilities such as background sync and precaching.

Progressive web applications are an exciting step for the web and are framework agnostic, meaning they can be built with simple HTML, CSS, and JavaScript, or using the latest JavaScript frameworks. In this section we have only scratched the surface of the power of these technologies. Tal Alter's book *Building Progressive Web Apps* (O'Reilly) offers a detailed look at the features and functionality of Progressive Web Applications.

16.4 Testing and Profiling a Progressive Web Application

Problem

You'd like to test that you've successfully fulfilled the requirements of a Progressive Web Application.

Solution

Use Lighthouse (*https://oreil.ly/hEdHB*) to audit performance, accessibility, best practices, SEO, and Progressive Web Application criteria. The easiest way to access Lighthouse is within the "Lighthouse" tab of Google Chrome Developer Tools. Visit the site (either in production or on a local web server) and click "Generate Report" (see Figure 16-4).

Lighthouse will then generate a report, making recommended improvements for any score reductions (see Figures 16-5 and 16-6).

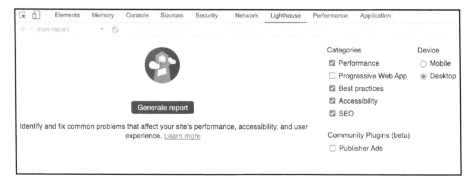

Figure 16-4. Lighthouse within Chrome Developer Tools

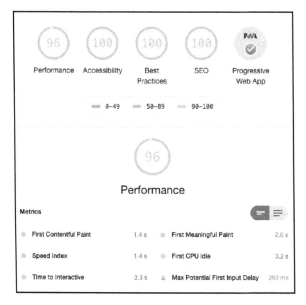

Figure 16-5. A high score demonstrates a performant application and successful progressive web app

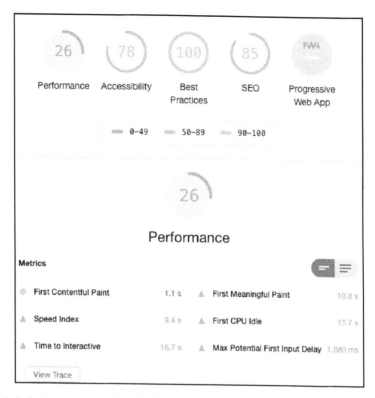

Figure 16-6. A site receiving a low Lighthouse score will also receive recommendations for improvement

> The general use of profiling non-Progressive Web Application sites with Lighthouse in the Chrome Developer Tools is covered in more detail in Recipe 11.4.

Discussion

Lighthouse is a tool for measuring web best practices, including performance and progressive web application compatibility. It comes built into the Chrome Developer Tools, but can also be installed as a Firefox extension.

In addition to being a browser tool, Lighthouse can be installed through npm and used on the command line or as a Node module. You would install Lighthouse the same as any other Node module:

```
$ npm install -g lighthouse
```

which can then be run by passing a URL as an argument:

```
$ lighthouse https://www.oreilly.com/
```

Passing a --view argument will open the results in your browser:

```
$ lighthouse https://www.oreilly.com/ --view
```

You can also specify an output filetype and location to store the report results:

```
$ lighthouse https://www.oreilly.com/ --view --output html --output-path ./report.html
```

And a *budget.json* file can be used to set and test against performance budget limitations. In a *budget.json* file, define the limitations to test against:

```
[
  {
    "path": "/*",
    "timings": [
      {
        "metric": "interactive",
        "budget": 3000
      },
      {
        "metric": "first-meaningful-paint",
        "budget": 1000
      }
    ],
    "resourceSizes": [
      {
        "resourceType": "script",
        "budget": 125
      },
      {
        "resourceType": "total",
        "budget": 300
      }
    ],
    "resourceCounts": [
      {
        "resourceType": "third-party",
        "budget": 10
      }
    ]
  }
]
```

> The Google Chrome team mantains a repository (*https://github.com/GoogleChrome/budget.json*) containing the documentation of *budget.json* options.

Testing locally from the command line can be helpful for local development, but the real power of Lighthouse as a code module is realized when used with continuous integration tools such as GitHub Actions, Circle CI, Jenkins, and Travis CI. The Lighthouse CI (*https://github.com/GoogleChrome/lighthouse-ci*) module enables you to perform Lighthouse testing in a continuous integration pipeline, such as on every GitHub pull request.

Here's a sample configuration for CircleCI:

```
version: 2.1
jobs:
  build:
    docker:
      - image: circleci/node:10.16-browsers
    working_directory: ~/your-project
    steps:
      - checkout
      - run: npm install
      - run: npm run build
      - run: sudo npm install -g @lhci/cli@0.3.x
      - run: lhci autorun
```

Full details on how to use Lighthouse in multiple CI environments are available in Google's Getting Started guide (*https://oreil.ly/7jnwx*).

16.5 Getting the Value of the Current URL

Problem

Your application needs to read the value of the current URL.

Solution

Use the href property of window.location to read the current value of the full URL:

```
const URL = window.location.href;
```

Discussion

window.location provides read-only information about the current URL or *location* of the document. The href property provides the full URL, which includes the protocol (such as HTTPS), hostname, the path to the current document, and any query strings. All together, this will match what is displayed in the user's URL bar:

```
const URL = window.location.href;
// logs https://www.jseverywhere.io/example
console.log(`The current URL is ${URL}`);
```

The global variable `location` is the same as `window.location`; however, I prefer the explicitness of using the `window` API.

The `href` property is not the only useful one. If you already know that the user is on your site, it may be more useful to access the `pathname` and `search` properties:

```
// user is at https://www.jseverywhere.io/example?page=2

const PATH = window.location.pathname;
// logs /example/
console.log(`The current path is ${PATH}`);

const QUERY = window.location.search;
// logs ?page=2
console.log(`The current query parameter is ${QUERY}`)
```

The full list of read-only properties of `window.location` are:

hash
    A hash value in the URL, such as #id

host
    The domain plus port

hostname
    The domain

href
    The full URL

origin
    The protocol, hostname, and port

pathname
    The path of the current document

port
    The server's port number value

protocol
    The protocol (HTTP or HTTPS)

search
    Query string values

16.6 Redirecting a URL

Problem

You need to use JavaScript to route a user to a different page.

Solution

Use either the `assign` or `replace` `window.location` method, depending on the goal of the redirect:

```
// route user to new page & preserve browser history
window.location.assign('https://www.example.com');
// route user to new page but do not preserve current page in history
window.location.replace('https://www.example.com');
```

The `window.location.assign` method will route a user to a new URL, but will preserve the routing page in the browser history. This means that a user will be able to use the browser's back button to navigate back to the page. Conversely, `window.location.replace` will replace the current URL in the history, disabling the ability to return to the current page.

Discussion

By using `window.location` methods, you are able to route a user to a new URL using JavaScript. This allows you to reroute a user or redirect a user based on a page interaction. `assign` and `replace` are not the only `window.location` methods at your disposal. The full list of methods is as follows:

`.assign()`
Navigates the user's browser to a given URL

`.reload()`
Reloads the page

`.replace()`
Navigates the user's browser to a given URL and removes the current document from the browser history

`toString()`
Returns the current URL as a string

By leveraging these methods, you will be able to use JavaScript to manipulate the route of the page, which can provide useful functionality for application UIs and interactive routing. Although these features can be very useful when developing applications, full page redirects should always be done with an HTTP redirect with the appropriate status code of 301 for permanent redirects or 302 for temporary redirects.

 Popular JavaScript frameworks come with a routing library or can be extended with a third-party routing library, which can be used for robust client-side routing.

16.7 Copying Text to a User's Clipboard

Problem

Your application needs to copy text, such as a share link, to the user's clipboard.

Solution

To copy text to a user's clipboard, place the text within a text `input` or `textarea` element and use the `navigator.clipboard.writeText` method to copy the text.

In your HTML, include the form element as well as a button. In the example, I'm setting an explicit `value` for the input element. This value could also be set by the user or dynamically in code:

```
<input type="text" id="copy-text" value="https://example.com/share/12345">
<button id="copy-button">Copy To Clipboard</button>
```

And in the corresponding JavaScript, add an event handler to the `button` element. When the button is clicked, use the `select` method to select the text within the `input` element followed by `navigator.clipboard.writeText()` to copy the text to the user's clipboard, as shown in Example 16-2.

Example 16-2. Copying text to the clipboard

```
const copyText = document.getElementById('copy-text');
const copyButton = document.getElementById('copy-button');

const copyToClipboard = () => {
  copyText.select();
  navigator.clipboard.writeText(copyText.value);
};

copyButton.addEventListener('click', copyToClipboard);
```

Discussion

Adding text to a user's clipboard from a text input box is a common UI pattern seen in web applications such as GitHub and Google Docs. This can be a useful feature to simplify the sharing of information or a URL for users. The input and button pattern demonstrated in the primary recipe is the most common use, but there may be times where you want to instead copy a user selection from the page's content. In this scenario, it may be useful to hide the form control. To do this, include the markup of the page content as well as a `textarea` or `input` element. In this example, I've used a `textarea` element and set the `tabindex` to remove it from the user's tab flow, then set `aria-hidden` to `true` so that screen readers know to ignore the element:

```
<p>Some example text<p>

<textarea id="copy-text" tabindex="-1" aria-hidden="true"></textarea>
<button id="copy-button">Copy the Highlighted Text</button>
```

In my CSS, I've hidden the element by placing it offscreen and giving it a height and width value of 0:

```
#copy-text {
  position: absolute;
  left: -9999px;
  height: 0;
  width: 0;
}
```

Finally, in my JavaScript I follow a similar pattern as Example 16-2, with the addition of using the `document.getSelection()` to get the value of any text that the user has selected on the page:

```
const copyText = document.getElementById('copy-text');
const copyButton = document.getElementById('copy-button');

const copyToClipboard = () => {
  const selection = document.getSelection();
  copyText.value = `${selection} – Check out my highlight at https://example.com `;
  copyText.select();
  navigator.clipboard.writeText(copyText.value);
}

copyButton.addEventListener('click', copyToClipboard);
```

Enabling easy sharing of web application content is a common pattern in the social web era. Using these techniques provides a pattern to simplify that interaction.

16.8 Enabling a Mobile-Like Notification in the Desktop Browser

Problem

You need a way to notify a user that an event has occurred or a long-running process is finished, even if your site isn't open in an active tab.

Solution

Use the Web Notifications API.

This API provides a relatively simple technique to pop up a notification window outside of the browser, so that if a person is currently looking at a web page in another tab, they'll still see the notification.

To use a Web Notification, you do need to get permission. In the following code, Notification permission is requested when a user clicks a button. If permission is granted, a notification is displayed:

```
const notificationButton = document.getElementById('notification-button');

const showNotification = permission => {
  // if the user didn't grant permission, exit the function
  if (permission !== 'granted') return;

  // content of the notification
  const notification = new Notification('Title', {
    body: 'Check out this super cool thing'
  });

  // optional: action to take when a user clicks the notification
  notification.onclick = () => {
    window.open('https://example.com');
  };
};

const notificationCheck = () => {
  // if notifications aren't supported return
  // alternately you could perform a different action
  // like redirect the user to email signup
  if (!window.Notification) return;

  // request permission from the user
  Notification.requestPermission().then(showNotification);
};

// on click, call the `notificationCheck` function
notificationButton.addEventListener('click', notificationCheck);
```

Discussion

Mobile environments have notifications that let you know when you've received a new "Like" on a Facebook post or a new email in your email client. Traditionally, we didn't have this capability in a desktop environment, though some might say this is a good thing.

Still, as we create more sophisticated web applications, it may help to have this functionality, particularly when our applications may take a significant amount of time. Instead of forcing people to hang around looking at a "working" icon on our pages, the web page visitor can view other web pages in other tabs, and know they'll get notified when the long-running process is finished.

In the solution, the first time the code creates a new notification, it gets permission from the web page visitor. If your application is created as a standalone web application, you can specify permissions in the manifest file, but for web pages, you have to ask permission.

Prior to the Notification permission request, you can also test to see if Notification exists, so an error is not thrown if it's not supported:

```
if (window.Notification) {
  Notification.requestPermission(() => {
    setTimeout(() => {
      const notification = new Notification('hey wake up', {
        body: 'your process is done',
        tag: 'loader',
        icon: 'favicon.ico'
      });
      notification();
    }, 5000);
  });
}
```

The Notification takes two arguments—a title string and an object with options:

body
    The text message in the body of the notification

tag
    A tag to help identify notifications for global changes

icon
    A custom icon

lang
    Language of notification

dir
    Direction of the language

You can also code four event handlers:

- `onerror`
- `onclose`
- `onshow`
- `onclose`

And you can programatically close the notification with `Notification.close()`, though Safari and Firefox automatically close the notification in a few seconds. All browsers provide a window close (*x*) option in the notification.

Extra: Web Notifications and the Page Visibility API

You can combine Web Notifications with the Page Visibility API to display the Notification only when the web page visitor isn't actively looking at the web page.

The Page Visibility API has broad support in modern browsers. It adds support for one event, `visibilitychange`, which is fired when the visibility of the tab page changes. It also supports a couple of new properties—`document.hidden` returns true if the tab page isn't visible, and `document.visibilityState`, which has one of the following four values:

- `visible`: When the tab page is visible
- `hidden`: When the tag page is hidden
- `prerender`: The page is being rendered but not yet visible (browser support is optional)
- `unloaded`: The page is being unloaded from memory (browser support is optional)

To modify the solution so that the notification only fires when the tabbed page is hidden, modify the code to check for `visbilityState`:

```
if (window.Notification) {
  Notification.requestPermission(() => {
    setTimeout(() => {
      if (document.visibilityState === 'hidden') {
        const notification = new Notification('hey wake up', {
          body: 'your process is done',
          icon: 'favicon.ico'
        });
        notification();
      } else {
        document.getElementById('result').innerHTML = 'your process is done';
      }
```

```
    }, 5000);
  });
}
```

Before creating the Notification, the code tests to see if the page is hidden. If it is, then the Notification is created. If it isn't, then a message is written out to the page instead.

16.9 Loading a File Locally in the Browser

Problem

You want to open an image file and output the metadata in the browser.

Solution

Use the File API:

```
const inputElement = document.getElementById('file');

function handleFile() {
  // read the contents of the file
  const file = this.files[0];
  const reader = new FileReader();
  // add 'load' event listener
  reader.addEventListener('load', event => {
    // once loaded do something with the contents of the file
  });
  reader.readAsDataURL(file);
}

inputElement.addEventListener('change', handleFile, false);
```

Discussion

The File API bolts onto the existing input element `file` type, used for file uploading. In addition to the capability of uploading the file to the server via a form upload, you can now access the file directly in JavaScript, and either work with it locally or upload the file to a server.

 For more on `FileReader`, check out MDN's page on the API (*http://mzl.la/1ya0o1k*), and a related tutorial (*http://mzl.la/1ya0qGs*).

There are three objects in the File API:

FileList
    A list of files to upload via `input type="file"`

File
    Information about a specific file

FileReader
    Object to asynchronously upload the file for client-side access

Each object has associated properties and events, including being able to track the progress of a file upload (and provide a custom progress bar), as well as signaling when the upload is finished. The `File` object can provide information about the file, including the filename, size, and MIME type. The `FileList` object provides a list of `File` objects, because more than one file can be specified if the input element has the `multiple` attribute set. The `FileReader` is the object that does the actual file upload.

Example 16-3 shows an application that uploads an image, embeds it in the web page, and displays some information about the image. The result is shown in Figure 16-7.

Example 16-3. Loading an image and metadata

```
<!DOCTYPE html>
<head>
  <title>Image Reader</title>
  <meta charset="utf-8" />
  <style>
    #result {
      width: 500px;
      margin: 30px;
    }
  </style>
</head>
<body>
  <h1>Image Reader</h1>
  <form>
    <label for="file">File:</label> <br />
    <input type="file" id="file" accept=".jpg, .jpeg, .png" />
  </form>
  <div id="result">
    <ul>
      <li>Image name: <span id="name"></span></li>
      <li>Image type: <span id="type"></span></li>
    </ul>
  </div>

  <script>
    const inputElement = document.getElementById('file');
    const result = document.getElementById('result');
    const nameEl = document.getElementById('name');
    const typeEl = document.getElementById('type');
```

```
    function handleFile() {
      // read the contents of the file
      const file = this.files[0];
      const reader = new FileReader();
      // add 'load' event listener
      reader.addEventListener('load', event => {
        // create the image element and display it within the result div
        const img = document.createElement('img');
        img.setAttribute('src', event.target.result);
        img.setAttribute('width', '250');
        result.appendChild(img);
        // display the image name and file type
        const name = document.createTextNode(file.name);
        const type = document.createTextNode(file.type);
        nameEl.appendChild(name);
        typeEl.appendChild(type);
      });
      reader.readAsDataURL(file);
    }

    inputElement.addEventListener('change', handleFile, false);
  </script>
</body>
```

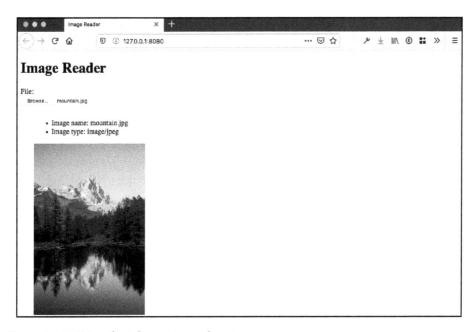

Figure 16-7. Using the File API to read an image

The File API is a W3C effort. For more information, you can read the latest draft (*http://.w3.org/TR/FileAPI*) or Mozilla's coverage (*http://mzl.la/1ya0qGs*).

16.10 Extending the Possible with Web Components

Problem

You need a component that encapsulates a specific look, feel, and behavior, and that you can include as easily as you'd include an HTML element, but don't want to use a web framework.

Solution

Consider Web Components, which allow you to create custom and reusable HTML elements. Web Components consist of a Template, custom elements, and shadow DOM. Each will be covered in the discussion.

Discussion

Think of a web page widget that's completely self-contained and you have some resemblance to Web Components, but only in the most shallow sense. Web Components, as a term, encompasses several different constructs. In the following sections, I'll cover each, provide examples, discuss polyfills, and what to expect in the future.

HTML templates

The `template` element is now part of the HTML5 specification. Currently it's supported in most modern browsers (*https://oreil.ly/SJZDC*). Within the `template` element, we include HTML that we want to group as a whole that isn't instantiated until it is *cloned*. It is parsed when loaded, to ensure it's valid, but it doesn't exist. Yet.

Working with templates is very intuitive. Consider a common practice with today's single-page JavaScript applications: taking returned data from a web service and formatting it as an unordered list (`ul`) (or new paragraph, or table, or whatever). Typically, we'd use the DOM methods to query for the existing `ul` element, create each list item (`li`) in the list, append text to the item, and append the item to the list.

What if we could cut out some of the steps? We could with the `template`. Given the following HTML:

```
<template id="hello-world">
  <p>Hello world!</p>
</template>
```

This is the JavaScript to add our "Hello World" template to a page:

```
const template = document.getElementById('hello-world');
const templateContent = template.content;
document.body.appendChild(templateContent);
```

In the example we access the `template` element, access the HTML element's content, and then append it to the HTML document using `appendChild()`. As I noted, templates are very intuitive, but you might be wondering, what's the point? All we've done is add more code for a process that's already simple, but templates are important for their use in Custom Elements, discussed in "Custom elements" on page 389, as well as the "Shadow DOM" on page 389.

Custom elements

The Web Components construct that has generated the most interest is the custom element. Instead of having to deal with existing HTML elements and their default behaviors and appearance, we create a custom element, package in its styling and behavior, and just attach it to the web page. A custom element can either extend an existing element or be "autonomous," meaning it is a completely new element. In the following example, I will extend the HTML `<p>` element to create a new element named `<hello-world>`. To do so, I will first need to define a class with any special methods for the element:

```
class CustomGreeting extends HTMLParagraphElement {
  constructor() {
    // always call super first in constructor
    super();

    // any additional element functionality can be written here
  }
}
```

Once the class is defined, I can register my element. Note that the element name must contain a hyphen to avoid any potential conflicts with existing HTML elements:

```
customElements.define("custom-greeting", CustomGreeting);
```

Now I can use my element in my HTML page:

```
<custom-greeting>Hello world!</custom-greeting>
```

Shadow DOM

I can't see *shadow DOM* without thinking of the fictional character "The Shadow." What a great character, and appropriate, too. Only The Shadow knew what evil lurked in the minds of men, and only the shadow DOM knows what lurks in its element's DOM.

Dragging ourselves away from fictional distraction, the shadow DOM is the most twisty of the Web Components. But intriguing, too.

First, the nonmysterious bits. The shadow DOM is a DOM, a tree of nodes just like we're used to when we access elements from the document element. The primary difference is that it doesn't exist, not in a way we know a DOM existing. When we create a *shadow root* of an element, then it comes into existence. But then, whatever the element used to have, is gone. That's the key to remember about the shadow DOM: creating it replaces the element's existing DOM.

By using the attachShadow method, you can attach a shadow root to any element:

```
const shadow = element.attachShadow({mode: 'open'});
```

The attachShadow method takes one parameter (mode), which accepts a value of either open or closed. Setting the value to open allows you to access the shadow DOM in the context of the page, like any other element. The most common shadow DOM use case is attaching a shadow DOM to a custom element as part of its constructor:

```
class CustomGreeting extends HTMLElement {
  constructor() {
    super();
    const shadow = this.attachShadow({mode: 'open'});
    const greeting = this.getAttribute('greeting') || 'world'
    shadow.innerHTML = `<p>
      Hello, <span class="greeting">${greeting}</span>
    </p>`;
  }
}
```

Though the above example contains two HTML elements, global CSS styles will not apply to a shadow DOM element. To style a custom element with a shadow DOM, we would create a style element within the custom element class and apply the styles:

```
class CustomGreeting extends HTMLElement {
  constructor() {
    super();
    const shadow = this.attachShadow({mode: 'open'});
    const greeting = this.getAttribute('greeting') || 'world'
    shadow.innerHTML = `<p class="wrapper">
      Hello, <span class="greeting">${greeting}</span>
    </p>`;

    // add css styles
    const style = document.createElement('style');

    style.textContent = `
      .wrapper {
        color: pink;
      }
```

```
    .greeting {
      color: green;
      font-weight: bold;
    }
    `;
  }
}
```

 The Polymer Project (*https://oreil.ly/874AX*) is a collection of libraries and tools for working with web components.

Web components are a very interesting part of the web standards ecosystem with great potential. HTML templates, custom HTML elements, and the shadow DOM provide a means for creating small, reusable UI components. This idea of lightweight components has been reflected in JavaScript libraries such as React and Vue.

16.11 Choosing a Front-End Framework

Problem

You are building a complex web application that requires a JavaScript framework. How do you choose the right framework?

Solution

There was a time when JavaScript frameworks seemingly came in and out of style faster than a fashion week runway. Thankfully, over the past few years the framework wars have slowed down and we have been left with a handful of excellent choices. Despite the slowdown of new development, it can still be challenging to choose the best framework for you and your project. When evaluating frameworks for a project, I recommend asking yourself the following questions:

Do I need a JavaScript framework?
　　Don't always reach for a framework by default. Oftentimes, simple sites and applications may be easier to write and maintain without a framework, while being more performant for a user.

What is the type of project I'll be developing?
　　Is this a personal project? A project for a client? An enterprise project with long-term support needs? An open source project? Consider the maintainers of your project and what will best meet their needs.

What is the level of community adoption and the longevity of the project?
> Consider the long-term support of the framework. Is it still an active project? Will it be supported by a large community to answer questions and fix bugs?

How well documented is the framework?
> Ensure that the documentation is easy to understand and complete.

What does the developer ecosystem for the framework look like?
> Evaluate the tooling, plug-ins, and metaframeworks.

Am I familiar with the framework?
> Is the framework something that you already know or have familiarity with or is this a learning project?

What will be the impact on my users?
> Perhaps the most important question of all. Determine if a framework will impact the performance, accessibility, or usability of your project.

While this is far from an exhaustive list, the authors of this book recommend looking at the following frameworks: React, Vue, Svelte, and Angular.

React

React (*https://reactjs.org*) is a UI-driven JavaScript framework developed and released by Facebook. React focuses on small visual components and commonly makes use of jsx, an XML syntax within JavaScript for rendering HTML components. React makes updates to the page more efficient by using a representation of the DOM, referred to as the virtual DOM (*https://oreil.ly/oK21x*).

Vue

Vue (*https://vuejs.org*) is a community-focused, UI-driven framework. Like React, Vue makes use of a virtual DOM to make page updates instantaneous. Many view Vue as an alternative to React. The feature set is similar, but Vue makes use of a more HTML-friendly template syntax and is community backed, rather than supported by Facebook. I'd recommend giving both React and Vue a spin to see which best matches you and your team's development style.

Svelte

Svelte (*https://svelte.dev*) takes a different approach from the other JS frameworks here. Similar to React and Vue, it is a UI-focused library, but rather than doing the bulk of the work in the user's browser, Svelte focuses on a compile step at development build time. The goal is to limit the tax on the user's browser so that developers can build performant applications.

Angular

Angular (*https://angular.io*) is a full-featured JavaScript framework, developed and released by Google. Angular survived the first wave of "framework" wars and has adapted to a component-based architecture that is similar to modern libraries. Unlike React, Vue, and Svelte, Angular is a fully featured framework out of the box, with in-app navigation, data and state management, and testing built into the framework. For many, particularly enterprise-focused teams, this can be a useful feature as it limits decision making when building new applications or adding features.

## PART III

Node.js

## CHAPTER 17

Node Basics

The dividing line between "old" and "new" JavaScript occurred when Node.js (referred to primarily as just Node) was released to the world. Yes, the ability to dynamically modify page elements was an essential milestone, as was the emphasis on establishing a path forward to new versions of ECMAScript, but it was Node that really made us look at JavaScript in a whole new way. And it's a way I like—I'm a big fan of Node and server-side JavaScript development.

In this chapter, we'll explore the basics of Node. At a minimum, you will need to have Node installed, as covered in Recipe 1.6 or Recipe 17.1.

17.1 Managing Node Versions with Node Version Manager

Problem

You need to install and manage multiple versions of Node on your development machine.

Solution

Use Node Version Manager (NVM) (*https://github.com/nvm-sh/nvm*), which allows you to install and use any distributed version of Node on a per-shell basis. NVM is compatible with Linux, macOS, and Windows Subsystem for Linux.

To install NVM, run the install script using either `curl` or `wget` in your system's terminal application:

```
## using curl:
curl -o- https://raw.githubusercontent.com/nvm-sh/nvm/v0.37.2/install.sh | bash
```

```
## using wget:
wget -qO- https://raw.githubusercontent.com/nvm-sh/nvm/v0.37.2/install.sh | bash
```

 If you are developing on Windows, we recommend using nvm-windows (*https://github.com/coreybutler/nvm-windows*), which is unaffiliated with the NVM project, but provides similar functionality for the Windows operating system. For instructions on how to use nvm-windows, consult the project's documentation.

Once you have installed NVM, you will need to install a version of Node. To install the latest version of Node, run:

```
$ nvm install node
```

You can also install a specific version of Node:

```
# install the latest path release of a major version
$ nvm install 15

# install a specific major/minor/patch version
$ nvm install 15.6.0
```

Once you've installed Node, you'll need to set a default version for new shell sessions. This can either be the latest version of Node that has been installed or a specific version number:

```
# default new shell sessions to the latest version of node
nvm alias default node
# default new shell sessions to a specific version
nvm alias default 14
```

To switch the version being used in a shell session, use the nvm use command followed by a specific installed version:

```
$ nvm use 15
```

Discussion

Using NVM allows you to easily download and switch between multiple versions of Node on your operating system. This can be incredibly useful when working with libraries that support multiple versions and legacy codebases. It also simplifies the management of Node within your development environment. You can view the list of releases and support timelines (*https://oreil.ly/9IY83*) for each release.

When using NVM, it's possible to list out all of the versions installed on your machine using the nvm ls command. This will show all of the installed versions, the default version for new shell sessions, and any LTS versions that you do not have installed:

```
$ nvm ls
        v8.1.2
        v8.11.3
       v10.13.0
->     v10.23.1
        v12.8.0
       v12.20.0
       v12.20.1
        v13.5.0
       v14.14.0
       v14.15.1
       v14.15.4
        v15.6.0
         system
default -> 14 (-> v14.15.4)
node -> stable (-> v15.6.0) (default)
stable -> 15.6 (-> v15.6.0) (default)
iojs -> N/A (default)
unstable -> N/A (default)
lts/* -> lts/fermium (-> v14.15.4)
lts/argon -> v4.9.1 (-> N/A)
lts/boron -> v6.17.1 (-> N/A)
lts/carbon -> v8.17.0 (-> N/A)
lts/dubnium -> v10.23.1
lts/erbium -> v12.20.1
lts/fermium -> v14.15.4
```

As you can see, I have several redundant patch versions of major releases installed on my machine. To uninstall and remove a specific version, you can use the `nvm unin stall` command:

```
nvm uninstall 14.14
```

Keeping track of which version of Node a project is designed to use can be a challenge. To make this easier, you can add an `.nvmrc` file to your project's root directory. The contents of the file is the version of Node that the project is designed to use. For example:

```
# default to the latest LTS version
$ lts/*

# to use a specific version
$ 14.15.4
```

To use the version specified in a project's `.nvmrc` file, run `nvm use` command from the root of the director.

For large projects, using a container technology, such as Docker, is an incredibly useful way to ensure version matching across environments, including deployment. The Node documentation has a helpful guide on Dockerizing a Node.js web app (*https://oreil.ly/phXQZ*).

17.2 Responding to a Simple Browser Request

Problem

You want to create a Node application that can respond to a very basic browser request.

Solution

Use the built-in Node HTTP server to respond to requests:

```
// load http module
const http = require('http');

// create http server
http
  .createServer((req, res) => {
    // content header
    res.writeHead(200, { 'content-type': 'text/plain' });

    // write message and signal communication is complete
    res.end('Hello, World!');
  })
  .listen(8124);

console.log('Server running on port 8124');
```

Discussion

A web server response to a browser request is the "Hello World" application for Node. It demonstrates not only how a Node application functions, but how you can communicate with it using a fairly traditional communication method: requesting a web resource.

Starting from the top, the first line of the solution loads the `http` module using Node's `require()` function. This instructs Node's modular system to load a specific library resource for use in the application. The `http` module is one of the many that come, by default, with a Node installation.

Next, an HTTP server is created using `http.createServer()`, passing in an anonymous function, known as the `RequestListener` with two parameters. Node attaches this function as an event handler for every server request. The two parameters are *request* and *response*. The request is an instance of the http.IncomingMessage object and the response is an instance of the http.ServerResponse object.

The http.ServerResponse is used to respond to the web request. The http.Incoming Message object contains information about the request, such as the request URL. If you need to get specific pieces of information from the URL (e.g., query string parameters), you can use the Node url utility module to parse the string. Example 17-1 demonstrates how the query string can be used to return a more custom message to the browser.

Example 17-1. Parsing out query string data

```
// load http module
const http = require('http');
const url = require('url');

// create http server
http
  .createServer((req, res) => {
    // get query string and parameters
    const { query } = url.parse(req.url, true);

    // content header
    res.writeHead(200, { 'content-type': 'text/plain' });

    // write message and signal communication is complete
    const name = query.first ? query.first : 'World';

    // write message and signal communication is complete
    res.end(`Hello, ${name}!`);
  })
  .listen(8124);

console.log('Server running on port 8124');
```

A URL like the following:

```
http://localhost:8124/?first=Reader
```

results in a web page that reads "Hello, Reader!"

In the code, the url module object has a parse() method that parses out the URL, returning various components of it (href, protocol, host, etc.). If you pass true as the second argument, the string is also parsed by another module, querystring, which returns the query string as an object with each parameter as an object property, rather than just returning a string.

In both the solution and in Example 17-1, a text message is returned as page output, using the `http.ServerResponse end()` method. I could also have written the message out using `write()`, and then called `end()`:

```
res.write(`Hello, ${name}!`);
res.end();
```

The important takeaway from either approach is you *must* call the response `end()` method after all the headers and response body have been set.

Chained to the end of the `createServer()` function call is another function call, this time to `listen()`, passing in the port number for the server to listen in on. This port number is also an especially important component of the application.

Traditionally, port 80 is the default port for most web servers (that aren't using HTTPS, which has a default port of 443). By using port 80, requests for the web resource don't need to specify a port when requesting the service's URL. However, port 80 is also the default port used by our more traditional web server, Apache. If you try to run the Node service on the same port that Apache is using, your application will fail. The Node application either must be standalone on the server, or run off a different port.

You can also specify an IP address (host) in addition to the port. Doing this ensures that people make the request to a specific host, as well as port. Not providing the host means the application will listen for the request for any IP address associated with the server. You can also specify a domain name, and Node resolves the host.

There are other arguments for the methods demonstrated, and a host of other methods, but this will get you started. Refer to the Node documentation (*http://nodejs.org/api*) for more information.

17.3 Interactively Trying Out Node Code Snippets with REPL

Problem

You want to easily run server-based Node code snippets.

Solution

Use Node's REPL (Read-Evaluate-Print-Loop), an interactive command-line version of Node that can run any code snippet.

To use REPL, type `node` at the command line without specifying an application to run:

```
$ node
```

You can then specify JavaScript in a simplified Emacs (sorry, no vi) line-editing style. You can import libraries, create functions—whatever you can do within a static application. The main difference is that each line of code is interpreted instantly:

```
> const add = (x, y) => { return x + y };
undefined
> add(2, 2);
4
```

When you're finished, exit the program with .exit:

```
> .exit
```

Discussion

REPL can be started standalone or within another application if you want to set certain features. You type in the JavaScript as if you're typing in the script in a text file. The main behavioral difference is you might see a result after typing in each line, such as the undefined that shows up in the runtime REPL.

But you can import modules:

```
> const fs = require('fs');
```

And you can access the global objects, which we just did when we used require().

The undefined that shows after typing in some code is the return value for the execution of the previous line of code. Setting a new variable and creating a function are some of the JavaScript that return undefined, which can get quickly annoying. To eliminate this behavior, as well as make some other modifications, you can use the REPL.start() function within a small Node application that triggers REPL (but with the options you specify).

The options you can use are:

prompt
> Changes the prompt that shows (default is >)

input
> Changes the input readable stream (default is process.stdin, which is the standard input)

output
> Changes the output writable stream (default is process.stdout, the standard output)

terminal
> Set to true if the stream should be treated like a TTY, and have ANSI/VT100 escape codes written

eval

> Function used to replace the asynchronous `eval()` function used to evaluate the JavaScript

useColors

> Set to `true` to set output colors for the `writer` function (default is based on the terminal's default values)

useGlobal

> Set to `true` to use the `global` object, rather than running scripts in a separate context

ignoreUndefined

> Set to `true` to eliminate the `undefined` return values

writer

> The function that returns the formatted result from the evaluated code to the display (default is the `util.inspect` function)

The following is an example application that starts REPL with a new prompt, ignoring the undefined values, and using colors:

```
const repl = require('repl');

const options = {
  prompt: '-> ',
  useColors: true,
  ignoreUndefined: true
};

repl.start(options);
```

The options we want are defined in the `options` object and then passed as parameters to `repl.start()`. When we run the application, REPL is started but we no longer have to deal with undefined values:

```
-> const add = (x, y) => { return x + y };
-> add(2, 2);
4
```

As you can see, this is a cleaner output without all those messy `undefined` printouts.

Extra: Wait a Second, What Global Object?

Caught that, did you?

One difference between JavaScript in Node and JavaScript in the browser is the global scoping. Traditionally in a browser, when you create a variable outside a function, using `var`, it belongs to the top-level global object, which we know as `window`:

```
var test = 'this is a test';
console.log(window.test); // 'this is a test'
```

Similarly, when using let or const in the browser, the variables are globally scoped, though not attached to the window object.

In Node, each module operates within its own separate context, so modules can declare the same variables, and they won't conflict if they're all used in the same application.

However, there are objects accessible from Node's global object. We've used a few in previous examples, including console, the Buffer object, and require(). Others include some very familiar old friends: setTimeout(), clearTimeout(), setInterval(), and clearInterval().

17.4 Reading and Writing File Data

Problem

You want to read from or write to a locally stored file.

Solution

Node's filesystem management functionality is included as part of the Node core, via the fs module:

```
const fs = require('fs');
```

To read a file's contents, use the readFile() function:

```
const fs = require('fs');

fs.readFile('main.txt', 'utf8', (err, data) => {
  if (err) throw err;
  console.log(data);
});
```

To write to a file, use writeFile():

```
const fs = require('fs');

const buf = "I'm going to write this text to a file";
fs.writeFile('main2.txt', buf, err => {
  if (err) throw err;
  console.log('wrote text to file');
});
```

The writeFile() function overwrites the existing file. To append text to the file, use appendText():

```
const fs = require('fs');

const buf = "\nI'm going to add this text to a file";
fs.appendFile('main.txt', buf, err => {
  if (err) throw err;
  console.log('appended text to file');
});
```

Discussion

Node's filesystem support is both comprehensive and simple to use. To read from a file, use the readFile() function, which supports the following parameters:

- The filename, including the operating system path to the file if it isn't local to the application

- An options object, with options for encoding, as demonstrated in the solution, and flag, which is set to r by default (for reading)

- A callback function with parameters for an error and the read data

In the solution, if I didn't specify the encoding in my application, Node would have returned the file contents as a raw buffer. Since I did specify the encoding, the file content is returned as a string.

The writeFile() and appendFile() functions for writing and appending, respectively, take parameters similar to readFile():

- The filename and path

- The string or buffer for the data to write to the file

- The options object, with options for encoding (w as default for writeFile() and a as the default for appendFile()) and mode, with a default value of 438 (0666 in Octal)

- The callback function, with only one parameter: the error

The options value of mode can be used to set the file's permissions if the file was created by write or append. By default, the file is created as readable and writable by the owner, and readable by the group and the world.

I mentioned that the data to write can be either a buffer or a string. A string cannot handle binary data, so Node provides the buffer, which is capable of dealing with either strings or binary data. Both can be used in all of the filesystem functions discussed in this section, but you'll need to explicitly convert between the two types if you want to use them both.

For example, instead of providing the *utf8* encoding option when you use `write File()`, you convert the string to a buffer, providing the desired encoding when you do:

```
const fs = require('fs');

const str = "I'm going to write this text to a file";
const buf = Buffer.from(str, 'utf8');
fs.writeFile('mainbuf.txt', buf, err => {
  if (err) throw err;
  console.log('wrote text to file');
});
```

The reverse—that is, to convert the buffer to a string—is just as simple:

```
const fs = require('fs');

fs.readFile('main.txt', (err, data) => {
  if (err) throw err;
  const str = data.toString();
  console.log(str);
});
```

The buffer `toString()` function has three optional parameters: encoding, where to begin the conversion, and where to end it. By default, the entire buffer is converted using the *utf8* encoding.

The `readFile()`, `writeFile()`, and `appendFile()` functions are *asynchronous*, meaning they won't wait for the operation to finish before proceeding in the code. This is essential when it comes to notoriously slow operations such as file access. There are synchronous versions of each: `readFileSync()`, `writeFileSync()`, and `appendFile Sync()`. I can't stress enough that you should *not* use these variations. I only include a reference to them to be comprehensive.

Advanced

Another way to read or write from a file is to use the `open()` function in combination with `read()` for reading the file contents, or `write()` for writing to the file. The advantages to this approach is more finite control of what happens during the process. The disadvantage is the added complexity associated with all of the functions, including only being able to use a buffer for reading from and writing to the file.

The parameters for `open()` are:

- Filename and path
- Flag

- Optional mode
- Callback function

The same `open()` is used with all operations, with the *flag* controlling what happens. There are quite a few flag options, but the ones that interest us the most at this time are:

r

  Opens the file for reading; the file must exist

r+

  Opens the file for reading and writing; an exception occurs if the file doesn't exist

w

  Opens the file for writing, truncates the file, or creates it if it doesn't exist

wx

  Opens the file for writing, but fails if the file *does* exist

w+

  Opens the file for reading and writing; creates the file if it doesn't exist; truncates the file if it exists

wx+

  Similar to w+, but fails if the file exists

a

  Opens the file for appending, creates it if it doesn't exist

ax

  Opens the file for appending, fails if the file exists

a+

  Opens the file for reading and appending; creates the file if it doesn't exist

ax+

  Similar to a+, but fails if the file exists

The mode is the same one mentioned earlier, a value that sets the *sticky* and *permission* bits on the file if created, and defaults to 0666. The callback function has two parameters: an error object, if an error occurs, and a *file descriptor*, used by subsequent file operations.

The `read()` and `write()` functions share the same basic types of parameters:

- The `open()` methods callback file descriptor
- The buffer used to either hold data to be written or appended, or read

---

- The offset where the input/output (I/O) operation begins
- The buffer length (set by read operation, controls write operation)
- Position in the file where the operation is to take place; *null* if the position is the current position

The callback functions for both methods have three arguments: an error, bytes read (or written), and the buffer.

That's a lot of parameters and options. The best way to demonstrate how it all works is to create a complete Node application that opens a brand new file for writing, writes some text to it, writes some more text to it, and then reads all the text back and prints it to the console. Since open() is asynchronous, the read and write operations have to occur within the callback function. Be ready for it in Example 17-2, because you're going to get your first taste of a concept known as *callback hell*.

Example 17-2. Demonstrating open, read, and write

```
const fs = require('fs');

fs.open('newfile.txt', 'a+', (err, fd) => {
  if (err) {
    throw err;
  } else {
    const buf = Buffer.from('The first string\n');
    fs.write(fd, buf, 0, buf.length, 0, (err, written) => {
      if (err) {
        throw err;
      } else {
        const buf2 = Buffer.from('The second string\n');
        fs.write(fd, buf2, 0, buf2.length, buf.length, (err, written2) => {
          if (err) {
            throw err;
          } else {
            const length = written + written2;
            const buf3 = Buffer.alloc(length);
            fs.read(fd, buf3, 0, length, 0, err => {
              if (err) {
                throw err;
              } else {
                console.log(buf3.toString());
              }
            });
          }
        });
      }
    });
  }
});
```

Taming callbacks is covered in Recipe 19.2.

To find the length of the buffers, I used `length`, which returns the number of bytes for the buffer. This value doesn't necessarily match the length of a string in the buffer, but it does work in this usage.

That many levels of indentation can make your skin crawl, but the example demonstrates how `open()`, `read()`, and `write()` work. These combinations of functions are what's used within the `readFile()`, `writeFile()`, and `appendFile()` functions to manage file access. The higher-level functions just simplify the most common file operations.

See Recipe 19.2 for a solution to all that nasty indentation.

17.5 Getting Input from the Terminal

Problem

You want to get input from the application user via the terminal.

Solution

Use Node's Readline module.

To get data from the standard input, use code such as the following:

```
const readline = require('readline');

const rl = readline.createInterface({
  input: process.stdin,
  output: process.stdout
});

rl.question(">>What's your name?  ", answer => {
  console.log(`Hello ${answer}`);
  rl.close();
});
```

Discussion

The Readline module provides the ability to get lines of text from a readable stream. You start by creating an instance of the Readline interface with `createInterface()` passing in, at minimum, the readable and writable streams. You need both, because you're writing prompts, as well as reading in text. In the solution, the input stream is `process.stdin`, the standard input stream, and the output stream is `process.stdout`. In other words, input and output are from, and to, the command line.

The solution uses the `question()` function to post a question, and provides a callback function to process the response. Within the function, `close()` is called, which closes the interface, releasing control of the input and output streams.

You can also create an application that continues to listen to the input, taking some action on the incoming data, until something signals the application to end. Typically that something is a letter sequence signaling the person is done, such as the word *exit*. This type of application makes use of other Readline functions, such as `setPrompt()` to change the prompt given the individual for each line of text; `prompt()`, which prepares the input area, including changing the prompt to the one set by `setPrompt()`; and `write()`, to write out a prompt. In addition, you'll also need to use event handlers to process events, such as `line`, which listens for each new line of text.

Example 17-3 contains a complete Node application that continues to process input from the user until they type in `exit`. Note that the application makes use of `process.exit()`. This function cleanly terminates the Node application.

Example 17-3. Access numbers from stdin until the user types in exit

```
const readline = require('readline');

let sum = 0;

const rl = readline.createInterface({
  input: process.stdin,
  output: process.stdout
});

console.log("Enter numbers, one to a line. Enter 'exit' to quit.");

rl.setPrompt('>> ');
rl.prompt();

rl.on('line', input => {
  const userInput = input.trim();
  if (userInput === 'exit') {
    rl.close();
    return;
  }
```

```
  sum += Number(userInput);
  rl.prompt();
});

// user typed in 'exit'
rl.on('close', () => {
  console.log(`Total is ${sum}`);
  process.exit(0);
});
```

Running the application with several numbers results in the following output:

```
Enter numbers, one to a line. Enter 'exit' to quit.
>> 55
>> 209
>> 23.44
>> 0
>> 1
>> 6
>> exit
Total is 294.44
```

I used `console.log()` rather than the Readline interface `write()` to write the prompt, followed by a new line, and to differentiate the output from the input.

See Also

Chapter 19 covers passing and reading command-line arguments in Node applications.

17.6 Getting the Path to the Current Script

Problem

Your application needs to read the path of the script that is being executed.

Solution

Use the __dirname or __filename variables, which are in the scope of the module executing it:

```
// logs the directory of the currently executed file
// ex: /Users/Adam/Projects/js-cookbook/node
console.log(__dirname);

// logs the directory and filename of the currently executed file
// ex: /Users/Adam/Projects/js-cookbook/node/example.js
console.log(__filename);
```

Discussion

The __dirname or __filename variables appear to be in the global scope, but they actually exist in the scope of the module itself. Let's assume that you have a project with the following directory structure:

```
example-app
|   index.js
├──dir1
|   |   example.js
|   └──dir3
|       |   nested.js
```

If you were to read the __dirname in the index.js file, it would be the path to the project's root directory. However, reading the __dirname in from a script in the *nested.js* file would read the path to the *dir3* directory. This allows you to read the path of a module as it's executed, rather than being limited to the parent directory itself.

A useful example of __dirname in action is when creating a new file or directory within the current directory. In the following example, the script creates a new subdirectory named *cache* within the current file's directory:

```
const fs = require('fs');
const path = require('path');
const newDirectoryPath = path.join(__dirname, '/cache');

fs.mkdirSync(newDirectoryPath);
```

17.7 Working with Node Timers and Understanding the Node Event Loop

Problem

You need to use a timer in a Node application, but you're not sure which of Node's three timers to use, or how accurate they are.

Solution

If your timer doesn't have to be precise, you can use setTimeout() to create a single timer event, or setInterval() if you want a reccurring timer:

```
setTimeout(() => {}, 3000);

setInterval(() => {}, 3000);
```

Both function timers can be canceled:

```
const timer1 = setTimeout(() => {}, 3000);
clearTimeout(timer1);
```

```
const timer2 = setInterval(() => {}, 3000);
clearInterval(timer2);
```

However, if you need more finite control of your timer, and immediate results, you might want to use `setImmediate()`. You don't specify a delay for it, as you want the callback to be invoked *immediately* after all I/O callbacks are processed but before any `setTimeout()` or `setInterval()` callbacks:

```
setImmediate(() => {});
```

It, too, can be cleared, with `clearImmediate()`.

Discussion

Node, being JavaScript based, runs on a single thread. It is *synchronous*. However, input/output (I/O) and other native API access either runs *asynchronously* or on a separate thread. Node's approach to managing this timing disconnect is the *event loop*.

In your code, when you perform an I/O operation, such as writing a chunk of text to a file, you specify a callback function to do any post-write activity. Once you've done so, the rest of your application code is processed. It doesn't wait for the file write to finish. When the file write has finished, an event signaling the fact is returned to Node, and pushed on to a queue, waiting for processing. Node processes this event queue, and when it gets to the event signaled by the completed file write, it matches the event to the callback, and the callback is processed.

As a comparison, think of going into a deli and ordering lunch. You wait in line to place your order, and are given an order number. You sit down and read the paper, or check your Twitter account while you wait. In the meantime, the lunch orders go into another queue for deli workers to process the orders. But each lunch request isn't always finished in the order received. Some lunch orders may take longer. They may need to bake or grill for a longer time. So the deli worker processes your order by preparing your lunch item and then placing it in an oven, setting a timer for when it's finished, and goes on to other tasks.

When the timer pings, the deli worker quickly finishes their current task, and pulls your lunch order from the oven. You're then notified that your lunch is ready for pickup by your order number being called out. If several time-consuming lunch items are being processed at the same time, the deli worker processes them as the timer for each item pings, in order.

All Node processes fit the pattern of the deli order queue: first in, first to be sent to the deli (thread) workers. However, certain operations, such as I/O, are like those lunch orders that need extra time to bake in an oven or grill, but don't require the deli worker to stop any other effort and wait for the baking and grilling. The oven or grill timers are equivalent to the messages that appear in the Node event loop, triggering a final action based on the requested operation.

You now have a working blend of synchronous and asynchronous processes. But what happens with a timer?

Both `setTimeout()` and `setInterval()` fire after the given delay, but what happens is a message to this effect is added to the event loop, to be processed in turn. So if the event loop is particularly cluttered, there is a delay before the the timer functions' callbacks are called:

> It is important to note that your callback will probably not be called in exactly (delay) milliseconds. Node.js makes no guarantees about the exact timing of when the callback will fire, nor of the ordering things will fire in. The callback will be called as close as possible to the time specified.
>
> —Node Timers documentation

For the most part, whatever delay happens is beyond the kin of our human senses, but it can result in animations that don't seem to run smoothly. It can also add an odd effect to other applications.

In Example 17-4, I created a scrolling timeline in SVG, with data fed to the client via WebSockets. To emulate real-world data, I used a three-second timer and randomly generated a number to act as a data value. In the server code, I used `setInterval()`, because the timer is reccurring:

Example 17-4. Scrolling timeline example

```
const app = require('http');
const fs = require('fs');
const ws = require('nodejs-websocket');

let server;

// serve static page
const handler = (req, res) => {
  fs.readFile(`${__dirname}/drawline.html`, (err, data) => {
    if (err) {
      res.writeHead(500);
      return res.end('Error loading drawline.html');
    }
    res.writeHead(200);
    res.end(data);
    return data;
  });
};

/// start the webserver
// connections on Port 8124 will be handled by the handler
app.listen(8124);
```

```
app.createServer(handler);

// data timer
const startTimer = () => {
  setInterval(() => {
    const newval = Math.floor(Math.random() * 100) + 1;
    if (server.connections.length > 0) {
      console.log(`sending ${newval}`);
      const counter = { counter: newval };
      server.connections.forEach(conn => {
        conn.sendText(JSON.stringify(counter), () => {
          console.log('conn sent');
        });
      });
    }
  }, 3000);
};

// Create a websocket connection handler on a different port
server = ws
  .createServer(conn => {
    console.log('connected');
    conn.on('close', () => {
      console.log('Connection closed');
    });
  })
  .listen(8001, () => {
    startTimer();
  });
```

I included console.log() to call in the code so you can see the timer event in comparison to the communication responses. When the setInterval() function is called, it's pushed into the process. When its callback is processed, the WebSocket communications are also pushed into the queue.

The solution uses setInterval(), one of Node's three different types of timers. The setInterval() function has the same format as the one we use in the browser. You specify a callback for the first function, provide a delay time (in milliseconds), and any potential arguments. The timer is going to fire in three seconds, but we already know that the callback for the timer may not be immediately processed.

The same applies to the callbacks passed in the WebSocket sendText() calls. These are based on Node's Net (or TLS, if secure) sockets, and as the socket.write() (what's used for sendText()) documentation notes:

> The optional callback parameter will be executed when the data is finally written out—this may not be immediately.
>
> —Node documentation

If you set the timer to invoke immediately (giving zero as the delay value), you'll see that the data sent message is interspersed with the communication sent message (before the browser client freezes up, overwhelmed by the socket communications—you don't want to use a zero value in the application again).

However, the timelines for all the clients remain the same because the communications are sent within the timer's callback function, *synchronously*, so the data is the same for all of the communications—it's just the callbacks that are handled, seemingly out of order.

Earlier I mentioned using `setInterval()` with a delay of zero. In actuality, it isn't exactly zero—Node follows the HTML5 specification that browsers adhere to, and "clamps" the timer interval to a minimum value of four milliseconds. While this may seem to be too small of an amount to cause a problem, when it comes to animations and time-critical processes, the time delay can impact the overall appearance and/or function.

To bypass the constraints, Node developers utilize Node's `process.nextTick()` instead. The callback associated with `process.nextTick()` is processed on the next event loop go around, usually before any I/O callbacks (though there are constraints, which I'll get to in a minute). No more pesky four-millisecond throttling. But then, what happens if there's an enormous number of recursively called `process.next Tick()` calls?

To return to our deli analogy, during a busy lunch hour, workers can be overrun with orders and so caught up in trying to process new orders that they don't respond in a timely manner to the oven and grill pings. Things burn when this happens. If you've ever been to a well-run deli, you'll notice the counter person taking the orders will assess the kitchen before taking the order, tossing in some slight delay, or even taking on some of the kitchen duties, letting the people wait just a tiny bit longer in the order queue.

The same happens with Node. If `process.nextTick()` were allowed to be the spoiled child, always getting its way, I/O operations would get starved out. Node uses another value, `process.maxTickDepth`, with a default value of 1000 to constrain the number of `process.next()` callbacks that are processed before the I/O callbacks are allowed to play. It's the counter person in the deli.

In more recent releases of Node, the `setImmediate()` function was added. This function attempts to resolve all of the issues associated with the timing operations and create a happy medium that should work for most folks. When `setImmediate()` is called, its callback is added after the I/O callbacks, but before the `setTimeout()` and `setInterval()` callbacks. We don't have the four-millisecond tax for the traditional timers, but we also don't have the brat that is `process.nextTick()`.

To return one last time to the deli analogy, setImmediate() is a customer in the order queue who sees that the deli workers are overwhelmed with pinging ovens, and politely states they'll wait to give their order.

 However, you do *not* want to use setImmediate() in the scrolling timeline example, as it will freeze your browser up faster than you can blink.

## CHAPTER 18

Node Modules

One of the great aspects of writing Node.js applications is the built-in modularity the environment provides. It's simple to download and install any number of Node modules, and using them is equally simple: just include a single `require()` statement naming the module, and you're off and running.

The ease with which the modules can be incorporated is one of the benefits of JavaScript *modularization*. Modularizing ensures that external functionality is created in such a way that it isn't dependent on other external functionality, a concept known as *loose coupling*. This means I can use a `Foo` module, without having to include a `Bar` module, because `Foo` is tightly dependent on having `Bar` included.

JavaScript modularization is both a discipline and a contract. The discipline comes in having to follow certain mandated criteria in order for external code to participate in the module system. The contract is between you, me, and other JavaScript developers: we're following an agreed-on path when we produce (or consume) external functionality in a module system, and we all have expectations based on the module system.

 One major dependency on virtually all aspects of application and library management and publication is the use of Git, a source control system, and GitHub, an extremely popular Git *endpoint*. How Git works and using Git with GitHub are beyond the scope of this book. I recommend the *Git Pocket Guide* by Richard Silverman (O'Reilly) to get more familiar with Git, and GitHub's own documentation (*https://github.com*) for more on using this service.

18.1 Searching for a Specific Node Module via npm

Problem

You're creating a Node application and want to use existing modules, but you don't know how to discover them.

Solution

Recipe 1.7 explains how to install packages with npm, Node's popular package manager (and the glue that holds the Node universe together). But you haven't yet considered how to *find* the useful packages that you need in npm's sprawling registry.

In most cases, you'll discover modules via recommendations from your friends and codevelopers, but sometimes you need something new. You can search for new modules directly at the npm website (*https://www.npmjs.org*). You can also use the npm command-line interface directly to search for a module. For instance, if you're interested in modules that do something with PDFs, run the following search at the command line:

```
$ npm search pdf
```

Discussion

The npm website provides more than just documentation for using npm; it also provides an interface for searching for modules. If you access each module's page at npm, you can see how popular the module is, what other modules are dependent on it, the license, and other relevant information.

However, you can also search for modules, directly, using npm. The process can take a fair amount of time and when it finishes, you're likely to get a huge number of modules in return, especially with a broader topic such as modules that work with PDFs.

You can refine the results by listing multiple terms:

```
$ npm search PDF generation
```

This query returns a much smaller list of modules, specific to PDF generation.

Once you do find a module that sounds interesting, you can get detailed information about it with:

```
$ npm view electron
```

You'll get useful information from the *package.json* of the module, which can tell you what it's dependent on, who wrote it, and when it was created. We still recommend checking out the module's npm website page and GitHub repository page directly.

There you'll be able to determine if the module is being actively maintained, get a sense of how popular the module is, review open issues, and look at the source code.

18.2 Converting Your Library into a Node Module

Problem

You want to use one of your libraries in Node.

Solution

Convert the library into a Node module. In Node, each file is treated as a module. For example, if the library is a file containing a function stored at /lib/hello.js:

```
const hello = val => {
  return console.log(`Hello ${val}`);
};
```

You can convert it to work as a Node module with the exports keyword:

```
const hello = val => {
  return console.log(`Hello ${val}`);
};

module.exports = hello;
```

Alternately, can also export the function directly:

```
module.exports = val => {
  return console.log(`Hello ${val}`);
};
```

You can then use the module in your application:

```
var hello = require('./lib/hello.js');

// logs 'Hello world'
hello('world');
```

Discussion

Node's default module system is based on CommonJS, which uses three constructs: exports to define what's exported from the library, require() to include the module in the application, and module, which includes information about the module but also can be used to export a function directly.

If your library returns an object with several functions and data objects, you can assign each to the comparably named property on module.exports, or you could return an object:

```
const greeting = {
  hello: val => {
    return console.log(`Hello ${val}`);
  },
  ciao: val => {
    return console.log(`Ciao ${val}`);
  }
};

module.exports = greeting;
```

or:

```
const hello = val => {
  return console.log(`Hello ${val}`);
};

const ciao = val => {
  return console.log(`Ciao ${val}`);
};

module.exports = { hello, ciao };
```

And then access the object properties directly:

```
const greeting = require('./lib/greeting.js')

// logs 'Hello world'
greeting.hello('world');
// logs 'Ciao mondo'
greeting.ciao('mondo');
```

Because the module isn't installed using npm, and just resides in the directory where the application resides, it's accessed by the file location and name, not just the name.

See Also

In Recipe 18.3, we cover how to make sure your library code works in both CommonJS and ECMAScript module environments.

In Recipe 18.4, we cover how to create an standalone module.

18.3 Taking Your Code Across Module Environments

Problem

You've written a library that you'd like to share with others, but folks are using a variety of Node versions with both CommonJS and ECMAScript modules. How can you ensure your library works in all of the various environments?

Solution

Use CommonJS modules with an ECMAScript module wrapper.

First, write the library as a CommonJS module, saved with the *.cjs* file extension:

```
const bbarray = {
  concatArray: (str, array) => {
    return array.map(element => {
      return `${str} ${element}`;
    });
  },
  splitArray: (str, array) => {
    return array.map(element => {
      return element.substring(str.length + 1);
    });
  }
};

module.exports = bbarray;
exports.concatArray = bbarray.concatArray;
exports.splitArray = bbarray.splitArray;
```

Followed by an ECMAScript wrapper module, which uses the *.mjs* file extension:

```
import bbarray from './index.cjs';

export const { concatArray, splitArray } = bbarray;
export default bbarray;
```

And a *package.json* file, which includes the type, main, and exports fields:

```
"type": "module",
"main": "./index.cjs",
"exports": {
  ".": "./index.cjs",
  "./module": "./wrapper.mjs"
},
```

Users of our module, using CommonJS syntax, can use the require syntax to import the module:

```
const bbarray = require('bbarray');

bbarray.concatArray('is', ['test', 'three']);
bbarray.splitArray('is', ['is test', 'is three']);
```

or:

```
const { concatArray, splitArray } = require('bbarray');

concatArray('is', ['test', 'three']);
splitArray('is', ['is test', 'is three']);
```

While those using ECMAScript modules can specify the `module` version of the library to use the ES `import` syntax:

```
import bbarray from 'bbarray/module';

bbarray.concatArray('is', ['test', 'three']);
bbarray.splitArray('is', ['is test', 'is three']);
```

or:

```
import { concatArray, splitArray } from 'bbarray/module';

concatArray('is', ['test', 'three']);
splitArray('is', ['is test', 'is three']);
```

 At the time of writing, it is possible to avoid the */module* naming convention for ECMAScript modules using the `--experimental-conditional-exports` flag. However, due to the current experimental nature and the potential of future changes in the syntax, we currently recommend against it. In future versions of Node, this will likely become the standard. You can read more about this approach in the Node documentation (*https://oreil.ly/Xzkid*).

Discussion

CommonJS modules have been the standard in Node since the beginning, and tools such as Browserify brought this syntax out of the Node ecosystem, allowing developers to use Node style modules in the browser. The ECMAScript 2015 (also known as ES6) standard introduced a native JavaScript module syntax, which was introduced in Node 8.5.0 and could be used behind an `--experimental-module` flag. Beginning with Node 13.2.0, Node ships with native support for ECMAScript modules.

A common pattern is to write a module using either the CommonJS or ECMAScript module syntax and use a compile tool to ship both as either separate module entry points or exported paths. However, this runs the risk of a module being loaded twice if it is loaded directly via one syntax by the application and either loaded directly or by a dependency using the other syntax.

In *package.json* there are three key fields:

```
"type": "module",
"main": "./index.cjs",
"exports": {
  ".": "./index.cjs",
  "./module": "./wrapper.mjs"
},
```

`"type"`

Specifies that this is a `module`, meaning that this library is using the ECMAScript module syntax. For libraries that exclusively use CommonJS, the `"type"` would be `"commonjs"`.

`"main"`

Specifies the main entry point of the application, for which we will point to the CommonJS file.

`"exports"`

Defines the exported paths of our modules. Through this consumers of the default `package` will receive the CommonJS module directly, while those using `package/module` will import the file from the ECMAScript module wrapper.

If we wish to avoid using the *.cjs* and *.mjs* file extensions, we may do so:

```
"type": "module",
"main": "./index.js",
"exports": {
  ".": "./index.js",
  "./module": "./wrapper.js"
},
```

See Also

In Recipe 18.5, we cover how to make sure your library code works across multiple module environments in both Node and the browser by using Webpack as a code bundler.

18.4 Creating an Installable Node Module

Problem

You've either created a Node module from scratch, or converted an existing library to one that will work in the browser or in Node. Now, you want to know how to modify it into a module that can be installed using npm.

Solution

Once you've created your Node module and any supporting functionality (including module tests), you can package the entire directory. The key to packaging and publishing the Node module is creating a *package.json* file that describes the module, any dependencies, the directory structure, what to ignore, and so on. You can generate a *package.json* file by running the `npm init` command in the root of the project's directory and following the prompts.

The following is a relatively basic *package.json* file:

```json
{
  "name": "bbArray",
  "version": "0.1.0",
  "description": "A description of what my module is about",
  "main": "./lib/bbArray",
  "author": {
    "name": "Shelley Powers"
  },
  "keywords": [
    "array",
    "utility"
  ],
  "repository": {
    "type": "git",
    "url": "https://github.com/accountname/bbarray.git"
  },
  "engines" : {
    "node" : ">=0.10.0"
  },
  "bugs": {
    "url": "https://github.com/accountname/bbarray/issues"
  },
  "licenses": [
    {
      "type": "MIT",
      "url": "https://github.com/accountname/bbarray/raw/master/LICENSE"
    }
  ],
  "dependencies": {
    "some-module": "~0.1.0"
  },
  "directories":{
    "doc":"./doc",
    "man":"./man",
    "lib":"./lib",
    "bin":"./bin"
  },
  "scripts": {
    "test": "nodeunit test/test-bbarray.js"
  }
}
```

Once you've created *package.json*, package all the source directories and the *package.json* file as a gzipped tarball. Then install the package locally, or install it in npm for public access.

Discussion

The *package.json* file is key to packaging up a Node module for local installation or uploading to npm for management. At a minimum, it requires a `name` and a `version`. The other fields given in the solution are:

description
: A description of what the module is and does

main
: Entry file for the module

author
: Author(s) of the module

keywords
: List of keywords that can help others find the module

repository
: Place where the code lives, typically GitHub

engines
: Node versions you know your module works with

bugs
: Where to file bugs

licenses
: License for your module

dependencies
: A list of dependencies required by the module

directories
: A hash describing the directory structure for your module

scripts
: A hash of object commands that are run during the module life cycle

There are a host of other options that are described at the npm website (*https:// oreil.ly/iXynV*). You can also use a tool to help you fill in many of these fields. Typing the following at the command line runs the tool that asks questions and then generates a basic *package.json* file:

```
$ npm init
```

Once you have your source set up and your *package.json* file, you can test whether everything works by running the following command in the top-level directory of your module:

```
$ npm install . -g
```

If you have no errors, then you can package the file as a gzipped tarball. At this point, if you want to publish the module, you'll first need to add yourself as a user in the npm registry:

```
$ npm add-user
```

To publish the Node module to the npm registry, use the following in the root directory of the module, specifying a URL to the tarball, a filename for the tarball, or a path:

```
$ npm publish ./
```

If you have development dependencies for your module, such as using a testing framework like Jest, one excellent shortcut to ensure these are added to your *package.json* file is to use the following, in the same directory as the *package.json* file, when you're installing the dependent module:

```
$ npm install jest --save-dev
```

Not only does this install Jest (discussed later, in Recipe 18.6), this command also updates your *package.json* file with the following command:

```
"devDependencies": {
  "jest": "^24.9.0"
}
```

You can also use this same type of option to add a module to dependencies in *package.json*. The following:

```
$ npm install express --save
```

adds the following to the *package.json* file:

```
"dependencies": {
  "express": "^3.4.11"
}
```

If the module is no longer needed and shouldn't be listed in *package.json*, remove it from the devDependencies with:

```
$ npm remove jest
```

And remove a module to dependencies with:

```
$ npm remove express
```

If the module is the last in either dependencies or devDependencies, the property isn't removed. It's just set to an empty value:

```
"dependencies": {}
```

npm provides a decent developer guide for creating and installing a Node module (*https://oreil.ly/ifa4e*). You should consider the use of an *.npmignore* or *.gitignore* file for keeping stuff *out* of your module. And though this is beyond the scope of the book, you should also become familiar with Git and GitHub, and make use of it for your applications/modules.

Extra: The README File and Markdown Syntax

When you package your module or library for reuse and upload it to a source repository such as GitHub, you'll need to provide how-to information about installing the module/library and basic information about how to use it. For this, you need a README file.

You've likely seen files named *README.md* with applications and Node modules. They're text-based with some odd, unobtrusive markup that you're not sure is useful, until you see it in a site like GitHub, where the README file provides all of the project page installation and usage information. The markup translates into HTML, making for readable web-based help.

The content for the README is marked up with annotation known as Markdown. The popular website Daring Fireball calls Markdown easy to read and write, but "Readability, however, is emphasized above all else." Unlike with HTML, the Markdown markup doesn't get in the way of reading the text.

Daring Fireball also provides an overview of generic Markdown (*https://oreil.ly/qkKRT*), but if you're working with GitHub files, you might also want to check out GitHub's Flavored Markdown (*https://help.github.com/en/github/writing-on-github*).

Here is a sample *REAMDE.md* file:

```
# Project Title

Provide a brief description of the project and what it does.
If the project has a UI, include a screenshot as well.

If more comprehensive documentation exists, link to it here.

## Features

Describe the core features of the project (what does it do?)
in the form of a bulleted list:

- Feature #1
- Feature #2
- Feature #3
```

```
## Getting Started

Provide installation instructions, general usage guidance, API examples,
and build and deployment information. Assume as little prior knowledge
as possible, describing everything in clear and coherent steps.

### Installation/Dependencies

How does a user get up and running with your project? What dependencies
does the project have? Aim to describe these in clear and simple steps.
Provide external links.

### Usage

Provide examples of how the project may be used. For large projects with
external documentation, provide a few examples and link to the full docs here.

### Build/Deployment

If the user will be building or deploying the project, add any useful guidance.

## Getting Help

What should users do and expect when they encounter bugs or get stuck using
your project? Set expectations for support, link to the issue tracker and
roadmap, if applicable.

Where should users go if they have a question? (Stack Overflow, Gitter, IRC,
mailing list, etc.)

If desired, you may also provide links to core contributor email addresses.

## Contributing Guidelines

Include instructions for setting up the development environment, code standards,
running tests, and submitting pull requests. It may be useful to link to a
separate CONTRIBUTING.md file. See this example from the Hoodie project:
https://github.com/hoodiehq/hoodie/blob/master/CONTRIBUTING.md

## Code of Conduct

Provide a link to the Code of Conduct for your project. I recommend using the
Contributor Covenant: http://contributor-covenant.org/

## License

Include a license for your project. If you need help choosing a license,
use this guide: https://choosealicense.com
```

Most popular text editors include Markdown syntax highlighting and previewing
capabilities. There are also desktop Markdown editors available for all platforms. I

can also use a CLI tool, like Pandoc (*https://oreil.ly/Cc4GX*), to covert the *README.md* file into readable HTML:

```
$ pandoc README.md -o readme.html
```

Figure 18-1 displays the generated content. It's not fancy, but it is eminently readable.

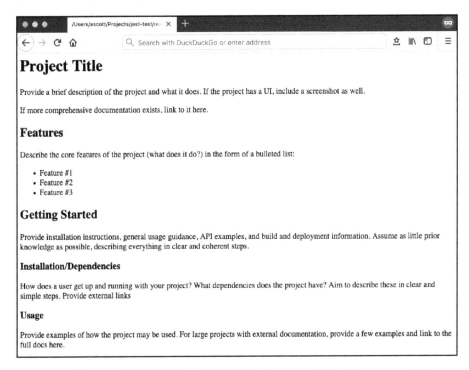

Figure 18-1. Generated HTML from README.md text and Markdown annotation

When you host your source code at a site such as GitHub, GitHub uses the *README.md* file to generate the cover page for the repository.

18.5 Writing Multiplatform Libraries

Problem

You've created a library that is useful both in the browser and in Node.js, and would like to make it available in both environments.

Solution

Use a bundling tool, such as Webpack, to bundle your library so that it works as an ES2015 module, CommonJS module, and AMD module, and can be loaded as a script tag in the browser.

In Webpack's *webpack.config.js* file, include the `library` and `libraryTarget` fields, which signify that the module should be bundled as a library and target multiple environments:

```
const path = require('path');

module.exports = {
  entry: './src/index.js',
  output: {
    path: path.resolve(__dirname, 'dist'),
    filename: 'my-library.js',
    library: 'myLibrary',
    libraryTarget: 'umd',
    globalObject: 'this'
  },
};
```

The `library` field specifies a name for the library that will be used in ECMAScript, CommonJS, and AMD module environments. The `libraryTarget` field allows you to specify how the module will be exposed. The default is `var`, which will expose a variable. Specifying `umd` will utilize the JavaScript Universal Module Definition (UMD) (*https://oreil.ly/VSpd0*), enabling the ability for multiple module styles to consume the library. To make the UMD build available in both browser and Node.js environments, you will need to set the `output.globalObject` option to `this`.

For more details on using Webpack to bundle code, see Chapter 17.

Discussion

In the example, I've created a simple math library. Currently, the only function is one called `squareIt`, which accepts a number as a parameter and returns the value of that number multiplied by itself. This is at *src/index.js*:

```
export function squareIt(num) {
    return num * num;
};
```

The *package.json* file contains Webpack and the Webpack command-line interface (CLI) as development dependencies. It also points the `main` distribution at the bundled version of the library, which Webpack will output to the *dist* folder. I've also added a build script that will run the Webpack bundler, aptly named `build`. This will allow me to generate the bundle by typing `npm run build` (or `yarn run build` if using Yarn).

```
{
  "name": "my-library",
  "version": "1.0.0",
  "description": "An example library bundled by Webpack",
  "main": "dist/my-library.js",
  "scripts": {
    "build": "webpack"
  },
  "keywords": ["example"],
  "author": "Adam Scott <adam@jseverywhere.io>",
  "license": "MIT",
  "devDependencies": {
    "webpack": "4.44.1",
    "webpack-cli": "3.3.12"
  }
}
```

Finally, my project contains a *webpack.config.js*, as described in the recipe:

```
const path = require('path');

module.exports = {
  entry: './src/index.js',
  output: {
    path: path.resolve(__dirname, 'dist'),
    filename: 'my-library.js',
    library: 'myLibrary',
    libraryTarget: 'umd',
    globalObject: 'this'
  },
};
```

With this setup, the command `npm run build` will bundle the library and place it within the *dist* directory of the project. This bundled file is what consumers of the library will use.

 To test the package locally, before publishing it to npm, run `npm link` from the root of the project directory. Then in a separate project, where you'd like to use the module, type `npm link <library name>`. Doing so will create a symbolic link to the package, as though it is globally installed.

Publishing the library

Once your library is complete, you will most likely want to publish it to npm for distribution. Make sure that your project is version controlled with Git and has been pushed to a public remote repository (such as GitHub or GitLab). From the root of your project's directory:

```
$ git init
$ git remote add origin git://git-remote-url
$ npm publish
```

Once published to a remote Git repository and the npm registry, the library can be consumed by running `npm install`, downloading or cloning the Git repository, or directly referencing the library in a web page using *https://unpkg.com/<library-name>*. The library can be consumed across the multiple JavaScript library formats.

As an ES 2015 module:

```
import * as myLibrary from 'my-library';

myLibrary.squareIt(4);
```

As a CommonJS module:

```
const myLibrary = require('my-library');

myLibrary.squareIt(4);
```

As an AMD module:

```
require(['myLibrary'], function (myLibrary) {
  myLibrary.squareIt(4);
});
```

And using a script tag on a web page:

```
<!doctype html>
<html>
  <script src="https://unpkg.com/my-library"></script>
  <script>
    myLibrary.squareIt(4);
  </script>
</html>
```

Handling library dependencies

Oftentimes a library may contain subdependencies. With our current setup, all dependencies will be packaged and bundled with the library itself. To limit the outputted bundle and to ensure that library consumers are not installing multiple instances of a subdependency, it may be best to treat them as a "peer dependency," which must also be installed or referenced on its own. To do so, add an `externals` property to your *webpack.config.js*. In the instance below, `moment` is being used as a peer dependency:

```
const path = require('path');

module.exports = {
  entry: './src/index.js',
  output: {
    path: path.resolve(__dirname, 'dist'),
    filename: 'my-library.js',
    library: 'myLibrary',
    libraryTarget: 'umd',
    globalObject: 'this'
  },
  externals: {
    moment: {
      commonjs: 'moment',
      commonjs2: 'moment',
      amd: 'moment',
      root: 'moment',
    }
  }
};
```

With this configuration, `moment` will be treated as a global variable by our library.

18.6 Unit Testing Your Modules

Problem

You want to make sure your module is functioning correctly and ready to be used by others.

Solution

Add *unit tests* as part of your production process.

Given the following module, named `bbarray`, and created in a file named *index.js*:

```
const util = require('util');

const bbarray = {
  concatArray: (str, array) => {
    if (!util.isArray(array) || array.length === 0) {
      return -1;
    }

    if (typeof str !== 'string') {
      return -1;
    }
```

```
      return array.map(element => {
        return `${str} ${element}`;
      });
    },
    splitArray: (str, array) => {
      if (!util.isArray(array) || array.length === 0) {
        return -1;
      }

      if (typeof str !== 'string') {
        return -1;
      }

      return array.map(element => {
        return element.substring(str.length + 1);
      });
    }
  }
};

module.exports = bbarray;
```

Using Jest (*https://jestjs.io*), a JavaScript testing framework, the following unit test (created as *index.js* and located in the project's *test* subdirectory) should result in the successful pass of six tests:

```
const bbarray = require('../index.js');

describe('concatArray()', () => {
  test('should return -1 when not using array', () => {
    expect(bbarray.concatArray(9, 'str')).toBe(-1);
  });

  test('should return -1 when not using string', () => {
    expect(bbarray.concatArray(9, ['test', 'two'])).toBe(-1);
  });

  test('should return an array with proper args', () => {
    expect(bbarray.concatArray('is', ['test', 'three'])).toStrictEqual([
      'is test',
      'is three'
    ]);
  });
});

describe('splitArray()', () => {
  test('should return -1 when not using array', () => {
    expect(bbarray.splitArray(9, 'str')).toBe(-1);
  });

  test('should return -1 when not using string', () => {
    expect(bbarray.splitArray(9, ['test', 'two'])).toBe(-1);
  });
```

```
    test('should return an array with proper args', () => {
      expect(bbarray.splitArray('is', ['is test', 'is three'])).toStrictEqual([
        'test',
        'three'
      ]);
    });
  });
```

The result of the test is shown in Figure 18-2, run using npm test.

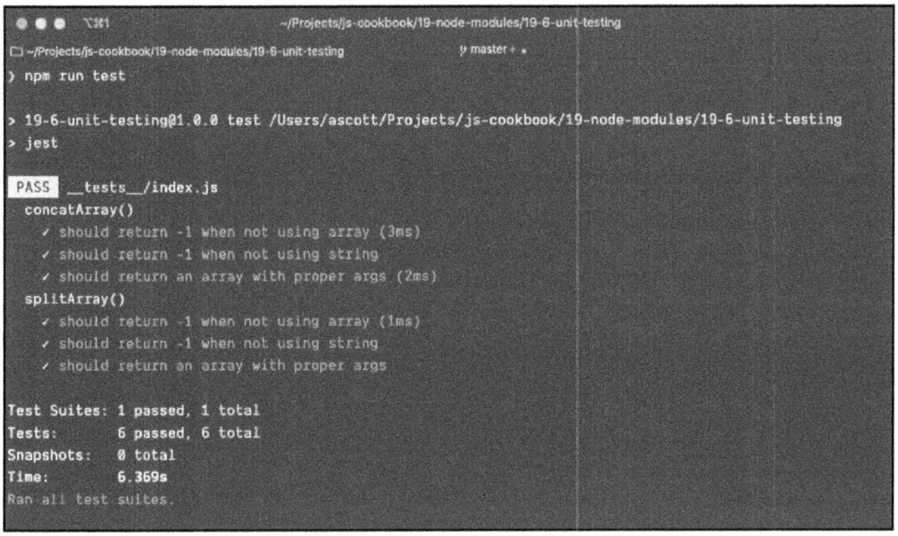

Figure 18-2. Running unit tests based on Jest

Discussion

A *unit test* is a way that developers test their code to ensure it meets the specifications. It involves testing functional behavior, and seeing what happens when you send bad arguments—or no arguments at all. It's called unit testing because it's used with individual units of code, such as testing one module in a Node application, as compared to testing the entire Node application. It becomes one part of *integration testing*, where all the pieces are plugged together, before going to *user acceptance testing*: testing to ensure that the application does what users expect it to do (and that they generally don't hate it when they use it).

Unit testing is one of those development tasks that may seem like a pain when you first start, but can soon become second nature. A good goal is to develop both tests and code in parallel to one another. Many developers even practice *test-driven development*, where unit tests are written prior to the code itself.

In the solution, we use Jest, a sophisticated testing framework. The module is simple, so we're not using some of the more complex Jest testing mechanisms. However, this provides an example of the building blocks of writing unit tests.

To install Jest, use the following:

```
$ npm install jest --save-dev
```

I'm using the `--save-dev` flag, because I'm installing Jest into the module's development dependencies. In addition, I modify the module's *package.json* file to add the following section:

```
"scripts": {
  "test": "jest"
},
```

The test script is saved as *index.js* in the *tests* subdirectory under the project. Jest automatically looks for files in a *tests* directory or files following the *filename.test.js* naming pattern. The following command runs the test:

```
$ npm test
```

The Jest unit tests makes use of *expect matchers* (*https://oreil.ly/E7RnY*) to test for the returned values.

## CHAPTER 19

Managing Node

The Node ecosystem reaches far and wide, from running scripts on a laptop to managing data on remote servers. The diversity of Node's core functionality, combined with the thousands of user-created modules, provides a rich environment for accomplishing nearly any programming task. However, this diversity can also present a challenge in navigating the options for accomplishing common tasks. This chapter demonstrates some of the common issues that Node developers may face.

19.1 Using Environment Variables

Problem

Your Node application requires different values in different environments, such as on your local machine and in production.

Solution

Use environment variables to set and read values in different environments. The core Node module `process` contains an `env` property, which will provide your application with access to any environment variables. In the following example, I am reading an environment variable named `NODE_ENV`:

```
process.env.NODE_ENV
```

To set an environment variable, you can specify a value ahead of running the `node` command to start the application. The following will set the `NODE_ENV` value to `development` and run the `index.js` script:

```
$ NODE_ENV=development node index.js
```

When working with projects with multiple environment variables, it is typically preferable to store those values locally in an *.env* file. Doing so in Node requires the `dotenv` package, which can be instaled from npm:

```
$ npm install dotenv --save
```

Now in your application code, require the module and initiate its configuration:

```
require('dotenv').config();
```

With this module, environment variables can be read from a *.env* file, rather than being passed as arguments to the command line. The *.env* file can consist of a number of environment variable values:

```
PORT=8080
DB_URI=mongodb://mongodb0.example.com:27017
KEY=12345
```

Discussion

The `process` object does not need to be imported as a module with a `require` statement as it is available globally to all Node programs. It is used to provide information about the current operating Node process, including the environment.

When reading an environment variable, it is often useful to use an `||` operator to specify a default value as a fallback for when a value is not provided in the environment. The following example will set the `port` variable to a value specified by a `PORT` environment variable, or `8080` if no environment variable value is provided:

```
const port = process.env.PORT || 8080;
```

The `dotenv` package is an npm module that allows you to load environment variables from a *.env* file. The usage is as straightforward as installing the package, combining the `require` statement, and initiating the configuration:

```
require('dotenv').config();
```

Once initiated and configured, the module will automatically read the values from a file named *.env* in the root of the project's directory. It is also possible to configure the package to read the file from an alternate location:

```
require('dotenv').config({ path: '/alternate/file/path/.env' })
```

If you choose to use ECMAScript modules with your Node project, first import the package as module and then separately initiate the configuration:

```
import dotenv from 'dotenv'

dotenv.config()
```

When working in a production environment, it is common for the host to set the environment variables. In that instance, you will not want to load the values from an *.env* file. A useful pattern is to only load the `dotenv` module in nonproduction environments:

```
if (process.env.NODE_ENV !== 'production') {
  require('dotenv').config();
}
```

> Never commit the *.env* file, and be sure to add it to your version control ignore list. These files are often used to store secure environment information, such as passwords or keys that should not be shared. A best practice is to instead include a file named *.env.example*, which contains blank or dummy values.

19.2 Managing Callback Hell

Problem

You want to do something with asynchronous operations, such as read the contents of a file and append it to a new file. Node provides this functionality using callback functions, but to use it asynchronously, you end up with nested code (noted by indentations) that makes the application unreadable and difficult to maintain.

Solution

Since Node version 8.0, we can use the `async/await` syntax along with the `promisfy` utility:

```
const fs = require('fs');
const { promisify } = require('util');

const readFile = promisify(fs.readFile);
const appendFile = promisify(fs.appendFile);

const readAppend = async (originalFile, secondaryFile) => {
  const fileData = await readFile(originalFile);
  await appendFile(secondaryFile, fileData);
  console.log(
    `The data from ${originalFile} was appended to ${secondaryFile}!`
  );
};

readAppend('./files/main.txt', './files/secondary.txt');
```

Node's built-in `promisify` utility is incredibly useful as it enables any function that follows the common error, values, callback style to return a promise. In Node 10+, filesystem operations can be used as promises natively by using the `fs.promises` API:

```
const fsp = require('fs').promises;

const readAppend = async (originalFile, secondaryFile) => {
  const fileData = await fsp.readFile(originalFile);
  await fsp.appendFile(secondaryFile, fileData);
  console.log(
    `The data from ${originalFile} was appended to ${secondaryFile}!`
  );
};

readAppend('./files/main.txt', './files/tertiary.txt');
```

Discussion

By design, Node code is asynchronous, or nonblocking, meaning that while the code is waiting on an operation, it can do something else. Oftentimes, however, we require that these operations happen in a specific order. Traditionally in Node, this was accomplished using callback functions. A callback function is a function that is called after the execution of a task. In the following example, the code reads a file and then performs an operation within the callback function:

```
fs.readFile(file, (error, data) => {
  if (error) {
    // handle error
  } else {
    // execute an operation after the file is read
  }
});
```

The `async/await` syntax allows you to write asynchronous code in a synchronous fashion. We cover `async/await` in detail in Chapter 10:

```
const waitOne = () => {
  return new Promise(resolve => {
    setTimeout(() => {
      console.log('It has been one second');
      resolve();
    }, 1000);
  });
};

const callWait = async () => {
  await waitOne();
};

callWait();
```

When working with a function that follows the common error, values, callback style, we can use Node's built-in `promisify` utility to return a promise:

```
const fs = require('fs');
const { promisify } = require('util');
```

```
const writeFile = promisify(fs.writeFile);
```

When using `async`/`await`, errors are handled within `try`/`catch` blocks:

```
try {
  await writeFile(file, buf);
} catch (error) {
  console.log(error);
  throw error;
}
```

As an example of how you can refactor existing code, the following example uses callbacks to write two lines to a file, read them back, and output the contents to the console:

```
const fs = require('fs');

const callbackHell = file => {
  const buf = Buffer.from('Callback hell first string\n');
  const buf2 = Buffer.from('Callback hell second string\n');

  // write or append the contents of the first buffer
  fs.writeFile(file, buf, err => {
    if (err) {
      console.log(err);
      throw err;
    }
    // append the contents of the second buffer
    fs.appendFile(file, buf2, err2 => {
      if (err2) {
        console.log(err2);
        throw err2;
      }
      // log the contents of the file
      fs.readFile(file, 'utf-8', (err3, data) => {
        if (err3) {
          console.log(err3);
          throw err3;
        }
        console.log(data);
      });
    });
  });
};

callbackHell('./files/callback.txt');
```

This is a relatively straightforward operation, but notice how quickly the indentation increases for the nested callbacks. We can clean it up using `async`/`await`:

```
const fs = require('fs');
const { promisify } = require('util');
```

```
const writeFile = promisify(fs.writeFile);
const appendFile = promisify(fs.appendFile);
const readFile = promisify(fs.readFile);

const fileWriteRead2 = async file => {
  const buf = Buffer.from('The first string\n');
  const buf2 = Buffer.from('The second string\n');

  // write or append the contents of the first buffer
  try {
    await writeFile(file, buf);
  } catch (error) {
    console.log(error);
    throw error;
  }

  // append the contents of the second buffer
  try {
    await appendFile(file, buf2);
  } catch (error) {
    console.log(error);
    throw error;
  }

  // log the contents of the file
  console.log(await readFile(file, 'utf8'));
};

fileWriteRead2('./files/async.txt');
```

This is much easier to understand without sacrificing the asynchronous code execution.

In each of the examples, I've used filesystem operations, but the `async`/`await` syntax is incredibly useful for a wide range of use cases in Node, including database interactions, fetching remote resources, hashing strings, and much more.

19.3 Accessing Command-Line Functionality Within a Node Application

Problem

You want to access a command-line utility, such as ImageMagick, from within a Node application.

Solution

Use Node's `child_process` module. For example, if you want to use ImageMagick's `identify`, and then print out the data to the console, use the following:

```
const { spawn } = require('child_process');

const identify = spawn('identify', ['-verbose', 'osprey.jpg']);

identify.stdout.on('data', data => {
  console.log(`stdout: ${data}`);
});

identify.stderr.on('data', data => {
  console.log(`stderr: ${data}`);
});

identify.on('exit', code => {
  console.log(`child process exited with code ${code}`);
});
```

Discussion

The `child_process` module provides four methods to run command-line operations and process returned data:

`spawn(command, [args], [options])`
> This launches a given process, with optional command-line arguments, and an `options` object specifying additional information, such as `cwd` to change directory and `uid` to find the user ID of the process.

`exec(command, [options], callback)`
> This runs a command in a shell and buffers the result.

`execFile(file, [args],[options],[callback])`
> This is like `exec()` but executes the file directly.

`fork(modulePath, [args],[options])`
> This is a special case of `spawn()`, and spawns Node processes, returning an object that has a communication channel built in. It also requires a separate instance of V8 with each use, so use sparingly.

The `child_process` methods have three streams associated with them: `stdin`, `stdout`, and `stderr`. The `spawn()` method is the most widely used of the `child_process` methods, and the one used in the solution. From the solution top, the command given is the ImageMagick `identify` command-line application, which can return a wealth of information about an image. In the *args* array, the code passes in the `--verbose` flag and the name of the image file. When the `data` event happens with the `child_process.stdout` stream, the application prints it to the console. The data is a buffer that uses `toString()` implicitly when concatenated with another string. If an error happens, it's also printed out to the console. A third event handler just communicates that the child process is exiting.

If you want to process the result as an array, modify the input event handler:

```
identify.stdout.on('data', (data) => {
    console.log(data.toString().split("\n"));
});
```

Now the data is processed into an array of strings, split on the new line within the `identify` output.

 Instead of using a child process, if you have either GraphicsMagick or ImageMagick installed, you can use the `gm` Node module (*http://aheckmann.github.io/gm*) for accessing the imaging capability.

Extra: Using Child Processes with Windows

The solution demonstrates how to use child processes in a macOS or Linux environment. There are similarities and differences between using child processes in Linux/Unix, and using them in Windows.

In Windows, you can't explicitly give a command with a child process; you have to invoke the Windows `cmd.exe` executable and have it perform the process. In addition, the first flag to the command is `/c`, which tells `cmd.exe` to process the command and then terminate.

Borrowing an example from *Learning Node* by Shelley Powers (O'Reilly), in the following code, the `cmd.exe` command is used to get a directory listing, using the Windows `dir` command:

```
const { spawn } = require('child_process');

const cmd = spawn('cmd', ['/c', 'dir\n']);

cmd.stdout.on('data', data => {
  console.log(`stdout: ${data}`);
});

cmd.stderr.on('data', data => {
  console.log(`stderr: ${data}`);
});

cmd.on('exit', code => {
```

```
  console.log(`child process exited with code ${code}`);
});
```

19.4 Passing Command-Line Arguments

Problem

You would like to be able to pass command-line arguments and read their values within your Node application.

Solution

For simple use cases, utilize the `process.argv` property, which returns an array containing any command-line arguments passed to the program when it is run. Since these values are an array, we can iterate over them to read (or in this example, print) their values:

```
process.argv.forEach((value, index) => {
  console.log(`${index}: ${value}`);
});
```

Now if I run my script, I can pass it command-line arguments, which will be printed to the console:

```
$ node index.js --name=Adam --food=pizza
```

Which will print the following:

```
0: /usr/local/bin/node
1: /Users/ascott/Projects/command-line-args/index.js
2: --name=Adam
3: --food=pizza
```

Node's `process` is a global object that allows a script to access information about the current Node.js process. The `argv` property or the `process` object contains the values of the arguments. The first index is always the path to the environment's Node executable, the second value of the array is always the path to the script itself, and the remaining items are the arguments in the order that they were passed to the script.

Discussion

Accessing arguments directly from Node's `process` object provides a straightforward way to retrieve command-line properties. However, parsing and making use of these values can prove tricky. Thankfully, utilizing the popular module Yargs (*https://oreil.ly/Ue9LF*) makes working with command-line arguments a more streamlined task:

```
const yargs = require('yargs/yargs');
const { hideBin } = require('yargs/helpers');
```

```
const {argv} = yargs(hideBin(process.argv));

console.log(argv);
```

Now if I rerun my script, passing it command-line arguments, the values will be printed to the console:

```
$ node index.js --name=Adam --food=pizza
# logs the following:
{ _: [], name: 'Adam', food: 'pizza', '$0': 'yargs/index.js' }
```

By using the Yargs module, you can easily read specific values and act on them in your script:

```
const yargs = require('yargs/yargs');
const { hideBin } = require('yargs/helpers');

const {argv} = yargs(hideBin(process.argv));

if (argv.food === 'pizza') {
  console.log('mmm');
}
```

By using command-line arguments, you can utilize information passed at runtime and react accordingly. Yargs can handle a lot more than reading input values, such as configuring help commands, enabling Boolean input values, limiting values to prede‐fined choices, and much more. I recommend consulting the Yargs documentation (*https://github.com/yargs/yargs#documentation*) for additional resources and documentation.

19.5 Creating a Command-Line Utility with Help from Commander

Problem

You want to turn your Node module into a Linux command-line utility, including support for command-line options/arguments.

Solution

To convert your Node module to a Linux command-line utility, add the following line as the first line of the module:

```
#!/usr/bin/env node
```

To provide for command-line arguments/options, including the ever-important --help, make use of the Commander module:

```
#!/usr/bin/env node
const program = require('commander');

program
  .version('0.0.1')
  .option('-n, --number <value>', 'A number to square')
  .parse(process.argv);

const square = Math.pow(program.number, 2);

console.log(`The square of ${program.number} is ${square}`);
```

 In Recipe 19.4 we discuss using the Yargs module, which simplifies the use of handling command-line arguments. Yargs is a great option for handling command-line argument inputs, while Commander is a fully featured module for building command-line-driven applications. We recommend taking a look at both options and choosing the one that is right for your use case.

Discussion

To convert a Node module to a command-line utility, first add the following line to the module:

```
#!/usr/bin/env node
```

Change the module file's mode to an executable, using CHMOD:

```
$ chmod a+x square.js
```

To run the above example, I would type the following in the terminal, from the project folder:

```
$ ./square.js -n 4
```

The command-line utility I created simply logs the square of a number. Let's look at a more complete example, which would create an image capture of a website using the Puppeteer (*https://github.com/puppeteer/puppeteer*) library. In a file named *snapshot.js*:

```
#!/usr/bin/env node
const program = require('commander');
const puppeteer = require('puppeteer');

program
  .version('0.0.1')
  .option('-s, --source [website]', 'Source website')
  .option('-f, --file [filename]', 'Filename')
  .parse(process.argv);

(async () => {
```

```
      console.log('capturing screenshot...');
      const browser = await puppeteer.launch();
      const page = await browser.newPage();
      await page.goto(program.source);
      await page.screenshot({ path: program.file });
      await browser.close();
      console.log(`captured screenshot at ${program.file}`);
  })();
```

We can then update the *package.json* file so that our command can be named and used directly (without the *.js* extension):

```
"main": "snapshot.js",
"preferGlobal": true,
"bin": {
  "snapshot": "snapshot.js"
},
```

Now if we run `npm link`, we can use the command directly on our local machine, without referencing the file directly:

```
$ snapshot -s http://oreilly.com -f test.png
```

Or you can use the *long option*, consisting of a double-dash (`--`) followed by a complete word:

```
$ snapshot --source http://oreilly.com --file test.png
```

And when you run the utility with either `-h` or `--help`, you get:

```
  Usage: snapshot [options]

  Options:

    -h, --help             output usage information
    -V, --version          output the version number
    -s, --source [website] Source website
    -f, --file [filename]  Filename
```

Running the following returns the version:

```
$ snapshot -V
```

Commander generates all of this automatically, so we can focus on our utility's primary functionality.

Publishing a command-line utility to the `npm` registry is the same as any other module:

```
$ npm publish
```

19.6 Keeping a Node Instance Up and Running

Problem

You're in a production environment and want to start up a Node application, keep it running forever, and reload it without downtime.

Solution

Use the `pm2` module to ensure the application is restarted if it's ever shut down:

```
$ pm2 start index.js
```

Discussion

`pm2` is a CLI tool that can be used to not only start a Node application, but to ensure the application is restarted if, for some reason, it's shut down.

Install `pm2` using npm:

```
$ sudo npm install pm2 -g
```

Then start your Node application, making use of `pm2`:

```
$ pm2 start index.js
```

The `start` action starts the Node application as a Unix *daemon* or background process. The utility can also make use of a number of options, which can all be listed with the `pm2 --help` command. A few that are particularly useful:

`-l`
    Create a log file

`-o`
    Log stdout from the script to the specified output file

`-e`
    Log stderr from the script to the specified error file

`-n`
    Name the application

`--watch`
    Watch for changes and restart the application

To start an application that includes these logs, use the flags and specify output files:

```
$ pm2 start  -l forever.log -o out.log -e err.log -n app_name index.js --watch
```

Some other helpful `pm2` actions are:

stop
    Stop the daemon script

restart
    Restart the daemon script

delete
    Delete the daemon script

describe
    Retrieve the details of a specific application

list
    List all running scripts

monitor
    Monitor logs, metrics, and application information

It can be very helpful to add an npm script to a project's *package.json* file to run the pm2 command:

```
"scripts": {
    "start": "pm2 start index.js",
}
```

With this addition, running npm start from the project's root directory will start the application using pm2. As an added bonus, this is often the default behavior of many Node application cloud hosting platforms.

19.7 Monitoring Application Changes and Restarting During Local Development

Problems

Development can get rather active, and it can be difficult to remember or time-consuming to restart an application each time the code has changed.

Solution

Use the nodemon utility to watch your source code and restart your application when the code changes.

To use, first install nodemon:

```
$ npm install -g nodemon
```

Instead of starting the application with node, use nodemon instead:

```
$ nodemon index.js
```

Discussion

The `nodemon` utility monitors the files within the directory where it was started. If any of the files change, the Node application is automatically restarted. This is a handy way of making sure your running Node application reflects the most recent code changes.

Generally, `nodemon` is not a tool you want to use in a production system. Instead, use a process manager such as `pm2`, as discussed in Recipe 19.6.

If the application accepts values when started, you can provide these on the command line, just as with Node, but precede them with the double dashes (`--`) flag, which signals to `nodemon` to ignore anything that follows and pass it to the application:

```
$ nodemon index.js -- -param1 -param2
```

When started, you should get feedback similar to the following:

```
[nodemon] 2.0.2
[nodemon] to restart at any time, enter `rs`
[nodemon] watching dir(s): *.*
[nodemon] watching extensions: js,mjs,json
[nodemon] starting `node index.js`
Listening on port 8124
```

If the code changes, you'll see something similar to the following:

```
[nodemon] restarting due to changes...
[nodemon] starting `node index.js`
Server running on 8124/
```

If you want to manually restart the application, type `rs` into the terminal where nodemon is running. You can also use a configuration file·or *package.json* configuration with the utility, monitor only select files or subdirectories, and even use it to run non-Node applications.

Here is a sample *package.json* configuration, which will instruct `nodemon` to use `verbose` mode and ignore specific directories:

```
{
  "nodemonConfig": {
    "verbose": true,
    "ignore": ["__tests__/*", "docs/*"],
  }
}
```

19.8 Scheduling Repeat Tasks

Problem

You have a task that needs to be run repeatedly at specific intervals.

Solution

Use `node-cron` (*https://oreil.ly/dYQHv*), which enables you to schedule tasks in Node using the GNU crontab syntax.

The following will log to the console every minute:

```
const cron = require('node-cron');

cron.schedule('* * * * *', () => {
  console.log('Log to the console every minute');
});
```

Discussion

To use the `node-cron` module, first install it with npm:

```
$ npm install node-cron
```

You can then use the `schedule` method along with the crontab syntax to create a scheduled task.

The crontab syntax can be a bit confusing if you have never encountered it before. In the above example, I've used an asterisk for each field, which stands for "first-last." We can replace the asterisks with the following values (in order):

- second (optional): 0–59
- minute: 0–59
- hour: 0–23
- day of month: 0–31
- month: 0–12 (or three-letter names)
- day of week: 0–7 (or three-letter names, 0 or 7 is Sunday)

The following will run at five minutes after midnight on the first day of every month:

```
const cron = require('node-cron');

cron.schedule('5 0 1 * *', () => {
  console.log('It is the first of the month!');
});
```

We can also include ranges. The following will run a job at midnight, on each weekday from June through September:

```
const cron = require('node-cron');

cron.schedule('0 0 * 6-9 1-5', () => {
  console.log('Summer workdays');
});
```

`node-cron` accepts two options: `scheduled` and `timezone`. The following will run a job at midnight in the same time zone as New York City:

```
var cron = require('node-cron');

cron.schedule('0 0 * * *', () => {
  console.log('Running a job at midnight ');
}, {
  scheduled: true,
  timezone: "America/New_York"
});
```

`scheduled` is a Boolean value that defaults to `true`. Cron jobs will not run if the value is set to `false`. `timezone` allows you to set a specific time zone for the schedule. For all the time zone names, see the Moment.js time zone page (*https://oreil.ly/VhAkl*).

19.9 Testing the Performance and Capability of Your WebSockets Application

Problem

You have an application that sends updated information on a frequent basis to every connected client, and you're concerned about performance and how the application will handle the load.

Solution

You'll want to perform both *speed (performance) tests* and *load testing*. See the discussion for details.

Discussion

Thanks to Node and WebSockets and other bidirectional communication techniques, we no longer have to use timers in web pages to hit servers for new data. The server itself can push the data to all the connected clients whenever the data is fresh. The animated, scrolling timeline in Example 17-4 demonstrates this type of application.

The question then becomes: yes, it's cool, but what does the coolness cost? Is my server going to crash and burn once 10 (100/1,000/10,000) clients connect? Will all the clients get the same response? The only answer to these questions comes from two types of tests:

- Speed or performance testing, which tests how fast the page loads, especially when the server is under stress
- Load testing that emulates many concurrent clients accessing the page at once

There are services that provide both types of testing, and if you're a large commercial operation and the reliability and performance of your application are critical, I definitely recommend taking advantage of them. Some, like Load Impact (*http://loadimpact.com*), even provide a decent trial of its product before committing. There are also tools you can use that will hit a page concurrently and then print out the load responses for each (or even graph it). Selenium (*http://seleniumhq.org*) is a very popular tool for performance testing.

The Node world also provides tools we can install easily and quickly with npm. They may not have exactly the same polish as the commercial tools, but they're certainly a lot cheaper. One tool to try is `loadtest`, which is an easier-to-run variation of ApacheBench (aka **ab**). You need to install it globally:

```
$ npm install -g loadtest
```

And then you run it from the command line. The following runs 200 requests per second (rps), with a concurrency of 10:

```
$ loadtest -c 10 --rps 200 http://mysite.com/
```

There are several other options, and ApacheBench is also an alternative that can be good for performance testing. However, the tests don't test the WebSockets connection because the request to the WebSockets server is contained in JavaScript that's never processed.

Another option is Thor, which is a load tester that's run directly against the Web-Socket server:

```
$ npm install -g thor
$ thor --amount 5000 ws://shelleystoybox.com:8001
```

This is an effective way of hammering (ahem) the WebSockets server with connections, but we're still not getting the back and forth communication to *really* test the entire application, front and back. The connections are made, and then dropped as quickly, so it's not really testing the communication as it exists if you and I were to access the application from our browsers. However, used with other tests that actually access the client page and process the WebSockets connection, they can help us determine if performance is going to be an issue with that many demands for connections (note: the app held up).

## CHAPTER 20

Remote Data

Data surrounds us. We create and interact with data throughout our daily lives, often in interesting and unexpected ways. When building Node applications, we often interact with data. At times, that data may be something that we've created for the application, or data that the user has entered into our system. However, it's also common to need to interact with data that comes from outside of our applications. This chapter covers best practices and techniques for working with remote data in Node applications.

20.1 Fetching Remote Data

Problem

You want to make a request to a remote server within your Node application.

Solution

Use `node-fetch`, one of the most popular and widely used modules, which brings the browser's `window.fetch` to Node. It's installed with npm:

```
$ npm install node-fetch
```

and can be used as simply as:

```
const fetch = require('node-fetch');

fetch('https://oreilly.com')
  .then(res => res.text())
  .then(body => console.log(body));
```

Discussion

node-fetch provides an API that closely mirrors the browser's window.fetch, allowing our Node programs to access remote resources. Like window.fetch, it offers support for the HTTP methods of GET, POST, DELETE, and PUT. In the case of GET, if the response indicates success (a status code of 200), you can then process the returned data (formatted as HTML in this instance) however you would like.

You can make a request for a JSON resource:

```
fetch('https://swapi.dev/api/people/1')
  .then(res => res.json())
  .then(json => console.log(json));
```

It's also possible to use the async/await syntax, including a try/catch block for error handling:

```
(async () => {
  try {
    const response = await fetch('https://swapi.dev/api/people/3');
    const json = await response.json();
    console.log(json);
  } catch (error) {
    console.log(error);
  }
})();
```

You can also stream a result to a file using the filesystem module:

```
const fs = require('fs');
const fetch = require('node-fetch');

fetch('https://example.com/image.png')
  .then(res => {
    const dest = fs.createWriteStream('image.png');
    res.body.pipe(dest);
  });
```

node-fetch can also handle POST, DELETE, and PUT methods, allowing you to send data to a server. In the following example, we make a POST request:

```
// example body for the request
const body = {
  id: 1,
  title: "Example"
};

fetch('https://example.com/post', {
    method: 'post',
    body:    JSON.stringify(body),
    headers: { 'Content-Type': 'application/json' },
  })
```

```
.then(res => res.json())
.then(json => console.log(json));
```

 `node-fetch` is a common and useful library for fetching remote data, but it is not the only one. Popular alternatives include Request (which, though still popular, is no longer actively maintained), Got, Axios, and Superagent.

20.2 Screen Scraping

Problem

You want to access specific content from a web resource from within your Node application.

Solution

Use the `node-fetch` and Cheerio modules to *screen scrape* a website.

First install the required modules:

```
$ npm install node-fetch cheerio
```

To scrape the page, make use of `node-fetch` to retrieve the content and then query the retrieved content with Cheerio:

```
const fetch = require('node-fetch');
const cheerio = require('cheerio');

fetch('https://example.com')
  .then(res => res.text())
  .then(body => {
    const $ = cheerio.load(body);
    $('h1').each((i, element) => {
      console.log(element.children[0].data);
    });
  });
```

Discussion

An interesting use of Node is to *scrape* a website or resource and then use other functionality to query for specific information within the returned material. A popular module to use for querying is Cheerio, which is a tiny implementation of jQuery core intended for use in the server. In the following example, a simple application is created to pull in all of the post titles on the O'Reilly Radar blog page. To select these titles, we use Cheerio to find links (a) contained within h2 elements that are within the `main` content. We then list the text of the link to a separate output:

```
const fetch = require('node-fetch');
const cheerio = require('cheerio');

fetch('https://www.oreilly.com/radar/posts/')
  .then(res => res.text())
  .then(body => {
    const $ = cheerio.load(body);
    $('main h2 a').each((i, element) => {
      console.log(element.children[0].data);
    });
  });
```

After the successful request is made, the HTML returned is passed to Cheerio via the `load()` method, and the result is assigned to a dollar sign variable ($), so we can select elements in the result in a manner similar to the jQuery library.

The element pattern of `main h2 a` is then used to query for all matches, and the result is processed using the `each` method, accessing the text for each heading. The output to the console should be the titles of all the articles on the main page of the blog.

A common use case is to download data when an API is not provided. In the following example, we're locating specific links on the page and piping the linked resource to a local file. I'm also using the `async/await` syntax to demonstrate how it may be used:

```
const path =
  'data-research/mortgage-performance-trends/mortgages-30-89-days-delinquent/';
const url = `https://www.consumerfinance.gov/${path}`;

(async () => {
  try {
    const response = await fetch(url);
    const body = await response.text();
    const $ = cheerio.load(body);
    $("a:contains('state')").each(async (i, element) => {
      const fetchFile = await fetch(element.attribs.href);
      const dest = fs.createWriteStream(`data-${i}.csv`);
      await fetchFile.body.pipe(dest);
    });
  } catch (error) {
    console.log(error);
  }
})();
```

We first fetch the page at the specific URL, which in this instance is a United States government website containing several linked CSV files. We then use Cheerio to locate all links on the page that contain the word "state." Finally, we fetch the linked-to file and pipe it to a local file.

Screen scraping can be a useful tool to have in your toolbox, but proceed with caution. Before scraping a website for use in a production application, be sure to consult its Terms of Service (ToS) or seek out permission from the site owner. Also be careful not to accidentally perform a denial-of-service attack (DDoS) by overloading the host's servers.

20.3 Accessing JSON-Formatted Data via a RESTful API

Problem

You want to access data formatted as JSON from a service through its API.

Solution

In a Node application, the simplest technique for accessing JSON-formatted data from an API is to use an HTTP request library.

In the following example, I'll again use node-fetch, much like in Recipe 20.1:

```
const fetch = require('node-fetch');

(async () => {
  try {
    const response = await fetch('https://swapi.dev/api/people/1/');
    const json = await response.json();
    console.log(json);
  } catch (error) {
    console.log(error);
  }
})();
```

The npm module got is a popular alternative to node-fetch:

```
const got = require('got');

(async () => {
  try {
    const response = await got('https://swapi.dev/api/people/2/');
    console.log(JSON.parse(response.body));
  } catch (error) {
    console.log(error.response.body);
  }
})();
```

Discussion

A RESTful API is one that is stateless, meaning that each client request contains everything necessary for the server to respond (doesn't imply any stored state between requests); it uses HTTP methods explicitly. It supports a directory-like URI structure, and transfers data formatted a certain way (typically XML or JSON). The HTTP methods are:

- GET: To get resource data
- PUT: To update a resource
- DELETE: To delete a resource
- POST: To create a resource

Because we're focusing on getting data, the only method of interest at this time is GET. And because we're focused on JSON, we're using client methods that can access JSON-formatted data and convert the data into objects we can manipulate in our JavaScript applications.

Let's look at another example.

The Open Exchange Rate (*https://openexchangerates.org*) provides an API that we can use to get current exchange rates, name-to-acronym for the different types of currencies, and the exchange rates for a specific date. It has a Forever Free plan (*https://oreil.ly/TjhFo*) that provides limited access to the API without cost.

It's possible to make two queries of the system (for current currency rate and name-to-acronyms), and when both queries finish, to get the acronyms as keys, and use these to look up the long name and rate in the results, printing the pairs out to the console:

```
const fetch = require('node-fetch');
require('dotenv').config();

const id = process.env.APP_ID;

(async () => {
  try {
    const moneyAPI1 = await fetch(
      `https://openexchangerates.org/api/latest.json?app_id=${id}`
    );
    const moneyAPI2 = await fetch(
      `http://openexchangerates.org/api/currencies.json?app_id=${id}`
    );

    const latest = await moneyAPI1.json();
    const names = await moneyAPI2.json();
    const keys = Object.keys(latest.rates);
```

```
    keys.forEach((value, index) => {
      const rate = latest.rates[keys[index]];
      const name = names[keys[index]];
      console.log(`${name} ${rate}`);
    });
  } catch (error) {
    console.log(error);
  }
})();
```

 Note that the id value will need to be replaced with your unique ID, assigned by the API provider when you create an account. In the example, I've used the dotenv module to load the stored value from a *.env* file.

The base currency is "USD" or the US dollar, and a here's a sampling of the results:

```
"Malawian Kwacha 394.899498"
"Mexican Peso 13.15711"
"Malaysian Ringgit 3.194393"
"Mozambican Metical 30.3662"
"Namibian Dollar 10.64314"
"Nigerian Naira 162.163699"
"Nicaraguan Córdoba 26.03978"
"Norwegian Krone 6.186976"
"Nepalese Rupee 98.07189"
"New Zealand Dollar 1.185493"
```

In the code snippet, I use async/await to make the queries, and then process the results when both queries are finished. In a production system, we'd most likely cache the results for however long our plan allows (hourly for the free API access).

See Also

The examples didn't need to *escape* the values used as parameters in the API requests, but if you do need to escape values, you can use Node's built-in query string.escape() method.

## CHAPTER 21

Building Web Applications with Express

Express (*https://expressjs.com*) is a lightweight web framework that has been the long-standing leader in web application development in Node. Similar to Ruby's Sinatra and Python's Flask, the Express framework by itself is very minimal, but can be extended to build any type of web application. Express is also the backbone of batteries included in web application frameworks, such as Keystone.js (*https://keystonejs.com*), Sails (*https://sailsjs.com*), and Vulcan.js (*http://vulcanjs.org*). If you are doing web application development in Node, you are likely to encounter Express. This chapter focuses on a handful of basic recipes for working with Express, which can be extended to build out all sorts of web applications.

21.1 Using Express to Respond to Requests

Problem

Your Node application needs to respond to HTTP requests.

Solution

Install the Express package:

```
$ npm install express
```

To set up Express, we require the module, call the module, and specify a port for connections in a file named *index.js*:

```
const express = require('express');

const app = express();
const port = process.env.PORT || '3000';

app.listen(port, () => console.log(`Listening on port ${port}`));
```

To respond to a request, specify a route and the response using Express's `.get` method:

```
const express = require('express');

const app = express();
const port = process.env.PORT || '3000';

app.get('/', (req, res) => res.send('Hello World'));

app.listen(port, () => console.log(`Listening on port ${port}`));
```

To serve static files, we can specify a directory with the `express.static` middleware

```
const express = require('express');

const app = express();
const port = process.env.PORT || '3000';

// middleware for static files
// will serve static files from the 'files' directory
app.use(express.static('files'));

app.listen(port, () => console.log(`Listening on port ${port}`));
```

To respond with HTML generated from a template, first install the templating engine:

```
$ npm install pug --save
```

Next, in the *index.js* file, set the `view engine` and specify the route that will respond with the template content:

```
app.set('view engine', 'pug')

app.get('/template', (req, res) => {
  res.render('template');
});
```

And then create a template file in the *views* subdirectory of the project with a new file. The template filename should match the name specified in `res.render`. In *views/template.pug*:

```
html
  head
    title="Using Express"
  body
    h1="Hello World"
```

Now requests to *http://localhost:3000/template* will return the template content as HTML.

Discussion

Express is a minimalist, but highly configurable framework for responding to HTTP requests and building out web applications. In the example, we set the port to `pro cess.env.PORT` or port 3000. In development, we can then specify a new port using an environment variable, such as:

```
$ PORT=7777 node index.js
```

or by using a *.env* file paired with the `dotenv` Node module. When deploying the application, the application hosting platform may require a specific port number or allow us to configure the port number ourselves.

With the Express `get` method, the application receives a request to a specific URI and then responds. In our example, when the application receives a request to the root URI (/), we respond with the text "Hello World":

```
app.get('/', (req, res) => res.send('Hello World'));
```

These responses can also be HTML, templates rendered to HTML, static files, and formatted data (such as JSON or XML).

Due to its minimal nature, Express itself contains minimal functionality, but can be extended using middleware. In Express, middleware functions have access to the `request` and `response` objects. Application-level middleware is bound to an instance of the `app` object through `app.use(MIDDLEWARE)`. In the example, we're making use of the built-in static files middleware:

```
app.use(express.static('files'));
```

Middleware packages can be used to extend Express's functionality in many ways. The `helmet` middleware package can be used to improve the Express security defaults:

```
const express = require('express');
const helmet = require('helmet');

const app = express();

app.use(helmet());
```

Templating engines simplify the process of writing HTML and allow you to pass data from your application to the page.

Here I am passing the data from the `userData` object to the template found at *views/user.pug*, which will be accessible at the */user* route:

```
// a user object of data to send to the template
const userData = {
  name: 'Adam',
  email: 'adam@jseverywhere.io',
```

```
    avatar: 'https://s.gravatar.com/avatar/33aab819d1ffa11fc4b31a4eebaf0c5a?s=80'
};

// render the template with user data
app.get('/user', (req, res) => {
  res.render('user', { userData });
});
```

Then in our template, we can make use of the data:

```
html
  head
    title User Page
  body
    h1 #{userData.name} Profile
    ul
      li
        image(src=userData.avatar)
      li #{userData.name}
      li #{userData.email}
```

The Pug templating engine is maintained by the Express core team and is a popular choice for Express applications, but its whitespace-driven syntax is not for everyone. EJS (*https://ejs.co*) is an excellent alternative that offers a more HTML-like syntax. Here's how the above example would look using EJS.

First, specify to install the ejs package:

```
$ npm install ejs
```

Then set EJS as the view engine in your Express application:

```
app.set('view engine', 'ejs');
```

And in *views/user.ejs*:

```
<!DOCTYPE html>
<html lang="en">
  <head>
    <title>User Page</title>
  </head>
  <body>
    <h1><%= userData.name %> Profile</h1>
    <ul>
      <li><img src=<%= userData.avatar %> /></li>
      <li><%= userData.name %></li>
      <li><%= userData.email %></li>
    </ul>
  </body>
</html>
```

21.2 Using the Express-Generator

Problem

You're interested in using Express to manage your server-side data application, but you don't want to manage all of the setup yourself.

Solution

To kickstart your Express application, use the Express-Generator. This is a command-line tool that generates the skeleton infrastructure of a typical Express application.

First, create a working directory where the tool can safely install a new application subdirectory. Next, run the `express-generator` command with npx:

```
$ npx express-generator --pug --git
```

I've passed two options with the command: `--pug` will result in the use of the Pug templating engine, while `--git` will generate a default *.gitignore* file in the project directory. For the full list of options, run the generator with the `-h` option:

```
$ npx express-generator -h
```

The generator creates a new directory with several subdirectories, some basic files to get you started, and a *package.json* file with all of the dependencies. To install the dependencies, change to the newly created directory and type:

```
$ npm install
```

Once all of the dependencies are installed, run the application using the following:

```
$ npm start
```

You can now access the generated Express application, using your IP address or domain and port 3000, the default Express port.

Discussion

Express provides a web application framework based on Node and with support for multiple templating engines and CSS preprocessors. In the solution, the options I chose for the example application are Pug as the template engine (the default) and the default of plain CSS (no CSS preprocessor). Though building the application from scratch enables a wider selection, Express supports only the following template engines:

`--ejs`
    Adds support for the EJS template engine

`--pug`
   Adds support for the Pug template engine

`--hbs`
   Adds support for the Handlebar template engine

`--hogan`
   Adds support for the Hogan.js template engine

Express also supports the following CSS preprocessors:

`express --css sass`
   Support for Sass

`express --css less`
   Support for Less

`express --css stylus`
   Support for Stylus

`express --css compass`
   Support for Compass

Not specifying any CSS preprocessor defaults to plain CSS.

Express also assumes that the project directory is empty. If it isn't, force the Express generator to generate the content by using the `-f` or `--force` option.

The newly generated subdirectory has the following structure (disregarding `node _modules`):

```
app.js
package-lock.json
package.json
/bin
    www
/node_modules
/public
    /images
    /javascripts
    /stylesheets
        style.css
        style.styl
/routes
    index.js
    users.js
/views
    error.pug
    index.pug
    layout.pug
```

The *app.js* file is the core of the Express application. It includes the references to the necessary libraries:

```
var createError = require('http-errors');
var express = require('express');
var path = require('path');
var cookieParser = require('cookie-parser');
var logger = require('morgan');

var indexRouter = require('./routes/index');
var usersRouter = require('./routes/users');
```

 Although the convention followed in this book is to use `const` and `let` to define variables, at the time of writing, the Express generator uses `var`.

It also creates the Express app with the following line:

```
var app = express():
```

Next, it establishes Pug as the view engine by defining the `views` and `view engine` variables:

```
app.set('views', path.join(__dirname, 'views'));
app.set('view engine', 'pug');
```

The *middleware* calls are loaded next with `app.use()`. Middleware is functionality that sits between the raw request and the routing, processing specific types of requests. The rule for the middleware is if a path is not given as the first parameter, it defaults to a path of `/`, which means the middleware functions are loaded with the default path. In the following generated code:

```
app.use(logger('dev'));
app.use(express.json());
app.use(express.urlencoded({ extended: false }));
app.use(cookieParser());
app.use(express.static(path.join(__dirname, 'public')));
```

The first several middleware are loaded with every app request. Among the middleware includes support for development logging, as well as parsers for both JSON and *urlencoded* bodies. It's only when we get to the `static` entry that we see assignment to specific paths: the static file request middleware are loaded when requests are made to the *public* directory.

The routing is handled next:

```
app.use('/', indexRouter);
app.use('/users', usersRouter);
```

The top-level web request (/) is directed to the routes module, while all user requests (/*users*) get routed to the users module.

 Read more about routing with Express in Recipe 21.3.

What follows is the error handling. First up is 404 error handling when a request is made to a nonexistent web resource:

```
app.use(function(req, res, next) {
  next(createError(404));
});
```

Next comes the server error handling, for both production and development:

```
app.use(function(err, req, res, next) {
  // set locals, only providing error in development
  res.locals.message = err.message;
  res.locals.error = req.app.get('env') === 'development' ? err : {};

  // render the error page
  res.status(err.status || 500);
  res.render('error');
});
```

The last line of the generated file is the module.exports for the app:

```
module.exports = app;
```

In the *routes* subdirectory, the default routing is included in the *routes/index.js* file:

```
var express = require('express');
var router = express.Router();

/* GET home page. */
router.get('/', function(req, res, next) {
  res.render('index', { title: 'Express' });
});

module.exports = router;
```

What's happening in the file is the Express router is used to route any HTTP GET requests to / to a callback where the request response receives a view rendered for the specific resource page. This is in contrast to what happens in the *routes/users.js* file, where the response receives a text message rather than a view:

```
var express = require('express');
var router = express.Router();
```

```
/* GET users listing. */
router.get('/', function(req, res, next) {
  res.send('respond with a resource');
});

module.exports = router;
```

What happens with the view rendering in the first request? There are three Pug files in the *views* subdirectory: one for error handling, one defining the page layout, and one, *index.pug*, that renders the page. The *index.pug* file contains:

```
extends layout

block content
  h1= title
  p Welcome to #{title}
```

It extends the *layout.pug* file, which contains:

```
doctype html
html
  head
    title= title
    link(rel='stylesheet', href='/stylesheets/style.css')
  body
    block content
```

The *layout.pug* file defines the overall structure of the page, regardless of content, including a reference to an automatically generated CSS file. The block content setting defines where the location of the content is placed. The format for the content is defined in *index.js*, in the equivalently named block content setting.

 The Pug templating engine (formerly known as Jade) was popularized by Express and offers a minimalist take on templating that makes use of whitespace in place of traditional HTML style tags. This approach may not be for everyone, and the Pug alternatives (Handlebars, Hogan.js, and EJS) all offer a more HTML-like syntax.

The two Pug files define a basic web page with an h1 element assigned a title variable, and a paragraph with a welcome message. Figure 21-1 shows the default page.

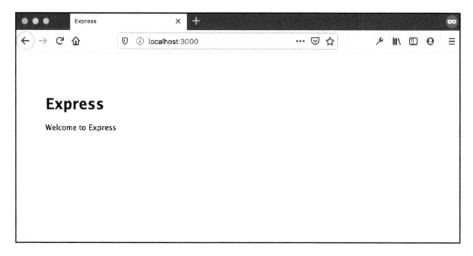

Figure 21-1. The Express-generated web page

Figure 21-1 shows that the page isn't especially fascinating, but it does represent how the pieces are holding together: the application router routes the request to the appropriate route module, which directs the response to the appropriate rendered view, and the rendered view uses data passed to it to generate the web page. If you make the following web request:

```
http://yourdomain.com:3000/users
```

you'll see the plain text message, rather than the rendered view.

By default, Express is set up to run in *development mode*. To change the application to *production mode*, you need to set an *environment variable*, NODE-ENV to "production." In a Linux or Unix environment, the following could be used:

```
$ export NODE_ENV=production
```

21.3 Routing

Problem

You want to route users to different resources in your application based on the request.

Solution

Use routes in Express to send specific resources based on the request path and parameters:

```
// respond with different route paths
app.get('/', (req, res) => res.send('Hello World'));
app.get('/users', (req, res) => res.send('Hello users'));

// parameters
app.get('/users/:userId', (req, res) => {
  res.send(`Hello user ${req.params.userId}`);
});
```

Discussion

In Express, we can return a response to the user when they make an HTTP request. In the above examples, I'm using `get` requests, but Express supports a number of additional methods. The most common of these methods are:

- `app.get`: request data
- `app.post`: send data
- `app.put`: send or update data
- `app.delete`: delete data

```
app.post('/new', (req, res) => {
  res.send('POST request to the `new` route');
});
```

Often we may want to enable multiple HTTP methods to a specific route. We can accomplish this by chaining them together:

```
app
  .route('/record')
  .get((req, res) => {
    res.send('Get a record');
  })
  .post((req, res) => {
    res.send('Add a record');
  })
  .put((req, res) => {
    res.send('Update a record');
  });
```

Often requests have parameters with specific values that we will make use of in our application. We can specify these in the URL using a colon (`:`):

```
app.get('/users/:userId', (req, res) => {
  res.send(`Hello user ${req.params.userId}`);
});
```

In the above example, when a user visits a URL at */users/adam123*, the browser will send the response of `Hello user adam123`. While this is a simple example, we could also make use of the URL parameter to retrieve data from our database, passing the information on to a template.

We're also able to specify formats for the request parameters. In the following example, I make use of a regular expression to limit the `noteId` parameter to a six-digit integer:

```
app.get('^/users/:userId/notes/:noteId([0-9]{6})', (req, res) => {
  res.send(`This is note ${req.params.noteId}`);
});
```

We are also able to use a regular expression to define an entire route:

```
app.get(/.*day$/, (req, res) => {
  res.send(`Every day feels like ${req.path}`);
});
```

The above example will route any request ending in day. For example, in local development a request to *http://localhost:3000/Sunday* will result in "Every day feels like Sunday" being printed to the page.

21.4 Working with OAuth

Problem

You need access to a third-party API (such as GitHub, Facebook, or Twitter) in your Node application, but it requires authorization. Specifically, it requires OAuth authorization.

Solution

You'll need to incorporate an OAuth client in your application. You'll also need to meet the OAuth requirements demanded by the resource provider.

See the discussion for details.

Discussion

OAuth is an authorization framework used with most popular social media and cloud content applications. If you've ever gone to a site and it's asked you to authorize access to data from a third-party service, such as GitHub, you've participated in the OAuth authorization *flow*.

There are two versions of OAuth, 1.0 and 2.0, which are not compatible with one another. OAuth 1.0 was based on proprietary APIs developed by Flickr and Google, was heavily web page focused, and didn't gracefully transcend the barrier among web, mobile, and service applications. When wanting to access resources in a mobile phone app, the app would have the user log in to the app in a mobile browser and then copy access tokens to the app. Other criticisms of OAuth 1.0 is that the process required that the authorization server be the same as the resource server, which doesn't scale when you're talking about service providers such as Twitter, Facebook, and Amazon.

OAuth 2.0 presents a simpler authorization process, and also provides different types of authorization (different flows) for different circumstances. Some would say, though, that it does so at the cost of security, as it doesn't have the same demands for encrypting hash tokens and request strings.

Most developers won't have to create an OAuth 2.0 server, and doing so is way beyond the scope of this book, much less this recipe. But it's common for applications to incorporate an OAuth client (1.0 or 2.0) for one service or another, so I'm going to present different types of OAuth use. First, though, let's discuss the differences between authorization and authentication.

Authorization isn't authentication

Authorization is saying, "I authorize this application to access my resources on your server." Authentication is the process of authenticating whether you are, indeed, the person who owns this account and has control over these resources. An example would be if I want to comment on an article at a newspaper's online site. It will likely ask me to log in via some service. If I pick my Facebook account to use as the login, the news site will most likely want some data from Facebook.

The news site is, first, authenticating me as a legitimate Facebook user, with an established Facebook account. In other words, I'm not just some random person coming in and commenting anonymously. Secondly, the news site wants something from me in exchange for the privilege of commenting: it's going to want data about me. Perhaps it will ask for permission to post for me (if I post my comment to Facebook as well as the news site). This is both an authentication and an authorization request.

If I'm not already logged in to Facebook, I'll have to log in. Facebook is using my correct application of username and password to authenticate that, yes, I own the Facebook account in question. Once logged in, Facebook asks whether I agree to giving the newspaper site the authorization to access the resources it wants. If I agree (because I desperately want to comment on a particular story), Facebook gives the news site the authorization, and there's now a persistent connection from the newspaper to my Facebook account (which you can see in your Facebook settings). I can make my comment, and make comments at other stories, until I log out or revoke the Facebook authorization.

Of course, none of this implies that Facebook or the news site are actually authenticating who I am. Authentication, in this case, is about establishing that I am the owner of the Facebook account. The only time *real* authentication enters the picture is in a social media context such as Twitter's authenticated accounts for celebrities.

Our development task is made simpler by the fact that software to handle authorization is frequently the same software that authenticates the individual, so we're not having to deal with two different JavaScript libraries/modules/systems. There are also several excellent OAuth (1.0 and 2.0) modules we can use in Node applications. One of the most popular is Passport (*http://www.passportjs.org*), and there are extensions for various authorization services created specifically for the Passport system. However, there are also very simple OAuth clients that provide barebones authorization access for a variety of services, and some modules that are created specifically for one service.

Passport.js is covered in Recipe 21.5. You can also read more about Passport and its various *strategies* supporting different servers at its website.

Now, on to the technology.

Client Credentials Grant

There are few web resources that nowadays provide an API you can access without having some kind of authorization credential. This means having to incorporate a round-trip directive to the end users—asking them to authorize access to their account at the service before the application can access data. The problem is that sometimes all you need is simple read-only access without update privileges, without a frontend login interface, and without having a specific user make an authorizing grant.

OAuth 2.0 accounts for this particular type of authorizing flow with the *Client Credentials Grant*. The diagram for this simplified authorization is shown in Figure 21-2.

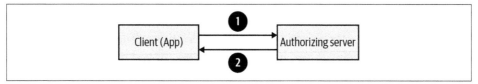

Figure 21-2. The Client Credentials Grant authorization flow

Twitter provides what it calls application-only authorization, which is based on OAuth 2.0's Client Credentials Grant. We can use this type of authorization to access Twitter's Search API.

In the following example, I used the Node module oauth to implement the authorization. It's the most basic of the authorization modules, and supports both OAuth 1.0 and OAuth 2.0 authorization flows:

```javascript
const OAuth = require('oauth');
const fetch = require('node-fetch');
const { promisify } = require('util');

// read Twitter keys from a .env file
require('dotenv').config();

// Twitter's search API endpoint and the query we'll be searching
const endpointUrl = 'https://api.twitter.com/2/tweets/search/recent';
const query = 'javascript';

async function getTweets() {
  // consumer key and secret passed in from environment variables
  const oauth2 = new OAuth.OAuth2(
    process.env.TWITTER_CONSUMER_KEY,
    process.env.TWITTER_CONSUMER_SECRET,
    'https://api.twitter.com/',
    null,
    'oauth2/token',
    null
  );

  // retrieve the credentials from Twitter
  const getOAuthAccessToken = promisify(
    oauth2.getOAuthAccessToken.bind(oauth2)
  );
  const token = await getOAuthAccessToken('', {
    grant_type: 'client_credentials'
  });

  // make the request for data with the retrieved token
  const res = await fetch(`${endpointUrl}?query=${query}`, {
    headers: {
      authorization: `Bearer ${token}`
    }
  });

  const json = await res.json();
  return json;
}

(async () => {
  try {
    // Make request
    const response = await getTweets();
    console.log(response);
  } catch (e) {
    console.log(e);
    process.exit(-1);
  }
  process.exit();
})();
```

To use the Twitter authorization API, the client application has to register its application with Twitter. Twitter provides both a *consumer key* and a *consumer secret*.

Using the oauth module, a new OAuth2 object is created, passing in:

- Consumer key
- Consumer secret
- API base URI (API URI minus the query string)
- A value of null signals OAuth to use the default */oauth/authorize*
- The access token path
- Null, because we're not using any custom headers

The oauth module takes this data and forms a POST request to Twitter, passing along the consumer key and secret, as well as providing a *scope* for the request. Twitter's documentation provides an example POST request for an access token (line breaks inserted for readability):

```
POST /oauth2/token HTTP/1.1
Host: api.twitter.com
User-Agent: My Twitter App v1.0.23
Authorization: Basic eHZ6MWV2RlM0d0VFUFRHRUZQSEJvZzpMOHFxOVBaeVJn
               NmllS0dFS2hab2xHQzB2SldMdzhpRUo4OERSZHlPZw==
               Content-Type: application/x-www-form-urlencoded;charset=UTF-8
Content-Length: 29
Accept-Encoding: gzip

grant_type=client_credentials
```

The response includes the access token (again, line breaks for readability):

```
HTTP/1.1 200 OK
Status: 200 OK
Content-Type: application/json; charset=utf-8
...
Content-Encoding: gzip
Content-Length: 140

{"token_type":"bearer","access_token":"AAAAAAAAAAAAAAAAAAAAAAAAAAAAAAAAAAAAA
%2FAAAAAAAAAAAAAAAAAAAAA%3DAAAAAAAAAAAAAAAAAAAAAAAAAAAAAAAAAAAAAAAAAAAAAAA"}
```

The access token has to be used with any of the API requests. There are no further authorization steps, so the process is very simple. In addition, since the authorization is at the application level, it doesn't require an individual's authorization, making it less disruptive to the user.

Twitter provides wonderful documentation. I recommend reading the "Application-only authentication overview" (*https://oreil.ly/ Mikyl*).

Read/write authorization with OAuth 1.0

Application-Only authentication is great for accessing read-only data, but what if you want to access a user's specific data, or even make a change to their data? Then you'll need the full OAuth authorization. In this section, we'll again use Twitter for the demonstration because of its use of OAuth 1.0 authorization. In the next recipe, we'll look at OAuth 2.0.

 I refer to it as OAuth 1.0, but Twitter's service is based on OAuth Core 1.0 Revision A (*http://oauth.net/core/1.0a*). However, it's a lot easier just to say OAuth 1.0.

OAuth 1.0 requires a digital signature. The steps to derive this digital signature, graphically represented in Figure 21-3, and as outlined by Twitter, are:

1. Collect the HTTP method and the base URI, minus any query string.
2. Collect the parameters, including the consumer key, request data, nonce, signature method, and so on.
3. Create a signature base string, which consists of the data we've gathered, formed into a string in a precise manner, and encoded just right.
4. Create a signing key, which is a combination of consumer key and OAuth token secret, again combined in a precise manner.
5. Pass the signature base string and the signing key to an HMAC-SHA1 hashing algorithm, which returns a binary string that needs further encoding.

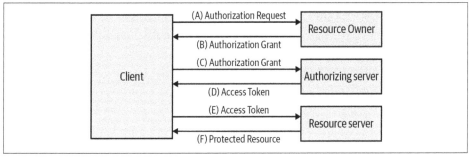

Figure 21-3. OAuth 1.0 authorization flow

You have to follow this process for *every* request. Thankfully, we have modules and libraries that do all of this mind-numbing work for us. I don't know about you, but if I had to do this, my interest in incorporating Twitter data and services into my application would quickly wane.

Our friend oauth provides the underlying OAuth 1.0 support, but we don't have to code to it directly this time. Another module, node-twitter-api, has wrapped all of the OAuth pieces. All we need do is create a new node-twitter-api object, passing in our consumer key and secret, as well as the callback/redirect URL required by the resource services, as part of the authorization process. Processing the request object in that URL provides us the access token and secret we need for API access. Every time we make a request, we pass in the access token and secret.

The twitter-node-api module is a thin wrapper around the REST API: to make a request, we extrapolate what the function is from the API. If we're interested in posting a status update, the REST API endpoint is:

```
https://api.twitter.com/1.1/statuses/update.json
```

The twitter-node-api object instance function is statuses(), and the first parameter is the verb, update:

```
twitter.statuses('update', {
        "status": "Hi from Shelley's Toy Box. (Ignore--developing Node app)"
        }, atoken, atokensec, function(err, data, response) {...});

twitter.statuses(
  'update',
  {
    status: 'Ignore learning OAuth with Node'
  },
  tokenValues.atoken,
  tokenValues.atokensec,
  (err, data) => { ... });
```

The callback function arguments include any possible error, requested data (if any), and the raw response.

A complete example is shown in Example 21-1. It uses Express as a server and provides a primitive web page for the user, and then uses another module.

Example 21-1. Twitter app fully authorized via OAuth 1.0

```
const express = require('express');
const TwitterAPI = require('node-twitter-api');

require('dotenv').config();

const port = process.env.PORT || '8080';
```

```
// keys and callback URL are configured in the Twitter Dev Center
const twitter = new TwitterAPI({
  consumerKey: process.env.TWITTER_CONSUMER_KEY,
  consumerSecret: process.env.TWITTER_CONSUMER_SECRET,
  callback: 'http://127.0.0.1:8080/oauth/callback'
});

// object for storing retrieved token values
const tokenValues = {};

// twitter OAuth API URL
const twitterAPI = 'https://api.twitter.com/oauth/authenticate';

// simple HTML template
const menu =
  '<a href="/post/status/">Say hello</a><br />' +
  '<a href="/get/account/">Account Settings<br />';

// Create a new Express application.
const app = express();

// request Twitter permissions when the / route is visited
app.get('/', (req, res) => {
  twitter.getRequestToken((error, requestToken, requestTokenSecret) => {
    if (error) {
      console.log(`Error getting OAuth request token : ${error}`);
      res.writeHead(200);
      res.end(`Error getting authorization${error}`);
    } else {
      tokenValues.token = requestToken;
      tokenValues.tokensec = requestTokenSecret;
      res.writeHead(302, {
        Location: `${twitterAPI}?oauth_token=${requestToken}`
      });
      res.end();
    }
  });
});

// callback url as specified in the Twitter Developer Center
app.get('/oauth/callback', (req, res) => {
  twitter.getAccessToken(
    tokenValues.token,
    tokenValues.tokensec,
    req.query.oauth_verifier,
    (err, accessToken, accessTokenSecret) => {
      res.writeHead(200);
      if (err) {
        res.end(`problems getting authorization with Twitter${err}`);
      } else {
        tokenValues.atoken = accessToken;
        tokenValues.atokensec = accessTokenSecret;
```

```
      res.end(menu);
    }
  }
);
});

// post a status update from an authenticated and authorized users
app.get('/post/status/', (req, res) => {
  twitter.statuses(
    'update',
    {
      status: 'Ignore teaching OAuth with Node'
    },
    tokenValues.atoken,
    tokenValues.atokensec,
    (err, data) => {
      res.writeHead(200);
      if (err) {
        res.end(`problems posting ${JSON.stringify(err)}`);
      } else {
        res.end(`posting status: ${JSON.stringify(data)}<br />${menu}`);
      }
    }
  );
});

// get account details for an authenticated and authorized user
app.get('/get/account/', (req, res) => {
  twitter.account(
    'settings',
    {},
    tokenValues.atoken,
    tokenValues.atokensec,
    (err, data) => {
      res.writeHead(200);
      if (err) {
        res.end(`problems getting account ${JSON.stringify(err)}`);
      } else {
        res.end(`<p>${JSON.stringify(data)}</p>${menu}`);
      }
    }
  );
});

app.listen(port, () => console.log(`Listening on port ${port}!`));
```

The routes of interest in the app are:

- /: Page that triggers a redirect to Twitter for authorization
- /auth: The callback or redirect URL registered with the app, and passed in the request
- /post/status/: Post a status to the Twitter account
- /get/account/: Get account information for the individual

In each case, the appropriate node-twitter-api function is used:

- /: Get a request token and request token secret, using getRequestToken()
- /auth/: Get the API access token and token secret, caching them locally, display menu
- /post/status/: status() with *update* as first parameter, status, access token and secret, and callback function
- /get/account/: account() with *settings* as the first parameter, an empty object, since no data is needed for the request, and the access token, secret, and callback

The Twitter authorization page that pops up is displayed in Figure 21-4, and the web page that displays account information for yours truly is displayed in Figure 21-5.

 Though it is no longer actively maintained, you can read more about the node-twitter-api module at its GitHub repository page (*https://github.com/reneraab/node-twitter-api*). Other libraries are more actively maintained and provide the same type of functionality, but I found node-twitter-api offers the simplest functional example for the purpose of demonstration.

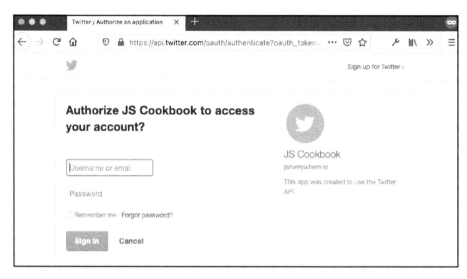

Figure 21-4. Twitter authorization page, redirected from the recipe app

Figure 21-5. Display of Twitter user account data in app

21.5 OAuth 2 User Authentication with Passport.js

Problem

You want to authenticate users in your application through a third-party service.

Solution

Use the Passport.js library paired with the appropriate strategy for the authentication provider you've chosen. In this example, I'll make use of the GitHub strategy, but the workflow will be identical for any OAuth 2 provider, including Facebook, Google, and Twitter.

You can make use of the GitHub strategy, first by visiting GitHub's website and registering a new OAuth application (*https://github.com/settings/applications/new*). Once the application is registered, you can integrate the Passport.js OAuth code into the application.

To begin, configure the Passport strategy, which will include the GitHub-provided client ID and client secret, along with the callback URL that you have specified:

```
const express = require('express');
const passport = require('passport');
const { Strategy } = require('passport-github');

passport.use(
  new Strategy(
    {
      clientID: GITHUB_CLIENT_ID,
      clientSecret: GITHUB_CLIENT_SECRET,
      callbackURL: 'login/github/callback'
    },
    (accessToken, refreshToken, profile, cb) => {
      return cb(null, profile);
    }
  )
);
```

To restore authentication state across HTTP requests, Passport needs to serialize and deserialize users:

```
passport.serializeUser((user, cb) => {
  cb(null, user);
});

passport.deserializeUser((obj, cb) => {
  cb(null, obj);
});
```

To preserve user logins across browser sessions, make use of the `express-session` middleware:

```
app.use(
  require('express-session')({
    secret: SESSION_SECRET,
    resave: true,
    saveUninitialized: true
  })
```

```
  );

  app.use(passport.session());
```

You can then authenticate requests using `passport.authenticate`:

```
  app.use(passport.initialize());

  app.get('/login/github', passport.authenticate('github'));

  app.get(
    '/login/github/callback',
    passport.authenticate('github', { failureRedirect: '/login' }),
    (req, res) => {
      res.redirect('/');
    }
  );
```

And reference the user object from requests:

```
  app.get('/', (req, res) => {
    res.render('home', { user: req.user });
  });
```

Discussion

OAuth is an open standard for user authentication. It allows us to authenticate users through third-party applications. This can be useful when allowing users to easily create accounts and log in to your applications, as well as for authenticating to use data from a third-party source.

OAuth requests follow a specific flow:

1. Your application makes an authorization request to the third-party service.

2. The user approves that request.

3. The service redirects the user back to your application, along with an authorization code.

4. The application makes a request to the third-party service with the authorization code.

5. The service responds with an access token (and optionally a refresh token).

6. The application makes a request to the service with the access token.

7. The service responds with the protected resource (in our case, the user account information).

Using Passport.js along with a Passport.js strategy for the OAuth provider simplifies this flow in an Express.js application. In this example, we'll build a small Express application that authenticates with GitHub and persists user logins across sessions.

Once we have registered our application with the service provider, we can begin development by installing the appropriate dependencies:

```
# install general application dependencies
npm install express pug dotenv
# install passport dependencies
npm install passport passport-github
# install persistent user session dependencies
npm install connect-ensure-login express-session
```

To store our OAuth client ID, client secret, and session secret values, we will use a *.env* file. Alternately, you could use a JavaScript file (such as a *config.js* file). It is critical that we not check this file into public source control, and I recommend adding it to your *.gitignore* file. In *.env*:

```
GITHUB_CLIENT_ID=<Your client ID>
GITHUB_CLIENT_SECRET=<Your client secret>
SESSION_SECRET=<A session secret - this can be any value you decide>
```

Next, we'll set up our Express application with Passport.js. In *index.js*:

```
const express = require('express');
const passport = require('passport');
const { Strategy } = require('passport-github');

require('dotenv').config();

const port = process.env.PORT || '3000';

// Configure the Passport strategy
passport.use(
  new Strategy(
    {
      clientID: process.env.GITHUB_CLIENT_ID,
      clientSecret: process.env.GITHUB_CLIENT_SECRET,
      callbackURL: `http://localhost:${port}/login/github/callback`
    },
    (accessToken, refreshToken, profile, cb) => {
      return cb(null, profile);
    }
  )
);

// Serialize and deserialize the user
passport.serializeUser((user, cb) => {
  cb(null, user);
});

passport.deserializeUser((obj, cb) => {
  cb(null, obj);
});

// create the Express application
```

```
const app = express();
app.set('views', `${__dirname}/views`);
app.set('view engine', 'pug');

// use the Express session middleware for preserving user session
app.use(
  require('express-session')({
    secret: process.env.SESSION_SECRET,
    resave: true,
    saveUninitialized: true
  })
);

// Initialize passport and restore the authentication state from the session
app.use(passport.initialize());
app.use(passport.session());

// listen on port 3000 or the PORT set as an environment variable
app.listen(port, () => console.log(`Listening on port ${port}!`));
```

You can then build your view templates, which can access the user data.

In *views/home.pug*:

```
if !user
  p Welcome! Please
    a(href='/login/github') Login with GitHub
else
  h1 Hello #{user.username}!
  p View your
    a(href='/profile') profile
```

In *views/login.pug*:

```
h1 Login
a(href='/login/github') Login with GitHub
```

In *views/profile.pug*:

```
h1 Profile
ul
  li ID: #{user.id}
  li Name: #{user.username}
  if user.emails
    li Email: #{user.emails[0].value}
```

Finally, we can set up our routes in the *index.js* file:

```
app.get('/', (req, res) => {
  res.render('home', { user: req.user });
});

app.get('/login', (req, res) => {
  res.render('login');
});
```

```
app.get('/login/github', passport.authenticate('github'));

app.get(
  '/login/github/callback',
  passport.authenticate('github', { failureRedirect: '/login' }),
  (req, res) => {
    res.redirect('/');
  }
);

app.get(
  '/profile',
  require('connect-ensure-login').ensureLoggedIn(),
  (req, res) => {
    res.render('profile', { user: req.user });
  }
);
```

This example was designed to closely match the Express 4.x Facebook example (*https://github.com/passport/express-4.x-facebook-example*), which provides well-documented code for working with Express and Facebook authentication. You can view hundreds of additional Passport.js strategies (*http://www.passportjs.org*).

21.6 Serving Up Formatted Data

Problem

Instead of serving up a web page or sending plain text, you want to return formatted data, such as XML, to the browser.

Solution

Use Node module(s) to help format the data. For example, if you want to return XML, you can use a module to create the formatted data:

```
const builder = require('xmlbuilder');

const xml = builder
  .create('resources')
  .ele('resource')
  .ele('title', 'Ecma-262 Edition 10')
  .up()
  .ele('url', 'https://www.ecma-international.org/ecma-262/10.0/index.html')
  .up()
  .end({ pretty: true });
```

Then create the appropriate header to go with the data, and return the data to the browser:

```
app.get('/', (req, res) => {
  res.setHeader('Content-Type', 'application/xml');
  res.end(xml.toString(), 'utf8');
});
```

Discussion

Web servers frequently serve up static or server-side generated resources, but just as frequently, what's returned to the browser is formatted data that's then processed in the web page before display.

There are two key elements to generating and returning formatted data. The first is to make use of whatever Node library to simplify the generation of the data, and the second is to make sure that the header data sent with the data is appropriate for the data.

In the solution, the `xmlbuilder` module is used to assist us in creating proper XML. This isn't one of the modules installed with Node by default, so we have to install it using npm, the Node Package Manager:

```
npm install xmlbuilder
```

Then it's a matter of creating a new XML document, a root element, and then each resource element, as demonstrated in the solution. It's true, we could build the XML string ourselves, but that's a pain. And it's too easy to make mistakes that are then hard to discover. One of the best things about Node is the enormous number of modules available to do most anything we can think of. Not only do we not have to write the code ourselves, but most of the modules have been thoroughly tested and actively maintained.

Once the formatted data is ready to return, create the header that goes with it. In the solution, because the document is XML, the header content type is set to `application/xml` before the data is returned as a string.

21.7 Building a RESTful API

Problem

You want to build a REST API using Node.js.

Solution

Use Express with the `app.get`, `app.post`, `app.put`, and `app.delete` methods:

```
const express = require('express');

const app = express();
const port = process.env.PORT || 3000;
```

```
app.get('/', (req, res) => {
  return res.send('Received a GET HTTP method');
});
app.post('/', (req, res) => {
  return res.send('Received a POST HTTP method');
});
app.put('/', (req, res) => {
  return res.send('Received a PUT HTTP method');
});
app.delete('/', (req, res) => {
  return res.send('Received a DELETE HTTP method');
});
app.listen(port, () => console.log(`Listening on port ${port}!`));
```

Discussion

REST stands for "Representational State Transfer," and is the most common architectural approach for building APIs. REST allows us to interact with a remote data source over HTTP, using the standard HTTP methods of GET, POST, PUT, and DELETE. We can make use of the Express routing methods to accept these requests.

In the following example, I'll create several routes that serve as API endpoints. Each endpoint will respond to an HTTP request:

/todos

> Will accept a get request for a list of todos as well as a post request for creating a new todo.

/todos/:todoId

> Will accept a get request that will return a specific todo as well as a put request, which will allow the user to update the todo content or completed state, and a delete request, which will delete the specific todo.

With these routes defined, we can develop a REST API that responds to these requests appropriately:

```
const express = require('express');

const port = process.env.PORT || 3000;
const app = express();
app.use(express.json());
app.use(express.urlencoded({ extended: true }));

// an array of data
let todos = [
  {
    id: '1',
    text: 'Order pizza',
    completed: true
  },
```

```
    {
      id: '2',
      text: 'Pick up pizza',
      completed: false
    }
  ];

  // get the list of todos
  app.get('/todos', (req, res) => {
    return res.send({ data: { todos } });
  });

  // get an individual todo
  app.get('/todos/:todoId', (req, res) => {
    const foundTodo = todos.find(todo => todo.id === req.params.todoId);
    return res.send({ data: foundTodo });
  });

  // create a new todo
  app.post('/todos', (req, res) => {
    const todo = {
      id: String(todos.length + 1),
      text: req.body.text,
      completed: false
    };

    todos.push(todo);
    return res.send({ data: todo });
  });

  // update a todo
  app.put('/todos/:todoId', (req, res) => {
    const todoIndex = todos.findIndex(todo => todo.id === req.params.todoId);
    const todo = {
      id: req.params.todoId,
      text: req.body.text || todos[todoIndex].text,
      completed: req.body.completed || todos[todoIndex].completed
    };

    todos[todoIndex] = todo;
    return res.send({ data: todo });
  });

  // delete a todo
  app.delete('/todos/:todoId', (req, res) => {
    const deletedTodo = todos.find(todo => todo.id === req.params.todoId);
    todos = todos.filter(todo => todo.id !== req.params.todoId);
    return res.send({ data: deletedTodo });
  });

  // listen on port 3000 or the PORT set as an environment variable
  app.listen(port, () => console.log(`Listening on port ${port}!`));
```

From the terminal, you can use `curl` to test our responses:

```
# get the list of todos
curl http://localhost:3000/todos

# get an individual todo
curl http://localhost:3000/todos/1

# create a new todo
curl -X POST -H "Content-Type:application/json" /
  http://localhost:3000/todos -d '{"text":"Eat pizza"}'

# update a todo
curl -X PUT -H "Content-Type:application/json" /
  http://localhost:3000/todos/2 -d '{"completed": true }

# delete a todo
curl -X DELETE http://localhost:3000/todos/3
```

Manually testing with `curl` can quickly become tedious. For API development, you may also want to make use of a REST client UI, such as Insomnia (*https://insom nia.rest*) or Postman (*https://postman.com*) (see Figure 21-6).

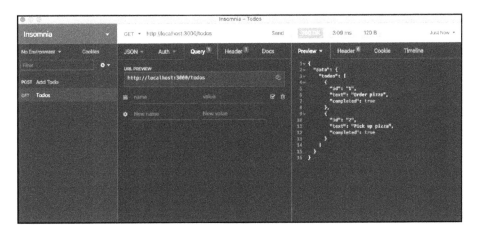

Figure 21-6. A GET request in the Insomnia REST client

In the above example, I'm using an in-memory data store. When building an API, you will most likely want to connect to a database. To do so, you can reach for a library such as Sequelize (*https://oreil.ly/NuXyR*) (for SQL databases), Mongoose (*https://oreil.ly/zP8Fr*) (for MongoDB), or an online data store such as Firebase (*https://oreil.ly/iZSFB*).

21.8 Building a GraphQL API

Problem

You would like to build a GraphQL API server application or add GraphQL endpoints to an existing Express application.

Solution

Use the Apollo Server package to include GraphQL type definitions, GraphQL resolvers, and the GraphQL Playground:

```
const express = require('express');
const { ApolloServer, gql } = require('apollo-server-express');

const port = process.env.PORT || 3000;
const app = express();

const typeDefs = gql`
  type Query {
    hello: String
  }
`;

const resolvers = {
  Query: {
    hello: () => 'Hello world!'
  }
};
const server = new ApolloServer({ typeDefs, resolvers });
server.applyMiddleware({ app, path: '/' });
app.listen({ port }, () => console.log(`Listening on port ${port}!`));
```

Apollo Server provides access to the GraphQL Playground (see Figure 21-7), which allows us to easily interact with the API during development (and in production, if desired).

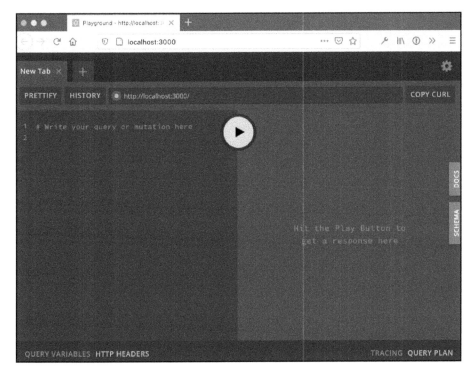

Figure 21-7. A GraphQL query in the GraphQL Playground

The GraphQL Playground also provides automatically generated documentation for the API, based on the type definitions you've provided (see Figure 21-8).

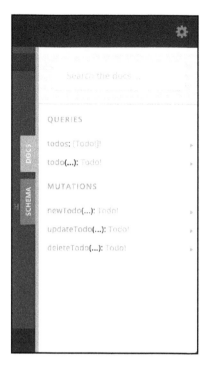

Figure 21-8. The generated documentation in GraphQL Playground

Discussion

GraphQL is an open source query language for APIs. It was developed with the goal of providing single endpoints for data, allowing applications to request the specific data that is needed. Apollo Server (*https://oreil.ly/toPLM*) can be used as a standalone package or integrated as middleware for popular Node.js server application libraries, such as Express, Hapi, Fastify, and Koa.

In GraphQL, a type definition schema is a written representation of our data and interactions. By requiring a schema, GraphQL enforces a strict plan for our API. This is because your API can only return data and perform interactions that are defined within the schema. The fundamental component of GraphQL schemas are object types. GraphQL contains five built-in scalar types:

- String: A string with UTF-8 character encoding
- Boolean: A true or false value
- Int: A 32-bit integer
- Float: A floating-point value

- ID: A unique identifier

Once the schema is written, we provide the API with a series of resolvers. These are functions that specify how the data should be returned in a query or changed within a data mutation.

In the previous example, we're using the `apollo-server-express` package, which should be installed alongside the `express` and `gql` packages:

```
$ npm install express apollo-server-express gql
```

To create a CRUD application, we can define our GraphQL type definitions and the appropriate resolvers. The following example mimics the one found in Recipe 21.7:

```
const express = require('express');
const { ApolloServer, gql } = require('apollo-server-express');

const port = process.env.PORT || 3000;
const app = express();

// an array of data
let todos = [
  {
    id: '1',
    text: 'Order pizza',
    completed: true
  },
  {
    id: '2',
    text: 'Pick up pizza',
    completed: false
  }
];

// GraphQL Type Definitions
const typeDefs = gql`
  type Query {
    todos: [Todo!]!
    todo(id: ID!): Todo!
  }

  type Mutation {
    newTodo(text: String!): Todo!
    updateTodo(id: ID!, text: String, completed: Boolean): Todo!
    deleteTodo(id: ID!): Todo!
  }

  type Todo {
    id: ID!
    text: String!
    completed: Boolean
  }
`;

// GraphQL Resolvers
```

```
const resolvers = {
  Query: {
    todos: () => todos,
    todo: (parent, args) => {
      return todos.find(todo => todo.id === args.id);
    }
  },
  Mutation: {
    newTodo: (parent, args) => {
      const todo = {
        id: String(todos.length + 1),
        text: args.text,
        completed: false
      };

      todos.push(todo);
      return todo;
    },

    updateTodo: (parent, args) => {
      const todoIndex = todos.findIndex(todo => todo.id === args.id);
      const todo = {
        id: args.id,
        text: args.text || todos[todoIndex].text,
        completed: args.completed || todos[todoIndex].completed
      };

      todos[todoIndex] = todo;
      return todo;
    },
    deleteTodo: (parent, args) => {
      const deletedTodo = todos.find(todo => todo.id === args.id);
      todos = todos.filter(todo => todo.id !== args.id);
      return deletedTodo;
    }
  }
};

// Apollo + Express server setup
const server = new ApolloServer({ typeDefs, resolvers });
server.applyMiddleware({ app, path: '/' });
app.listen({ port }, () => console.log(`Listening on port ${port}!`));
```

In the above example, I'm using an in-memory data store. When building an API, you will most likely want to connect to a database. To do so, you can reach for a library such as Sequelize (for SQL databases), Mongoose (for MongoDB), or an online data store such as Firebase.

The defined queries return data directly from the API, while the mutations allow us to perform changes to the data, such as create a new item, update an item, or delete an item.

Index

Symbols
!= operator, 74
\# (private field), 181
$ (terminal command line), 15
${} (template literal expression), 44
* (universal selector), 269
+ operator
    concatenation, 43
    joining numbers to strings, 38
; (semicolon), cookie value, 326
< angle bracket, 74, 80
<= comparison operator, 74
= operator, 80
== operator, 74
=== operator, 74, 168
> angle bracket, 74, 80
>= comparison operator, 74
\ (backslash character/escape sequence), 41, 50
_ (underscore character), 179, 181
` (backtick character), 44
{} (curly brackets), 44, 200
|| operator, 440
… (spread operator), 94, 97, 107, 155, 164

A
aboutAudio() event handler, 357
abstraction layers, logging, 236
accessibility
    automatically updated regions, 298-299
    for forms, 292-298
    to HTML elements, 263, 269-271
    public versus private fields in constructor, 175
    removing elements from page view, 285

video controls, 360
accessor descriptor, 158
accumulator, 110
add() method, Set, 113
addEventListener() method, 267
Agile development paradigm, 246
Airbnb JavaScript Style Guide, 25
AJAX, 301, 305
alert boxes, 294
all() method, 211-213, 217
allSettled() method, 213
Alter, Tal
    Building Progressive Web Apps (O'Reilly), 373
AMD (Asynchronous Module Definition), 432, 434
Angular framework, 393
anonymous functions, 120, 203
any() method, 213
ApacheBench, 456
Apollo Server package, 496-500
app.js file, 471
appendChild() method, 279, 389
appendFile() function, 406
appendText() function, 405
application manifest, 366, 370-372
application-only authentication, 478
arc length, calculating, 71
areArraysEqual() method, 91
arguments object, 124, 126, 136
argv property, 447
ARIA alert role, 294, 297
aria-atomic attribute, 299
aria-invalid attribute, 293-297

aria-live region attribute, 299
aria-relevant attribute, 299
aria-required attribute, 298
arrays (Array object), 87-116
    breaking down into separate variables,
        93-94
    checking that object is an array, 88
    cloning of, 95-97
    combining values in single calculation,
        110-112
    converting function arguments into, 94, 121
    converting sets to, 114
    copying portion of array by position, 98-99
    emptying of, 101
    equality testing for two arrays, 90-93
    exact matches, searching for, 104-105
    extracting items meeting specific criteria,
        100-101
    flattening of two-dimensional, 103-104
    iterating over all elements in, 88-90
    joining, 187
    key-indexed collection of items, 114-116
    merging of, 97-98
    methods for processing, 89
    nonduplicated value collection, 113
    passing to function expecting list of values,
        94
    reducing, 110
    removing artifacts from, 53
    removing duplicate values, 102
    removing/replacing elements, 107-108
    searching for items meeting specific criteria,
        105
    sorting array of objects by property value,
        108-109
    transforming every element, 109
    validating contents of, 112-113
arrow syntax, 117, 121-124
artifacts, removing from arrays, 53
assertion tests, 243
assign() method
    Object, 165
    window.location, 379
async function, await keyword in, 214-217, 304,
    441
async keyword, 218-220
Asynchronous Module Definition (see AMD)
asynchronous programming, 201-226

await and async for waiting for promise,
    214-217
callback function change to promise,
    208-211
callback hell, managing in Node, 441-444
concurrent multiple promise execution,
    211-213
error handling, 232-233, 235
generator function, 218-220
Node timers and, 414
page updating during loop, 202-204
Promise object, using function that returns,
    204-207
reading/writing files, 407
web workers, 220-226
attachShadow() method, 390
attribute selectors, 269, 294
audio element, 356-357
authentication
    versus authorization, 477
    Passport.js, 486-491
authorization frameworks, 485-491
automatically updated regions, 298-299
await keyword, 201, 214-217, 219, 304, 441

B

Babel, 182, 242
base case, recursive functions, 142
bidirectional communication, client-server,
    320-322, 455
BigInt type, 61, 72-74
binary data, sending and loading into image,
    318-319
bind() method, 137, 138-141
blob() response type, 206, 318
Bostock, Mike, 352
breakpoint, setting, 253-255
browser, 4, 253-261
    (see also web apps/APIs)
    debugging JavaScript, 253-255
    developer console, 4-9
    identifying unused JavaScript, 257-259
    lazy evaluation in browser-based consoles,
        6, 87
    Lighthouse for measuring best practices,
        259-261
    local file loading, 385-388
    notifications in, 382-385
    responding to requests in, 400-402

runtime performance analysis, 255-257
security and access to error details, 234
Building Progressive Web Apps (O'Reilly), 373
button element, for click handler, 267

C

cacheVersion, 369
call stack, 143
callback function
    arguments supported, 110, 117-121
    asynchronous programming and, 201
    change to promise, 208-211
    with every() and some() methods, 113
    forEach() method and, 110
    function binding and, 139-140
    Node management, 441-444
    Node timers, 414, 417
    Readline module, 411
    with reduce() method, 110
    validating array contents, 113
CamelCase notation, 275
Canvas, 348, 355
canvas element, 354-356
captureStackTrace() method, 239
capturing parentheses (x), 54
case conversion of first letter in strings, 58
case-insensitive string comparison, 45-46
CDATA (character data) markup, 345-348
ceil() method, 66
chaining, method, 48, 186-188, 206, 352
change event, 310, 311
character data (CDATA) markup (see CDATA)
charAt() method, 59
checkbox status check, 279
checked property, 279
Cheerio, 459-460
child element discovery with Selectors API,
    272-273
childNodes property, 264, 265
child_process module, 445-446
Chrome Developer Tools (see DevTools)
CI (continuous integration) tools, 376
circular arc length, calculating, 71
class expression, 175
class keyword, 174-175
class value change to an HTML element, 273
classes, 173-200
    adding properties to, 177-182
    adding static methods to, 188-190

constructors and, 174, 176-177, 183-186,
    194
creating objects with static method, 190-192
inheriting functionality from another class,
    192-197
method chaining support, 186-188
modularization, 197-200
parent and child, 192-195
reusable class, 173-177
string representation, 182
classlist property, 273
clear method, DOM Storage, 335
clear() method, Set, 114
clearImmediate() function, 414
CLI (command-line interface) tools
    accessing functionality in Node, 444-446
    curl, 495
    init (npm), 16
    passing arguments in Node, 447-448
    utility using Commander module, 448-450
click events, 267, 283
click functionality, adding, 267-268
Client Credentials Grant, 478-480
client-server communication
    bidirectional, 320-322, 455
    long polling, 322-324
    sharing cookies across domains, 319-320
    with Websockets, 320-322
cloning
    arrays, 95-97
    objects, 164-168
closures, 117, 129-130, 134
cloud-based programming environments, 34
code
    enforcing standards with linter, 24-28, 44
    JavaScript playground, 31-34
    programming approaches, 246
    running blocks of code in console, 7-9
    sharing across module environments,
        422-425
    simplifying with destructuring assignment,
        127-128
    strings (see strings (String object))
    styling consistently with formatter, 28-31
    test code coverage, 247-250
    unit tests of, 242
    validation of, 36
code editor, choosing, 2-3
code snippets, REPL for trying out, 402-404

code splitting, 364
command-line interface (see CLI)
Commander module, 448
CommonJS, 242, 423, 432, 434
composition pattern, 195
computed property names, 149
computed styles, 276
concat() method, 97, 103
concatenation of strings, 43-45
console, using, 4-9
console.error() method, 234
console.log() method, 4, 183
const keyword, 101
constants, storing to refer to by name, 170-171
constructors
    classes and, 174, 176-177, 183-186, 194
    multiple, 176-177
    objects and, 145, 167
    public versus private fields in, 175
container technology, 400
contains() method, 274
continuous integration tools (see CI)
controls attribute, audio element, 356
cookies, 319-320, 325-328
Coordinated Universal Time (see UTC)
copying text to user clipboard, 380-381
© copyright symbol, 40
CORS (Cross-Origin Resource Sharing), 320
createAttribute() method, 276
createElement() method, 278, 287
createInterface() function, 411
createServer() method, 400
createTextNode() method, 276, 287
credentialed requests, 319
credit card validation library, 291
cross-domain communication, 319-320
Cross-Origin Resource Sharing (see CORS)
CRUD (Create-Read-Update-Delete), 499
Crypto object, 63
cryptograpically secure random numbers,
    63-65
CSS (Cascading Style Sheet)
    attribute selectors, 274-275, 294
    changing properties, 273
    preprocessor, 469
    shadow DOM element, 390
    visibility of properties, 285
CSS-style selector strings, 272
curl command-line tool, 495

currency format, 462
current date and time, 75-77
currentTime attribute, 359
custom classes, constructor pattern in making,
    183-186
custom elements in HTML, 389

D
D3 for the Impatient (O'Reilly), 352
D3 library, 350-353
Daring Fireball, 429
data
    CDATA markup, 345-348
    cookies, 319-320, 325-328
    Express's return of formatted, 491-492
    Fetch API to request, 223, 301-305
    form, 289-292, 306-310
    IndexedDB database management, 338-344
    localStorage client-side storage item,
        334-338
    persistence of, 129, 325-344
    reading/writing to files, 405-410
    remote data (see remote data)
    sessionStorage for client-side storage,
        328-334
    types, 35, 37
data descriptor, 158
database management (IndexedDB), 338-344
dates (Date object), 75-86
    adding days to a date, 79-80
    comparing, 80
    converting ISO 8601 format to, 77-79
    current date and time, 75-77
    formatting date value as string, 84-86
    methods available, 75
    testing for equality, 80-81
    tracking elapsed time between, 82-83
debugger statement, 254
debugging, 253-255, 265
Decimal type, 67
decimal values, 66-68, 70-70
decodeURI() function, 229
deep copy of an object, 166-168
default parameters, 124
defineProperty() method, 157, 181
degrees, converting to radians, 71
delete() method, Set, 114
deleting rows from table, 283
dependencies, managing, 17, 434

describe() function, 243
destructuring assignment, 93-94, 127-128
developer console, using, 4-9
development environment, setting up, 1-34
    choosing code editor, 2-3
    developer console, 4-9
    enforcing code standards with linter, 24-28
    experimenting in playground, 31-34
    filling in boilerplate with Emmet shortcuts,
        11-13
    npm package manager, 13-21
    strict mode to catch mistakes, 9-11
    styling code consistently with formatter,
        28-31
    test server setup, 21-24
development mode, 474
development run task, 23
DevTools (Chrome Developer Tools), 253-261,
    265
_dirname variable, 412
display property, 285
Docker, 400
document object, 264
document.cookie object, 325
DOM (Document Object Model), 263
    inserting new element in, 278
    nodes (elements), 264-265
    pruning, 283
    sessionStorage, 328-334
    shadow DOM, 389
    SVG and, 345
DomParser API, 316-317
dot-syntax, 149
dotenv package, 441
Drasner, Sarah
    SVG Animations (O'Reilly), 348
duplicate values, removing from arrays, 102

E
ECMAScript, 73
    (see also ES6)
    adoption of standard, 263
    BigInt and, 73
    modularization, 283, 422-425
    using with Node project, 440
Eich, Brendan, 263
EJS template system, 468
elapsed time between dates, tracking, 82-83
element object, 265

elements, 264
    (see also HTML5)
    in arrays, 88-90, 107-108, 109
    assigning variables, 93
    button, 267
    canvas element, 354-356
    DOM, 278, 390
    img (see images (img element))
    media, 354-360
    parent and child, 263-265
    script elements, 346
email validation, regular expression, 59-60
EME (Encrypted Media Extensions), 360
Emmet editor feature, 11-13
emojis, inserting into strings, 42-43
encodeURI() function, 229
encrypted files, 360
Encrypted Media Extensions (see EME)
endcodeURIComponent() method, 325
ended event, 356
enum (enumerated identifier), 170-171
environment variables, 439-441
equality operators, 74
equality testing, 80-81, 90-93
Error class, 239
Error() function, 237
errors (Error object), 227-240
    in asynchronous programming, 232-233,
        235
    catching and neutralizing, 227-230
    catching different types, 230-232
    debugging, 253-255, 265
    detecting unhandled, 233-236
    floating point rounding, 66
    in forms, 292-298
    handling with fetch(), 304-305
    list of types, 231
    logging tools, 236
    long polling, 322-324
    RangeError, 231, 238
    ReferenceError, 238
    strict mode to catch mistakes, 9-11, 157
    SyntaxError, 238
    throwing custom error object, 239-240
    throwing standard error object, 237-239
    TypeError, 157, 231
ES6 (ECMAScript 2015)
    classes in JavaScript and, 173, 197-200
    multiplatform libraries, 431, 434

sharing code across module environments, 424-425
unit tests of code, 242
escape sequence, 41, 50
ESLint, 24, 30, 44
event handlers
aboutAudio(), 357
onblur, 293
onsuccess, 340
upgradeneeded, 341
window.error, 234
event loop, 414-415
events
addEventListener(), 267
change, 310, 311
click, 267, 283
ended, 356
input event listener, 291
mouseover or mouseout, 287
onchange, 336
play, 356
storage, 335
timer, 139
visibilitychange, 384
window.unhandledrejection, 235
every() method, 112
exception, Error object, 228
exec() method, 445
execFile() method, 445
expect() function, 242
Express framework, 465-500
Express-Generator, 469-474
formatted data, returning, 491-492
GraphQL API, 496-500
OAuth, 476-491
responding to HTTP requests, 465-468
RESTful API, 492-495
routing, 474-476
extends keyword, 192

F

Facebook, 477
factorials, 141
factory functions, 136-137, 149
factory methods, 176
fail-fast behavior, 213
Fetch API, 223, 301-305
fetch() method, 302
binary data request, 318-319

form submission, 306
long polling, 322-324
XML, 316-317
XMLHttpRequest(), 306
Fibonacci Sequence, 141
File API, 385-388
File object, 385
FileList object, 385
_filename variable, 412
FileReader object, 385
files
app.js file, 471
encrypted, 360
execFile() method, 445
loading locally in browsers, 385-388
.mjs format, 198
.nvmrc format, 399
package.json file, 16, 18-20, 362, 425-428
reading/writing data in Node, 405-410
README, 429-431
test.js file, 242
WAV format, 357
fill attribute, 346
filter() method, 100
find() method, 105-106
findIndex() method, 102, 105-106
Firefox Developer Edition, 253
flat() method, 103
flattening of two-dimensional arrays, 103-104
floating point rounding errors, 66
floor() method, 62, 66
for await loop, 219
for loop, 88, 90
forEach() method
adding values to HTML table, 282
Array object, 89, 110
results from querySelectorAll() with, 266
foreignObject element, 355
fork() method, 445
formatting
code, 28-31
data, 491-492
dates, 77-79, 84-86
JSON formatted strings, 310, 315
numbers, 38-40, 69, 462
RESTful API and JSON-formatted data, 461-463
FormData object, 308-310
forms

error highlighting, 292-298
fetching remote data submissions, 306-310
populating selection lists, 310-314
validating data, 289-292
for…in loop, 153
for…of loop, 88, 132
fragile base class problem, 195
freeze() method, 160, 161
from() method, 114
frontend frameworks, 391-393
fs module, 405-410
full-duplex communication (see bidirectional
    communication)
function constructor, 117, 183-186
function expression, 118
function keyword, 131
function objects, 117, 139, 184-186
Function type, 37, 117
functional programming, 87, 89, 90
    (see also arrays; promises)
functions, 117-143
    accepting unlimited arguments, 125-126
    anonymous, 120, 203
    arrow, 121-124
    async, 214-217, 304, 441-444
    bind() method, 137
    binding() method, 138-141
    callback (see callback function)
    constructors and, 175
    converting arguments into arrays, 117, 121
    default parameters, 124
    generator function, 131-135, 218-220
    higher order, 137
    inner and outer, 129-130
    Jest's matcher functions, 241-246
    literals in, 126-128
    method-like, 184
    named, 121, 126-128
    partial application, 135-138
    passing array to function expecting list of
        values, 94
    passing as arguments to other functions,
        117-121
    recursive algorithms, 141-143
    reducer, 110
    returning Promise object, 204-207
    storing state with closure, 129-130

G
generator function, 131-135, 218-220
Generator object, 131
getAttribute() method, 275
getBoundingClientRect() method, 287
getComputedStyle() method, 276
getDate() method, 79
getElementsByTagName() method, 270-271,
    278
getElementsByTagNameNS() method, 355
getItem() function, 332
getRandomValues() method, 63-65
getSelection() method, 381
getSVGDocument() method, 349
getTime() method, 79
Git Pocket Guide (O'Reilly), 419
GitHub, 419, 429, 487
global flag (g), 50
global methods
    parseFloat(), 283
    parseInt(), 283
global objects, Node versus JavaScript, 404
global variables, 129, 283
global versus local installation of developer
    tools, 17
Google Chrome Developer Tools (see Dev-
    Tools)
Google Lighthouse (see Lighthouse)
Goyvaerts, Jan
    Regular Expressions Cookbook (O'Reilly),
        52
GraphicsMagick, 446
GraphQL API, 496-500

H
has() method, Set, 114
hexadecimal to decimal value, converting,
    70-70
hidden property, 384
higher order functions, 137
hover-based pop-up info windows, 287-289
href property, 377
hrtime.bigint() method, 83
HTML5, 49, 263-299
    (see also DOM)
    accessibility to elements, 263-265, 269-271
    audio element, 356-357
    automatically updated regions, 298-299

canvas element integration with SVG, 354-356

checkbox status check, 279

child element discovery with Selectors API, 272-273

class value change to an element, 273

click functionality, 267-268

copying text to user's clipboard, 380-381

custom elements, 389

deleting rows from table, 283

document tree organization, 264

filling in boilerplate with Emmet shortcuts, 11-13

hiding page elements, 285-286

highlighting form errors, 292-298

hover-based pop-up info windows, 287-289

importance of escaping, 49

parent and child elements, 263-265

replacing tags with named entities, 48-49

results from querySelectorAll() with forEach(), 266

select element, 311-313

shared attributes, finding elements with, 269

style attribute setting, 274-276

table values, adding up, 280-282

template element, 388

text, adding to paragraph, 276-278

validating form data, 289-292

video element, 356, 357-360

Web Components and, 388-391

HTTP

  cookie sharing across domains, 319-320

  mixed content security issue, 321

  responding to Express requests, 465-468

  responding to Node server request, 400

  RESTful API methods, 462, 493

http module, 400

I

I/O operations, Node and, 414-415

id property, 157

IDB library, 341-344

IE (Internet Explorer), 266, 305

ImageMagick, 445

images (img element), 206

  (see also SVG)

  accessing, 206-207, 269-271

  discovering child elements, 272-273

  hover-based pop-up info windows, 287-289

sending as binary data, 318-319

video, 356, 357-360

immutability, array, 90

in operator, 150

includes() method, 46, 104

IncomingMessage object, 401

IndexedDB, 338-344

indexOf() method

  Array object, 104-105, 107

  String object, 47, 52

inheritance, 151, 153, 192-197

init command (npm), 16, 425

input event listener, 291

insertBefore() method, 278

instanceOf operator, 92, 145-147, 230

integration testing, 437

Internet Explorer (see IE)

Intl.DateTimeFormat object, 86

Intl.NumberFormat object, 39, 69

isArray() method, 88

isFinite() method, 69

isFrozen() method, 161

isNan() method, 69

ISO 8601 format, converting dates, 77-79

iterative versus functional approaches to array processing, 90

J

Janert, Philipp

  D3 for the Impatient (O'Reilly), 352

JavaScript

  history, 263

  playground, 31-34

Jest, 241-246, 247, 436-438

joining arrays, 187

jQuery, 263, 459

JSON

  accessing data RESTfully, 461-463

  BigInt issue, 74

  formatted strings, 310, 315

  parsing of returned, 314-316

JSONP (JSON with padding), 316

K

key-indexed collection of items, 114-116

key-value syntax, 149

key/value pairs, 308, 315

keyboard navigation, 268

keys() method, 153

L

lastIndexOf() method, 104
lazy evaluation, browser-based consoles, 6, 87
lazy loading, 365
leaky abstraction, Unicode characters, 43
length property, 335
Levithan, Steven
    Regular Expressions Cookbook (O'Reilly),
       52
libraries
    converting to Node modules, 421-422
    credit card validation, 291
    D3, 350-353
    handling dependencies, 434
    IDB, 341-344
    multiplatform, 431-435
    sharing across environments, 422-425
    Workbox, 373
    writing tests first before, 246
Lighthouse, 259-261, 373-377
linter, enforcing code standards with, 24-28, 44
lists
    arrays passing to function expecting list of
       values, 94
    extracting from strings, 52-53
    populating selection lists, 310-314
lite-server, 21-24
literal functions, 126-128
live regions, 298-299
Load Impact, 456
load testing, Node, 456
local versus global installation of developer
    tools, 17
locale identifiers, 39
localeCompare() method, 45, 109
localStorage functionality, 329, 334-338
long option, 450
long polling a remote data source, 322-324
loose coupling, 419
loose equality, testing for, 74

M

makeString() function, 135
Map object, 114-116
map() method, 53, 96, 110
Markdown syntax, 429-431
markup, escaping, 49
matchAll() method, 54, 55
matcher functions, 242, 245

Math object, 61-66, 71
media, working with, 345-360
    adding JavaScript to SVG, 345-348
    audio file playing, 356-357
    canvas element integration, 354-356
    D3 tool to create SVG bar chart, 350-353
    video control, 356, 357-360
    web page script, accessing SVG from,
       348-350
merging of arrays, 97-98
message property, 228, 237
messageType property, 225
method chaining, 48, 186-188, 206, 352
methods
    adding new, 174
    adding to class, 188-190
    array processing, 89
    creating method-like functions, 184
    creating objects, 190-192
    date, 75
    factory, 176
    global, 283
    promises, 205-206, 208, 210
    versus properties, 180-181
    RESTful API, 462, 493
middleware packages for Express, 467
minification of JavaScript, 363
.mjs files, 198
mobile web loading time issue, 363-365
module object, 200
modules, 216, 419-438
    (see also web apps/APIs)
    await keyword in, 216
    child_process, 445-446
    classes with modules, 197-200
    Commander, 448
    converting library into module, 421-422
    fs module, 405-410
    of global variables, 283
    http, 400
    installable, 425-431
    multiplatform libraries, 431-435
    npm in search for specific module, 420-421
    pm2, 451-452
    Readline, 410-412
    strict mode in, 160
    taking code across environments, 422-425
    unit testing of, 435-438
    url module object, 401

xmlbuilder, 492
Yargs, 447
mouseout event, 287
mouseover event, 287
mulberry32() function, 133
multiple constructors, 176-177

N

name property, 228
named entities, replacing HTML tags with,
    48-49
named functions, 121, 126-128
namespaces, 197-200, 346
NaN values, 102
nesting, 139
new keyword, 145, 184, 185
next() method, 131
Node, 397-500
    callback hell, 441-444
    command-line functionality, 444-448
    command-line utility using Commander,
        448-450
    downloading package with npm, 16-18
    environment variables, 439-441
    with Express (see Express framework)
    global process object, 83
    HTTP server, 400
    input from terminal, 410-412
    installing/maintaining with npm, 13-21,
        362, 397
    keeping Node instance up and running,
        451-452
    Lighthouse as code module, 375-377
    modules (see modules)
    package.json file, 18-20
    path to current script, 412
    reading and writing file data, 405-410
    remote data, 457-463
    REPL for trying out code snippets, 402-404
    require() function, 400
    responding to browser request, 400-402
    restarting app during local development,
        452-453
    scheduling repeat tasks, 454-455
    terminal and shell, 14-15
    testing WebSockets app, 455-456
    timers and event loop, 413-418
    Twitter API, 478-485
    updating package with npm, 20-21

version management, 397-400
    Web Crypto API, 63
node object, 265
Node Version Manager (see NVM)
node-cron module, 454-455
node-fetch module, 457-461
NodeList, 265, 266, 282
nodemon utility, 452-453
nodeName property, 265
nodes, DOM, 264-265
Node_env environment variable, 439
nondestructive changes, 95
nonduplicated value collection, 113
nonenumerable properties, 165
notifications in desktop browser, 382-385
now() property, 191
npm (Node package manager)
    creating installable module for, 425-429
    installing, 13-21, 362
    Lighthouse, 375-377
    maintaining Node with, 397
    publishing a library to, 434
    in search for specific module, 420-421
    with Webpack, 363
:nth-of-type() selector, 280
Number type, 61, 73, 73
Number() function, 68
numbers, 61-74
    BigInt for manipulating very large, 72-74
    calculating circular arc length, 71
    converting between degrees and radians, 71
    converting decimal to hexadecimal value,
        70-70
    converting string to number, 68-69
    cryptograpically secure random, 63-65
    formatting, 38-40, 69, 462
    generating random, 61-65
    preserving accuracy in decimal values,
        66-68
    pseudorandom generator, 62, 133-135
    rounding to specific decimal place, 65-66
numeric value, converting to formatted string,
    38-40
NVM (Node Version Manager), 14, 397-400
nvm-windows, 398
.nvmrc file, 399

O

OAuth framework, 476-491

authorization versus authentication, 477
    Client Credentials Grant, 478-480
    Passport.js for authentication, 486-491
    read/write authorization, 481-485
object literal, 126-128, 147-150, 176
object-oriented programming, 173
objects (Object type), 145-171, 403
    (see also regular expressions)
    altering behavior with prototypes, 185
    cloning of, 164-168
    constructors and, 145, 167
    converting to JSON formatted strings, 310
    creating with static method, 190-192
    customizing how property is defined,
      156-159
    deep copy of, 166-168
    enum creation with Symbol(), 170-171
    global, 403
    identifying properties, 150-151
    identifying types, 145-147
    iterating over all properties of, 152-154
    literal, 126-128, 147-150, 176
    merging properties of two, 155
    preventing changes to, 159-161
    Proxy class for intercepting and changing
      actions on, 161-164
    sorting array by property value, 108-109
    testing for empty, 154
    unique object property keys, 168-170
octal numbers, 70
onblur event handler, 293
onchange event, 336
onsuccess event handler, 340
Open Exchange Rate, 462
open() function, file system, 407-410
open() method, IndexedDB, 340

P

package.json file, 16, 18-20, 362, 425-428
page updating during loop, 202-204
Page Visibility API, 384
paragraphs
    adding text to, 276-278
    inserting new in div element, 278
parameters
    default, 124
    fetch, 302
    named function, 126-128
    rest, 125

undefined, 138
parent and child classes, 192-195
parent and child elements in HTML, 263-265
parentNode property, 270
parse() method
    Date object, 77
    JSON, 314, 315
    url module object, 401
parseFloat() method, 69, 280
parseInt() function, 280
partial application, 135-138
Passport.js, 486-491
pathname property, 378
patterns
    building creational, 191
    finding all instances in strings, 54-57
    replacing with new strings, 49-52
Performance analysis, 255-257
Performance object, 83
performance testing, Node, 455
permissions, Web Notification, 382
play event, 356
playgrounds, 31-34
pm2 module, 451-452
Pnpm package manager, 14
polling, 322-324
polyfills, 266, 283, 305, 365
Polymer Project, 391
pop() method, 101
pop-up info windows, 287-289
POST request, 307-310
postMessage() function, 221, 223
Prettier code formatter, 28
preventDefault() method, 235, 268
primitive types, 145, 146
private class fields, 181
process object, 447
process.exit() function, 411
process.nextTick() function, 417
profiling, web apps/APIs, 373-377
progressive web applications (see PWAs)
promises (Promise object), 201
    in asynchronous generator function, 218
    await and async for waiting for promise,
      214-217
    callback function change to promise,
      208-211
    concurrent multiple promise execution,
      211-213

error handling, 232, 235
methods, 205-206, 208, 210
using function that returns, 204-207
promisfy utility, 441
properties
adding to class, 177-182
CSS, 273, 274, 285, 294
customizing definitions, 156-159
defining new, 150-151
Error object, 228
identifying, 150-151
iterating over all properties of objects,
152-154
keeping private, 179
merging of two objects', 155
methods for finding, 153
versus methods, 180
naming, 150, 169
nonenumerable, 165
preventing addition of, 160
sorting array by property value, 108-109
unique keys, 168-170
prototype chain, 147, 151, 153, 184, 195-197
prototypes, 173, 174, 184-186
Proxy class/object traps, 161-164
pseudorandom number generator, 62, 133-135
Pug templating engine, 468, 471-473
push() method, 100
PWAs (progressive web applications), 366-377

Q

query string, 229
querySelector() method, 272
querySelectorAll() method, 266, 272, 282
question() function, 411

R

race() method, 213
radians, converting to degrees, 71
radix, 70
random numbers, generating, 61-65
random() method, 61, 133
RangeError, 231, 238
React framework, 392
read() function, 407-410
read/write authorization, OAuth 1.0, 481-485
readFile() function, 406
reading and writing file data, 405-410
Readline module, 410-412

README files, 429-431
RealFaviconGenerator, 372
rect element, 353
recursive algorithm, 141-143
redirecting a URL, 379-380
reduce() function, 110
reduce() method, 110
reducer function, 110
redundancy, reducing, 135-138
reference types, 155
ReferenceError, 238
RegEx object, 50, 55
region attributes, 299
regular expressions, 40, 49-52
(see also strings)
basic use of, 50
cookie value matching, 328
email address validation, 59-60
replacing HTML tags with named entities,
48-49
special characters, 40-42, 51
Regular Expressions Cookbook (O'Reilly
Media), 52
reload() method, 379
remote data, 301-324
fetching, 301-314, 457-459
form submission, 306-310
HTTP cookie sharing across domains,
319-320
long polling a remote data source, 322-324
in Node, 457-463
parsing of returned JSON, 314-316
RESTful API and accessing JSON-formatted
data, 461-463
screen scraping, 459-461
selection list population from server,
310-314
sending binary data and loading into image,
318-319
WebSockets for client-server communication, 320-322
XML, fetching and parsing, 316-317
XMLHttpRequest to request data, 305-306,
320
removeChild() method, 283
REPL (read-evaluate-print-loop), 402-404
replace() method
String object, 49, 50
window.location, 379

replaceAll() method, 47, 49
RequestListener function, 400
require() function, 400
rest operator, 93
rest parameter, 125
RESTful API, 461-463, 492-495
reusable class, creating, 173-177
reviver function, 314
round() method, 65, 82
rounding numbers to specific decimal place,
    65-66
routing, Express, 474-476
rows, deleting from table, 283
runtime performance analysis, 255-257

S
Scalable Vector Graphics (see SVG)
scale functionality, D3, 352
scheduling repeat tasks in Node, 454-455
scope, 135, 184
screen scraping, 459-461
script elements, 346
seal() method, 160
search property, 378
security issues
    browser access to error details, 234
    encrypted media and playback functional-
        ity, 360
    mixed content (HTTP and HTTPS), 321
seed value, pseudorandom number generator,
    133
select element, 311-313
selection list population from server, 310-314
Selectors API, 272-273
Selenium, 456
semver (semantic versioning), 20
sendText() function, 416
sensitivity property, 45
ServerResponse end() method, 402
ServerResponse object, 401
service workers, 226, 367-369, 372
sessionStorage functionality, 328-334
Set object, 102, 113
set() method, 114
setAttribute() method, 274-276
setDate() method, 79
setHours() method, 81
setImmediate() function, 414
setInterval() function, Node, 413, 416

setInterval() method, web workers, 204
setItem() function, 332
sets, converting to arrays, 114
setTimeout() function
    asynchronous programming, 118, 139, 202,
        202
    Node, 413
shadow DOM, 389
shadow root of HTML element, 390
shallow compare, 91
shallow copies, 96, 99, 165
shared attributes, finding elements with, 269
shared workers, 226
shell, 14
short-circuit evaluation, 36
showMessage() function, 118
side effect, 365
significant digits, 39
Silverman, Richard
    Git Pocket Guide (O'Reilly), 419
slice() method
    Array object, 96, 99, 107
    String object, 53, 59
socket.write() function, 416
some() method, 112
sort() method, 97, 108
spaces, removing from strings, 58
spawn() method, 445
special characters
    inserting into strings, 40-42
    list of regular expressions, 51
speed testing, Node, 455
splice() method, 99, 107
split() method, 53
stack property, 228
start() function, 403
startsWithE() method, 100
state, functions storing with closure, 129-130
static keyword, 188
static methods
    adding to class, 188-190
    creating objects, 190-192
storage event, 335
Storage object, 328-334
strict equality, 74
strict mode
    catching mistakes with, 9-11, 157
    customizing propery definition, 157
    in modules, 160

stringify() method, 74, 315
strings (String object), 35-60, 182
    (see also regular expressions)
    case-insensitive string comparison, 45-46
    checking for existing, nonempty, 35-38
    checking for specific substring, 46
    converting numeric value to formatted,
        38-40
    converting to dates, 77-79
    converting to numbers, 68-69
    CSS-style selector, 272
    date value formatted as, 84-86
    extracting lists from, 52-53
    finding all instances of patterns in, 54-57
    inserting emojis into, 42-43
    inserting special characters into, 40-42
    JSON formatted, 310, 315
    providing better representation for class,
        182
    replacing all occurrences of, 47
    replacing HTML tags with named entities,
        48-49
    template literals for clearer concatenation,
        43-45
    uppercase conversion of first letter, 58
    whitespace removal from beginning and
        end of, 57-58
structured programming, 246
style attribute, 274-276
style property, 274
substrings
    checking for specific, 46
    replacing matched, 54
super() keyword, 194, 239
Svelte framework, 392
SVG (Scalable Vector Graphics)
    adding JavaScript to, 345-348
    canvas element integration in HTML,
        354-356
    D3 tool to create SVG bar chart, 350-353
    web page script access, 348-350
SVG Animations (O'Reilly), 348
Symbol type, 169
Symbol() method, 169-171
SyntaxError, 238

T
tables
    adding up values, 280-282

deleting rows from, 283
tagged templates, 45
TDD (Test-Driven Development), 246, 437
template element, 388
template literals for clearer concatenation,
    43-45
templating engines, 467
Temporal object, 83
terminal, using in Node or npm, 14, 410-412
termination condition, recursive functions, 142
test code coverage, 247-250
test server setup, 21-24
test() function, 242
test() method, 59
Test-Driven Development (see TDD)
test.js file, 242
testing, 241-250
    assertion tests, 243
    for empty objects, 154
    for equality, 80-81, 90-93
    integration, 437
    load testing, 456
    for loose equality, 74
    matcher functions list, 245
    Node modules, 435-438
    Node speed and performance, 455
    with REPL, 402-404
    user acceptance, 433, 437
    web apps/APIs, 373-377
    WebSockets app, 455-456
    writing unit tests, 241-246
text
    adding to paragraphs, 276-278
    copying to user clipboard, 380-381
    working with in Node, 277, 287, 405, 416
Text node, 277
this keyword
    arrow function syntax and, 268
    classes, 185, 189
    constructors, 175
    Function, 137, 139-141
    static methods, 189
Thor, 456
throw statement, 231, 237, 239-240
timers
    event, 139
    Node, 413-418
toBe() function, 242
toExponential() method, 38

toFixed() method, 38
toJSON() method, 74
toLowerCase() method, 45, 47
toPrecision() method, 38
toString() method
    child_process module, 446
    classes and, 182
    file system, 407
    Number object, 38, 70
    window.location, 379
toThrow() function, 245
toUpper() method, 58
tree shaking, 364
trim() method, 53, 57-58
truthy values, 245
try...catch block, 229, 304
Twitter API, 478-485
type conversion, 38-40
type property, 157
typed arrays (see binary data)
TypeError, 157, 231
typeof operator, 36-37, 146
types, identifying object, 145-147

U

UglifyJS, 363
undefined parameter, 138
unique identifiers, 169
unit testing
    matcher functions list, 245
    Node modules, 435-438
    writing tests with Jest, 241-246, 437
Universal Module Definition (UMD), 432
unscoped function, 139
upgradeneeded event handler, 341
uppercase conversion of first letter in strings,
    58
url module object, 401
URLs
    current value, 377-378
    redirecting, 379-380
user acceptance testing, 433, 437
UTC (Coordinated Universal Time), 76, 84

V

validation
    array contents, 112-113
    form data, 289-292
validator.js library, 290

variables
    assigning elements to, 93
    breaking array into separate, 93-94
    confirming, 35-38
    environment, 439-441
    global, 129, 283
video element, 356, 357-360
visibility property, 285
visibilitychange event, 384
visibilityState property, 384
VS (Visual Studio) Code, 2, 3
Vue framework, 392

W

WAI-ARIA (Web Accessibility Initiative-
    Accessible Rich Internet Applications),
    292-299
waterfall project design, 246
WAV file format, 357
web apps/APIs, 361-393
    accessing JSON data via RESTful, 461-463
    bundling JavaScript, 361-363
    copying text to user clipboard, 380-381
    DomParser API, 316-317
    Express (see Express framework)
    Fetch API, 223, 301-305
    File API, 385-388
    frontend framework, 391-393
    loading files locally, 385-388
    mobile web loading time issue, 363-365
    notifications in desktop browser, 382-385
    Page Visibility API, 384
    progressive web applications, 366-377
    redirecting a URL, 379-380
    Selectors API, 272-273
    testing and profiling, 373-377
    Twitter API, 478-485
    URL current value, 377-378
Web Components, 388-391
Web Crypto API, 63
Web Notifications API, 382-385
Web Worker API (Worker object), 203, 220-226
Webpack, 361-363, 364-365, 432, 434
WebSockets, 320-322, 455-456
while loop, 132
whitespace characters, 50-51, 57-58
window API, 378
window.crypt property, 63
window.error event handler, 234

window.location, 377
window.unhandledrejection event, 235
Windows OS, Node on, 398, 446
withCredentials property, 320
Workbox library, 373
write() function, 407-410
writeFile() function, 406
writeText() method, 380

X

XHTML, CDATA and, 347
XML

fetching and parsing of, 316-317
formatting with Node, 491-492
SVG (see SVG)
xmlbuilder module, 492
XMLHttpRequest() (XHR) method, 305-306,
    320

Y

Yargs module, 447
Yarn package manager, 14
yield keyword, 131

About the Authors

Adam D. Scott is an engineering leader, web developer, educator, and artist based in Connecticut. He has worked at the crossroads of technology and education for over a decade, teaching and writing curriculum on a range of technical topics. This is his seventh book.

Matthew MacDonald is a tech writer and long-ago Microsoft MVP who's written enough heavy books to prop open all the doors in his house. Visit his website (*https://prosetech.com*) to learn about his free JavaScript book for kids, or to follow his semi-regular hot-takes programming publication, *Young Coder*.

Shelley Powers has been working with, and writing about, web technologies—from the first release of JavaScript to the latest graphics and design tools—for more than 12 years. Her recent O'Reilly books have covered the semantic web, Ajax, JavaScript, and web graphics. She's an avid amateur photographer and web development aficionado, who enjoys applying her latest experiments on her many websites.

Colophon

The bird on the cover of *JavaScript Cookbook* is a little egret (*Egretta garzetta*). This small white heron, the smallest and most common in Singapore, is a lot like the new world snowy egret. Its original breeding distribution included the large inland and coastal wetlands in warm temperate parts of Europe, Asia, Africa, Taiwan, and Australia. Little egrets in warmer locations are permanent residents, while the northern birds migrate to Africa and southern Asia.

Adult little egrets are 55–65 cm long with an 88–106 cm wingspan and weigh 350–550 grams. Their plumage is all white. They have long black legs, yellow feet, and slim black bills. In the breeding season, adults have two long nape plumes, gauzy plumes on their backs and breasts, and red or blue skin between their bills and eyes.

Little egrets are lively hunters with a wide variety of techniques: they patiently stalk prey in shallow waters; stand on one leg and stir the mud with the other to scare up prey; and stand on one leg and wave the other foot over the water's surface as a lure. They eat fish, insects, amphibians, crustaceans, and reptiles. They nest in colonies on platforms of sticks in trees or shrubs, reed beds, or bamboo groves, often with other wading birds. Many of the animals on O'Reilly covers are endangered; all of them are important to the world.

The cover illustration is by Karen Montgomery, based on a black and white engraving from Cassell's *Natural History*. The cover fonts are Gilroy Semibold and Guardian Sans. The text font is Adobe Minion Pro; the heading font is Adobe Myriad Condensed; and the code font is Dalton Maag's Ubuntu Mono.

O'REILLY®

There's much more where this came from.

Experience books, videos, live online training courses, and more from O'Reilly and our 200+ partners—all in one place.

Learn more at oreilly.com/online-learning